W9-BCN-083

RESTAURANT MANAGEMENT
Customers, Operations, and Employees
Second Edition

Robert Christie Mill

School of Hotel, Restaurant, and Tourism Management
Daniels College of Business
University of Denver

Upper Saddle River, New Jersey 07458

Library of Congress Cataloging-in-Publication Data

Mill, Robert Christie.
  Restaurant management : customers, operations, and employees /
Robert Christie Mill.—2nd ed.
      p. cm.
  Includes bibliographical references and index.
  ISBN 0-13-027364-3
  1. Restaurant management.   I. Title.
  TX911.3.M24 M55 2000
  647.95'068—dc21   00-027168

Publisher: Dava Garza
Acquisitions Editor: Neil Marquardt
Associate Editor: Marion Gottlieb
Production Editor: Patty Donovan, Pine Tree
    Composition
Production Liaison: Barbara Marttine Cappuccio
**Director of Manufacturing
    and Production:** Bruce Johnson
Mananging Editor: Mary Carnis
Manufacturing Manager: Ed O'Dougherty
Art Director: Marianne Frasco
Cover Design Coordinator: Miguel Ortiz
Marketing Manager: Ryan DeGrote
Editorial Assistant: Susan Kegler
Cover Design: Marianne Frasco
Cover Art: Stock Illustration Source, Inc. /
    Rebecca Molayem
**Interior Design, art production
    and page layout:** Pine Tree Composition
Printing and Binding: R. R. Donnelley & Sons

Dedication

*For Christian, Jordan,
and Mikayla*

Prentice-Hall International (UK) Limited, *London*
Prentice-Hall of Australia Pty. Limited, *Sydney*
Prentice-Hall Canada Inc., *Toronto*
Prentice-Hall Hispanoamericana, S.A., *Mexico*
Prentice-Hall of India Private Limited, *New Delhi*
Prentice-Hall of Japan, Inc., *Tokyo*
Prentice-Hall Singapore Pte. Ltd.

10 9 8 7 6 5 4 3 2
ISBN 0-13-027364-3

CONTENTS

Chapter 5
Pricing and Designing the Menu   108

Chapter 9
Kitchen Equipment and Interiors:
Selection, Maintenance, and Energy Management   237

Chapter 10
Sanitation and Food Safety

Chapter 11
Controlling Costs   289

Chapter 12
Employee Selection   318

Chapter 13
Training and Development 354

Chapter 14
Motivating the Employee 378

Chapter 15
Restaurant Manager 2000   413

PREFACE

In writing this book I wanted to identify the crucial elements involved in the successful operation of a restaurant and show their interrelationships. In providing what John Fuller, the former head of the Scottish Hotel School, called the "meal experience," the restaurant manager brings together three elements: customers, the operation (consisting of food and beverage items as well as the physical facility), and employees. The operator's task is to manage these elements to produce satisfied customers. How to do this is the thrust of this book.

In Chapter 1 we provide a financial overview of the restaurant industry while looking at the major factors affecting the growth of the business and considering the factors that make the difference between success and failure in running a restaurant.

In Chapters 2 through 6 we consider the first of the three elements of the meal experience: the customer. The eating habits of the various segments of the market are described in Chapter 2 and the major trends in customer behavior that affect the business are identified. Chapter 3 goes on to show how to develop a marketing plan to attract one or more of the segments identified in Chapter 2. The importance of promotion as a marketing tool is recognized in Chapter 4 as we consider how and when to use various types of advertising to bring people in the front door. The role of the menu as a crucial part of the marketing effort is covered in Chapter 5, with sections on pricing and design to develop the strongest possible promotional vehicle. The culmination of the marketing effort to the customer is the provision of high-quality service, the topic of Chapter 6. The features that make the service encounter unique are identified and strategies developed to provide service to the customer that will result in satisfied patrons who want to return and who will tell their friends to visit.

Chapters 7 through 11 deal with the physical facilities. In Chapter 7 we show how the front of the house can be designed to positively impact on the psychological needs and behavior of the customer. The effect on employee productivity of the design of the back of the house is also covered. Chapter 8 follows the flow of food and beverage items from supplier to customer through the various departments within the operation in developing procedures for effective purchasing, receiving, storing, and issuing of items used. The various production and service systems are compared within the context of developing effective cost control. Chapter 9 focuses on kitchen equipment and interiors. Guidelines are given on the proper procedures to follow in selecting, cleaning, and repairing kitchen equipment. Readers are shown how to develop a comprehensive energy management program. The importance of sanitation and food safety is stressed in Chapter 10. The major sanitation problems faced by restaurant managers are identified and procedures developed for preventing foodborne diseases. A program to build effective employee habits is presented. In the final chapter in this section, Chapter 11, we show how to analyze financial statements systematically to determine the profitability of the operation.

In the third section of the book we examine the role of employees. Chapter 12 deals with employee selection, identifying the work groups that managers will turn to increasingly in the next decade. The legal environment within which managers must operate is described and the steps involved in staffing the operation are noted and guidelines given on how to improve the quality of employees selected. The design of effective orientation, training, and development programs is covered in Chapter 13, together with tips on how to develop the skills necessary to be an effective trainer. The topic of employee motivation is dealt with in Chapter 14. Suggestions are given as to why employees behave the way they do, and techniques are developed that will allow managers to channel and maintain employee behavior through the implementation of various process theories of motivation. In the final chapter we examine the National Restaurant Association's report on the manager in the year 2000, indicating the major skills and knowledge that will be required of restaurant managers by the turn of the century.

ACKNOWLEDGMENTS

I am grateful to Professor John Fuller who, as head of the Scottish Hotel School, first brought the phrase "the meal experience" to my attention.

While the layout for the book languished on a piece of paper for over twenty years it was Prentice Hall's Robin Baliszewski who believed in the concept sufficiently to push the idea into reality. I am also indebted to the reviewers who gave their experience and knowledge to suggest excellent improvements: John D. Britto, San Joaquin Delta College; Stephen E. Carlomusto, Johnson and Wales University. Many thanks to Marion Gottlieb of Prentice Hall who oversaw production of this second edition and Patty Donovan of Pine Tree Composition, Inc., who, as a superb project manager, greatly improved this text.

Last, but by no means least, this book would not have been completed were it not for the heroic efforts of Michael R. Rogers, Jill Lamoureaux, and Terra J. Pugh, my research assistants, who updated quick bites, completed the index, and vastly improved the instructor's guide. I, of course, take full responsibility for any and all errors.

CHAPTER ONE

INTRODUCTION

learning objectives

By the end of this chapter you should be able to:

1. Identify the major factors affecting the growth of the restaurant industry.
2. Identify the common denominators of restaurants.
3. Provide a financial overview of the restaurant industry in the United States.
4. Identify the reasons that restaurants fail.
5. Identify the major reasons contributing to the financial success of a restaurant.
6. Identify the skills necessary to manage a restaurant.

The Best Restaurant in the World

The menu should be a personal expression of the chef and at the same time respect the traditions of both classic and regional good taste.

Dishes should be simple and unfussy and garnishes kept to a minimum and entirely edible.

The kitchen must be capable of cooking seafood with the same degree of refinement as it does meat and poultry.

Breads and desserts must be made on the premises.

There should be a good cheese selection.

The wine list must have great depth and breadth.

There should be a first-rate selection of brandies, dessert wines and other spirits.

The restaurant should be elegant but unpretentious.

The restaurant must take reservations.

There should be no tables any guest might possibly perceive to be an "A" or "B" table, and table settings, from silverware to napery, should be of the finest quality.

A member of the service staff should always be in sight of every table and be ready for any request but must never intrude on a table's conversation.

The generosity of spirit at the restaurant should endure from the moment a guest enters the door until the moment the guest leaves.

Source: John Mariani, restaurant critic, quoted in *Dining Out.*

THE FOOD SERVICE INDUSTRY

The importance of the foodservice industry can be seen from the following figures [1]:

- The restaurant industry provides work for almost 8 percent of those employed in the United States.
- Forty four percent of the consumer's food dollar goes to meals and snacks prepared away from home.
- There are almost 800,000 locations offering food service in the United States.
- The restaurant industry employs more than 10 million people. This number is projected to reach 12 million by 2006.
- More than 37 percent of all adults have, at some time during their lives, worked in the restaurant industry.
- Almost 50 billion meals are eaten each year in restaurants and school and work cafeterias.

The foodservice industry as a whole had projected 1999 food and drink sales of almost $354 billion from three segments: commercial, noncommercial restaurant, and military restaurant services. The military restaurant services part of the business accounts for just 0.3 percent of the total and includes services in officers' and NCO clubs and military exchanges. The noncommercial restaurant sector accounts for just under 9 percent of total sales and includes catering operations in offices, factories, hospitals, schools and colleges. Sales in the commercial restaurant services sector account for an overwhelming 91 percent of the total. From 1996 to 1999, revenues in all three segments of the foodservice industry grew from $308 billion to $354 billion [2]. The 1999 figures for the various segments of the commercial sector were as follows [3]:

Segment	Revenue (billions)	1996–1999 Compound Annual Growth Rate
EATING PLACES		
Fullservice restaurants	$117,278,905	5.2%
Limited service (fast food)	110,408,547	4.7
Commercial cafeterias	4,190,798	2.9
Social caterers	3,352,804	5.4
Ice-cream, frozen custard, yogurt stands	2,877,959	3.9
Bars and taverns	11,459,442	3.7
MANAGED SERVICES		
Manufacturing and industrial plants	6,023,016	5.9%
Commercial and office buildings	1,740,235	5.0
Hospitals and nursing homes	2,331,379	3.6
Colleges and universities	5,378,230	7.6
Primary and secondary schools	2,116,670	6.2
In-transit restaurant services (airlines)	2,242,798	5.0
Recreation and sports centers	3,127,055	4.8
LODGING PLACES		
Hotel restaurants	$17,629,158	5.2%
Motor-hotel restaurants	429,711	0.4
Motel restaurants	614,590	0.1
OTHER		
Retail-host restaurants	$16,584,521	7.2%
Recreation and sports	4,603,311	4.4
Mobile caterers	1,218,576	5.3
Vending and nonstore retailers	7,747,605	4.6

In this book we focus on the two largest segments of the commercial industry: quick- and full-service restaurants.

INDUSTRY TRENDS

The restaurant industry does not operate in a vacuum. Industry trends directly reflect changes in the society within which the business operates. The manager who is aware of (and, better still, able to anticipate) these trends is in a position to take advantage of opportunities in the marketplace. This involves conducting a scan of the environment. The National Restaurant Association (NRA) offers periodic analyses of trends as they affect the restaurant industry.

Tableservice Trends

In its 1998 survey of tableservice restaurant trends the NRA found that [4]:

- One of the biggest concerns of tableservice operators is winning customer loyalty. Operators, especially those with lower average check sizes, report it is more difficult to maintain customer loyalty than it was two years ago.
- Tableservice restaurants derive a large proportion of their revenue from repeat customers.
- At restaurants with an average check of less than $8, local customers are responsible for 80 percent of annual revenues; at restaurants where the average check is $25 or more, business is split equally between local customers and visitors.
- Half of all operators report that their customers are more value conscious than they were two years ago.

---

quick bite 1 . 1
Hot Concepts: Atomic Burrito

As bagel shops across the country close by the dozen, James E. Blacketer would like to jump into the now-empty stores. The stores' sizes and layouts are a good fit for Blacketer's new Atomic Burrito chain. Blacketer, the president and chief executive of Western Country Clubs, Inc. (WWCI), entered into a joint venture with the struggling Wichita, Kansas–based New York Bagel Enterprises Inc. The agreement will switch eight of the bagel stores to Atomic Burrito stores in college towns in Texas, Oklahoma, Kansas, Tennessee, Missouri, and Nebraska. The joint venture allows WCCI to save building costs. The conversions are expected to only cost $200,000 to $250,000.

Atomic Burrito's checks average from $6.25 to $6.50. Burritos are priced from $3.95 for a regular-size veggie burrito, to $7.95 for a two-pound "Super Atomic" size burrito. Customers can pick other ingredients including rice, cheese, beans, pico de gallo, diced tomatoes, cilantro, onions, jalapenos, lettuce, and bell peppers. For a little extra, customers can order sour cream, avocado, guacamole, or queso. Other menu items include quesadillas, salads, and tacos, including a "Baja fish taco."

Atomic Burrito is decorated in a fun style with bright colors. The restaurant's theme includes a small, mad-scientist character carrying a huge burrito. The outlets have room for about 100 in the dining room and about 20 more on a patio. The chain receives about 60 percent dine-in business and would like to become a hangout for college students after the bars close.

Source: Hamstra, Mark. "Atomic Burrito hopes to fill bagel chain's excess sites." *Nation's Restaurant News,* v. 32, no. 51, December 21, 1998, p. 110.

- To get customers to return operators are offering items that are popular (vegetarian items continue their rise in popularity), are offering complete dining experiences, and are making more use of such things as gift certificates.
- The task of finding qualified and motivated employees is identified as the most common concern of operators.
- Employee referrals, walk-ins, and newspaper ads are seen as the most effective ways of recruiting new employees.
- More operators are using off-site preparation of food items as a way of dealing with labor problems and increasing productivity.

Sources of Information

How can an operator be proactive by identifying changes before they occur rather than reactive and attempting to respond to changes after they happen? The key is to become a trend watcher. In its formal setting, trend watching involves reading or watching news media, keeping track of issues and events, noting the data, and using them to predict what might happen in the future.

In one study [5], restaurateurs were given a choice of the following sources of information:

- family members and personal friends
- other restaurant owners
- trade associations

Atomic Burrito

- printed sources
- customers
- food and equipment vendors
- bankers, lawyers or accountants

The most frequently used sources were family and friends, food and equipment vendors and printed materials. A complete watch of printed and other media would involve keeping track of events as reported by the four major television networks: ABC, CBS, NBC, and Fox, the three national news magazines: *Newsweek, Time,* and *U.S. News & World Report;* and several influential newspapers, including the *Chicago Tribune, Los Angeles Times, New York Times, Wall Street Journal,* and *Washington Post.* For busy restaurateurs such a watch could become a full-time job. For the specialist trends can be evaluated by reading trade magazines, the front page of the *Wall Street Journal, USA Today,* and a technical

---

quick bite 1.2
Pressured Lifestyles

Consumers today frequently feel that they have too many things to do and not nearly enough time to do it. Over three-fourths of consumers (77%) relate that they are always looking for new ways to save time. Most of these consumers agree that utilizing restaurants helps them to save valuable time.

Although consumers feel that dining out is too expensive to do often, they are willing to trade dollars for time. This willingness to pay for time is a likely cause for the rise in takeout sales. More than two-thirds of all adults feel that takeout or delivery food allows them more time for other activities and therefore the majority also feels that they are worth the expense.

Consumers need for time saved also contributes to on-premises dining as well. More than 40% of consumers say that they are cooking fewer meals at home than they used to. An even greater percentage, 56%, of adults say that they are not entertaining at home as often as they used to either. As a result, more and more consumers are willing to spend money dining out in order to spend time with family and friends.

Continuing demographic trends, such as more working mothers, connected with a strong economy and satisfied patrons have given more customers the ability and desire to regularly socialize in restaurants. Over two-thirds of adults feel that going out to a restaurant to socialize with family and/or friends is a better way to make use of their free time than attending to guests at home. This trend is extending to holidays as well. Almost 60% of consumers agree that those who get takeout or catered meals on holidays have more leisure time to enjoy with family and guests.

Source: "1999 Highlights." *Restaurants USA,* v. 18, no. 11, December 1998, p. F13.

Major Issues

The National Restaurant Association is the industry's watchdog in Washington. The NRA makes sure to monitor legislative issue that will effect operations across the country. Major upcoming issues that the NRA sees as important:

- Health-care reform

The NRA has and will continue to work with employer groups to encourage Congress to adopt a reform package that will make health insurance more affordable for operators to provide to their employees. An element of a health-care bill that the NRA promotes is the Association Health Plans (AHP) proposal that would allow employers to obtain health coverage through a trade association-sponsored plan.

- Social Security reform

By 2030, Social Security is expected by many to run out of funds. This is partially due to the immense number of baby boomers that will be leaving the workforce. The NRA advocates the adoption of a reform plan that will retain the existing benefit levels for those already retired or nearing retirement age. The espoused plan will protect all retirees with a minimum guaranteed amount and will allow workers to invest at least part of their FICA contributions to personally controlled retirement accounts. In order for a plan to be accepted by the NRA, it should not raise payroll taxes.

- Business-meal deductibility

The NRA will continue to attempt to convince lawmakers to restore business-meal deductibility to 100%. The NRA considers business meals as tools for middle-class business owners, not extravagant "three-martini" lunches as so often viewed by lawmakers.

- Minimum wage

Although proponents of increased minimum wage failed to pass legislation 1998, they are not likely to give up. NRA's position on increasing minimum wage is that hiking up the minimum wage leads to decreased hours, layoffs and canceled hiring plans.

Source: "A New Year Means New Challenges for Restaurateurs on Capitol Hill." *Restaurants USA,* v. 19, no. 1, January 1999, p. 8.

Courtesy of Bruegger's Bagel Bakery.

precursor publication. Precursor publications are those that influence main-stream journalists by uncovering trends before they occur. The *Wall Street Journal* is not particularly good at forecasting what might happen in the future because by the time an item appears in the *Journal,* it is already fact. For general issues, magazines such as *Demography, Science News,* and *Utne Reader* have been found to be useful precursor publications.

COMMON DENOMINATORS

A useful way to explore the industry is to consider the factors that are common to all restaurants [6].

Utility versus Pleasure

Restaurants are built for utility or pleasure. Utility restaurants are filling stations, seeing to the need we all have for periodic refueling during the day. Restaurants that are built for pleasure appeal to more than the need to refuel. The importance of good food and wine is shared with the desire to dine in comfortable surround-ings. Some suggest that up to 75 percent of meals eaten away from home in the United States are for utilitarian purposes and the other 25 percent are for pleasure.

Imagine the following progression of foodservice operations:

- Vending machines
- Fast-food operations
- Cafeterias
- Coffee shops
- Family restaurants
- Dinner houses
- Luxury restaurants

As the utility of a concept decreases, the pleasure component increases. Going from high utility to high pleasure, we move from vending machines through luxury restaurants.

> *High utility/low pleasure*
> Vending machines
> Fast-food operations
> Cafeterias
> Coffee shops
> Family restaurants
> Dinner houses
> Luxury restaurants
> *High pleasure/low utility*

Service and Menu Price

Restaurants can also be classified on the basis of the degree of service offered. The level of service offered can range from full service to self-service. In full- or table-service operation, servers take menu orders from customers and deliver those items to the table. This level of service requires more square feet of space per seat than that required by any other type of operation.

Counter service allows customers to sit at a counter facing the production area. A minimum of space is needed because the production area where the food is prepared and the service area where the food is served are one and the same. Tray service is used in such operations as airlines and hospitals. Food is delivered to the passenger or patient already plated on a tray. Room service is common in hotels. Orders are placed from the room by the guest, and the meal is arranged on a tray or table and delivered to the room by service personnel.

In *self-service* operations customers serve themselves. This type of service is appropriate for serving large numbers of people in a relatively short period of time. Self-service operations may be found in cafeterias where customers pick up a tray and serve themselves from items displayed in a cafeteria line or in several areas in freestanding style. Buffet service is increasingly popular for breakfast at hotels, as it allows customers to get what they want for one price and to serve themselves as quickly as they wish. Some restaurants use buffet service for a particular meal, typically lunch or Sunday brunch.

Takeout service allows customers, for example, to pick up something on the way home from work and to enjoy it wherever they wish, whether in the privacy of their own homes or in their cars. Vending machines serve in-between meal snacks or simple meals that can be served cold or cooked by the customer in a microwave oven provided at the scene.

An increase in service typically comes with an increase in menu prices. The vending machine, relatively inexpensive, is totally self-service; a luxury restaurant may offer table-side carving. The progression from low prices and low levels of service to high prices and maximum service is the same as before.

> *Low service/low prices*
> > Vending machines
> > Fast-food operations
> > Cafeterias
> > Coffee shops
> > Family restaurants
> > Dinner houses
> > Luxury restaurants
> *High service/high prices*

Menu prices are also a function of when a meal is eaten, the cost of labor, the space per customer, and the cost of that space. Meals taken in the evening, when customers are more likely to stay longer, cost more than lunch meals, when customers stay for less time and the restaurateur can increase customer and seat turnover by selling the table again.

Since the restaurant business tends to be highly labor intensive, the cost of labor is a major determinant in the price of a meal—the more service, the greater the labor cost and the higher the price. There is also a relationship between the cost of space and menu prices. The cost of a facility is, in great part, determined by the size of the facility—the larger the operation, the more it costs to build. Part of the decision that must be made is how much of the facility should be revenue producing (where customers are served) compared to non-revenue producing (for example, kitchen, storage, and service areas). Less space given over to producing revenue means that more revenue per square foot must be generated from that space. In addition, the more square footage per customer (for example, greater space between the tables), the more it will cost the customer in menu prices.

Food Preparation Method

Restaurants have the option of preparing food from scratch or buying convenience items and finishing them in the operation. The decision as to which mix to operate under has many ramifications. Using convenience items will result in greater food cost but lower labor cost. The level of expertise needed by employees will be less if convenience items are used. The experience of the prevailing labor force may thus be a factor in the decision whether to make or buy. Different types of equipment may also be needed, depending on whether items are prepared from scratch or purchased as convenience items. Finally, the image of the operation may be a factor in this decision. A luxury restaurant, seeking an upscale image, may advertise preparation from scratch as part of its message. Most operations make some items while purchasing others in a convenience form.

Menu Development

All restaurants have menus. However, the format of the menu will vary greatly depending on a variety of factors.

Frequency of Change. Menus can range from those that are completely fixed to those that change completely daily. The former is simpler to plan for than the latter. Menus that are completely fixed are used in fast-food and specialty operations. Changes are made only when individual menu items are dropped or added for reasons of popularity or profitability.

In some operations the menu is essentially fixed but changes are made depending on the season of the year or when daily specials are added. In the former case menus may change two or four times a year to accommodate seasonally popular items. Salads and lighter items may predominate in the summer, while stews and other hearty items provide the mainstay in the winter. Certain popular items may be kept year-round.

Daily specials help where there is repeat business. Customers who tire of the regular menu may find the specials appealing. The appeal to the customer also comes from the perception that if a dish is prepared that day, it is fresher or specially prepared. For the operator, daily specials can be a way of recycling leftovers. The baked chicken from one day becomes chicken à la king the next.

Daily changes can be cyclical or complete. Cyclical changes are used when the customer base is captive: that is, when they are tied to a particular operation such as in institutional feeding such as college dorms or prisons. In such an operation a menu is repeated on a cycle that can range from two to six weeks in length. A complete change would be appropriate for a captive audience in a resort setting where people stay for two weeks at a time. In this situation the entire menu is often changed daily.

Types of Offerings. Menus tend to be à la carte, table d'hôte, or some combination of the two. On à la carte menus, items are priced individually. The appetizers, entrees or main course, potatoes, vegetables, and desserts are priced separately. A table d'hôte menu features a complete meal at a set price, with, for example, a choice of appetizer, main course, and dessert from several options. A combination menu might price appetizers and desserts separately while including salad, bread, potato, and vegetable in the price of the entree. An advantage of à la carte menus is their perception of being classier. They certainly tend to be more expensive. By packaging a dessert in with the main course, the average check—total revenue divided by the number of customers—can be increased. People are "forced" to buy an item—the dessert—they might not purchase otherwise. If they feel the value is there, they will be satisfied and the restaurateur will have sold an item that would not have been purchased had it been priced separately.

Size of Menu. Restaurants range from those that have a limited menu to those that offer an extensive menu. A limited menu offers fewer choices to the customers and relies on creating a large number of customers willing to purchase a small number of menu items. Care must be taken that the items offered are desired by a relatively large percentage of people.

A limited menu restricts the number of customers. If all the restaurant offers is salads and a party of four is eating out together, one person in the party who does not like salads can lose the restaurant four customers. For this reason fast-food operations tend to start out with a basic product and as the concept moves through the life cycle, add items to the menu to attract a larger base of people.

A limited menu allows people to make a very quick decision as to what to eat. This may appeal to customers who do not want to make extensive decisions at mealtimes. It also speeds customer turnover.

A limited menu also means less waste. For every item on the menu, there is a waste factor. It may occur as spoilage in storing; it may be that too much is made of a particular item and the remainder must be thrown out. Thus the more items on the menu, the more items will have to be ordered, stored, issued, prepared, and served. Inventory costs will be higher, as will waste costs.

The major advantage of an extensive menu is that there is a greater chance that one or more items on the menu will appeal to more people, thus increasing the menu range.

OVERVIEW OF RESTAURANT CHAINS

Full-service Restaurants

The recent strength in the sales of full-service restaurants has been as a result of a strong economy and upbeat consumers who felt that, even if a job was lost, another would be readily found [7]. Despite this, or perhaps because of this, operators face increasing competition, especially at restaurants with higher prices, where the perception of value received by customers is less than with lower priced operations.

Limited-service Restaurants

Sales growth at quick-service restaurants has traditionally come from increases in the number of outlets. As growth in the number of outlets has slowed recently, so has sales. Some companies are emphasizing the concept of return-on-investment on an individual location basis, further slowing expansion. In addition, a number of chains are reducing the proportion of restaurants in the company that operate as company stores, selling them to their better franchisees.

Quick-service operators are increasingly feeling the competition from grocery stores and convenience stores. Some are increasing their marketing efforts in an attempt to differentiate themselves from the competition. In 1997 they spent 4 percent of sales on advertising. One-third expect to spend more while just under two-thirds say they will continue to spend the same [8].

Customer satisfaction is increasing—the percentage of customers who feel that the value received meets or exceeds their expectations increased from 65 percent in 1995 to 76 percent in 1998 [9].

The 1998 top-10 restaurant chains were [10]:

Rank	Chain	Concept	U.S. Systemwide Sales (millions)
1	McDonalds	Sandwich	$18,123
2	Burger King	Sandwich	8,245
3	Taco Bell	Sandwich	5,000
4	Wendy's	Sandwich	4,994
5	Pizza Hut	Pizza	4,800
6	KFC	Chicken	4,200
7	Aramark Global Food/Leisure Services	Contract	3,437
8	Subway	Sandwich	3,100
9	Hardee's	Sandwich	2,394
10	Domino's Pizza	Pizza	2,300

Sandwich Chains

Sandwich chains account for 42 percent of top-100 chain U.S. systemwide sales. The first edition noted that customers have difficulty differentiating among the various sandwich chains and that, to do well, they must return to identifying what differentiates them from the competition. The answer, according to industry practice, seems to be promotional tie-ins. The lack of differentiation in the sandwich market may mean that the toy becomes the deciding factor, particularly when children exert a major factor in the choice of restaurant.

Noting the move by sandwich chains to highlight promotional tie-ins, many industry observers joke that some restaurants are toy stores that sell food on the side. Responding to increased competition for market share, chains are increasingly building on the hype created by entertainment companies and toy collectors. McDonalds pioneered the movement in 1997 with its Teeny Beanie Babies promotion. By making the premium appealing to collectors, return sales were all but assured. The challenge for management is to turn the customer, initially attracted by the promotion, into a long-term returning customer after the toys are gone. It is suggested that the competition to design toy tie-ins leaves the smaller chains at a distinct disadvantage. Reaching a deal with Hollywood or a TV network is something that only the larger chains can pull off.

In an effort to streamline operations some top chains have been revamping the back-of-the-house to improve efficiency and allow them to improve speed, freshness and individuality of orders. The top-five sandwich chains were [11]:

Rank	Chain	U.S. Market Share (%)
1	McDonalds	35
2	Burger King	16
3	Taco Bell	10
4	Wendy's	10
5	Subway	6

Contract Chains

Accounting for 12 percent of top-100 U.S. systemwide sales, contract catering covers sales by foodservice management firms. The recreation segment is increasingly seen as prestigious as foodservice plays a more important role at sporting events. As sports facilities become places of entertainment the event is only part of a restaurant–play area–shopping–museum complex. As the facility is enhanced, so customer expectations of the food served increase. The top chains are:

Rank	Chain	U.S. Market Share (%)
1	Aramark Global Food	24
2	LSG Sky Chefs/Sky Chefs	9
3	Sodexho Marriott Corporate Serv.	8
4	Sodexho Marriott Healthcare Serv.	8
5	Sodexho Marriott Education Serv.	7

Dinner Houses

In an effort to compete, dinner-house operators are launching new growth vehicles, remodeling aging stores, and actively searching for concepts that can be expanded. Dinner houses made up 10 percent of top-100 chain revenue in 1998. In that year the top chains were:

Rank	Chain	U.S. Market Share (%)
1	Applebee's Neighborhood Bar & Grill	17
2	Red Lobster	16
3	Olive Garden	12
4	Outback Steakhouse	12
5	Chili's Grill & Bar	11

quick bite 1.4
The Restaurant Industry Dollar

	A	B	C
Sales			
Food sales	97.0%	78.4%	100.0%
Beverage sales (alcoholic)	5.6	21.9	0.0
Total sales	100	100	100
Cost of sales			
Food cost	33.6	34.6	32.3
Beverage cost	30.0	30.0	0.0
Total cost of sales	33.3	33.5	32.3
Gross profit	66.7	66.5	67.7
Operating expenses			
Salaries and wages	30.4	28.3	26.9
Employee benefits	3.4	4.1	2.2
Direct operating expenses	5.2	5.5	5.2
Music and entertainment	0.0	0.1	0.0
Marketing	1.6	2.1	3.9
Utility services	3.6	2.9	2.9
Restaurant occupancy costs	4.7	5.3	6.6
Administrative and general	2.3	3.8	2.1
Repairs and maintenance	1.6	1.7	1.4
Total operating expenses	60.9	61.0	60.1
Interest expense	Insufficient data		0.5
Income before income taxes	4.7	3.6	5.7

Source: Restaurant Industry Operations Report, 1998 (Washington, DC: Deloitte & Touche and the National Restaurant Association, 1998), pp. 25, 55, 85. Note: (1) All figures are medians based on 1997 data. (2) All ratios are based on a percentage of total sales except food and beverage costs, which are based on their respective sales. A, full-service restaurants, average check per person under $10.00; B, full-service restaurants, average check per person $10.00 and over; C, limited-service fast food restaurants.

Pizza Chains

Pizza chains account for 9 percent of top-100 U.S. systemwide sales. After several years of discounting, the pizza chains found that reduced prices and two-for-ones produced volume but did little for profits. Some chains are beginning to focus on core marketing and operational strategies at the expense of low-price promotions. The general trend towards prepared foods benefits pizza with its takeout and home delivery. Home delivery, in turn, has benefited from recent advances in delivery bag technology.

The top chains in 1998 were:

Rank	Chain	U.S. Market Share (%)
1	Pizza Hut	44
2	Domino's Pizza	21
3	Little Caesar's Pizza	11
4	Papa John's Pizza	11
5	Sbarro, The Italian Eatery	4

Family Chains

In an attempt to maintain market share against competitors from other sectors of the industry, family chains are struggling to keep their 7 percent market share of the top-100 chains. Much remodeling and "reimaging" is going on as the chains look to update a rather tired image and to differentiate themselves from casual and quick-service restaurants. Denny's, for example, is remodeling all of its units as "Denny's Diner 2000" restaurants with jukeboxes and revolving pie cases. Lunch and dinner menus are being improved, and breakfast is advertised as a differentiating factor. While the present focus is on the family, industry observers see a 10-year trend towards appealing to aging baby-boomers who want high-quality food and value but are turned off by the noisy casual dinner houses.

The top chains are:

Rank	Chain	U.S. Market Share (%)
1	Denny's	22
2	Shoney's	11
3	Cracker Barrel Old Country Store	11
4	International House of Pancakes	11
5	Perkins Family Restaurants	9

Chicken Chains

Chicken chains are responsible for 6 percent of top-100 U.S. systemwide sales. The top-five chicken chains in 1998 were:

Rank	Chain	U.S. Market Share (%)
1	KFC	57
2	Boston Market*	13
3	Popeyes	11
4	Chick-fil-A	10
5	Church's Chicken	8

*Boston Market filed for chapter 11 bankruptcy in 1998. As this book went to press its future was uncertain.

Food Trends

Catering to patron's changing tastes is difficult. Inventive chefs will seek new and innovative menu items that will give them an edge over the competition. Occasionally, one may even create a new culinary trend. However, there is no guarantee that the fad will last; some fade immediately, while others remain favorites for decades. It is important that when considering new items, chefs and managers must keep in mind their customer's concern for their waistlines and wallets. Past major food trends include salad bars, mesquite-grilled meats, pineapple pizzas, wine coolers, nouvelle cuisine, fern bars, croissant sandwiches, self-serve bars, chicken nuggets, oat bran and over-the-top food presentations. New trends that are expected to take off in the new millennium are ethnic foods and ingredients along with vegetarian and organic items. According to culinary professionals, the following items are what's in and what's out:

Hot/Trendy Items	Cool/Passé Items	Everlasting Favorites
• Infused oils	• Taco salad	• Asparagus
• Pan-seared	• Fondue au fromage	• Spinach
• Espresso/specialty coffee drinks	• Cream-based sauces	• Berries
• Asian/Thai	• Chef's salad	• Lime
• Meatless/vegetarian dishes	• Blackened	• Cantaloupe

When America's top chefs were surveyed, the overwhelming majority named ethnic cuisines, foreign flavors and imported ingredients at the top of their trends list. The fact that ethnic and imported goods are easier to obtain than before is a bonus for operators. This trend towards ethnic fare is one result of an increasingly diverse population. Large minority segments of the population are having a tremendous effect on the tastes of the nation. The growing Asian and Pacific Islander populations are increasing the use of ingredients such as ginger and lemongrass, commonly thought of as Asian.

One of the most popular ethnic foods is Thai cuisine. Thai dishes often use fish, fresh fruits and vegetables as well as various herbs and spices. The combination of these ingredients create meals that are low in fat and sodium but are high in flavor and texture that appeal greatly to health-conscious individuals. Ethnic cuisine is also having a great impact on all menu items; chefs creating new dishes are focusing less on style and concentrating more on simple substance. Ethnic cuisines also inspire the use of new popular ingredi-

(continued)

ents such as quinoa, a staple of the ancient Incas; couscous, a North African staple; and chipotle chilies from Mexico and South America.

Vegetarian and Organic

Just a decade ago, an operator would have a hard time getting customers to consider a vegetarian dish. However, vegetarian dishes have become popular menu items, especially as entrees. Many of the finest chefs have created vegetable menus or added meatless/vegetarian dinner selections to the menu. Over 50% of tableservice operators with an average per-person check size of $15 or more reported that their customers are ordering vegetarian dishes more frequently than before.

Organic produce has also gained popularity as patrons have begun to lean toward healthier lifestyles. Many operators agree that organic foods are a hot commodity. However, because of the high price of organic fruits and vegetables, restaurants with an average check size of $25 or more are more likely to offer organically grown items. Yet, as organic items become more popular, prices are likely to fall allowing more restaurateurs to add them to their menus.

Source: "1999 Highlights." *Restaurants USA*, v. 18, no. 11, December 1998, pp. F26–F28.

This segment of the industry continues characterized by the introduction of new products and concepts and development in nontraditional outlets. Typical of the new prototypes are the snackable items—popcorn chicken and honey barbecue wings of KFC, the quick-casual Cajun Kitchen of Popeyes, and country fried steak at Churchs.

Grill-Buffet Chains

Grill-Buffet chains, which account for 2 percent of top-100 chain sales, have lately been resizing units to suit local markets. Expansion is increasingly into smaller cities where competition is less. The 1998 top grill-buffet chains were:

Rank	Chain	U.S. Market Share (%)
1	Golden Corral	32
2	Ryan's Family Steak House	25
3	Ponderosa Steakhouse	20
4	Western Sizzlin'	12
5	Sizzler	11

WHY RESTAURANTS FAIL

By some estimates, one out of every three restaurants fails in the first year of operation. One study of publicly held companies identified the following events described as unique in the bankruptcy process of restaurant firms. They are [12]:

- Net losses
- Management turnover
- Loan default
- Royalty default
- Credit accommodation
- Decline in unit sales
- Renegotiation of franchise contract

There are a variety of reasons for the high failure rate in this business [13]. Very simply put:

profit = sales − costs

---

quick bite 1.6
Employees and Competition

Labor is increasingly a problematic issue for restaurateurs. In 1998, the national unemployment level reached 4.5%, a figure so low it has rarely been seen in peacetime economies. The low rate is causing operators to face tough recruitment-and-retention problems. The labor shortage is effecting both table-service and quick-service facilities where operators say that finding qualified and motivated labor will be the top challenge they face in 1999.

Competition is a second big challenge for operators. Competition in the restaurant industry is growing. Almost 4 out of 5 consumers said that they have a much larger selection of outlets available to them today than they did several years ago. And with 815,000 locations across the country that provide foodservice, the consumer has many choices.

As a result of the labor shortage and increased competition, many operators are taking extra steps to retain the quality employees they currently have. These restaurateurs realize that in order to be successful into the new millennium they must encourage a culture that promotes employee satisfaction and ultimately leads to customer satisfaction.

Source: "1999 Highlights." *Restaurants USA*, v. 18, no. 11, December 1998, pp. F4–F5.

Thus, to achieve profitability it is necessary to increase sales while reducing costs. By increasing costs through such things as bigger portion sizes or more service, a restaurant becomes more attractive to customers, thereby increasing sales. The reverse is also true. Costs can be trimmed by having fewer employees or cheaper cuts of meat, which might lead to the loss of customers, thereby reducing sales. We focus our discussion of the reasons that restaurants fail on the two sides of the profit equation: sales and costs.

Failure to Increase Sales

Same Concept. Many failures occur because management stays with the same concept for too long. Like other products and services, restaurants have a life cycle. In the early stages of a new operation, the restaurant goes through an introductory stage in which the concept is introduced into the marketplace. If all goes well, the operation experiences a period of growth, in which sales are increasing at an increasing rate. As the concept matures, sales continue to increase but at a decreasing rate. If no action is taken, a period of decline sets in, during which sales fall. Throughout the life-cycle curve, profits lead sales. That is, a downturn in profits precedes a downturn in sales. In this way it is possible to get advance warning about where the restaurant is in the cycle.

If advance notice is given and the operation changes, it is possible to go through a period of rejuvenation rather than decline. Fast-food restaurants attempted this a few years ago when they added breakfast items to their menus as a response to a slowdown in sales. One way to rejuvenate an operation is to sell a product or service at additional times: hence the breakfast menu. They made a similar decision when they expanded internationally. The domestic market was becoming saturated, and future growth necessitated overseas expansion. This is another way to rejuvenate—sell to another market.

Lack of Creativity. Lack of sales often comes from a lack of imagination and creativity in developing new ideas. We are conditioned to believe that "new is good." Increasingly, the public is looking for new ways to do things, new items on the menu, new experiences in general. Managers cannot afford to rely on the

"It's a sad commentary on the state of franchise relations...that in many cases the franchisor is the franchisee's biggest competitor."
—GARY AUSTERMAN,
FRANCHISEES' ATTORNEY

Problems between franchisor and franchisee is one of the causes of restaurant failure. *Source: Nation's Restaurant News*, October 9, 1995, p. 118.

status quo. Flexibility is the key—operators need to adopt an attitude that encourages them and their employees to seek constant improvement in their restaurants.

Falling sales may be due partially to the human tendency to react to new situations rather than to anticipate them. There are constant changes in the marketplace. Changing economic conditions may include a demand for less expensive menu items; increased concern over alcohol abuse leads to less consumption of alcohol. The reactive manager waits until trends work their way through society and manifest themselves in a different, reduced, or nonexistent customer base. The proactive manager reads newspapers and magazines, attends industry forums where trends are discussed, anticipates the likelihood of events happening, identifies their potential effects on the business, and changes the operation accordingly before the effects of the changes are felt. In other words, the proactive manager plans rather than simply operates the business.

Failure to Control Costs

Most restaurants operate on relatively small profit margins. Cost control is very important in ensuring a profitable margin. In foodservice operations, the principal areas of cost are labor, food, and beverages. Keeping a close watch on these three areas helps ensure profitability.

Productivity.   To a large extent, high employee costs are a result of poor productivity. Productivity is the ratio of outputs (sales, profits, etc.) to inputs (time, costs, etc.). Typically, this ratio is less for service industries than for manufacturing concerns. In fact, the National Restaurant Association has estimated that the restaurant industry is only half as productive as the manufacturing industries. To the extent that service is important to customers, it is difficult to achieve a sales increase by reducing staff. However, labor cost savings of 10 to 20 percent can be expected through improved employee scheduling alone, resulting in a savings of 3 to 6 percent of sales [14].

Cost Cutting.   Many operators fall into a cost-cutting mode that is counterproductive. When sales drop managers are often tempted to cut costs to compensate for reduced sales. Advertising may be reduced; employee uniforms are not laundered as frequently; less expensive cuts of meat replace menu staples. As a result, the customers who remain become disenchanted with the operation and leave. The focus often is on cutting costs when it should be on increasing sales.

This comes about because of the cost structure of restaurant's. So many of a restaurant's costs are fixed; they do not vary as sales volume varies. The mortgage or lease payment must still be made whether there is one customer or a thousand; the restaurant must be lit regardless of the number of patrons. As a consequence, only a limited amount of cost cutting can take place. In operations where a high proportion of costs are fixed, the break-even point—the point at which sales generated exactly equals costs incurred—is higher than for businesses in which a large proportion of the costs are variable. A variable cost is one that varies proportionately with sales volume (Figure 1.1).

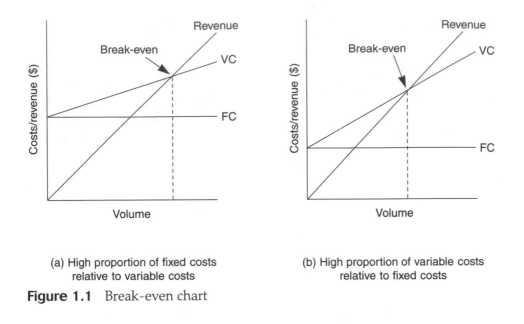

(a) High proportion of fixed costs
relative to variable costs

(b) High proportion of variable costs
relative to fixed costs

Figure 1.1 Break-even chart

However, once the break-even point has been passed, the only costs incurred are variable costs. In restaurants, the variable costs are relatively small compared to the fixed costs. As a result, once an operation has reached a sales volume above the break-even point, the profit potential from a relatively small increase in sales volume becomes great. Managers might therefore better focus their attention on increasing sales rather than on spending time seeking to minimize costs. This is not to negate the importance of cost control; it is, rather, to suggest that with a finite amount of management time available, profits might be increased more by focusing on the sales side of the profit equation than on the cost side.

SUCCESS FACTORS

The key to a successful operation is to develop the right concept, execute it skillfully, give timely service, and meet customer expectations [15].

Right Concept

For the immediate future the "right" concept will be one that gives off energy, meets customer needs for a convenient location and hassle-free experience, does not require that customers dress up, and offers an ethnic flair.

Execution

Employees are the key to execution of the concept. This involves finding the right kinds of people and training them to provide the level of service demanded by the customer. Table service operators identify "finding qualified labor" as either the number-one or number-two issue (depending on the average check of the

quick bite 1.7
Challenges for Success

Labor

The strong economy experienced in the late 90s has spurred restaurant sales; however, the same economic growth results in a tight labor market. As a result, operators find themselves faced with the challenge of finding qualified and motivated workers. The growing number of 16-to-24 year olds—the restaurant industry's primary labor pool—is not enough to relieve the pressure restaurateurs face when attempting to find quality employees.

The competition for labor is fierce; operators not only compete against each other for quality employees, but also against retail and other service businesses. Highly valuable employees can often take their pick from numerous offers and frequently change jobs. 30% of operators say that their hourly employees tend to work for a shorter tenure than two years ago, while 10% feel that their salaried employees are working shorter tenures.

Satisfaction

Many restaurateurs are beginning to offer rewards to hourly and salaried employees to increase satisfaction and productivity. Incentives provided by management range from pay raises and bonuses to benefits such as profit sharing and health insurance. Recognition programs such as "Employee of the Month" are also popular reward systems with operators. Effective rewards can be very inexpensive and might include an afternoon off, a special pin or a simple "thank you."

Training is an excellent way to increase employee satisfaction while increasing customer satisfaction at the same time. Almost 60% of quick-service operators report that they will designate a larger portion of their budget in 1999 to training than they did in 1998. Many tableservice operators are recruiting employees right from the educational system through school-to-career initiatives and scholarship programs.

Technology

More and more restaurateurs are investing in technology to increase efficiency and productivity while increasing customer service. 45% of operators plan to allocate a larger portion of their 1999 budget to technology than they designated in earlier years. 39% said that they would allocate the same amount as they did in 1998.

Many quick-service outlets will use self-service, customer-activated ordering terminals in the future. However, most do not currently use these terminals. Technology also effects the method of payment customers choose to

(continued)

use. The use of credit cards is increasing, especially due to the use of debit cards. 70% of restaurateurs reported an increase in credit card use from two years before.

Expansion and Renovation

Quick-service operators will continue to prioritize expansion and renovation. Expansion is one of the largest sources of growth for restaurant chains whether through entering new markets or increasing their presence in existing markets. However, saturation in many markets has slowed the rate of expansion in contrast with prior years. Renovation can increase sales in existing locations through remodeling and equipment improvements. 58% of quick-service operators reported that they intend to increase expenditures for renovation in 1999.

Source: "1999 Highlights." *Restaurants USA*, v. 18, no. 11, December 1998, p. F15–F16

operation) facing them today. A primary factor in this regard is the economic health of the country. When the economy is strong, fewer people are willing to enter the foodservice industry. The reverse is also true.

To ensure that employees have the skills to perform to a standard, employers should provide a full range of activities for employees. This begins with a handbook explaining company policies, written job descriptions, and an orientation program. Training manuals are an integral part of a training program, but films or videos are used increasingly in part to overcome language difficulties. A complete system includes regular job performance evaluations to ensure that standards are being maintained.

Service

As noted earlier, service is a major concern for both customers and operators. Indeed, service complaints dominate, far exceeding customer complaints about food or atmosphere. Five elements have been identified as important: providing timely service, answering customer questions, handling complaints, delivering accurately totaled guest checks, and recommending appropriate menu items. Customers seem most satisfied with the accuracy of the check and the server's ability to answer questions, although only 75 percent rated staff as "good" or "excellent" on these items. Almost two-thirds of respondents rated servers "good" or "excellent" in recommending appropriate menu items.

The two most common complaints in the categories above concern speed of service and inattentive staff. The former can involve service that is too slow or the feeling of being rushed. It is important to tailor the speed of service to the individual and the occasion. In the latter case, customers are upset by having to summon employees to give an order or by waiting for a check. For customers, the wait seems longest after the meal is over. Delays during a meal seem shorter than waits either before or after the meal. Customers are most dissatisfied with the way that complaints were handled. The subject of service is dealt with in more detail in Chapter 5.

Meeting Customer Expectations

Increasingly, customers have higher expectations, demanding more attention and friendlier service. Most customers seem satisfied with food quality, dining area cleanliness, comfort of the atmosphere, freshness of the ingredients, and portion size. Indeed, the only area where satisfaction is less than 50 percent relates to noise level. As the customer base ages this is expected to become of even greater concern. Rising expectations manifest themselves in a desire for a better price/value relationship.

MANAGEMENT SKILLS: BASIC FUNCTIONAL AREAS

The National Restaurant Association has identified the following nine functional areas as representative of a restaurant manager's job [16]. They are rank-ordered based on mean importance ratings by restaurant managers.

Outback Steakhouse's management compensation plan gives managers ownership in their operation.

1. Cost control and financial management: monitoring, controlling, and reporting the profitability indicators for the store.
2. Supervision of shift operations: running each shift efficiently, effectively, and in accordance with procedures.
3. Organizing and planning shift operations: making preparations for each shift so that operations run smoothly and efficiently.

---

quick bite 1.8
Road to the Top

Anne Albertine, manager, product and culinary development

Anne Albertine has no problem keeping busy as Taco Bell Corp.'s only product development staff member with any culinary experience. Albertine, while serving as Taco Bell's manager of product and culinary development, helps to shape the taste of America. Albertine was hired on at Taco Bell after serving five years at Nike sportswear company in their product development department. Although it may seem strange for a graduate of University of Massachusetts, Amherst with a culinary arts certificate to end up at Nike, according to Albertine she just kind of fell into the job. The job market wasn't great in the restaurant industry at the time she graduated.

When Albertine decided that she wanted to get back into food, she furthered her education earning a degree at Portland, Oregon's Western Culinary Institute and then apprenticed at chef Michel Richard's Citrus in Los Angeles. After taking more classes in London and Napa Valley Albertine landed the position at Taco Bell. According to Mary Wagner, Taco Bell's chief technology and quality officer, Albertine has exactly the right mix of skills for her position. Due to her experience in product development at Nike, Albertine understands the sense of timing and urgency.

Albertine's experience with French, Mexican and Japanese cooking has helped her develop the foods and flavors at Taco Bell. Albertine was involved in Taco Bell's recent Gorditas line, whose launch was the QSR chain's most successful to date. However, Albertine spends the majority of her time working on Taco Bell's Project Gold, the revamping of the entire chain's menu. Albertine's goal is to provide customers with better quality in order to gain more credibility for the chain, bringing in a wider variety of customers.

Albertine feels that Mexican food is a great platform. She especially enjoys the many flavors and expressions of food available. Mexican food provides Taco Bell with many opportunities that burger places just don't have. According to Albertine, "What we're doing, too, is trying to stretch Americans' tastes and introduce some flavors that they may not have had before and make us more accessible to them."

Source: Cavanaugh, Bonnie. "Anne Albertine: From sportswear to foodservice: Developing a winning product every time." *Nation's Restaurant News*, v. 33, no. 4, pp. 10–11.

4. Unit coordination and control: communicating and coordinating among store managers and their supervisors and others in the organization.
5. Customer relations: improving customers' dining experiences.
6. Motivating employee performance: monitoring, enhancing, and controlling employee performance.

---

 quick bite 1.9
Hot Skills

Administration 2000

One of the greatest administrative skills a restaurant manager will need in 2000 is computer proficiency for tasks including scheduling needs and demand forecasting. These computer skills will be needed as more foodservice organizations begin to use comprehensive computer-based information systems. Managers need advanced computer skills as routine administrative tasks become computerized through stand-alone computer or a networked system.

Managers will also need the ability to deal with a multicultural work force. Managers will be required to deal with a growing ethnically diverse workforce. One of the greatest skills a manager can obtain to address this trend is to become multilingual.

Interpersonal skills are necessary to interact with a diverse staff and are also beneficial in the teaching and training aspect that is needed for all employees. Training will become more important in the future and the time spent on it will outweigh that spent on paperwork.

The Top 10 Most Likely Developments for Managers in Administration 2000:

1. Need for greater computer skills
2. Ability to supervise an ethnically diverse staff
3. Ability to teach and train employees
4. Must have better people management skills
5. Ability to motivate employees
6. Must be flexible with employees, especially in scheduling
7. Must spend more time on training employees
8. Must spend more time managing human resources and less time on paperwork
9. Need for understanding government and regulatory law and compliance
10. Must be able to manage time

Adapted from: National Restaurant Association, *Foodservice Manager 2000.* (Washington DC: National Restaurant Associaton, 1992).

7. Employment and development of crew members: recruiting, selecting, developing, and retaining crew members.
8. Communication with outside sources: communicating with management, marketing, and community resources outside the store.
9. Monitoring and maintaining facility and equipment: keeping all physical assets operational and in good repair.

The following three functional areas are identified as most important.

Employment/Development of Crew

Managers will find that human resource issues will become a top priority. They will thus be spending more time training employees. One area in which this will be necessary is in the basics of service. Managers will need better skills in managing people and in teaching and training employees. They will also have to develop a higher commitment to their employees' career development.

Supervision of Shift Operations

The challenge for managers in this area will involve supervising a more culturally diverse staff. Through their employees, they will have to stress service as a competitive point of difference. Higher levels of service will have to be provided in a more cost-effective manner. This will also be done in an environment that will place more stringent regulations on food handling and sanitation.

---

 q u i c k   b i t e   1 . 1 0
Industry Structure in 2010

According to the National Restaurant Association the most likely developments regarding industry structure in 2010 are:

- To be successful, operators will have to provide the highest levels of service in addition to quality food.
- There will be continued and intense competition.
- Chain operations will make up a larger share of the market.
- Most chains will operate multiple concepts.
- Government will play a larger role in food safety.

Source: Restaurant Industry 2010: The Road Ahead (Washington, D.C.: National Restaurant Association, 1999), pp. 8, 23.

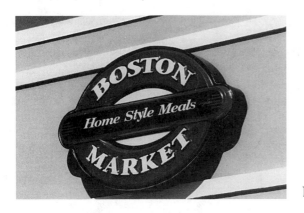

Boston Market

Motivating Employee Performance

Finding and motivating employees will become even more important than it is today. Managers will need excellent interpersonal skills as they empower employees to provide better service, becoming more like team leaders and coaches.

In Chapter 15 we look more closely at the skills necessary for restaurant managers as we approach the next century.

ENDNOTES

1. Deloitte & Touche LLP, *1998 Restaurant Industry Operations Report*, (Washington, DC: National Restaurant Association, 1998), p. 6.

2. 1999 Restaurant Industry Forecast, *Nation's Restaurant News*, December 1998, p. F8.

3. Ibid.

4. National Restaurant Association, *Tableservice Restaurant Trends, 1998* (Washington, DC: National Restaurant Association, 1998).

5. Claire D. Schmelzer and James R. Lang, "Networking and Information Sources of Independent Restaurateurs," *Hospitality Research Journal*, vol. 14, no. 2, 1990, pp. 327–338.

6. Donald E. Lundberg, *The Restaurant: From Concept to Operation* (New York: John Wiley & Sons, 1985), pp. 18–22.

7. "1998 Restaurant Industry Forecast," *Nation's Restaurant News*, December 1998, p. F11.

8. Ibid., p. F11.

9. Ibid., p. F10.

10. "NRN Top 100," *Nation's Restaurant News*, June 28, 1999, pp. 97–158.

11. Ibid, p. 148.

12. Francis A. Kwansa and H. G. Parsa, "Business Failure Analysis," *Hospitality Research Journal*, vol. 14, no. 2, 1990, pp. 23–34.

13. Lewis J. Minor and Ronald F. Cichy, *Foodservice Systems Management* (Westport, CT: AVI Publishing Company, 1984), pp. 18–23.

14. Robert Christie Mill, *Managing for Productivity in the Hospitality Industry* (New York: Van Nostrand Reinhold, 1989), p. 53.

15. *Job Analysis Report for Unit Manager and Assistant Manager* (Washington, DC: Educational Foundation of the National Restaurant Association, 1988).

16. National Restaurant Association, *Foodservice Manager 2000, Current Issues Report* (Washington, DC: National Restaurant Association, 1992), p. 7.

CHAPTER TWO

UNDERSTANDING THE CUSTOMER

learning objectives

By the end of this chapter you should be able to:

1. Describe the eating habits of various segments of the restaurant market.

2. Identify the six major decision scenarios for the dinner market.

3. Identify major ongoing trends in customer behavior that will affect the restaurant industry.

Customers love to hear the sound of their own names, we were told. Constantly reinforce the positive and distract from the negative or embarrassing; when the kitchen runs out of a customer's favorite dish, withhold the bad news until you have some good news to bring. Create an aura of comfort and confidence. People go to a restaurant to feed their emotions, not their stomachs. (Some customers want to feel important, others to be entertained; some want the staff to take a personal interest in them, others want to be left alone. Find out precisely what each customer needs.)

Source: Jeffrey Steingarten, *The Man Who Ate Everything* (New York, NY: Vintage Books, 1997).

INTRODUCTION

An understanding of the restaurant customer is useful as long as the limitations of such a study are appreciated. It is useful as a way of seeing the big picture: Why do people eat out, and what are the characteristics of this activity? However, any attempt to characterize the restaurant customer will result in a picture that while valid in the aggregate will probably not be accurate for any particular operation. Thus, although this chapter will be useful to managers overall, it will be necessary to develop a marketing plan (Chapter 3) to make the picture relevant to the individual operation.

MARKET CATEGORIES

One way to make market categories relevant is to think of the foodservice industry as being arranged in three general categories: the captive market, the mass market, and the status market (Figure 2.1).

Captive Market

The captive market—in institutions, industrial or school settings, and airplanes—is limited in the choice of what is available. These customers have little choice in what to eat, when and where to eat, and the price if a charge is made. The primary concern here is "how we eat."

When people are given little or no choice in the mechanics of the eating experience, there is a tendency to rebel. Having little or no choice in these matters is like being treated as a child. As a child, adults told us when to eat, what to eat, how to eat, and how much to eat. When people grow up, they want to make these decisions for themselves and resent being put back in the role of a child. Take, for example, eating on a plane. Passengers are locked into their seats, served when it is convenient for the cabin staff to do so, and remain trapped in place until the staff decides to collect the platters.

Research in British mental institutions has shown some rather sophisticated behavior on the part of patients regarding food. Hoarding of food, midnight snacks, and secret parties allowed the patients to exhibit some degree of control over their food intake—control that was not allowed in the way they were served their meals.

There is some indication that traditional complaints about institutional food have less to do with the food and more to do with the way the food is served and the lack of control the customers have in that process. Allowing some degree of

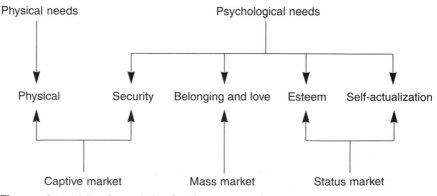

Figure 2.1 Needs and the food service industry.

Cool Blue's

As the son of a handicapped father, Richard Baressi, owner of Cool Blue's seafood and pasta restaurant and blues club, accessibility is a major issue. Baressi's father, who had multiple sclerosis, let him realize firsthand the difficulties of handicapped restaurant patrons. Yet, Baressi is concerned with all handicapped customers, including the blind.

Dining in a restaurant can be a tension-filled event for the visually impaired. A blind patron may feel embarrassed and self-conscious requiring someone else read the menu to him or her. However, considerate restaurateurs like Baressi have begun investing in braille and large print menus for their visually impaired guests, including many senior citizens.

In order to help make his restaurant more convenient for his visually impaired patron, Baressi enlisted the help of Brailling Enterprises Inc., a firm located in Sharon, Massachusetts that provides braille consulting services to restaurants, hotels and educational facilities. The business also furnishes materials and other services to increase safety, independence, and comfort of blind and visually impaired patrons.

When an establishment provides braille menus, visually impaired customers are given a feeling of self-confidence and self-reliance, making their dining experience more pleasurable. The menus also allow blind and visually impaired patrons to look over the menu several times before making a decision rather than asking the waiter or someone else to repeat it over and over again. Providing large print menus for seniors is a good move for any restaurateur, especially as the baby boomers begin to age.

Due the benefits of braille menus, it is a wonder why all restaurants do not provide them. However, the Americans with Disabilities Act (ADA) has a loophole that says a restaurant is in compliance as long as a server is willing to read the menu to a patron. Yet, according to Baressi, braille menus are in the long run a smarter, more cost-effective choice than having a busy waiter read the menu repeatedly.

Source: Strauss, Karyn. "On the Menu: Cool Blue's." *Nation's Restaurant News,* v. 33, no. 5, February 1, 1999, p. 39.

choice in how, when, and where food is served may result in fewer complaints and more satisfied customers.

McDonalds is one company that combined cost and availability in their initial marketing thrust. The first national advertising campaign for McDonalds did not mention food or beverage. It said: "You deserve a break today; so get out and get away—to McDonald's." They were talking to the busy mother, trying to balance the needs of home, children, and often, a job outside the home. This person was hungry, the children were hungry, and the conflicting demands of the mother's life left her exhausted. The "solution" was a trip to McDonalds. Catering to physical needs, McDonald's offered a break from the work of preparing food by serving food at low cost to the customer.

Mass Market

The mass market looks for food in a social setting. This large segment of the market encompasses everyone from teenagers grabbing a burger in the company of friends and families eating out together to special dates and anniversary dinners. Whatever the occasion, the primary concern is the same: with whom we eat.

Status Market

The status market is more concerned with where we eat. To see and be seen is more important than what is on the menu. The choice of restaurant to which a business client is taken for lunch indicates what status the client "deserves." At the same time, the prices on the menu are, in part, a measure of the status accorded the host by his or her company. The person who selects the restaurant or suggests an item from the menu takes responsibility for that suggestion. If the experience is good, the recommendation is complimented and the recipient gets to bask in the admiration of others. The reverse is also true: More than an overcooked steak is on the line.

It should be emphasized that at different times of the week, the same person can be concerned with the satisfaction of different needs. An executive may grab a salad at Wendy's for lunch on Monday, dine with her husband at a romantic getaway on Tuesday, and treat a business client to lunch in an upscale club on Wednesday. In the first instance the concern is physical—to refuel; in the second it is belonging and love—to create the mood for romance; and in the third it is esteem—to impress the client. The key for the operator is to understand the underlying motivation for the dining experience and to organize all elements of the marketing mix to meet those needs and wants.

CUSTOMER CHARACTERISTICS

The typical American, aged 8 or older, has an average of four commercially-prepared meals a week—2.2 lunches, 1.3 dinners, and 0.7 breakfasts [1]. Men eat out more frequently than do women. Those between 18 and 24 eat an average of six commercially-prepared meals a week while those over 65 average 2.5 meals a week. Segments that have a higher-than-average propensity to commercially-prepared meals include African Americans, those of Hispanic origin, residents of Southern states, and employed female heads of households. Those less likely include households earning less than $25,000 a year, unemployed females, and households without children.

A brief look at some important market characteristics follows.

Repeat Customers

Repeat business accounts for anywhere from 60 percent (operations with an average check of $8 or less) to 80 percent (operations with an average check of $25 or more) of total revenue for restaurants. Frequent diners are responsible for three quarters of all dinner occasions when the meal is purchased outside the home [2]. Restaurateurs focus on providing value as a way of getting first-timers back. Half report that customers are more value conscious than before. It is more difficult than ever to maintain customer loyalty.

Frequent diners have two major characteristics [3]. They eat dinners out at least seven times a month; and they have distinct behavior patterns in their dining habits. There are, in fact, five subsegments of this market—each with unique behavior patterns. The "Too Tired to Cook" group purchases an average of 4.8 dinners a week away from home. They use full-service restaurants, carryout, and grocery stores. They want quick, easy, and relatively healthy dinner choices. The "Busy Parents" are constantly on the move and pick up dinner on the way home or between events. Pleasing the children is particularly important. They want something that is fast, easy, has drive-thru access, and value-for-money deals.

"Care Seekers" are older adults and empty-nesters. They want home-cooked dishes they are familiar with, friendly service, and discounts. The "Urban Sophisticates" tend to eat out at higher-priced restaurants. For them, the restaurant selected is an extension of their lifestyle. Fresh ingredients and made-to-order items are important as are unique, trendy foods and ingredients as well as

---

quⅰck bⅰte 2.2
Changing Demographics

Where is the Market Potential?

Population Projections by Age, 2000–2010

	Population (thousands)			Percent Distribution	
	2000	**2005**	**2010**	**2000**	**2010**
18–24	25,231	26,918	27,155	9.4	9.6
25–34	37,149	35,997	37,572	13.8	13.3
35–44	43,911	40,951	37,202	16.4	13.2
45–54	37,223	41,619	43,207	13.9	15.3
55–64	24,158	29,762	35,430	9.0	12.5
65–74	18,243	18,410	21,039	6.85	7.4
75+	16,639	17,864	18,323	6.2	6.5

Source: Statistical Abstract of the United States, 1991 (Washington, DC: U.S. Government Printing Office, 1992).

wine and beer tastings. Finally, the "Flavor Savorers" select a restaurant based on a particular cuisine or because of a signature menu item. Being known as the best place for a specific type of food will attract this group.

Boomers

Although generation-Xers eat out more often, baby-boomers, those born between 1946 and 1964, spend more when they dine out. Restaurant spending is influenced by household income as well as the age and employment status of the head of the household. The proportion of the food dollar spent on food away from home increases as household income rises. Households with incomes of

---

quick bite 2.3
Family Dining

As adults begin to call for spicier and more ethnic cuisine, family-dining restaurants are answering. However, this change in style does not mean that these restaurants are giving up the perennial favorites. They are merely reacting to changing consumer preferences. Operators are adapting for fear that patrons will find other outlets to provide them with the foods they crave.

As family restaurants attempt to cater better to adults, many are also renewing their focus on kids. Many operators are beginning to concentrate on children by offering them meals based on taste preferences rather than on kids-meal enticements commonly used by quick-service chains. The prevailing attitude in the family segment is retain traditional flavors, but be sure to experiment with trends or else you will be out of business.

The lines between the family dining and the casual dining segments are beginning to blur. One major reason is the number of cooking shows appearing on cable TV. These shows feature cuisines that many consumers have never seen before, such as Cajun. Customers want to try new things. One family chain, Cracker Barrel, is beginning to offer regional dishes to its traditional menu in order to appeal to more customers. When Bob Evans added new menu items, their same-store sales increased by 5%.

The attempt to capture family business is much more difficult than before. Family eating patterns are shifting and families will now eat almost anywhere. Up to 10% of the tables at an upscale steakhouse may be occupied by families on any given night. There is a growing sophistication of taste and family restaurants must respond in order to retain business. However, it is important for a family restaurant to stay focused. When an operator has a strong family concept, it is unwise to give that up moving towards casual dining; a core menu is still the strongest selling point in the family segment.

Source: Cebrzynski, Gregg. "Family Restaurants Explore Bolder Tastes for Adults, New Meals for Kids." *Nation's Restaurant News,* v. 33, no. 9, March 1, 1999, pp. 47–50.

$70,000 or more before taxes spend almost half of their food budget on restaurant meals [4]. The baby-boomer age group is at the peak of earning capacity and can afford to spend on eating out.

Multicheck Households

Just under two-thirds of all married-couple households have two or three paycheck earners [5]. This increases the amount of disposable income available for eating out, among other things. More money is also available as the income gap between men and women in the workforce has narrowed over the years. Combined with the busy lifestyle of both husband and wife working outside of the home, these income factors add up to tremendous market potential.

Households with two or more people in them and two paycheck earners spend more than 40 percent more than households with one earner on food away from home. The impact is greatest in higher-check upscale restaurants. Households with two earners account for over twice as many visits to higher-check upscale restaurants than households with one earner.

Families with Children

Families with children represent another frequent-dinner segment. These busy parents have little time to cook. Full-service restaurants with lower per-person check sizes make the greatest effort to appeal to this segment of the market. To cater to this segment of the market restaurants are offering [6]:

- Child-size portions at lower prices
- Children's favorite menu items
- Entertainment for children, such as coloring books
- Promotions to attract families with children

Children's tastes change as they get older. Children under 6 order pizza, milk, cold cereal, hamburgers/cheeseburgers, macaroni and cheese, cookies, gelatin, and french fries. Popular for kids between 6 and 17 are pizza, tacos, french fries, nachos, and hamburgers/cheeseburgers [7]. Children in general are also becoming more adventurous eaters. While Mexican and Asian foods are ordered a small percentage of the time, the incidence of both is on the rise. Pasta, breakfast sandwiches, rice, and juice are all increasing in popularity.

Minorities

Fueled by strong population and income growth, minorities are becoming an increasingly attractive market segment for restaurateurs [8]. For both lunch and dinner whites are less likely than African-Americans, Asians or Hispanics to eat out. About 37 percent of Hispanics report they are on-premises restaurant customers for lunch compared to 33 percent for African-Americans and Asians. In addition, all three groups are substantially more likely than whites to order take-out and delivery and to visit quick-service restaurants and convenience stores.

Hispanic and African-American females are more likely to be customers than minority males. This is probably explained by the relatively large proportion of minority females in the workforce. Usually, the likelihood of eating out decreases with age. This, however, is not true for Hispanics who are just as likely to eat out as they grow older compared to younger Hispanics. This segment, together with African-Americans, are more likely than whites in the same income bracket to eat out. While lower incomes mean that many minority customers do not have the same amount of disposable income as do whites, their increased propensity to eat out indicates that, as incomes rise, they will likely be interested in more and different kinds of restaurant experiences.

Takeout and Delivery

Picking up on the customers' need for convenience, more restaurants are offering takeout and delivery service. In 1998 more than 75 percent of U.S. households made at least one carryout or delivery purchase in a typical month. Daily Users purchase takeout foods every day. One in five takeout customers is a daily user, accounting for half of all takeout sales [9]. Together with Frequent Users, they are responsible for 80 percent of all takeout business.

Daily Users are young, mobile, and more likely to be men. Frequent Users tend to be young couples and young parents. The pressures of balancing work and family push them to takeout meals. While fast food restaurants account for over 40 percent of takeout meals, carryout places (15 percent), delivery (14 per-

Men prefer red meat! *Source:* Monfort Foodservice advertisement.

Restaurant Management: Customers, Operations, and Employees

cent), full-service restaurants (11 percent), and grocery stores (6 percent) all vie for a piece of the action.

Seniors

Senior citizens are regarded as a frequent dinner customer. As noted above, this "care-seekers" category includes older adults and empty-nesters. Such things as early-bird specials, all-you-can-eat buffets, senior-citizen discounts, and

---

q u i c k   b i t e   2 . 4
Resort Fine Dining

According to operators in the resort sector of the hospitality industry, fine dining is an integral part of the resort experience. The upscale restaurants that serve the resort market are presented with unique challenges and benefits. It is important to offer a memorable experience to guests, especially for on-site restaurants, because with high-end room rates come high end expectations.

Fine dining increases in importance each year as consumers begin to age and develop more sophisticated tastes. As the traveling "baby boomer" population increases in age, they require a more comfortable environment and more options. As a result, many resorts are giving more attention to their fine dining establishments and putting more upscale spins on their casual dining venues.

As the resort industry becomes more competitive, more emphasis is placed on food service and quality. Successful resorts must offer more than institutional type food. Healthy menu items are becoming more popular as resorts institute spa facilities. And because service is essential in a resort setting, restaurants must be flexible and open. Guests may request unusual items or room service. The resort restaurant must provide more services than a dinner-house restaurant.

Because many guests stay exclusively on resort property, menu options must be extremely varied. One popular trend in resort fine dining is a chef's menu, which offers between four and seven courses. This type of special menu allows for extra pampering. Resort guests typically seek both cutting edge culinary trends and perennial favorites. Seasonality has a major impact on many resort menus as well. One Colorado ski resort offers hearty plates of simple foods with fresh ingredients in the wintertime and lighter dishes offering Colorado's natural bounty of fruits, vegetables and fish in the summertime.

Despite customer's growing expectations for food quality and service in the fine dining experience, their expectations include the ability to remain comfortable—which rules out strict dress codes. When people are on vacation, they don't want to be restricted. The guest should be able to relax and enjoy the meal.

Source: Ruggless, Ron. "Upscale Dining Demand Spurs Resorts to Hone Service, Quality." *Nation's Restaurant News*, v. 33, no. 12, March 22, 1999, pp. 53–56.

Generation Y

Internet usage is rapidly increasing and although it is impossible to sell a hamburger on the World Wide Web, it is possible to attract customers in different ways. One advertising executive suggests an on-line food fight to target Generation Y, those born after 1977. Generation Y is the first generation to grow up with digital technologies from birth. Kids can have fun without doing harm; it empowers them to break rules without getting in trouble. These food fights can take place in special gaming rooms set up in quick-serve and casual dining venues.

Members of Generation Y see computers and other technology as extensions of themselves socially, intellectually and emotionally. The use of the internet has allowed this generation of young people to build extended families for themselves. These kids also believe that being smart is attractive.

Members of this generation are more optimistic about the future than their predecessors, Generation X, and are more sophisticated for their age. These youths feel enabled by technology and feel that they have more control over their lives because of the technology.

Restaurants need to empower these adolescents; passive giveaways won't work. Generation Y is seeking active involvement. The implication for restaurants is that they need to become entertainment destinations incorporating things such as cyber-cafes and video arcades. Many members of this generation frequent quick-serve chains after school to substitute for an empty home.

These customers provide restaurants with the opportunity to create more of a community environment than a simple place of transaction. The fast-food restaurant serves as a alternative home and their friends as a substitute family. Restaurants need to take advantage of this shift and make a goal of encouraging restaurant patrons to communicate with each other.

One Burger King in Manhattan, seizing an opportunity, installed a bank of computers and gave away free internet time with the purchase of a value meal. The restaurant found the concept so popular that it is now allowing customers to send virtual postcards to friends, which facilitates brand building.

Technology has additional applications for restaurants. One application that could improve casual dining is monitors in waiting areas that allow patrons to order before they are seated. Customers are occupied, the food is ready when they sit, and table turns increase.

Source: Cebrzynski, Gregg. "Restaurants May Want to Get Wired to Reach Generation Y Youths." *Nation's Restaurant News,* v. 33, no. 10, March 8, 1999, p. 14.

quick bite 2.6
Convenient Competition

Home Meal Replacement is both an opportunity and a threat for many operators. Competition is intense and convenience stores are making their way onto the field. According to Sharon Powell, vice president for fresh foods merchandising at 7-Eleven, "Our biggest challenge is to get people to trust convenience stores for good food."

In 1994, Southland Corp., 7-Eleven's parent, combined their distribution centers with commissaries to create the Deli Central fresh-food concept. The concept has been growing since. The proprietary name, Deli Central, describes the signature line of ready-to-eat entrees, sandwiches, salads, fruits, pizzas, Mexican foods, vegetables, desserts and breakfast foods. These items are made fresh each day and delivered to stores before dawn each morning.

Store managers order freshly made items via a computer network installed specially for the program. The manager has total control over what is ordered and is responsible for eliminating waste and stock-outs.

Items ordered are prepared at the commissary/distribution units that all have a USDA office and inspector on-site to oversee the food-handling practices. According to Powell, the commissaries were developed because it is too difficult to guarantee quality on items prepared in-store. From the commissary, the items are labeled with the date and time they were prepared and loaded into temperature-controlled trucks. Any items that are not used before the next delivery are donated to local soup kitchens, pantries or emergency shelters.

Recipes for Deli Central items are created by chefs from around the country and tested by customers for appeal, taste, portion size, appearance and price. Individual operators also track regional items by noting customer's buying patterns. With the program in place, 7-Eleven officials feel that they can keep pace with today's changing market and stay competitive.

Source: Weiss, Shari. "Fast and Fresh: Convenience-store Chains like 7-Eleven Must Convince Customers to Trust Them to Provide Fresh Food 24 Hours a Day." *Nation's Restaurant News,* March 29, 1999, v. 33, n. 13, p. 14.

so-called "comfort foods" like roast chicken and meatloaf [10] attract this segment of the market. To appeal to this group operators offer such things as smaller portions at lower prices, special services, such as a shuttle to the restaurant, and early-bird specials.

THE BUYING PROCESS

Various internal and external factors combine to influence how customers choose where, when, how, and why to eat out. The vehicle used to explore this will be a national study prepared by the National Restaurant Association on the dinner market [11].

In comparing results from the 1989 report (summarized in the first edition of this book) and the 1996 report, two issues have taken on greater importance. First, "convenience" is more important. There are two aspects of convenience for the customer: (1) convenience in terms of time, and (2) in terms of effort. When customers are in a hurry they are particularly concerned with location, easy access, speed of service, reasonable prices, and the availability of all-inclusive meals. This need for time-convenience is increasingly being met by carryout and drive-thru options. Some 20 percent of dinners are eaten in the car. When convenience is seen as an escape from effort more attention is paid to the taste of the food, the hours of the operation and the existence of special deals. This customer is more indulgent [12]. Second, there is the issue of value: How does the customer perceive "value," and what have operators done to initiate "value pricing"? Value is perceived differently depending on the type of outlet. The taste of the food is the strongest contributor to value across all categories of restaurant except for sit-down restaurants with an average check of over $20 where knowledgeable servers takes precedence. In addition to taste, fast food restaurant customers look for the freshness of the ingredients combined with how reasonable the prices are, how close the outlet is, and speed of service. Reasonable prices define value for cafeterias and buffets. In sit-down restaurants where the average check is less than $10 the uniqueness of the food combined with the convenience of the location, the hours of operation and the friendliness of the service create a picture of value for the customer. Where the average check is over $20 the uniqueness of the food and easy access and good parking are important after the level of knowledge of the servers. Where the check varies from $10 to $20, value means having original food, reasonable prices, easy access, no waiting, friendly service, and entertainment.

Decision Scenarios

This report divides all dinner decisions into six basic decision scenarios that seek to satisfy three goals [13]:

The goal of *social pleasure* or *togetherness* is met through:

Celebration/special occasion where the accent is on enjoying each other's company. These meals tend to be on Saturdays, the decision is made well in advance, the meals last one and a half hours, the party is large, and coupons are not used.

Kids where the (adult) decision-maker is primarily concerned with pleasing one or more children. The size of the group is large, the decision is made that day (50 percent of the time an hour or less in advance), hamburger and pizza are the favorite choices, and coupons are used. Customers tend to be younger parents of children and females.

The goal of *eating pleasure* is met through:

A craving where the focus is on satisfying the desire for a particular type of food, irrespective of how healthy it might be. Cravings occur every day of the week, early in the evening. Oriental, pizza, and general menu are the typical choices, the average time spent at the restaurant is one hour, and children are typically not present.

Home cooking where the desire is for healthy, wholesome food. Meals are taken before 6:00 P.M., the decision being made not very far in advance.

The goal of *lifestyle support* or *convenience* is satisfied by:

Pressed for time where the customer is in a hurry and has little time available. These visits tend to be on weekdays, early in the evening. Children are part of the group one-third of the time with hamburgers being the most common menu choice and the average time spent being less than half an hour.

No energy/fatigue when the diner is tired and wants to take it easy. Weekdays, relatively early in the evening, is the common pattern where the decision on where to go is made at the last minute. Hamburger and pizza are, again, the most common choices. Meals last about a half-hour and coupons are used relatively often. Most customers are young couples without children.

The breakdown of dinner need by type of restaurant is shown in Table 2.1. The indications are [14]:

When customers eat dinner at . . .	The needs they seek to satisfy are . . .
fast food restaurant	pressed for time/kids/no energy/ fatigue
self-service cafeteria/buffet	home cooking/craving
sit-down restaurant (under $10)	home cooking/craving/celebration
sit-down restaurant ($10–$20)	craving/celebration
sit-down restaurant ($20 +)	celebration/craving

Customer Expectations

Respondents to this survey identified some 28 different expectations for when they went out to dine. They are broken into the following seven broad categories [15].

Hallmarks of a Great Place

- Great-tasting food
- Fresh food/ingredients
- Comfortable atmosphere
- Reputation/recommendation
- Friendly people/service
- Portion size
- Variety of menu choices
- Knowledgeable servers

Table 2.1   Dinner need states by type of restaurant

	Fast Food Restaurants	Self-Service Cafeterias	Sit-Down Restaurants		
			Under $10	$10–$20	Over $20
Social Pleasure					
Celebration	3%	14%	17%	38%	55%
Kids	19%	12%	7%	3%	1%
Eating Pleasure					
A Craving	10%	18%	28%	43%	38%
Home Cooking	13%	39%	29%	11%	3%
Lifestyle Support					
Pressed for Time	37%	10%	9%	2%	2%
No Energy/Fatigue	18%	8%	10%	3%	2%

Source: National Restaurant Association, *Dinner Decision Making* (Washington, DC: National Restaurant Association, 1996), pp. 49–50.

- Unique or original food
- Interesting place to go

Timing

- Speed of service
- Hours of operation
- No waiting

Location

- Convenient
- Easy access/good parking
- Close to other places I had to stop

Pricing

- Reasonable prices
- All-inclusive meal
- Special deals/coupons

Amenities

- Reservations accepted
- Credit cards accepted
- Alcohol served
- Entertainment

Appeal to kids

- Kids like it
- Children's menus/things to do for kids

Dieter's choices

- Healthy foods
- Low-calorie/low-fat foods

Celebration/Special Occasion. The National Restaurant Association identifies the likelihood of eating at a restaurant on holidays and special occasions as follows [16]:

Holiday/Occasion	Percent who eat out
Your birthday	55%
Mother's Day	30
Valentine's Day	21
Father's Day	17
Easter	14
New Year's Eve	12

When customers go out for a celebration or special occasion they have high expectation in terms of all of the above hallmarks of a great place, most all of the amenities noted above and having an all-inclusive meal. On the other hand, they have lower expectations in terms of speed of service, the convenience of the location, how reasonable the prices are, having special deals and low-calorie foods, and appealing to kids.

Kids. When "kids" is the major motivator all of the kids and timing characteristics and most of the location characteristics are important. In addition, there are high expectations that prices be reasonable, special deals, including coupons, are available, entertainment is offered, and checks are accepted. It is less important that servers are knowledgeable, the food is unique, it is an interesting place, reservations and credit cards are accepted, and alcohol is served.

A Craving. When customers crave a particular type of cuisine all of the hallmarks of a great place and most of the amenities characteristics (especially the availability of alcohol) are important. In addition, there are high expectations for easy access and good parking. The "kids" factors, speed of service and being close to where the customer had to stop were not so important.

Home Cooking. For those seeking to satisfy the need for home cooking *all* of the characteristics of the hallmark of a great place, timing, location, dieter's choices, and most of the pricing characteristics are important. There are also high expectations for a children's menu and check acceptance. Conversely, there are

Road to the Top: Barbara Timm-Brock, Chief Product Officer

After holding executive positions with The Olive Garden, Pizza Hut and Grand Metropolitan PLC/Pillsbury Co., Barbara Timm-Brock accepted the chief product officer position at AFC's Cinnabon and Chesapeake Bagels, Bakery & Café concepts including 358 units. Timm-Brock is responsible for supplying new methods for front- and back-of-the-house operations, developing menu strategy and new products. Her degree in chemical engineering and M.S. in management of technology from the University of Minnesota helps her to lead research and development and quality control for the company. Timm-Brock's background in strategic planning and team building has allowed her to fit right in to her position at AFC.

Timm-Brock considers the bakery café category one of the most exciting in the business. She enjoys creating an environment in which people can come to get a welcome and warm feeling. However, her goal is to grow the category even further now that consumers are looking at bakery cafes as more than a place to get a quick bite for breakfast or a snack. Timm-Brock's main motivation for joining AFC was the company's culture and passion for quality and freshness. Timm-Brock envisions growing awareness of the Cinnabon name to more than 80%, the share it currently has, by offering new products.

Timm-Brock is persistent in practicing good management skills by practicing quality, teamwork and leadership. According to former co-worker, Rosemary Rose, Timm-Brock has an ability to inspire others with her give-and-take approach. She helps others learn to balance their personal and professional lives. "In many ways her insights and vision are exceptional," according to Rose. "They can almost be a little scary. And that's a good thing. It's easy to look for quick fixes, but she helped you see the longer vision."

Timm-Brock began her career in foodservice at Pillsbury Co. in 1984 in a position as senior associate scientist for new product development. As Timm-Brock worked her way up the corporate ladder, she earned the position of program leader/senior research scientist for new ventures leading multidisciplinary teams developing products like Cornbread Twists, Toaster Strudels and Azteca Mexican products. This teamwork experience carries over for Timm-Brock who would like to see success for her entire team at AFC.

Source: Cebrzynski, Gregg. "Barbara Timm-Brock: Individual Success Comes Through Team Success for AFC Enterprises' New Chief Product Officer." *Nation's Restaurant News,* v. 33, no. 4, pp. 36–40.

quick bite 2.8
Consumer Needs in 2010

According to the National Restaurant Association, the most likely developments regarding consumer needs in 2010 are:

- The percentage of the food dollar spent away from home will continue to increase.
- Customers will seek higher quality takeout food.
- Customers will be more knowledgeable and value conscious.
- Convenience will be of great concern to customers.
- Operators will respond to changing demographics by increasing marketing to seniors.

Source: Restaurant Industry 2010: The Road Ahead (Washington, D.C.: National Restaurant Association, 1999), p. 14.

lower expectations for the acceptance of reservations and having alcohol and entertainment available.

Pressed for Time. Location, speed of service, and reasonable prices are important when customers are pressed for time. Expectations are lower for all of the hallmarks, amenities, or dieter's choices. Having good parking, an all-inclusive meal, or a children's menu is also less important.

No Energy/Fatigue. Customers eating out because they are tired have greater expectations for speed of service, reasonable prices, special deals, and most of the above location characteristics. All of the dieter's choices, "kids" factors, and most of the hallmark and amenity characteristics, except for great-tasting food, portion size, menu variety, and check acceptance, are less important. These customers also have lower expectations for good parking and an all-inclusive meal.

ENDNOTES

1. "Craving to Eat Out," *Restaurants USA,* October 1996, pp. 40–43.

2. "Customer Loyalty Key to Success," *Restaurants USA,* February 1994, pp. 41–43.

3. "Dining Out—A Habit-Forming Experience," *Restaurants USA,* September 1997, pp. 39–40.

4. "A Booming Boomer Business," *Restaurants USA,* August 1996, pp. 40–42.

5. "Multicheck Households Spark Sales," *Restaurants USA,* April 1998, pp. 45–46.

6. "Restaurants Build Loyalty Among Seniors and Families," *Restaurants USA,* March, 1998, pp. 45–46.

7. "The Boomer Echo," *Restaurants USA*, March 1997, pp. 39–41.

8. "Diverse Diners," *Restaurants USA*, January 1999, pp. 39–41.

9. "Tracking Takeout," *Restaurants USA*, June/July 1998, pp. 39–41.

10. "Restaurants Build Loyalty Among Seniors and Families," *Restaurants USA*, March, 1998, pp. 45–46.

11. National Restaurant Association, *Dinner Decision Making* (Washington, DC: National Restaurant Association, 1996).

12. Ibid, p. 11.

13. Ibid, pp. 6–7.

14. Ibid, p. 51.

15. Ibid, pp. 54–56.

16. "'Tis The Season To Eat Out—Holiday Dining Update," *Restaurants USA*, November 1996, pp. 40–42.

CHAPTER THREE

DEVELOPING A MARKETING PLAN

learning objectives

By the end of this chapter you should be able to:

1. List the steps involved in producing a marketing plan.

2. Describe how to conduct a customer, property, and competitor analysis.

3. Compare and contrast the various ways by which a market can be segmented.

4. Identify the elements of the marketing mix for restaurant operations.

5. Describe how to monitor each step of a marketing plan to ensure its effectiveness.

"The customer is king."
Cesar Ritz

"The customer is usually right."
Lettuce Entertain You

"We put our guests second."
Danny Meyer

Source: Darrenburg, Andrew and Karen Page, *Dining Out* (New York, NY: John Wiley & Sons, Inc., 1998).

MARKETING DEFINED

The American Marketing Association defines marketing as the "process of planning and executing the conception, pricing, promotion, and distribution of ideas, goods, and services to create exchanges that satisfy individual and organizational objectives" [1]. This definition indicates that marketing is much more than advertising, much more than sales promotion. Marketing encompasses everything from developing the concept, product, and/or service to how it should be priced, promoted, and made available to people. It works only if an exchange is made between buyer (the individual) and seller (the organization) that benefits both. The buyer receives something of value and the organization receives revenue.

Robert Reid developed a definition that brings together the financial concerns of management and the need to satisfy consumer needs. His definition encompasses three items [2]:

1. Determining the needs and wants of consumers.
2. Creating the mix of products and services that will satisfy these needs and wants.
3. Promoting and selling the product–service mix to generate a level of income satisfactory to the management and stockholders of the organization.

J. C. Penney is thought to have put it this way: "If you satisfy the customers but fail to get the profit, you'll soon be out of business; if you get the profit but

Bahama Breeze.

Hot Concepts

Bahama Breeze

The main idea at Bahama Breeze to bring the islands to the mainland. One *Orlando Sentinel* reviewer determined Bahama Breeze to be a top-echelon experience, "Go ahead and strike up the marimba," the reviewer, Scott Joseph, proclaimed. "Bahama Breeze is as refreshing as the wind in the Virgin Islands. It is fun, creative and, best of all, flavorful."

Darden Restaurants owns and operates five Bahama Breeze units and is headquartered in Orlando, Florida. Four of the Caribbean-themed units are beginning to break the $100,000 weekly sales hurdle. The chain's test markets include Memphis, Tennessee, and Orlando and Tampa, Florida.

The restaurants possess an unusual and original island-flavored menu that includes house-made soups, sauces and desserts. The atmosphere is a relaxed Caribbean one in which a variety of over 500 tropical drinks are served to live music. The unique ambiance is one reason that wait lists extend beyond the industry standard of the nine o'clock slowdown.

Many customers find the restaurant so entertaining that they consider it "an evening of pleasure on par with dinner paired with entertainment." One British couple and their grown children spent two of their vacation nights at Bahama Breeze. According to Gary Heckel, president of the diner-only chain, the company's mission is to give every patron a reason and a desire to return by giving them a great experience through a variety of small details.

According to executive vice president, Gary Sweatt, "This concept combines the elements of a great island restaurant with a great bar, but food is the primary focus." As a result of the Bahama Breeze successes thus far, Darden plans to open and operate as many as 50 restaurants in the next five years. Although the units focus on food, bar sales account for as much as one-third each unit's total revenues.

Darden not only focuses on making its customers happy, but also its managers. The company, which stresses fun, hustle and passion, pays many of its general managers at Bahama Breeze locations more than $100,000 annually. And according to Sweatt, the highly paid managers lead to high returns. As a result, their turnover rate is under 20% for management and under 80% for hourly staff.

Source: Hayes, Jack. "Bahama Breeze: Bringing Paradise to the Mainland." *Nation's Restaurant News*, May 17, 1999, v. 33, no. 20, pp. 54–56.

fail to satisfy the customers, you'll soon be out of customers." The idea is to generate profits by producing satisfied customers.

Inherent in these definitions are several ideas. First, there is the focus on the customer. Marketing is a way of thinking about the business that makes satisfying customer needs paramount. Second, there is the practical implication that businesses cannot be all things to all people—they cannot satisfy all the needs and wants of all the people. Some choice must be made as to which segments of the market are to be targeted. Third, there is an appreciation of research to determine customer needs and wants. The idea of sequential steps—that products and services are developed only after customer needs and wants have been identified—is a fourth idea. Customer satisfaction is the fifth idea. It is not enough to promote and sell the service. Customer satisfaction implies that the operation must not only bring customers in, it must bring them back. Finally, the idea of exchange means that the satisfaction of customers' needs must bring economic benefit to the organization.

DEVELOPING A MARKETING PLAN

Six steps are involved in the development of a marketing plan [3]:

1. Conduct a marketing audit.
2. Select target markets.
3. Position the property.
4. Determine marketing objectives.
5. Develop and implement action plans.
6. Monitor and evaluate the marketing plan.

Conduct a Marketing Audit

There are three parts to the marketing audit; it is an analysis of the customers, the property or operation, and the competition. Given the foregoing definitions of marketing, it is appropriate to look first at customers.

Customers. The purpose of the customer, property, and competitive analysis is to develop a profile of the customers and to evaluate, in an unbiased way, how the operation stacks up relative to the competition in providing what they want.

Information about the customers breaks down as follows:

- Who are they?
- Where do they come from?
- When do they visit, and when is the decision made?
- How do they reach us?
- Why do they come and how satisfied are they?

quick bite 3.2
Technology and Customer Trends

Realizing changing customer attitudes and buying behavior is important to the success of any restaurant. It is essential for restaurateurs to identify and track patrons in order to anticipate, manage and adjust to change. Several technologies exist that allow operators to do just that as well as profile their customers and segment them demographically.

These important marketing tools are becoming more and more afford-able as the millennium approaches. The technologies allow restaurateurs to collect extensive data on individual customers and integrate it with sales and diner frequency information. From the intelligence collected operators can identify trends and create sales and marketing plans.

Customer information can be effectively analyzed using the following steps:

1) Determine a viable customer sample: An appropriate customer sample will be representative of the restaurant's entire customer base. A representative sample will include a cross section of patrons from an extended period of time who portray all dayparts and weekparts. For example, if 30% of a store's weekly sales are generated on Friday and Saturday night, than 30% of the sample should represent Friday and Saturday night customers. The most important aspect of a sample is that it is representative of the true customer base.

2) Tracking transaction data and customer loyalty with credit card data: One effective way that customers can be identified is by tracking them through credit card usage. All credit card transactions are recorded in point-of-sale systems with a total sales amount, date and credit card number. Additionally, credit card processors can often provide up to six months of historical transaction data. Any credit card data collected can be analyzed for sales and frequency information.

3) Identifying and profiling customers from credit cards: Using a "search and match process," a store's own credit card records can be matched to large consumer databases similar to those used by mail order houses and large retail chains. As much as 60 percent of patrons can be identified by their full names, addresses, and important demographic and psychographic information. This information can be used to segment customers into distinct categories and profiled by their purchasing habits.

4) Tracking and rewarding customers with loyalty program: Frequent diner programs are the most common way for restaurateurs to track customers. When used in conjunction with POS systems, operators can gain detailed sales, menu performance and customer repeat visits information.

(continued)

In addition to being a mere "tactical" tool to provide rewards for customer frequency, these programs can be used to make strategic decisions using "customer-centric" data.

5) Tracking customers by phone numbers: Many restaurants have takeout/delivery software programs that use customers phone numbers to identify them.

6) Using the data to build sales: Once the data is collected by one of the above methods, some software programs and other services are available to help operators analyze the data and make recommendations to increase the store's sales.

Source: Bogardus, Charlotte. "The Right Tools Can Help Operators Identify and Track Customers for the Millennium." *Nation's Restaurant News,* v. 33, no. 3, January 18, 1999, pp. 32, 55.

This information can come from sales histories, employees and management staff, the customers themselves, and outside research sources. Sales histories should be kept for six distinct dining segments [4].

1. Weekday breakfast: Monday–Friday
2. Weekday lunch: Monday–Friday
3. Weekday dinner: Monday–Thursday
4. Weekend breakfast: Saturday and Sunday
5. Weekend lunch: Saturday and Sunday
6. Weekend dinner: Friday–Sunday

Note that while weekday breakfast and lunch run from Monday through Friday, weekday dinner runs from Monday through Thursday. The breakdown is in terms of the characteristics of the meal. Friday dinner is regarded by customers as part of the weekend.

For each day it would be appropriate to collect data on:

- Number of customers
- Total sales in dollars
- Number of meals sold
- Number of beverages sold
- Number of appetizers sold
- Number of side items sold

- Number of desserts sold
- Number of breakfast customers
- Breakfast sales in dollars
- Number of lunch customers
- Lunch sales in dollars
- Number of dinner customers
- Dinner sales in dollars
- Average entree in dollars
- Average check in dollars
- Number of beverages, appetizers, side items, and desserts per customer
- Average breakfast, lunch, and dinner check
- Daily sales as a percentage of the week
- Breakfast, lunch, and dinner sales as a percentage of day's sales
- Weekend and weekday sales as a percentage of week's sales

The information collected basically breaks down into how many people the restaurant serves, how much customers spend, what they order, and how the restaurant's business is spread throughout the week. From this analysis we can see when business is strong and, more important, when it is weak. In addition, specific objectives can be set to improve sales of specific items or numbers of customers.

A core store panel provides the head office with information from the field through the collection of data from a representative sample of stores. The sample chosen should be representative of the company's geographic distribution and sales volume. Data should be collected on [5]:

- Sales by day and week
- Transaction count
- Product sales mix
- Advertising activities
- Promotional activities
- Competing activities
- Weather

On an informal basis, management and staff can provide information about the customers because they are constantly in contact with them. While such data are not scientific, they can give a picture of the items that are selling and why, what customers like and do not like, and what types of people visit at different times during the week. In addition to providing useful information, asking the opinion of employees makes them feel important and can serve as a motivational tool.

More formal questionnaires can be used to collect information on the customer base. The key in developing a questionnaire is to develop the research objectives first, decide on the questions that will provide answers to the information being sought, select an appropriate research methodology, and conduct the research.

A simple category of data that can easily be collected and is very useful is customer zip codes. Most restaurants attract customers from a relatively small area. Some consultants estimate that 80 percent of a restaurant's business comes from within a three-mile radius. Having servers and/or cashiers ask for customers' home and work zip codes, management can readily identify where customers come from.

The best way to find out what a restaurant is doing well and poorly is to ask customers. The key to increasing sales and customer count is to identify the characteristics of existing customers and to use that profile as a basis for attracting more customers who fit that profile.

One way to get this information is from a focus group. A focus group consists of six to ten former or existing customers, led by a discussion leader, who express their feelings about various aspects of the operation. Questions go from the general to the specific and concentrate on motivations, feelings, and gut-level issues. Although not statistically reliable, such sessions can indicate a great deal about what motivates customers.

Customer comment cards are a favorite way of collecting information. There is probably a positive bias built into any research conducted in the restaurant. Most customers will not complain in the restaurant unless there is something really wrong. An average or mildly unpleasant experience may not result in negative comments from the customer until they leave the operation.

Property. The property analysis is an unbiased evaluation of the strengths and weaknesses of the operation. A "typical" checklist would evaluate the property and the competition as to the following factors [6]:

- Menu variety
- Menu appeal
- Food/beverage quality
- Food/beverage taste
- Food/beverage consistency
- Portion size
- Pricing
- Service speed
- Service quality
- Service friendliness
- Cleanliness
- Promotional activity
- Visibility
- Image
- Atmosphere

quick bite 3.3
Location or Concept: Which Comes First?

Keith Goldman suggests two approaches when deciding what kind of restaurant to open and where it should be located. The approach taken depends on whether the location or the concept is preselected.

Preselected Location

1. Analyze secondary data: area growth, resident demographics, and sales data.
2. Conduct primary market study to determine current market potential. Analysis of the competition and potential market through focus groups and interviews.
3. Analyze life-cycle trends and identify gaps in the marketplace where growth segments are not being served.
4. Select dominant market segments.
5. Determine customer profiles: behavior and eating habits.
6. Select concept to meet the needs of the segment(s) selected.

Preselected Concept

1. Define the characteristics of the concept.
2. Analyze potential customers by age and region, identifying their eating preferences.
3. Select the customer profile that best fits selected concept.
4. Collect secondary data for several different potential locations.
5. Conduct primary market studies of potential locations.
6. Select market area through zip-code demographics indicating the highest concentration of your target market.

Source: Keith Goldman, "Concept Selection for Independent Restaurants," *Cornell Hotel and Restaurant Administration Quarterly*, December 1993, pp. 59–72.

- Facility
- Sales level
- Point of sale
- Happy-hour offerings

The problem is that such a list does not indicate how important these things are to the customer. A better starting point is to look at the operation from the viewpoint of the customer. By identifying the factors important to customers and using these items as a checklist to evaluate both the operation and the competition, a focus on the customer is assured. For example, if a restaurant features an excellent salad bar but that factor is unimportant to the customers, is the salad bar a strength, a weakness, or a neutral factor?

Suppose that one segment of the dinner market seeks out places that excel in five things:

1. Food quality
2. Nice place
3. Cleanliness
4. Friendly people
5. Fresh food and ingredients

If the operation appeals to this segment of the market, they could identify from them just what is meant by each of these five factors and use the resulting list as the basis for evaluating the property and the competition.

Some restaurants use mystery shoppers to evaluate the operation. These people should always remain anonymous and conduct random evaluations. There are typically three or four visits the first month, followed by monthly visits thereafter. Management receives a report on the exterior, interior, and signage of the facility in addition to comments on the appearance, performance, and service provided by the employees.

Competition. A competing facility is any operation that seeks to attract the business being sought by the restaurant under consideration.

A competitive analysis compares competing facilities with the operation under study. The purpose of such an analysis is to discover [7]:

1. Profitable market segments being served by competitors that are not being served at the operation under study.
2. Some competitive benefit or advantage the property has that cannot be matched by the competition.
3. Weaknesses in the marketing strategy of the competition that can be capitalized on.

A competitive analysis involves getting as much relevant information as possible and includes eating at the facility and evaluating the advertising.

Select Target Markets

The idea behind selecting market segments is that people are different in what they want from a dining experience and that it is not possible to be all things to all people. Market segmentation involves dividing a heterogeneous market into smaller homogeneous segments. While the members of a segment have characteristics similar to each other, they differ from people in another market segment.

In this way operators can more effectively target marketing efforts to those people who are most likely to patronize the restaurant.

Segmentation Variables. Marketers segment the market on the basis of one or more variables. The major variables used are geographic, demographic, psychographic, usage or behavioral, and benefits sought. Geographic segmentation involves identifying the geographic limits of the trading area and appealing to people within the boundaries of that area. The National Restaurant Association estimates that people will travel an average of 15 to 18 minutes for special-occasion meals. A radius of 18 minutes' driving time from the operation would be a geographic segmentation of the market.

Demographic segmentation involves dividing the market on the basis of such things as age, income, gender, family size, stage in the family life cycle, educational level, occupation, ethnicity, religion, nationality, and social class. In earlier chapters we discussed the eating-out patterns of various market segments. The National Restaurant Association notes that high-spending households have the following demographic characteristics [8]:

- Income of $30,000 +
- Head of household 35 to 54
- Household size of two or more with two or more earners
- Household head either employed as a manager and professional, technical, sales and clerical, or self-employed
- Lives in the East or Northeast

Psychographic segmentation divides people based on their attitudes, interests, and opinions. For example, the NRA identifies five market segments based, in part, on their lifestyle [9]. They are:

- "Too tired to cook" who want convenience and eating pleasure
- "Busy parents" who want to please the children
- "Care Seekers" who want familiar, home-cooked dishes, friendly service, and discounts
- "Urban sophisticates" who are trend-hungry
- "Flavor savorers" who are driven by cravings

Segmenting on the basis of use or behavior is based on the oft-quoted 80–20 rule. This rule states that 80 percent of the business comes from 20 percent of the customers. If the operator can identify the frequent customers who make u p a substantial part of the business, he or she can do a more effective job of marketing.

The Simmons Market Research Bureau, Inc. breaks restaurant use into five segments: nonprospects (those who are never likely to become users), prospects (those who might become users), light users (1 to 5 times per month), medium users (6 to 13 times per month), and heavy users (over 14 times per month). Heavy

Wine Tastings

Winemaker dinners have traditionally been one of the best-known and most successful wine events held in restaurants. Patrons seeking an individual and educational wine and dining experience find the set-menu dinners with wine experts to be very rewarding. However, the popularity of wine seems to be at an all-time high and new types of wine events popping up all over the country.

The Sunset Grill in Nashville, Tennessee has offered a wine tasting event for the past three years. The weekly "Casual Wine Tasting" helps to build traffic in the restaurant during the off season. Owner Randy Rayburn holds the seminar for an hour and a half at a cost of $10 per person. The tastings are informal and include light hors d'oeuvres and many different wines. For more serious wine lovers, The Sunset Grill provides a weekly hour-long in-depth class. The advanced class also costs $10 per person and attracts some 50 to 100 people a week.

The B.O.B. in Grand Rapids, Michigan uses their "Wine School" to attract an older clientele. The "Wine School" is a weekly series of classes held for two hours once a week. Each class has an individual theme; some themes include "Chardonnays of the World," "Celebration Wines for the Holidays," and "Wines of Australia." According to Bill Koski, general manager, the cost per person varies according to the price of the wines served, but usually averages about $7.95. The classes are lead by a local wine expert and feature five wines per week.

B.O.B.'s classes have an informal and friendly tone and provide information about the wines including their origin, how they are made and what to serve them with. The classes were developed to generate traffic and create publicity rather than create profit. The seminars usually draw approximately 75 people a week, approximately 8 new people each week. Often attendees stay to eat or drink additional glasses. According to Koski, the classes have had long-lasting benefits.

Source: Wiegand, Ronn. "Operators Implement Wine Seminars, Cook Up Restaurant Traffic." *Nation's Restaurant News*, v. 33, no. 1, January 4, 1999, p. 53.

users account for 44.8 percent of total restaurant revenue in a typical month, medium users account for 40.8 percent, and light users bring in the remaining 14.8 percent of revenue. Giving the light user an index of 100, the heavy user has an index of 522. For every $1 spent by a light user, a heavy user spends $5.22 [10].

Benefit segmentation separates people out on the basis of the benefits sought from the meal experience. As identified in Chapter 2, there are five different decision scenarios for people dining out. These are:

1. Fun time
2. Nice meal out
3. Craving
4. Making sure that everyone is getting something to eat
5. Easiest thing available

Those eating out for a "fun time" believe that they deserve a treat or reward and feel like having fun. They have the time to plan the event, and price is not very important to them. On the other hand, the "easiest thing available" group eat out when they are tired and pressed for time. They choose options with the least number of hassles. For them, speed of service and a convenient location are important benefits they look for.

Market segments should be selected on the basis of size, likelihood of growth, competitive position, the cost of reaching the segment, and how compatible the segment is with the company's objectives and resources.

Revenue Grid.   For an existing business a revenue grid and an analysis of activity can be helpful in selecting workable market segments. A revenue grid identifies how much revenue is brought in from the various segments of the market presently being served. A useful rule of thumb in marketing is: "Attract customers similar to those already being attracted." For some reason the restaurant attracts a certain kind of clientele. An examination of the existing customer base broken down by how much sales each segment brings in is an excellent start to identifying future potential. In other words, find out who the customers are and seek to find more people with similar characteristics.

An analysis of business activity will tell when business is good and, more important, when it is bad. This can suggest areas of importance for increasing sales. The marketplace can then be searched for prospective market segments consisting of people who eat out when the operation needs the business. The segments are then evaluated relative to the criteria noted above to determine their suitability.

Position the Property

Positioning Statement.   The image that customers have of an operation is its position in the marketplace. A good positioning statement accomplishes several things. First, it creates an image in the minds of the customers as to what it stands for. In the foodservice business, as in any other, image is reality. People make decisions based on their perceptions rather than on the reality of the situation. If the image is positive—that the restaurant offers good value—the decision may be made to eat out there. Image alone will not induce the customer to buy. That willingness comes from a variety of promotional means described later.

The actual meal experience offers a reality check to the guest. The actual experience may be less than expected. The result is a disappointed customer. The image portrayed by the operation must be positive enough to encourage people

quick bite 3.5
Repositioning

Often an operator's best defense against declining sales is a new image. However, as the Shoney's chain has discovered repositioning a business in the customer's mind can be a complex task. In order to combat two concurrent years of declining sales, the family chain Shoney's Restaurants employed a new marketing strategy. The "neighborhood-based" plan resulted from the operator's restructuring of management.

Shoney's repositioning plan included going back to "ground zero," readdressing their positioning statement, their target market and products offered to them. According to Shoney's senior vice president of marketing, Kent W. Smith, the chain will attempt to build on its neglected brand equity for the most part through new marketing initiatives. Part of Shoney's current image problem is that they have strayed from their positioning in the past by trying to enter the casual dining segment. However, according to Smith, the chain is now committed to marketing Shoney's brand as "your neighborhood family restaurant."

In order to reinforce their new image Shoney's appointed local-store marketers to work with unit managers and regional managers in order to develop neighborhood-focused marketing programs. Some of Shoney's tactics include working with neighborhood charities and community groups that will encourage repeat business. Even simply organizing a charity car wash can go a long way in creating a "friendly neighbor" image.

Another attempt Shoney's has made to focus on their family restaurant position is by creating a "Family Fun Night" which creates an entirely different environment than on a normal night. The special evening includes loud music, clowns and drawings for inexpensive prizes. According to Smith, "Family Fun Night" has energized stores and increased sales. However, one essential issue that Shoney's new plan does not address is how to differentiate themselves from other family restaurants and theme restaurants.

Source: Cebrzynski, Gregg. "Shoney's Starts from Ground up with Marketing Strategy." *Nation's Restaurant News*, v. 33, no. 3, January 18, 1999, pp. 8, 70.

to visit the operation. The actual meal experience must be equal to or greater than the image for the guest to leave satisfied.

Second, the positioning statement will describe the benefits the restaurant offers to the guests. Restaurants offer features but people buy benefits. Customers, in fact, "buy" a bundle of benefits. When going out for a meal, different people look for different things. For some, a large variety of menu choices is important. For others, price is a major concern. Still others emphasize privacy. Since people buy benefits, the operation must communicate what benefits it offers to its potential customers.

Third, it differentiates the property from the competition. Everyone offers "good food," "atmosphere," and "value." But just what is it that makes one restaurant different from the other? Why should I come to your place rather than the restaurant across the street?

The key is to find a difference, an advantage, that is difficult for the competition to replicate. Every business seeks a unique selling point or a competitive differential advantage, something that makes it different from the competition that can be used to advantage. The nature of business means that unique selling points are subject to the principle of perishable distinctiveness. If one restaurant develops an advantage that makes it more attractive to customers, the competition becomes aware of that advantage and seeks to copy it, thus neutralizing the previously unique selling point. That which made the restaurant distinctive is gone; it is perishable. "What can separate me from my competition that is difficult, if not impossible, for them to copy?" This is the third element that must be answered from a positioning statement.

It should readily be seen that a positioning statement can come only after an analysis has been made of the market, the property, and the competition. The key is to identify what the target market wants (the benefits) from a dining-out experience and how one operation is perceived (in the minds of the customers) as providing these benefits compared to the competition.

Perceptual Maps. Perceptual maps can be useful tools in developing a positioning statement. A perceptual map is a visual representation of two elements: the relative importance of various benefits to guests and their perception of how well a facility does in providing these benefits. In essence, customers from the market segment being sought are asked two questions: "What things are important to you when dining out?" and "How well do you think restaurant X does in providing these things?" The benefits considered important to customers can be identified from informal discussions with guests or from a focus group session. The focus group can identify what the members like and dislike about the company and the competition. The results are qualitative rather than quantitative. They will not disclose percentages, but they will indicate "gut issues." From such a group a list of benefits sought when dining out can be obtained. For example, it may be that customers decide that the benefits they are looking for when dining out are:

A Prices in their range	K Consistency
B Nice place	L Special deals and coupons
C Cleanliness	M Variety
D Friendly people and service	N No lines and no waiting
E Extensive choice	O Size of the portions
F Speed of service	P Food presentation
G Food quality	Q Convenience of location
H Value for money	R Comfortable seating
I Kids like it	S Fresh food and ingredients
J Hours open	T Unique or original food

This list can then be used to construct a questionnaire to be presented to a sample of present and prospective customers who are asked to rate the importance of these items to them on a scale of 1 (very important) to 5 (not important). Those customers are then asked how well the restaurant under study does in providing these things, again on a scale of 1 (totally) to 5 (not at all). The resulting scores can be placed on a matrix as in Figure 3.1.

Crosshairs are drawn on the graph such that half of the 20 items are above the horizontal line and half below, and half of the 20 items are to the left of the vertical line and half to the right. The result is four quadrants. In the upper right section, quadrant 1, are items that are not important to the customers and which they think the restaurant does not satisfy. In this example guests say that the following factors are not important to them and, furthermore, the restaurant does not, in their mind, provide these things:

- Prices in their range
- Extensive choice
- Kids like it
- Hours open
- Variety

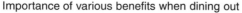
Importance of various benefits when dining out

Figure 3.1 Perceptual map.

Restaurant Management: Customers, Operations, and Employees

Quadrant 2 contains factors that, again, are not important to the guests. However, in this case they do think that the restaurant provides these:

- Friendly people and service
- Speed of service
- Food presentation
- Fresh food and ingredients
- Unique or original food

Quadrants 3 and 4 are made up of factors that customers consider important. In quadrant 3 are factors that they perceive the restaurant does not do a good job of providing. In quadrant 4 are factors the customers think the operation does do well on.

The factors in quadrant 3 are:

- Nice place
- Food quality
- Value for money
- Consistency
- Special deals and coupons

The remaining factors, in quadrant 4, are:

- Cleanliness
- No lines and no waiting
- Size of the portions
- Convenience of location
- Comfortable seating

From these findings the restaurant can identify where it stands in the minds of its customers and determine appropriate actions. The factors in quadrants 1 and 2 should be ignored. Customers tell us that these items are not important to them. If they are not important to the customers, they are not important to the foodservice operation. There will be a tendency for restaurants to want to play to their strengths. The customers perceive that the restaurant offers friendly service that is fast and includes original dishes made with fresh ingredients and presented well. However, these factors just are not very important to them. The facility that markets to guests on factors not important to them will not attract those people.

The important items are in quadrants 3 and 4. These factors are important to guests. But they do not believe that the restaurant is a nice place that offers consistent, good-quality food, special deals, and delivers value for money. They do believe that it is clean, offers correctly sized portions, comfortable seating, and a convenient location with no lines.

At this point it is necessary to do a reality check. How accurate are the customers' perceptions? The answer will determine the appropriate action. Where the image is negative but the actual situation is positive, we need to improve the image. For example, it may be that special deals are offered but customers are unaware of them. Where the image is negative and the actual situation is negative, or when the image is positive but the actual situation is negative, the product or service must be changed. For example, if people believe that consistency is a problem and it really is a problem, the food served must be improved so that it is consistent. Similarly, if the perception is that the seats are comfortable, but in reality they are not, that also must be changed. If customers are drawn to a restaurant expecting comfortable seats, the visit will show that they are not and the customer will be dissatisfied. Finally, where the image is positive and the actual situation is positive, we have the basis for a positioning statement.

Similar perceptual maps can be drawn for the competition to determine just where, in the minds of the customer, we are perceived as doing a better job of providing benefits important to them. The resulting positioning statement will be based on research that has identified the benefits the customer is looking for, what is provided to satisfy these desired benefits, and how the restaurant differs from the competition in providing these desired benefits. In essence, the positioning statement says: "For _____ seeking _____, we provide _____."

The first blank should be filled with the segment of the market being considered, the second blank identifies the benefits being sought, and the third space says what will be provided to satisfy customers.

Determine Marketing Objectives

Criteria. The very act of setting objectives increases the likelihood that they will be achieved. The reason is that management now has something to work toward. Developing objectives gives managers a way to determine the extent to which they are moving forward and to allow them to change strategies if positive movement is not being made. It allows for a way of keeping score. This in itself is a motivational tool as well as a method of assigning responsibility and rewarding the achievement of results.

To be useful, objectives should be set for each segment of the market to which the restaurant is appealing. Each market segment is different in terms of dining and spending patterns and the extent to which the operation is presently successful in its marketing effort. For seniors it may be appropriate to increase the number of such customers, whereas for businesspeople it may be more appropriate to have existing customers patronize the operation more frequently.

Second, objectives should be results oriented. This usually means specifying an improvement in volume, revenues, or market share. It is only by identifying the desired results that management can set targets and, later, measure to see whether the effort has been successful.

Objectives should also be set in quantitative rather than qualitative terms. The problem with qualitative objectives (for example, "to improve service") is that the measurement of such objectives is open to subjective judgment.

There should be a time element to each objective. It is not enough to say that the foodservice operation wants to increase its customer count by 100 customers a week. A time limit must be set as to when this objective should be achieved.

Life-cycle Curve. Objectives have to be set consistent with where the operation is in the product life-cycle curve. The concept of a product life cycle is that a business goes through various stages during its lifetime. A business is introduced into the marketplace and will grow, mature, and decline. Different marketing objectives are appropriate at the various stages of the life cycle. In the introductory stage, the key is to create awareness and trial on the part of customers; in the growth stage, sales are increasing at an increasing rate and market share should be maximized; in the maturity stage, sales are increasing but at a decreasing rate and profits should be maximized while market share is defended; and finally, in the decline stage of the life cycle, sales are decreasing and expenditures are reduced and as much is extracted from the business as possible.

Buying Process. It is also important to set objectives that are consistent with where customers are in their buying process. The concept of a buying process is that potential customers go through a series of stages in their own minds before making a purchase. They must first be made aware of the existence of the operation. Then they need to have information outlining the operation's benefits to them. At this point, if the campaign is successful, customers form a positive attitude about the restaurant, develop a preference for it, are convinced they should go there, actually visit the restaurant, and if satisfied, return. The objectives set will vary depending on where the market is in this process.

At the awareness stage, the objective is to expose people to the operation. How successful we are can be measured by identifying the number of people exposed to the message: number of readers, viewers, and so on.

At the knowledge or comprehension stage, when customers are trying to identify what the restaurant can offer them, the objective is to transmit information. How well this has been accomplished can be determined by measuring the percentage of readers or viewers who remember essential parts of the message.

The objective in the attitude stage is to changes people's attitudes about the operation. The success of a program can be determined by measuring consumer attitudes before and after the campaign to determine whether or not a change has occurred. Similarly, during the preference stage—where the objective is to create a preference in the mind of the customer—preference surveys before and after the campaign can be done. It may be, for example, that prior to the campaign one restaurant places sixth out of 10 on a list of preferred operations. If the restaurant places third, after the program, the campaign can be called a success.

The conviction stage seeks to have customers do something. The number of actions taken—phone reservations made, for example—can be measured. Purchase is measured by the number of people who come in the door or who order the item being promoted. Finally, adoption—where the objective is repeat purchase—can be measured by the percentage of customers who are repeats.

Develop and Implement Action Plans

Implementing an action plan actually involves developing and executing a specific marketing mix for each segment of the market being sought. It involves developing the means to carry out the job, developing a budget to accomplish the plan, and assigning responsibility for the plan.

The marketing mix has been variously defined by different authors. Originally comprised of product planning, pricing, distribution, promotion, servicing, and market research, it has been standardized into the "four P's" of product, price, promotion, and place. Other elements have been suggested to make the four P's suitable for the hospitality industry. It is suggested that the marketing mix for foodservice operations consists of four elements: product–service mix, price, promotion–communication, and place–distribution mix [11]. The mix chosen will vary depending on the industry, the position of the operation in the marketplace, and how it fares presently relative to the competition.

Product–Service Mix. The product–service mix consists of the various products and services offered by the operation in an attempt to satisfy customer needs. It covers such things as the options on the menu, quality, reputation, image, the furnishings and decor, the exterior structure and interior layout, and the various service features of the operation. It includes elements that the customer pays for either directly or indirectly. The price charged for the steak on the plate covers not only the meat itself but also the plate it is served on, the napkins used, background entertainment, and even the view from the table, the "price" of which is reflected in the cost of buying the facility and is passed on to the customer in the prices charged. Even the status of visiting a particular restaurant is something that is paid for in increased prices.

According to Lewis and Chambers [12], the following factors are associated with successful new products and services:

- The ability to identify customer needs.
- Using existing company know-how and resources.
- Developing new products in the company's core markets.
- Measuring performance during the development stage: screening and testing ideas before spending money on development.
- Coordinating between research and development and marketing.
- An organizational environment that encourages entrepreneurship and risk taking.
- Linking new product development to corporate goals.

Price. Several points regarding price bear mentioning. First, the importance of price comes from the fact that it is one-half of the price–value relationship that customers seek. If, in the minds of the guest, the value received is less than the price paid, the experience will be viewed negatively. Second, in the foodservice business much of the pricing that goes on is product-driven pricing. That is, restaurants often have a particular facility that has various fixed costs and items on the menu that can increase in their cost to the restaurateur. The operator has to meet these costs by finding a segment of the market willing to pay the price for the product. However, it should always be remembered that the customer is the final arbiter of whether the price charged is acceptable. The latter concept, consumer-driven pricing, has often been ignored in the restaurant industry [13]. In the 1970s, restaurants responded to price increases of various food items by raising prices—in effect, passing their price increases on to the customer. After awhile, customers decided that the prices charged were more than the value received. As a result, many customers traded down.

---

 quick bite 3.6
Outback Steakhouse

Outback Steakhouse does it "just right." Outback has been extremely consistent in their marketing messages, effectively reinforcing their positioning in consumers' minds. Branding expert Scott Davis says that this makes Outback Steakhouse one of the strongest brands in the restaurant industry. According to Davis, who heads the Brand Asset Management Practice for Chicago-based Kuczmarski & Associates, Outback is one of the few restaurants in the U.S. who has been so loyal and consistent to its message and its brand.

A campaign developed by TBWA/Chiat/Day, New York, sticks to the message presented by Outback's familiar tagline, "No rules, just right." One TV spot in particular presents young, athletic people on the beach ignoring the sign warning against loud music and fun. The Australian-accented announcer remarks, "You know that little voice in your head that makes you feel guilty for having too much of a good thing? Yeah, we don't either." The campaign reinforces Outback's image as a spot to relax and unwind from everyday stress. The spots also focus on the quality of the chain's menu. The commercials appeal to a human and emotional side of consumers, which persuades them to stay loyal to the chain.

One of the unique aspects of Outback's "No rules, just right" motto is that it extends into the company's philosophy. According to Outback's vice president of marketing, Nancy Schneid, the chain's employees are trained that there are "no rules, just right" when it comes to customer satisfaction. Future advertising by Outback will feature their take-away service that will help Outback maintain its No. 1 position against competitors.

Source: Cebrzynski, Gregg. "Outback Ads 'Just Right,' Holds Fast to Brand Message." *Nation's Restaurant News*, v. 32, no. 51, December 21, 1998, p. 8.

FREE 8" Cheese Pizza
or only **$2.00** for a
12" Pizza
with purchase of any 16" pizza
(toppings extra)

Not valid with any other offers. Please mention coupon
when ordering. Coupon required. Expires 8/1/97.

$2.00 off
any order over $15.00
or **$1.00 off**
any order over $12.00

Not valid with any other offers. Please mention coupon
when ordering. Coupon required. Expires 8/1/97.

$3.00 off
any order over $15.00

NEW! *For Pick-up Only*

Not valid with any other offers. Please mention coupon
when ordering. Coupon required. Expires 8/1/97.

Jay Solomon suggests using coupons for bringing in business on slow nights.

Fast-food restaurants gained business from table-service restaurants, and convenience stores benefited from customers who saw fast-food prices increase. Many customers decided to stay home and eat, satisfying their desire for quality by eating better at home. The smarter operators recognized this customer resistance and adjusted concepts and prices accordingly. The point is that the customer, not the product cost, will determine whether an item will sell.

Promotion–Communication Mix. The promotion–communication mix consists of all of the communications between the company and the customer and consists of media advertising, word of mouth, merchandising, promotion, public relations, publicity, and personal selling. These items are covered in greater detail in Chapter 4.

Place–Distribution Mix. The channels that connect the company and its various customers are referred to as the distribution mix. Channels can either be direct or indirect. A direct channel of distribution means that the restaurant communicates directly with its customers. In indirect distribution there are one or more intermediaries between the restaurant and its customers. For example, a restaurant may decide to be listed in a discount book sold by high school students as a fundraising device. A restaurant may decide to become part of a package tour being promoted by a tour operator. The decision to accept credit cards also brings an intermediary—the credit card company—between the restaurant and the customer.

There are several factors to consider before deciding the form of distribution. If there is an existing or a proposed distribution network, it may be in the interests of the operator to use it. If the seniors in the local high school propose to sell discount books as a fundraiser, it is probably easier to tap into that effort rather than to duplicate it by distributing fliers on the restaurant directly to the parents and friends of the students.

Several years ago the Scottish Tourist Board began a program called A Taste of Scotland. Restaurants were asked to provide a special menu using

---

quick bite 3.7
Campaigns—McDonalds Brand Campaign

McDonalds is one of the largest QSR advertisers. In a recent campaign, McDonalds advertised choices and the fact that they have even more choices than ever. In fact, McDonalds has even more of everything including fun, smiles and memories. McDonalds hopped on to the retro craze and used Donna Summer's famous song "She Works Hard for the Money," but adapted the lyrics to remind customers where they can go for fun and food at prices that will make them come back.

Arnold Communications of Boston created the ad campaign. The commercials did not sell Happy Meals or Big Macs, but it is an effort at brand building for one of the most recognizable brands in the world. McDonalds is attempting to build a "brand context" for future promotions to fit into. Because a restaurant can't give discount deals all the time, it needs to emphasize the intangible benefits of fun and memories to produce a substantial return on investment.

McDonalds "More for Your Money" campaign was designed to furnish an umbrella theme for local promotions. The message was a simple one of value—McDonalds is the right place to eat for everyone in the world—and the message came through clearly in the commercials by the variety of people depicted in the ads. The true question is whether or not the campaign actually explained what McDonalds is all about and had any meaning for consumers who already understand that McDonalds provides value and a pleasant experience or else they would not return consistently as they do.

Regardless of customer awareness, focusing on brand image is important even for established brands. Brand image tells what a brand stands for, why its is important to consumers and why customers should believe in the brand.

Source: Cebrzynski, Gregg. "McDonalds Brand Campaign Promises More of Everything." *Nation's Restaurant News*, v. 33, no. 12, March 22, 1999, p. 14.

locally produced items and to price it within a certain range. In return, the Scottish Tourist Board listed them in a booklet distributed to tourists which informed them of the operations participating in the scheme. Again, the network provided by the board was not available to the individual operation.

People in the indirect channel of distribution between the restaurant and the customer make their money by helping generate sales. They do not get paid unless a sale is made. Thus the selling cost for the restaurant is a variable one. This compares to the selling cost for direct distribution, which is a fixed cost. The promotion is directed by the operator directly to the customer and must be paid for in full whether it attracts one customer or a thousand. On the other hand, it must be remembered that everyone between the restaurant and the customer must get a cut of the selling price charged by the operation. If a menu item regularly sells for $18 and the restaurant sells that item directly to the customer, it receives $18. However, if a credit card is used, a percentage of the sale is paid to the credit card company and the bank handling the collection. The bus operator willing to bring in two busloads of tourists three times a week during the season will pay less than the $18 because he or she is buying in bulk and expects to pay less by buying wholesale. Every restaurant manager would prefer to sell every meal for the retail price. At times during the day, or the week, or the year, however, the business is not there to pay the full asking price. This is when, and only when, discounts paid to intermediaries can be justified.

The key for the operation is to know when it wants the business and to know the cost structure sufficiently well to realize how low it can price the product and still make money. As a minimum, it is important to know what the break-even point is. As discussed in Chapter 1, the break-even point for a food-service facility is that point at which the operation exactly breaks even. No profits are made; no costs are incurred. At the break-even point, total revenues taken in exactly equal total costs incurred. The important distinction here is that after the break-even point, the only costs incurred by the operation are variable costs. If break-even can thus be assured, the product can be priced to cover variable costs. Anything over the variable cost is profit.

A third factor to consider is the image of the intermediary. The image of the people or organizations distributing the product represent, for the customer, the image of the restaurant being sold. Operators would want to ensure that this image is consistent with the one they want to portray.

When sales are made directly, they are made through the employees of the restaurant. Those employees are employed by the operation and should therefore be more motivated to ensure the success of the restaurant than others in the channel who are not employees. The operator needs to determine the needs and wants of those in the channel to ensure a match with her or his own needs.

A final factor to consider is who has the power in the channel. To the extent that a restaurant relies on a tour operator to bring in a significant amount of business, that operator has increased power to demand better prices and services at the risk of taking the business to another restaurant. Recently, a number of restaurants in the northeast were successful in their attempts to reduce the percentages paid to American Express. The individual operation must balance the various forms of direct and indirect distribution in such a way that it feels in charge of its own destiny rather than being at the mercy of others in the channel.

Budget.   A crucial part of the action plan is the budget that is developed to carry it out. Various means have been used to develop a budget. A common way of developing a budget is to base it on a percentage of sales. Restaurants typically spend from 0.4 to 6.8 percent of sales on marketing depending on whether it is a full- or limited-service, limited-menu with no table-service facility, or a cafeteria. This option can work with businesses with a high percentage of repeat business. However, if sales go down in a particular year, the following year's marketing budget will be cut when it should probably be increased.

Another option is to spend in line with what the competition is spending. This effectively puts one's fate in the hands of the competition, who may not know what they are doing.

A third option is to spend what the business can afford. This approach is a reactive way of deciding action plans.

The fourth approach is the best but also the most difficult. Action plans are developed that will be successful and an amount budgeted to ensure their completion. At this point the desired budget may have to be modified in light of the amount of money available. However, the point is first to determine how much is needed to do the job, then determine if the business can afford it, rather than vice versa.

Monitor and Evaluate the Marketing Plan

It is easy to see when a marketing plan is successful—there are more customers coming in more often and paying a higher average check. Equally, it is easy to determine when a plan has not worked—fewer customers coming in as often and spending less. What is difficult, however, is to determine why the plan failed. The exciting part of putting a marketing plan in place is the operation of the plan. But the most important and most overlooked part is determining whether or not it was successful and how and where it succeeded or went wrong. Even when the plan is evaluated, it is often done after the event as a kind of postmortem. This may help ensure the success of the next marketing effort. However, it does nothing for the existing campaign.

The marketing plan must be monitored at each step of the way to ensure that it is on track, and corrective action must be taken at each step of the way if it is off track. The first point at which a plan can falter is in the selection of the correct market segment. No matter how good an advertising campaign, if it is directed at the wrong people, it will not work. For control purposes, the restaurateur needs to ask:

- Do I know what my customers want?
- Do I know what people in the marketplace, who are not yet my customers, want?
- Do I know the characteristics of the target market I want to attract?

quick bite 3.8
Road to the Top

Brian J. Kolodziej, vice president for culinary operations

Brian J. Kolodziej's associate's degree in culinary arts from Johnson & Wales, his experience in fine dining, and an extreme interest in food has helped him to revitalize Chili's casual-dining menu, which has traditionally been known for burgers, ribs and appetizers. Following Kolodziej's lead, Chili's menu has added contemporary items including more soups, salads, and sandwiches.

Many executives at Brinker International give Kolodziej's menu ideas credit for helping to increase same-store sales over the past two years. About half of Chili's menu has changed in the past two years under Kolodziej's direction. Part of his strategy is to create a "food-culture" program, making food awareness the highest priority in the chain's restaurants. Kolodziej is set on providing guests with a variety of choices by combining Chili's casual-dining menu with his fine dining background gained from The Mansion on Turtle Creek and the Adolphus Hotel.

Kolodziej rose through the ranks at Brinker International after beginning as a corporate chef for Kona Ranch Steakhouse in Oklahoma City and the Spageddies casual Italian dining concept, both which Brinker later dropped from their portfolio. As vice president for culinary operations for Chili's, Kolodziej took a menu that had been there since the '70s and revitalized it. He instituted a new bun, new choices, new builds, and a new attitude in presentation and service. Kolodziej kept the core menu items and revived them by changing their ingredients and presentations.

Kolodziej has helped to make Chili's food as good as it can be. He understands food, but also sees the big picture, according to Doug Brooks, chief operating officer for Brinker International. He understands the necessity of marketing and operations in his culinary ideas. According to Brooks, Kolodziej is extremely organized and a great manager. However, according to Kolodziej, the main idea is to be creative and have fun. "We never realize," he concludes, "just how hard we are working."

Source: Ruggless, Ron. "Brian J. Kolodziej: Menu Development Is the Forte of Chili's VP Who Believes in Getting Back to 'Food First.'" *Nation's Restaurant News,* v. 33, no. 4, pp. 132–133.

Assuming that the answer to all the questions above is "yes," the next step is to evaluate the objectives that have been set. The objectives should be:

- Specific
- Measurable
- Achievable

- Realistic
- Time-based
- Consistent with the operation's place in the product life-cycle curve
- Consistent with the customer's place in the buying process

In monitoring the theme of the program, research is essential to determine the extent to which it is desirable and believable in the eyes of the target market.

quick bite 3.10
Restaurant Marketing in 2010

According to the National Restaurant Association the most likely developments regarding restaurant marketing in 2010 are:

- Marketing will make more use of consumer databases to more effectively target customers.
- There will be an increase in branding and cross-brand marketing.
- Loyalty marketing will become more highly developed.

Source: Restaurant Industry 2010: The Road Ahead (Washington, D.C.: National Restaurant Association, 1999), p. 14.

Additionally, it must be action oriented. In other words, will it produce action on the part of potential customers?

In selecting the appropriate promotional mix, the key concern is whether or not the message is being placed where it will be seen, heard, and/or read by the target market. Media planning involves making decisions on the timing, frequency, size, and position of promotional messages. At this stage messages should be tracked to see whether they meet the objectives set earlier. Were customers exposed to the message? Did the message convey to them the necessary information about the operation? Were their attitudes about the facility changed as a result of the message? Did they develop a preference for the operation because of the message? Were they driven to action by the message? Will they come back again? Finally, the budget must be examined along two lines: (1) is it sufficient to meet the objectives set, and (2) is it an amount that the business can afford?

ENDNOTES

1. "AMA Board Approves New Marketing Definition," *Marketing News*, March 1, 1985, p. 1.

2. Robert D. Reid, *Hospitality Marketing Management*, 2nd ed. (New York: Van Nostrand Reinhold, 1989), p. 8.

3. James R. Abbey, *Hospitality Sales and Advertising* (East Lansing, MI: Educational Institute of the American Hotel and Motel Association, 1989), p. 34.

4. Tom Feltenstein, *Foodservice Marketing for the '90s* (New York: John Wiley & Sons, 1992), pp. 51–54.

5. Ibid., p. 29.

6. Ibid., p. 23.

7. Abbey, *Hospitality Sales and Advertising*, p. 37.

8. National Restaurant Association, "A Booming Boomer Business," *Restaurants USA*, August 1996, p. 41.

9. National Restaurant Association, "Dining Out—A Habit-Forming Experience," *Restaurants USA*, September 1997, p. 39.

10. Eric N. Berkowitz, Roger A. Kerin, Steven W. Hartley, and William Rudelius, *Marketing*, 3rd ed. (Homewood, IL: Richard D. Irwin, 1992), p. 204.

11. Abbey, *Hospitality Sales and Advertising*, p. 20.

12. Robert C. Lewis and Richard E. Chambers, *Marketing Leadership in Hospitality: Foundations and Practices* (New York: Van Nostrand Reinhold, 1989), p. 327.

13. Ibid., p. 354.

CHAPTER FOUR

PROMOTING
THE OPERATION

learning objectives

By the end of this chapter you should be able to:

1. Describe the various stages in the promotional process.
2. Compare and contrast the various methods of establishing a promotional budget.
3. Describe the functions of advertising.
4. Identify the criteria used in selecting which media should be used.
5. Compare and contrast the effectiveness of various media.
6. Identify the key parts of a successful sales promotion: merchandising effort and public relations campaign.

Value is what you get divided by what you pay.
Aric D. Nissen, Country Kitchen International

THE PROMOTIONAL PROCESS

Objectives of Promotion

Modern marketing calls for more than developing a good product, pricing it attractively, and making it available to target customers. Restaurants must also communicate with their customers.

Management communicates with customers—both existing and potential—through what is known as the promotional mix. The end goal of promotion is behavior modification: We want to initiate or change the behavior of customers such that they will dine with us.

Specifically, promotion seeks to inform, persuade, and remind. For new or remodeled restaurants the task is to inform the public about the operation; for existing operations the job is to persuade customers to visit; to existing customers it is necessary to keep them consciously aware of the operation so that when they think about eating out, one restaurant immediately springs to mind.

Steps in the Process

The communications process is illustrated in Figure 4.1. A target market is identified, objectives set, the content and form of the message established, the promotional mix determined, appropriate media selected, and a budget established. It is important to set up controls at each step of the way to determine whether the campaign is on track.

Target market.   The various segments of the market have been covered in earlier chapters. To determine whether the correct market has been chosen, the operator must answer the following questions:

- Do I know what my customers want?
- Do I know what the marketplace wants?
- Do I know the characteristics of the target market I want to attract?

Objectives.   To determine the objectives of the campaign it is important to determine where the operation is in the life-cycle curve and where the customers are in the buying process. The concept of a life-cycle curve involves the notion that a business goes through various stages. The length of time in each stage will vary from business to business. At each stage, different operational strategies are important. Typically, a business will be introduced into the marketplace, then go through stages of growth, maturity, and decline or rejuvenation. In the first stage, the new or remodeled concept is introduced into the marketplace. At this point, potential customers are unaware of the operation. The objective is to inform customers of the restaurant's existence.

If all goes well the restaurant goes through a period of growth. One characteristic of the operation is that sales or customers are increasing at an increasing rate. Perhaps there was a 5 percent increase in sales last year, a 7 percent increase this year, and a projected 8 percent increase next year. At this point, customers are obviously aware of the operation and the objective is to persuade.

In the mature stage of the life cycle, sales and/or customers are increasing but at a decreasing rate—last year's growth of 6 percent is replaced this year by a growth of 5 percent and a projected growth next year of 3 percent. Profits begin to peak before sales decline. The promotional objective is to differentiate the operation from the competition.

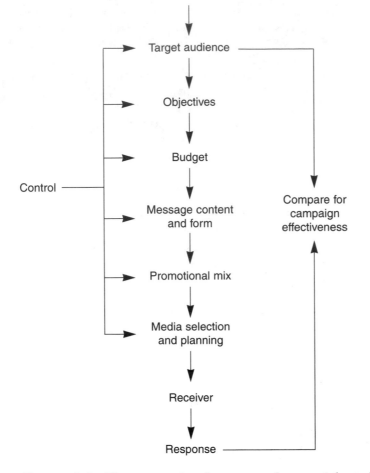

Figure 4.1 The promotional process. *Source:* Adapted from Robert Christie Mill and Alastair M. Morrison, *The Tourism System: An Introductory Text,* 2nd ed. (Upper Saddle River, NJ: Prentice Hall, 1992), p. 448.

If no remedial action is taken, the business will go into the decline stage of the cycle. Sales and/or customers are going down. At this point it is important to take the appropriate steps to get out of that particular business segment.

Remedial action can be taken to rejuvenate the business to produce another spurt of growth. This might involve getting existing customers to come in more often and/or at different times of the day, going after another segment of the market, or introducing new items on the menu (or a change of theme altogether). A number of the fast-food chains noticed a slowdown in sales as the industry entered the mature stage of the life cycle and introduced breakfast menus as a way of rejuvenating sales. In addition, many expanded overseas to reach an entirely new market.

Restaurant Management: Customers, Operations, and Employees

Hot Concepts

Del Taco

Del Taco has been in business for over 35 years as a quickservice operator. Yet the chain has just recently began aggressively expanding into new markets. The concept is counting on those who have moved from their current Southern California locations to provide them with an existing customer base in locations such as Phoenix, Arizona. The company is planning on developing 16 new sites in the Phoenix area by the end of 2000 according to president of the 340-unit Del Taco, based in Laguna Hills, California.

The company currently has four units operating in Arizona, the first one opened in May 1999. The first Del Taco is company owned while the other three Arizona stores are franchised. The planned freestanding units will be approximately 2,100-sqaure feet and will be patterned after a "'Concept 2000' prototype, which features colorful graphics, 15-foot ceilings and a drive-thru," according to Paul Hitzelberger, Del Taco's executive president of franchise development relations.

In addition to the sixteen locations planned for Arizona, Del Taco will increase its number of stores in the 10 states they operate in by at least 47 stores in 1999. Further long-term plans for the company include opening more than 1,000 units in 20 to 25 states by 2004. Why the rapid growth? Del Taco is preparing an attack on the Tex-Mex quickserve giant, Taco Bell, which has more than 7,000 units globally and almost $5 billion in sales for 1998.

Del Taco prices their items similar to Taco Bell and follows many of the new menu item introductions with similar ones of their own. The Del Taco chain has created a great deal of rivalry in the markets in which they compete. Taco Bell's Gorditas introduction was immediately followed by Del Taco' Big Fat Taco sandwich.

Del Taco is even chomping at the heels of Taco Bell's chihuahua with one ad that makes fun of the Taco Bell mascot and its executives. The chain's average check of almost $5 at newer locations have resulted from the introduction of the BBQ Big Fat Taco which feature a choice of beef, chicken or steak for $1.59. Most of the stores are open 24 hours and 65 percent of sales are generated by drive-thru service.

Many industry analysts praise Del Taco's menu for offering American items such as hamburgers and fries as well as Mexican entrees. The choice helps to eliminate the veto vote, which prevent many families and groups from eating Mexican. Many analysts expect Del Taco to become the Burger King of the Mexican quickserve market as long as they retain the capital to continue growth. However, since Del Taco is a privately held company that does not plan on going public, this could be their biggest challenge.

Source: Spector, Amy. "In a Dog-Eat-Dog World, Del Taco Bites into Giant Chihuahua's Market Share." *Nation's Restaurant News,* May 17, 1999, v. 33, n. 21, p. 8.

quick bite 4.2
Designing Successful Advertising

An effective display ad originates with a fresh message and is complemented with visual flair, a hot headline and a memorable tag line. In order to create a convincing ad, it is important to understand what message the ad should convey. The following points are some helpful tips for creating successful advertising.

- Use a simple message.

If customers are given too much to remember, they may not remember anything from the ad at all. One way to handle possible information overload is to gather all of the messages about the restaurant customers should know and wade through it. Out of these possible messages one memorable message should be picked, one that will attract the most customers.

- Stress benefits, not features.

In order to be effective, an ad must tell customers what's in it for them. The idea is to translate the restaurant's best features into benefits that the patron desires. The customer should be an active participant in the ad—change "friendly and fun atmosphere" to "enjoy our friendly and fun atmosphere with your friends and family."

- Excel above and beyond the competition.

An effective ad must display how a restaurant is better than the competition. Search competitors' ads to find advantages held by the restaurant that the competition does not have or offer. One way to discover the restaurant's advantage is to ask frequent customers why they return. Whatever attribute of the restaurant appeals to them can become the heart of the display ad.

- Use words and pictures in concert.

Readers look to the visual first and then read the headline followed by the logo. The visual should match the text. If the ad states that the restaurant has the best service, the graphic should reinforce this idea perhaps with a photograph of a waiter conversing with a customer. Color can also enhance an ad; research shows that four-color ads are read nine times more than black-and-white ads.

(continued)

quick bite 4.2

Designing Successful Advertising (*continued*)

- Do's and don'ts.

The typeface used for a display ad should fit the ad's overall message. If the ad claims inexpensive meals then the typeface should give a cheap look, conversely, an expensive restaurant should use an elegant typeface in its ad's headlines. Yet, elaborate typefaces should not be used in the text because it can make reading difficult. Size is also important. One element should dominate the ad; equal-sized elements can confuse readers. The first thing people see in the ad, whether headline or graphic, should tell people the primary benefit. Finally, the tag line should be noteworthy and reinforce a buying decision. Famous taglines include: "Did somebody say McDonalds?" and "Come see the softer side of Sears."

Source: Perry, Phillip M. "Show and Tell: The Recipe for Display Ad Success." *Restaurants USA,* v. 19, no. 1, January 1999, pp. 13–17.

For control purposes objectives should be SMART—that is, they should be specific, measurable, achievable, realistic, and time-bound. To make the objective specific, it is necessary to quantify it. It is not enough to "increase awareness"; it is necessary to "reach 1000 prospects." The sheer fact that a specific target has been set increases the chances of reaching it.

Similarly, objectives must be measurable. There is no way that an objective of "increasing awareness" can be measured; it is just too vague. It is possible, however, to determine whether or not 1000 people have been exposed to a promotional message. Newspapers count circulation, radio stations count listeners, and direct mailings can be tabulated.

If objectives are not achievable, setting them becomes a meaningless exercise. They must also be realistic in the eyes of the people whose job it is to meet the objectives. If objectives are set at an unrealistically high level—"we want to sell an additional 200 bottles of wine next week"—the servers who are charged with the task of selling the wine will not even try, realizing that it is impossible.

Finally, objectives must be time-bound. There must be a time frame within which the objective is to be achieved. If there is no time frame, it becomes impossible to determine whether the objective has been reached.

Message Content and Form.   A variety of themes can be developed as part of a promotional campaign. A restaurant may stress reputation, food taste or type, quality, or service. The "proper" message is one that is desirable, believable, exclusive, and action-oriented. It must make the customer want what is being offered; it has to be believed; it should "belong" to one operation and no one else; and it should induce action on the part of the customer.

Message Consistency

Marketing plans use multiple tools that many would not consider as part of marketing including the company name, logo, corporate colors, letterhead and signage. However, it is essential to the success of any company that all of these tools and any other implemented work together to create a strong and unforgettable corporate image. Often companies use so many different styles that none of their messages hold together.

Always presenting messages in the same tone to patrons, whether it's light-hearted and fun or serious and conventional, results in a consistent image. Basically, a consistent image gives a company a voice of its own that speaks to customers, bringing success. Selecting an image requires a great deal of planning and organization. The same effort must go into every message put forth by a firm. When the message remains consistent and the image works, a company develops a unique position in the minds of consumers, which often guarantees their imminent loyalty.

The following items are important to remember when creating a company image:

Think like a customer . . .

In order to successfully package an image, operators need to think like their customers and address any item that can add to their enjoyment, comfort and ease. For example, a maternity store may provide parking for "expecting mothers only" or a children's clothing store may provide a play area for kids.

Match language and corporate persona . . .

All communication should match the image of a company in order to follow good marketing practice. For example, Caesar's Palace in Las Vegas begins each of its marketing letters with "Hail!" rather than the traditional "Dear," and one New York deli inquires whether or not patrons would like to "schlep" their leftovers home. Signage is a great way to replace boring messages into unique ones. Instead of the traditional "Place Order Here" sign, a more daring restaurant may opt for a "What do you want?" sign.

Colors speak loudly . . .

Colors should be used as consistently as words. Colors will forever be linked to a business in the customer's mind. Colors that having connotations and meanings themselves can reinforce an image. For example, silver means high-tech and green means money. Even shapes and sizes can present their own meaning in logos and other designs.

(continued)

Promotional Mix.　The major elements of the promotional mix are [1]:

- Advertising: any paid form of nonpersonal presentation and promotion of ideas, goods, or services by an identified sponsor.
- Personal selling: oral conversations, either by telephone or face to face, between salespersons and prospective customers.
- Sales promotion: short-term incentives to encourage purchase or sales of a product or service.
- Merchandising: materials used in-house to stimulate sales, including brochures on display, signs, posters, tent cards, and other point-of-purchase promotional items.
- Public relations and publicity: the nonpaid communication activities involved in maintaining or improving relationships with other organizations and individuals.

The principles and practices involved in the proper selection of the various parts of the promotional mix will make up much of the remainder of this chapter.

Media Selection and Planning.　Various elements of the promotional mix involve using paid or unpaid media. While selecting appropriate media will be covered in more detail later, the key control question is this: "Is my message in a place where it will be seen, read, and/or heard by my customers?"

Budget.　The place of budgeting in the promotional process will depend on the approach to promotion taken by the operation. In a bottom-up approach, objectives will be set, the methods of reaching the objectives determined, and a budget agreed upon that will do the job. All too often, however, a top-down approach is used whereby the budget is determined first and objectives set relative to the amount of money available. Budgets can either be set according to industry standards, to what the competition is spending, to what amount of money is available, or to meet the agreed-upon objectives.

Full-service restaurants spend an average of 1.6 to 2.2 percent of sales on marketing expenses [2]. The problem with an average is just that—it is an average. This figure represents a number for newly opened operations (which probably need to promote more) and established facilities, which may not need to promote as much. This figure should only be used as a very rough starting point.

Often a manager, noticing that the competition has taken out an advertisement in the local paper, responds with an ad of his or her own. Although it can be important to match the competition, this policy has two major drawbacks: It means that the manager's actions are being "controlled" by the competition and assumes that the competition knows what it is doing!

For many managers promotion is seen as a cost of doing business rather than as an investment. Too often the refrain is, "I can't afford to advertise" to which the answer is, "You can't afford not to." Promotional expenses must be planned for in advance as a part of doing business rather than being relegated to the category of an "extra" for which money may or may not be available after all other bills have been paid.

The best and most difficult method of establishing a budget is to identify the objectives and set a budget sufficient to meet the objectives. At the same time, it must be an amount that the business can afford. Promotion is more art than science. There is no scientific way to determine how many advertisements it will take to produce x number of customers. For this reason alone, there is a common tendency to view budgeting as a top-down effort.

Response.   If promotion is communication, it does not work unless communication occurs, unless the object of the communication receives it and responds. If each step of the process has been controlled, there is a greater chance that the campaign will be a success and that customers will respond to an advertisement, buy the bottle of wine from the server, or order the appetizer noted on the tent card.

This final part of the control process is vital. Did the promotion do what it was intended to do? Can we trace the impact on sales to a particular effort? Only through such tracking can a cost-benefit analysis be done in an effort to measure the effectiveness of the various parts of the promotional effort.

Customer Use of Information

According to the National Restaurant Association [3], while restaurateurs typically use advertisements in magazines and newspapers or direct mail to tempt customers into their restaurants for the first time, these types of information sources are used by fewer than one out of five adults who are looking for a new restaurant. Twenty-eight percent of adults report they are likely to select a new tableservice restaurant on the basis of a television advertisement while one-third are likely to use a restaurant guide. Eight percent are likely to use the Internet, a figure expected to increase dramatically in the future. Word-of-mouth remains the most popular source of information used by prospective customers in selecting a new restaurant. Younger people and those with lower incomes are less likely to use the recommendations of friends than are older people and those in higher income brackets. However, across all age and income groups, personal recommendations are overwhelmingly the most used information source. This emphasizes the importance of providing excellent value and service, the subject of Chapter 6.

ADVERTISING AGENCIES

When to Use an Agency

A foodservice company can handle its own promotional campaign or it can hire an advertising agency. Some owners, managers, and key personnel are clever with words and ideas. They may actually be better than some professionals at creating ads and promos. They may need only occasional outside services and suppliers to help them promote their businesses. Other operators may not be so fortunate or creative; they may wish to contract with outside companies for publicity services and suppliers to help them promote their businesses. Another option could be to create an in-house advertising agency—that is, an agency within the firm.

Operators of many small or beginning businesses have little choice. Their advertising budget is not big enough to justify hiring an independent agency, much less setting up a house agency. These operators must look after their own promotion, calling on representatives of local media for expertise. Fortunately, many local broadcast or print media prepare advertising quite competently. The restaurateur has only to coordinate the themes and timing of the various efforts—and be sure that he or she is buying what is needed. It is always worth remembering that advertising salespeople are paid for selling advertising, and believing in their service, they will sell as much as they can.

Agencies are paid in a variety of ways [4]. Often, they receive commissions from the media in which the message is placed. The usual commission is 15 percent of the cost of the advertisement. If an advertisement cost $400, for example, the client would pay the agency the $400. The agency would subtract 15 percent ($60) and pay the media $340.

Agencies also charge the client for production and creative services involved in creating the advertisement. Typically, these fees consist of monthly retainers in addition to hourly charges for creative work, photography, and typesetting. Finally, agencies charge for advertisements on which commissions are not paid, such as direct mail and local newspaper advertising.

How to Select an Agency

When an agency wants a restaurant's business, or a restaurateur wants to hire an agency, it is customary to arrange an agency presentation. The larger the account and billing, the more attractive the company will be to agencies.

An agency presentation can be accomplished over a simple lunch or may take the form of a full-blown display of what the agency can do. A presentation will include a description of the personnel of the agency and some representative work they have performed successfully for others. A list of past and present clients will usually be offered for reference checks. The pitch can be conducted in the client's offices or at the agency. Most agencies prefer to use their facilities to avoid interruptions and to put on a proper show.

Presenting agencies will try to sell an entire marketing plan rather than just a media plan. Even if they do not know the idiosyncracies of the business, they may be able to lay out a plan of attack to help a restaurateur get more mileage out of an ad budget.

If the restaurateur's budget is large enough to interest them, it is wise to listen to more than one agency's presentation. It is not wise to make a hasty decision. References of past and present clients of the agencies that are being considered should be checked before committing to an outside agency.

Most agencies will not represent more than one client in a given business or industry. If an agency already has a restaurant or hospitality account, it will probably be prepared to quit or lose it before taking another.

Before making a decision, the agency offices should be toured and meetings held with the personnel. The person who will be working with the account representing the client should be identified. Agency personnel who do not own a piece of the action in their agencies tend to move about in their industry just as restaurant people change jobs in theirs. It may become an important issue if an account executive leaves the agency. An account may be bound by an employment agreement that forbids agency personnel from taking clients along to a new agency.

Studying how an advertising agency works will help improve cooperation with the agency's efforts. An outside agency representative can instruct a client in how they operate, purchase media, perform research, order graphic artwork and photography, handle copyrighting, and conduct publicity. In the process a restaurateur will sign all insertion orders and okay all copy. It is important for clients to receive copies of all work done on their behalf.

The agency relationship should begin with a complete understanding of how all items, services, and media are to be purchased. Both parties must exert every possible effort to be open to what the other is doing for their mutual good. Both client and agency must anticipate problems and discuss them beforehand to establish the best possible relations and to achieve the best results.

Most client–agency relationship and agreements, either oral or written, can terminate almost immediately. Agencies know that they cannot work where they are not wanted. There should be one item that should be understood when a split occurs—all bills and invoices should be paid by the client to the agency or be guaranteed to all other suppliers and media. When this is fully done, the agency should relinquish all the materials and support information that belong to the client.

ADVERTISING

As noted above, advertising can be defined as any paid form of nonpersonal presentation and promotion of ideas, goods, or services by an identified sponsor.

Functions of Advertising

Advertising seeks to inform, persuade, and remind. It can accomplish a number of things [5]: It presents information to the customer about the operation, it encourages first-time visits, it enhances the image of a particular company or operation, and it reinforces the behavior of customers who have eaten there in the past.

Types of Campaigns

National/Local. Advertising campaigns can be either national or local. National advertising uses network media—television, radio, and magazines—to reach a national audience. The effort is essentially directed toward promoting the general name or image of the company rather than toward any one establishment. At the local level promotions are tailored to the local market in an attempt to promote specific restaurants.

Cooperative Agreements. To maximize use of the promotional dollar, individual restaurants can enter into cooperative agreements whereby a number of individual operations pool their resources to produce an advertisement promoting eating out in general or restaurants in a geographic area. This allows an individual facility to advertise in media that it could not afford on its own. Individual managers must determine whether or not the benefits of inclusion outweigh the costs.

Another example of cooperative advertising is when restaurants who are members of chains cooperate with the corporate office in producing a promotion. A national chain would pay the "national rate" for a series of advertisements in print, television, or radio. This rate is higher than the "local rate," that paid by a local business. By splitting the cost of the campaign 50–50 and having the local business book the advertisement, the company gets a lower rate while the individual business effectively doubles its advertising budget.

Media Selection Criteria

A variety of criteria are used to determine which media should be used. The most important criteria are the cost per contact, total cost, market selectivity, geographic selectivity, source credibility, visual quality, noise level, life span, pass-along rate, and timing flexibility.

The cost per contact, usually expressed as cost per thousand (CPM), refers to the cost of reaching 1,000 people. The total cost is the actual cost of the message. Market selectivity refers to the extent to which an advertiser can reach a specific market segment. In recent years magazines aimed at a general readership have given way to a variety of magazines targeted toward specific groups of people. This makes it easier to reach particular segments of the market.

Similarly, geographic selectivity refers to the ability to reach a particular part of the country, state, or town. Many magazines run regional editions while small townships put out local papers. Source credibility considers how believable the medium is viewed to be by the reader or listener. Certain media offer better quality visuals than others. Generally speaking, the quality of visuals in newspapers is poor.

When an advertisement competes with other activities for a person's attention, the noise level is said to be high. If the tendency is to give total attention to the message, the noise level is said to be low.

Life span and pass-along rate are closely related. A newspaper has a life span of one day. One person reads it and usually discards it. A magazine, on the other hand, is kept around longer and may be read by someone other than the person who purchased it. A radio advertisement has an even shorter life span than that of a newspaper, as the message cannot be referred to again. Among other things, this means that radio advertisements have to be repeated a number of times to have any kind of impact.

Finally, timing flexibility refers to the lead time needed to run or change an advertisement.

Newspapers

Effectiveness.   Newspapers, as noted above, are the primary advertising medium for tableservice restaurants. They generally offer the most cost-effective means of reaching potential consumers, both in terms of total cost and cost per contact. Market selectivity is low, and geographic selectivity is average. It is possible, for example, to zero-in on specific towns. The trust factor appears to be low and the visual quality less than average. To counteract a high noise level, low life span, and pass-along rate, newspapers offer a great deal of flexibility in the timing of advertisements.

Copy/Layout.   When using a newspaper advertisement copy, layout and photographs/sketches must be considered. The copy consists of the headline and body. The headline of the ad must catch the reader's attention while the body includes the details. A good advertisement starts with a headline that is enticing, provocative, and attention-grabbing. A clever, punch headline with few words is preferable to one that attempts to tell the entire story.

Size/Shape.   Choosing a different size and shape is one way to make an ad stand out. If most other ads are 1/4-page vertical, a 1/4-page horizontal space may attract more attention.

Suppress the urge to crowd as much information as possible into an ad. The most successful ads tell a simple story in clear, concise language. Ads jammed with too many facts and figures are least likely to be read. All ads create certain types of impressions. A simple test can determine what stands out most in an ad. The ad is turned upside down to see what is most noticeable. People are used to reading left to right, top to bottom. Once a page is turned upside down, the viewer's mind's eye becomes disoriented and he or she cannot read according to learned methods. At first, an ad may look like a big blur, but later the viewer will be able to detect the most outstanding element in the ad, the one that will have the most impact on readers. If that element is not the one intended, the ad needs to redesigned. If the big blur remains and the viewer finds it difficult to determine any outstanding elements, the ad needs to be redesigned.

Restaurant Management: Customers, Operations, and Employees

A catchy headline, a strong graphic, a bold price, or any other single element should be prominent.

Radio

Radio is an immediate medium for quick news and information. Advertising time can readily be bought and commercials produced quickly for relatively low cost. It is selective for broad market segments and has a high geographic selectivity. Credibility is low and noise level high, while timing flexibility is better than average.

Station Formats. In seeking a share of the market, radio stations have created many individual formats that reach different target audiences efficiently. Radio station formats include talk, Spanish, middle-of-the-road, top 40, R & B, classical, contemporary, religious, adult contemporary, nostalgia/big band, news/talk, oldies, disco, educational, jazz, progressive rock, beautiful music, blues/soft, and gospel music. Individual stations claim that their listeners are loyal and selective because of their strong preferences for a station's format and their personal identification with the particular interests reflected by the station.

Effectiveness. Radio uses words and sounds to describe products and services and special occasions. Radio plays on the imagination of the listeners and attempts to sell the sizzle rather than the steak.

Many radio stations in a market result in fragmented audiences. Radio advertising can therefore be costly and inefficient when many stations are needed to reach a broad cross section of target audiences. Radio cannot show or demonstrate products or services. The advertising message usually must remind people of things they know. New, unique, or complicated ideas may be difficult to express. Radio is a transient medium. Messages cannot be kept for later reference. Listeners, for example, must remember addresses and telephone numbers. Coupon offers are out.

The Federal Trade Commission (FTC) regulates the percentage of total air time that can be devoted to commercials. Many listeners, however, believe that some radio stations are over commercialized, particularly at peak periods. Advertising messages therefore need strong creative treatment to be noticed and remembered.

Commercial formats. Commercials generally come in two formats: 30 and 60 seconds. The half-minute spots do not cost 50 percent of the cost of full-minute spots. The expense is so close that many advertisers use 60-second commercial spots for the greatest cost efficiency. Also, 30-second commercials are very brief. A 30-second spot involves 65 to 70 words of copy, while a 60-second commercial generally accommodates 125 to 135 words of copy.

Television

Unquestionably, television is the powerhouse medium. It combines most of the advantages of sight, sound, immediacy, dramatization, and emotional involvement of the viewers in a way that no other medium can match. It is also expensive. It can make customers aware of what there is to offer, at a price that requires considerable planning and budgeting.

Effectiveness.   Television is the dominant medium. It reaches people of every type and is of average market selectivity while covering large areas of geography quite efficiently. However, television is inefficient when advertisers need to reach a highly selected group of people. It cannot isolate distinctively differing groups of people as does radio with its highly categorized formats.

Television can also show how a product or service works, and it provides strong name identification. It builds awareness rapidly and, by its intensity, increases audience perception of commercial message. As a medium it is not credible, the noise level is high, and the timing flexibility is low.

Television ads cannot be saved for later reference or couponing. In addition, commercial time is generally short and, like radio spots, television messages must have an immediate impact on viewers. Television cannot be used for long, complicated explanations.

Magazines

Effectiveness.   There are almost as many different kinds of magazines as there are different kinds of restaurants. Therefore, a magazine will pinpoint the market by the type of publication chosen. However, any bona fide publication seeking advertisers should provide information concerning its readership, circulation, and advertising costs to permit a restaurateur to determine where it should fit into the advertising program.

Some magazines devote special sections to restaurant advertising. Frequently, the readership of such columns is high and comparable to an editorial feature of the same length. Most magazines are read by the same people, issue after issue. An eating establishment whose advertisement is noted regularly becomes a part of the readers' subconscious mind. An acceptance is established because of the familiarity of name or message.

Yellow Pages

Effectiveness.   Yellow Pages advertisements are important in every promotional campaign. They provide good value for the investment. It is important to have the advertisement draw in the reader. However, to compete with all the listings in the Yellow Pages, many restaurants find it advantageous to place an ad close to their listing or to have their business name set in bold type.

In Yellow Pages advertising the name, address, and phone number of the restaurant are highlighted for people who have sought out the restaurant section for a specific interest. If a person is scanning the pages to decide on a place to dine, an advertisement has an opportunity to direct him or her to the establishment.

Layout.   Advertising space in the Yellow Pages is sold in standard-size units. The sizes are usually one-fourth of a page, one-eighth of a page, and one-sixteenth of a page. The rates vary according to the number of phone books printed. Based on a cost per thousand impressions, it is not an expensive medium. The total bill, a combination of rate and production costs, can be paid in advance or prorated to coincide with the restaurant's regular service billing.

Signs and Billboards

Signs and billboards can be found on location, on highways, or on buildings. The message should be brief, yet eye-catching. Gigantic signs are now being constructed that swing and shimmer at the slightest touch of wind. Changeable copy panels make it possible to advertise daily menu changes and even provide public service messages from time to time. Generally, a contract for painted display advertising runs for one, two, or three years. The contract specifies the number of times that copy will be renewed or changed during the contract period. It is a rule of thumb in the outdoor advertising business that the message should be renewed or changed every four months. Many advertisers consider outdoor reminder advertising to be supportive rather than primary in nature. Outdoor posters must be brief with just a few bold, easy-to-read words to tell a story or theme.

Direct Mail

Direct mail marketers send mailings that include letters, glossy advertisement, samples, and foldouts to prospects on their mailing list.

Advantages. Direct mail offers a number of advantages to the restaurateur. This form of advertising has a high degree of control as the manager decides to whom the message is to be sent. The number of pieces mailed can be tailored to the size of the budget available. It is highly audience selective in that the mailing lists are developed from customer lists or from lists obtained from mailing-list houses, which can provide lists of names broken down into a variety of specific segments. Direct mail is increasing in popularity because it permits high target-market selectivity.

It is also highly flexible, in that the message can be personalized to different market segments. There is some question as to whether or not it is cluttered. Certainly, people are unlikely to be doing anything else when they read their mail. On the other hand, so much mail is now regarded as "junk mail" that any and all nonpersonal mail stands a good chance of being thrown out unopened unless the piece is carefully designed. The ability to assess responses from a mailing by enclosing a coupon or a phone number allows easy measurement of the results of a campaign.

Disadvantages. Direct mailings tend to have a high discard rate, high total cost, and long lead time. A rule of thumb is that a direct mailing gets a 1 to 3 percent response rate. This means that for every 100 letters sent out, the operator will receive only an average 2 percent response rate to a mailing. To get 100 customers with a response rate of 2 percent would require a mailing of 5,000 pieces. The response rate can be improved by having a high-quality list and a mailing that is targeted to the needs of the potential customers being sought.

It is estimated that between 15 and 30 percent of mailing lists change each year. The cost of updating lists, in addition to the low response rate, can result in

quick bite 4.4
Direct Mail Campaigns

Restaurateurs often do very little to promote their operation due to cost constraints. However, direct mail is an effective and inexpensive way to promote any business. The trick to effective direct mail is getting people to read it. One method of catching consumers' attention is using attractive picture postcards. In addition sending mail that emulates wedding invitations can be as effective as using more expensive air envelopes. These six direct mail tactics can boost unit sales if done right.

Exotic picture postcards. The benefit to sending postcards is a lower mailing rate. The postcard rate is usually about 10 cents less than regular postage. In addition, if a customer gets a postcard from Florida, they will read it especially if it has a clever line like "Don't Mickey Mouse around with your next meal."

From Trash to Treasure. One tactic for direct mail is to send out an unattractive, non-noteworthy, simple postcard that is bound to be thrown out. One week letter, send the same postcard in a normal business envelope. Crumple up the postcard, then flatten it out and add a Post-it® note that reads, "'Please don't throw this away again! This is important!'"

Something Borrowed. Something New. Creating a direct mail piece that looks like a wedding invitation is sure to get a response. Use an invitation theme like, "You're Cordially Invited To A Free Dessert (with purchase of any entrée)." Invitations are expensive, but can be easily copied with textured paper and envelopes. Use a "LOVE" stamp rather than bulk mail number or meter.

Fake Next-Day Air. Direct mail houses often sell envelopes that look amazing like next-day air packages, but they can be sent for normal postage.

Good Fortune. Many promotional companies offer unique and inexpensive items that an operator can send to customers. One example is custom-made fortune cookies, which predict that a customer will visit the restaurant for a free dinner (with the purchase of one).

Greeting Cards. Greeting cards are a great way to retain customers that a restaurant already has. They are cheap and readily available. They should however be used in unusual ways including Thanksgiving cards, which many people don't receive, birthday cards and Valentine's Day cards. Boss's Day and Secretary's Day cards can often be used to boost lunch business.

Source: Slutsky, Jeff & Slutsky, Marc. "6 killer direct marketing tactics." *Restaurant Hospitality,* May 1998, v. 82, n. 5, pp. 88–92.

a relatively high cost to conduct a campaign. Implementing direct mail through a list house can furnish a lengthy list. If you were to send a mailing to each name, it could develop into a high-priced expenditure.

Mailing Lists.   A properly conducted campaign requires the preparation of up-to-date mailing lists, designing of the piece, processing of the bulk mailing, and responding to inquiries. This can involve a long lead time, ultimately resulting in higher costs.

Commercial lists can be purchased or rented from companies specializing in the development of such items. They can also be obtained from general lists through business directories or membership rosters of associations, or from house lists developed by the restaurant itself. The best source for a mailing list is the property's own customers. The major problem is that such a list takes time to develop. To "prime the pump" a general list tied to the zip codes within a three- to five-mile radius of the operation is probably the second-best alternative.

Types of Mailings.   The most appropriate options for restaurants are letters, newsletters, and menus. Letters are very simple to prepare and can be used for such things as announcements, invitations, and so on. Newsletters to regular customers can be sent monthly, bimonthly, or quarterly, to keep the property in the customer's conscious awareness. As with all direct mail, newsletters should be filled with information that is interesting and important to customers. Seasonal messages and recipes and informative tips regarding food and wine are some of the items to consider. Many people select a restaurant based on the type of menu. For them, mailing the menu itself may induce people to try the operation, particularly a new facility.

Mailing can be either first class, suitable for letters and postcards; third-class single piece, best for booklets and brochures; and third-class bulk, for newsletters or other items mailed in bulk. The latter is the least expensive, but takes longer than first class to be delivered. A variety of restrictions and regulations must be met for the use of third-class mailing.

Success Factors.   To be successful a mailing piece should follow the five P's [6]. First, it should form a picture in the mind of the customer. We think in terms of pictures, not letters or words. Second, it must offer a promise and show how the promise will be fulfilled. The promise should be something that is important to the customer.

Next, the message must prove to the reader that what is being promised is true. "Proof" might come in the form of testimonials, success stories, or statistics. Fourth, the message should push the customer to action—ask for the sale. This might involve making a reservation, sending in a coupon, or showing up for dinner.

Finally, there should be a postscript. In reading a direct mail piece, most people first read the letterhead, then check to look at the signature and to see if there is a P.S. Interest can be generated by means of a clever postscript.

The effectiveness of a direct mail campaign is measured by the number of responses generated. As noted earlier, one of the advantages of direct mail is that the results are readily measurable against the costs involved.

INTERNET

Use of the Internet as a source of information as well as an advertising vehicle is expected to increase rapidly in the next decade. To get the most out of a Web page [7] it is important to downplay the advertising aspect of the page and play up the information aspect. Viewers tend to get turned off by pages they consider too "advertising-aggressive." The objective is to get prospective customers to add the restaurant page to their electronic address book and return often. The Web page has to be integrated into other marketing efforts. Use the page to refer people to newspaper advertisements which, in turn, should list the electronic address of the restaurant. The initial impression is important—browsers may stay for as little as five seconds before moving on. Emphasizing a customer benefit may get them to stay. Lead with a banner that will teach them something such as information on wine and food pairings.

The site should be simple to navigate around and downloading pages should be easy and fast. Like other advertisements, the information should be updated on a regular basis to encourage repeat visits. Including links to other related sites is regarded as good "Netiquette" and professional. Finally, the Web page by itself will be of little use. As noted above, it should be mentioned in all other promotions and advertisements as well as on menus and business cards.

PERSONAL SELLING

Personal selling consists of oral conversations, either by telephone or face to face, between salespersons and prospective customers. In a restaurant situation, personal selling occurs outside the operation as staff attempt to book business and inside as employees try to "sell up," get customers to increase the amount spent. The latter topic is dealt with in Chapter 6.

SALES PROMOTION

Incentives

Sales promotion consists of short-term incentives to encourage the purchase of a product or service. Consumer promotions may include coupons, premiums, patronage rewards, contests, sweepstakes, and games.

Promotions may be open or contingent. Open offers do not require the customer to do anything other than buy the product. Special meals and discounts are examples of open offers. The advantage to the restaurant is that the promotion will have broad customer appeal since no effort to redeem a coupon, for example, is required. On the other hand, the restaurateur has no idea how many people will take advantage of the promotion. More people may show up than was anticipated, creating bad will if items being promoted are not available or high costs if they are.

A contingent offer requires the customer to do something: clip a coupon, eat out three times within a month, or make a specific purchase. The redemption

Incentives and promotions enhance perceived value and attract customers to restaurants. More than 51% of adults indicated that they would take advantage of two-for-one specials and considered it a value-packed promotion. Women were also more likely than men to give a positive response to promotions and to use coupons in general than men were.

Complete-meal and all-you-can-eat specials are most popular with younger customers. Almost 55% of consumers age 18 to 34 said that they were likely to use an all-you-can-eat special, compared with only 28% of those 65 and older. Those 55 and older (nearly 38%) prefer early-bird specials.

Promotion Usage—Percentage of consumers who are likely to use the following types of incentives or promotions when eating out or ordering takeout food.

Type of Incentive or Promotion	Percent Likely to Use
Two-for-one	51%
Coupons	44%
Complete-meal specials	44%
All-you-can-eat specials	42%
Price reductions for off-peak hours dining	33%
Senior-citizen discounts	30%
Early-bird specials	24%
Games and sweepstakes	14%

Source: "1999 Highlights." *Restaurants USA,* v. 18, no. 11, December 1998, p. F9.

rate is more easily controlled, although fewer customers will be attracted. The latter method is preferred for cost-control reasons.

Because of their short-term nature—good promotions have an expiration date—they can have the benefit of stimulating sales during the period of the promotion. Promotions cannot be used as the sole or even most important part of the marketing effort. If the business makes too much use of promotions there is a danger that customers will wait for the next promotion before they buy. This, in essence, is what has happened in the pizza business. Many, if not most, households will simply not buy pizza unless they have a coupon for a discount or two-for-one.

Coupons. Coupons are certificates that give the customer a savings when they purchase a product, as in a two-for-one meal purchase. This is the most

quick bite 4.6
Quick-Serve Promotions

Snowstorms and credit limits often lead to the decline of foodservice sales in the periods immediately following Christmas and New Year's Eve. As a response, many quick-service restaurants begin to roll out the promotions during January and February in order to increase business. Not only do operators launch new menu items, debut ad campaigns or resort to tried and true promotions, but they also use the after-holiday periods to advertise low-fat and healthy items.

One of the largest challenges for operators when considering promotions is sustaining year-after-year growth. Some popular promotions include Weinerschnitzel's chili-cheese burger and chili-cheese dog for $2 and corn dog for 59 cents and A&W Restaurant's onion ring and cheddar-melt burger combo. However, some restaurant chains simply promote the low-calorie and low-fat menu items available instead of using promotions. Subway uses this technique, which has a very strong appeal after the holidays, comparing its product with the competition.

Many chains, including Subway, do not discount or have any special product emphasis and instead focus on relevant brand messages. According to Kevin Armstrong, Subway's marketing director, discounting is too difficult for franchisees and it does not make economic sense. Subway has not seen any negative impact on their margins due to their lack of discounting.

Source: Zuber, Amy. "Winter Weather, Holiday Bills Spur QSR Promos." *Nation's Restaurant News,* v. 33, no. 2, February 11, 1999, pp. 3, 41–44.

widely used special offer, surpassing such things as restaurant specials, combination offers, or senior discounts. A 15 to 20 percent discount is needed to induce customers to buy.

Coupons offering free products are used to generate customer trial. Thus the measure of success is whether or not the customer count increased. A successful trial promotion would attempt to get customers to buy something they would not ordinarily order. For this reason, a free beverage with a sandwich is not a good idea, as most people will order a beverage anyway. It might be better in this situation to offer free onion rings.

Premiums.   Premiums consist of items given away free or at reduced cost. The best and most successful premium has been glasses. The reasons? Glasses break, so households continually need them and it is easy to tie them into popular movies or sports teams. Premiums should be structured to sell higher-priced items—a larger drink, for example, and to encourage repeat visits—collecting all six glasses in the set.

Patronage Rewards. Patronage rewards are cash or other awards for regular use. Restaurants might start a VIP club and establish an awards system based on how many times customers come in or how much they spend. Punching a customer card means that the card is carried around in the customer's purse or wallet, thereby acting as an advertising reminder.

Contests, Sweepstakes, Games. Contests, sweepstakes, and games give customers the chance to win something. A contest calls for the customer to submit an entry, a jingle, a guess, or a suggestion, to be judged by a panel that will select the best entries. A sweepstake calls for names to be entered into a drawing. A game presents customers with something every time they buy that may or may not help win them a prize.

Key Steps

In setting up a promotion the objective needs to be determined, the target market selected, a strategy for implementing the promotion outlined, ways to promote the promotion identified, and evaluation methods set up.

Objective. The purpose or objective of the promotion needs to be determined up front. The objective can be thought of as the problem to be solved. Typically, promotions are used to attract new customers, keep existing customers happy, speed up slow periods, or to spotlight specials. The implementation of the promotion will differ depending on what the objective is.

Target Market. As part of the objective it is necessary to identify the market segment to whom the promotion is to be directed. As stated above, the promotion will be to either existing or potential customers. Existing customers have already tried the restaurant and know what to expect. They will require less information on the facility than will new customers, who will have to be sold on trying out the facility.

The promotions used must be compatible with the set of objectives. Slow periods can be offset by coupons, contests, packages, gift certificates, or discounts. Low check averages are best dealt with through coupons, product samples, contests, or premiums. Contests and product samples can help if existing customers are bored and want something new and different. The point is that the promotion selected will depend on the objective or problem to be solved.

Strategy. The success of a promotion will depend on how it is promoted. The concept of vertical integration is important here. Vertical integration means that the same message is given to the target market through a variety of interconnected means. For example, a Halloween-theme evening could be promoted through radio spots announcing the promotion, newspaper ads with cut-out coupons for specials, local promotions inviting kids to wear costumes, and in-house activities with posters in the restaurant and an employee costume contest. The important point is that all methods are coordinated to complement each other in promoting the event.

Promotion. Restaurants may split the cost of a promotion by hooking up with a supplier interested in moving his or her product. Similarly, cross-promotions can occur with a noncompeting business. A restaurant close to a theater may offer a discount to theater patrons upon presentation of the theater ticket.

Disclaimers and disclosures are often overlooked in putting together a promotion. The following guidelines are important [8]:

- Product size and specifications. Clearly identify the menu item and size being promoted.
- Price/discount. Highlight the price savings by stating the regular price and the promotional price.
- Where to find the offer. In smaller markets, identify your location; in larger markets, stating that the offer is good at participating restaurants will suffice.
- Expiration date. Make this date clear and easily readable.
- What to do. Let the customers know precisely what is expected of them: whether they must bring in the coupon, or buy two meals within a certain period of time.
- Avoid double hits. State that the offer is not good with any other promotional offer.
- Limitation. If the offer is limited to a number, state the number. It may be one per customer or one per household, for example.
- Time and day restrictions. Since one of the purposes of a promotion is to stimulate sales during slow periods, it may be necessary to note the times when the promotion is in effect.

Evaluation.   It is important to determine whether the promotion has been effective. The true measure of a promotion is whether or not there was an increase in sales activity. This requires a comparison of sales activity—number of customers, sales in dollars, average check, and so on—before and after the promotion. If a promotion were being targeted for the month of August, the July sales figures would serve as the base. This year's August figure would have to be adjusted in light of sales trends to give an accurate picture. Suppose, for example, that sales revenue in July of this year were up 6 percent over those of the preceding year. A reasonable expectation would be that even without a promotion, sales figures for this August would be up 6 percent over sales in the preceding year. Any increase above 6 percent in this August's sales figures would then be attributed to the promotion.

A target for increased sales that will be necessary to cover the cost of a promotion can be determined if the restaurateur knows the promotional costs and his or her cost structure. As identified in preceding chapters, costs can be either fixed or variable. The variable costs—food or beverage, labor, discounts, and supplies—should be determined as a percentage of sales and totaled. This total is subtracted from 100 and the resulting percentage figure divided into the promotional cost in dollars to determine the sales necessary to cover the promotional costs.

For example, if a sandwich that normally sells for $9 costs $3.50, the food cost percentage is 39 percent. If it is being discounted by 15 percent, and extra employee costs and extra supplies are estimated at 5 and 1 percent of sales, respectively, total variable expenses for the promotion are 39 plus 15 plus 5 plus 1, or 60 percent. Subtracting this from 100 leaves 40. If the cost of the promotion is estimated at $350, the sales necessary to break even on the promotion are $350 divided by 40 percent, or $875.

Working backward, $875 in increased sales will result in $525 of extra costs ($875 multiplied by 60 percent). The remaining $350 ($875 minus $525) represents the cost of the promotion. Anything more than an increase in sales of $875 will result in increased profit; anything less will result in a loss. For example, sales of $1200 will result in $720 in costs (60 percent of $1200). When the cost of the promotion—$350—is subtracted, the resulting profit is $370.

MERCHANDISING

Merchandising consists of materials used in-house to stimulate sales. The difference between merchandising and promotions is that promotions are used to get customers in the door, whereas merchandising occurs once the customer is inside the restaurant. Merchandising includes brochures on display, signs, posters, tent cards, and other point-of-purchase promotional items.

Purpose

The purpose of merchandising is twofold: to retain a store's loyal customer base, and to increase the percentage of total business generated by these loyal customers. In the former case, this means developing ways to prevent core customers from becoming bored with the restaurant. In the latter situation, it involves ways to increase the visitation and/or average check of existing customers.

Effectiveness

One of the primary merchandising tools available is the menu itself. By changing the menu periodically, or through the development of daily or holiday specials, a restaurant can continually offer something new and different to its customers.

Effective merchandising can also come from displays and samples of food. It is said that we eat with our eyes rather than our mouths. Nowhere is this as true as in the way in which desserts are sold. The presence of a dessert tray can be very effective in increasing sales. Similar displays for wine, entrees, and salads as well as table-side preparation can be equally effective.

Care must be taken that the number of tent cards and promotional materials not overwhelm the customer. The intent is to prevent boredom, not create confusion because of all the choices available.

Many operators with limited advertising/promotional budgets will learn to develop ongoing and ever-changing activities for their guests and personnel to enjoy. The element of surprise and fun can be one of a restaurant's major strong points.

New themes, catchy ideas, and fresh gimmicks require careful planning and follow-through. Meals will, as always, be the star attraction, but the presentation may need serious rehearsal and trial runs. Customers enjoy being invited to dress rehearsals. The wrinkles can be ironed out for unveiling in such a way that competition will pale in comparison.

Merchandising of Beverages

Beverages can be merchandised in a variety of ways. Easy access can be made by having portable bars in the lobby while customers are waiting for a table. Once seated, the drink order should be taken and delivered right away. Some restaurants promote a happy hour with free hors d'oeuvres to attract cocktail business. The price and quality of hors d'oeuvres must be kept in mind. The price of the hors d'oeuvres must be absorbed by the price of the drink, and the quality must be indicative of the facility.

---

 quick bite 4.7
Co-op Mail Programs

In order to supplement their mass-marketing efforts and in an attempt to reach and capture narrowly defined markets, a number of chains including KFC, Miami Subs and Domino's Pizza have experimented with a co-op-mailing program.

The chains utilized the Carol Wright targeted database program created by Cox Direct. The Carol Wright envelope package typically contains 20 or more ads from product and service marketers. The envelopes are sent to customers in clusters of ZIP codes within a certain radius of the store's locations.

The mailings have been very successful according to one Domino's executive. Per-unit sales increased $600 after the first mailing trial. However, the increase cannot solely be attributed to the coupons in the mailers.

The Carol Wright program targets dual-income families with median incomes of $52,000 and who have children up to 17 years old, providing many marketers, such as Domino's, with a perfect demographic fit. Domino's traditionally targets families with children.

Determining the success of the mailer compared with other advertising media is difficult to do. Although Domino's tracks all coupon redemptions through a computer program, all of their marketing plans are integrated so that consumers are exposed to several different messages.

Sales manager of the Cox Direct restaurant program, Brendon M. Carroll, sees the co-op-mailing program a complement to marketer's existing media plans, not a substitute. The mailings cost approximately $20 to $25 per thousand households. According to the national print management company for Pizza Hut, for every dollar spent on the co-op program, Pizza Hut receives a return of $1.40.

Source: Cebrzynski, Gregg. "Chains Test Targeting Efficiency of Co-op Mail Program." *Nation's Restaurant News,* v. 33, no. 7, February 15, 1999, p. 22.

Restaurant Management: Customers, Operations, and Employees

Serving wine in a variety of glasses. *Source:* Cardinal International catalog, Wayne, New Jersey.

Another area to expand into is wine sales. Wine merchandising must be realistic and uncomplicated for the consumer. Many people find wine intimidating and will not order for fear of the unknown or fear of looking foolish. An awareness can be generated through wine displays, lists, and verbal reminders from wait staff. The ability of employees to sell is a major merchandising tool.

PUBLIC RELATIONS AND PUBLICITY

Public relations includes everything that a restaurant does to maintain or improve its relationship with other organizations. Publicity is the use of nonpaid communications such as press releases and press conferences [9].

Businesses have a number of different "publics": individuals and organizations with whom and with which it interacts. These range from employees and their families, unions, and owners to customers, competitors, government, hospitality schools, and the media. It is the job of public relations to represent the operation favorably to these publics.

Word of Mouth

The value of public relations is that although the organization gives up total control of the message, the resulting message is very persuasive because it is perceived as being more objective than a commercial advertisement. Word-of-mouth publicity is by far the most desirable form of advertising. It means that someone was sufficiently impressed with your establishment to discuss it with others. An endorsement by a friend is usually enough to cause a person to try a place. Potential customers are bombarded with every sort of advertising every day. Advertisers are always proclaiming how great their places, foods, quality, service, and prices are. Customers can get tired of all the exaggerated promises, especially when a few places do not measure up to what was promised. Understandably, people tend to be skeptical and often discount an advertiser's claims. In short, there is a gap between what advertisers say and what customers believe. There is, however, little or no gap when a friend recommends an eating place to another friend. The friend has no motive for profit or gain; therefore, the suggestion is appreciated and believed.

While the power of word of mouth has been demonstrated time after time, it takes too long to develop positive word of mouth into sufficient numbers of customers to ensure the financial success of the establishment. It has been argued that the role of advertising is primarily to expose people to the fact that the facility is out there but that it will take word of mouth to induce actual patronage. This is probably true of more expensive purchases such as weddings or anniversary parties but is less true for an individual or family decision to eat out.

Similarly, editorial and commentary reviews in the media are not suspect. Readers, listeners, and viewers have more trust in these reviews than in advertising messages. The idea, then, is to get the media to write or talk about a business without the suggestion that they are in it for personal profit. Newsworthy events, for example, are not considered by masses as being commercial. If it is news, it is fact.

Implementation

Implementing a program of public relations requires care. Objectives need to be set that tie into the overall marketing plan. Public relations activities can be continuous, preplanned short-term activities, or unpredictable, short-term activities [10].

Continuous activities.   Continuous activities can include such things as:

- Being involved in the local community by donating food for local charity events
- Being involved in industry organizations, serving as an officer, and/or giving seminars
- Communicating to various publics through newsletters
- Engaging in a variety of employee relations programs, such as employee-of-the-month awards, sending birthday cards, or employee incentive programs
- Keeping in regular touch with the media by offering yourself as an industry spokesperson
- Continually updating media kits and photographs to meet editorial deadlines

- Preparing annual or periodic reports to owners
- Acting as guest lecturer at hospitality and/or local schools
- Becoming involved with government agencies in a proactive rather than a reactive way
- Developing a format for keeping in touch with customers through newsletters or other means

Preplanned Short-Term Activities. Preplanned short-term activities revolve around something of interest such as an opening, a prestigious award, or a special employee. This type of information is typically communicated through a press release—an announcement or short article written in an attempt to attract the attention of the media. If something is to be printed or viewed, it must, in the opinion of the editor or director, be of interest to readers or viewers. For press releases, this should be kept in mind. An item of "major" importance to a restaurateur may be of little or no interest to the average reader or viewer.

Press Release. A good press release should answer the questions "who, what, when, where, why, and how." Ideally, this information will be summarized in the opening paragraph. In addition to being newsworthy, the press release should be dated, list a contact person and phone number, indicate when the information can be released (usually, the indication is that the information is "for immediate release"), be typed double-spaced, have an eye-catching headline, be printed on specially designated paper, be no more than two pages in length, and be factual.

As a restaurateur with many things going on, there is the opportunity to make news with virtually everything. Consider these new possibilities even before the restaurant doors are opened:

- Releases to the press on the signing of a lease or the construction of a building to house a restaurant
- Advance announcement of the number of local people who will be employed
- Notices of the grand opening
- Arrangements with public figures to appear at a fundraising opening

Press conferences can be held when there is something really important to announce to the media. The press should be given a summary in writing of the news story in addition to being given the opportunity to ask questions.

Ceremonies and openings offer yet another opportunity for a planned event. Remember, the event will probably be more important to the company than to the media. The task is to make it equally important to readers or viewers.

Unpredictable Events. The third type of activity involves events that are unpredictable. These usually involve some type of activity wherein the purpose for the restaurant is to avoid negative publicity. It may be that patrons became ill after eating at the restaurant or that an employee is a suspect in a crime. The rules of thumb are:

Cameron Mitchell, managing general partner/president

Cameron Mitchell realized the restaurant business was for him one busy Friday working at Max & Erma's casual-dining restaurant in Columbus, Ohio. "It was a Friday afternoon, and we were busy. It was the energy. I loved the action and the enthusiasm. I fell in love with it." That night he went home and wrote down his career goals, which ended with becoming the president of a restaurant company at 35; he has accomplished all of his goals.

Mitchell graduated with honors from the Culinary Institute of America. In 1993, he opened his first restaurant, Mitchell's Contemporary American Cuisine. The upscale bistro was an immediate success and is now considered one of his company's smaller restaurants. Mitchell has opened eight restaurants in five years and has plans for two more on the drawing table. Mitchell credits his establishments' successes with the market situation in Columbus, which had been hurting for great restaurants despite the saturation of mediocre operations in the market.

The "Grumpy Gourmet," Doral Chenoweth, Columbus' premier restaurant critic, hails Mitchell as the most popular restaurateur in town. According to Chenoweth, professional servers and chefs leave other restaurants to work for Mitchell because of his engaging personality and good treatment of employees, not to mention his incentive program.

Mitchell has built a successful company on the philosophies that associates come first and the answer to any question is yes. Mitchell once took 50 of his managers to Disney World for a three-day weekend to reward their hard work. One method of keeping associates happy is by granting unusual scheduling requests for students, single parents or any other employee.

According to David Miller, Mitchell's vice president of operations, Mitchell has many qualities that lead to his success including surrounding himself with good people and recognizing his weaknesses and addressing them. Mitchell also believes in giving back to a community that serves him well by serving on boards and other committees for organizations like the United Way Leadership Group and the Cystic Fibrosis Foundation.

Mitchell is considering expanding into markets other than Columbus, but he is not in any hurry to build a larger company. He is happy with his company's current rate of business and feels content all-around. "I am living my dream right now," he says. "My life is just terrific. I couldn't be happier."

Source: Walkup, Carolyn. "Cameron Mitchell: Goal-driven Operator Says He's Already Living His Dream." *Nation's Restaurant News,* v. 33, no. 4, pp. 160–162.

quick bite 4.9
Restaurant Promotion in 2010

According to the National Restaurant Association the most likely developments regarding restaurant promotion in 2010 are:

- Restaurants will join with suppliers and retailers in joint marketing programs.
- Operators will make more use of credit card promotional activities.

Source: Restaurant Industry 2010: The Road Ahead (Washington, D.C.: National Restaurant Association, 1999). p.14.

- Tell the truth.
- Do not cover things up.
- Collect the facts and communicate these to the media.
- Take action to correct the situation.

The best measure of a public relations plan is: Did it meet its objective? When people are asked if they have frequented a particular business and reply "No, but it has a good name," the goal of public relations has been reached.

ENDNOTES

1. T. F. Chiffriller, *Successful Restaurant Operation* (Boston: CBI Publishing Company, 1982), p. 278.

2. National Restaurant Association, "Fullservice Finances," *Restaurants USA*, October 1998, p. 43.

3. National Restaurant Association, "Drawing Diners to Your Door," *Restaurants USA*, May 1998, pp. 41–43.

4. Robert D. Reid, *Hospitality Marketing Management*, 2nd ed. (New York: Van Nostrand Reinhold, 1989), pp. 284–286.

5. Ibid., p. 233.

6. James R. Abbey, *Hospitality Sales and Advertising* (East Lansing, MI: Educational Institute of the American Hotel and Motel Association, 1989), pp. 336–337.

7. Phillip M. Perry, "Honing Your Home Page," *Restaurants USA*, September 1997, pp. 21–25.

8. Tom Feltenstein, *Foodservice Marketing for the '90s* (New York: John Wiley & Sons, 1992), pp. 101–102.

9. Alastair M. Morrison, *Hospitality and Travel Marketing* (Albany, NY: Delmar Publishers, 1989), p. 420.

10. Ibid., pp. 429–440.

CHAPTER FIVE

PRICING AND DESIGNING THE MENU

learning objectives

By the end of this chapter you should be able to:

1. Identify the functions of the menu.
2. Identify trends in menu content.
3. Compare the three different philosophies of pricing the menu.
4. Illustrate by means of examples the various methods of menu pricing.
5. Describe the different methods of listing prices on a menu.
6. Compare and contrast the different methods for measuring the strength of a menu.
7. Give specific guidelines on the design, layout, and pricing of a menu to increase the average check while boosting the sales of specialty items.

People want to have raspberries in January and chestnuts in July. That's the problem in the United States: people cannot wait. There should be a law that you can use products only seasonally.
Sirio Maccioni, quoted in *Dining Out*

Source: Dornenburg, Andrew and Karen Page, *Dining Out* (New York, NY: John Wiley & Sons, Inc., 1998).

IMPORTANCE OF THE MENU

A menu lists the various product offerings of a restaurant. However, it does much more than that. First, it is a contract with the customer, an indication that what is described on the menu is what will be delivered to the customer. At a minimum the menu should identify the name of each dish, the major ingredients, and how

---

 quick bite 5.1
Hot Concepts

General Cinemas Theatres

General Cinemas Theatres debuted a huge success in the Chicago-area suburb of Lombard, Illinois. As a result, GC is expanding its luxury cinema-restaurant concept by opening larger units in more cities across the nation. The premium theatres are housed in the same building as the GC traditional screen theatres. Movies are shown on multiple screens in some locations beginning in 45-minute intervals in order to regulate traffic flow. The theaters are similar to the first-class section on an airplane. White tablecloth restaurant service is provided in a bistro that adjoins theaters and a full bar. The food selection at the bistro is limited to a wide variety of appetizers including Maryland crab cakes and spinach-and-artichoke dip; a smaller selection of entrees includes prime rib and an assortment of desserts.

The theaters offer specials associated with the picture playing. For example, during a Bond movie, customers can have their martinis "shaken, not stirred" or order double magaritas during *The Mask of Zorro.* Patrons can eat in the restaurant or the theater that features individual cherrywood dining tables. Those who chose not to eat during the show are seated in high backed leather seats in a plush, carpeted auditorium.

Coffee and dessert after the movie is a popular option in the bistro area. Popcorn is free in the premium theaters and all patrons must be 21 or over due to the alcohol consumption. A concierge service and a coat check are services offered with the price of the ticket, as well as valet parking in the evening. Prices of tickets vary from city to city; however Lombard tickets sell for $15.00 on evenings and weekends.

While premium theaters are leading the way, foodservice is expanding at traditional theaters as well. Loews Cineplex Entertainment has expanded concession stand offerings at their movie theaters to include chicken wings, curly fries, chicken tenders, popcorn shrimp, mozzarella sticks, nachos Grande and jalapeño poppers. The company installed kitchens in the center of the main concession area in each of their theaters to allow the items to be cooked to order.

Source: Strauss, Karyn. "General Cinema Expands Premium Cinema Concept." *Nation's Restaurant News,* April 12, 1999, v. 33, n. 15, pp. 30–32.

the dish is prepared. Second, it is an essential part of the marketing effort. As a merchandising tool the menu seeks to do certain things. Properly priced, designed, and presented, the menu can increase the average check, boosting sales of specialty items while complementing the overall atmosphere of the facility.

MENU CONTENT

As a backdrop to looking at menu content it is instructive to consider changes in food consumption of the part of the American public [1]. Table 5.1 indicates increases and declines in per capita consumption between the early to mid-80s and the early to mid-90s. Frozen yogurt, kiwi fruit, and bottled water experienced the greatest gains during this period while oat consumption also increased dramatically. This reflects the benefits of cutting back on fat and increasing grain and fruit consumption. This also reflects the increased number of varieties of fresh

**Table 5.1   Changes in annual consumption:
1980–1984 to 1990–1994**

GAINERS	
Item	**Percent Gain**
Frozen yogurt	+1,000%
Kiwi fruit	+267
Bottled water (gallons)	+186
Mangoes	+146
Oat products	+137
Skim milk (gallons)	+129
Noncitrus fruit juices	+112
Limes	+106
Diet noncarbonated soft drinks (gallons)	+101

LOSERS	
Item	**Percent Decline**
Veal	−43%
Plain whole milk (gallons)	−38
Cottage cheese	−28
Canned green peas	−28
Distilled spirits (gallons)	−26
Fresh grapefruit	−19
Beef	−14
Cane and beet sugar (refined)	−14
Eggs (number)	−11

fruits and vegetables that are available. The United States Department of Agriculture (USDA), for example, reports that supermarket produce departments have increased the number of products they carry from 150 in the mid-1970s to 250 in the mid-1980s and 400 by the mid-1990s. People are eating more salad vegetables—sweet bell peppers, broccoli, spinach, onions, carrots, and tomatoes. Since the early 1980s any increase in lettuce consumption has come from the sale of specialty varieties such as red and green leaf, romaine and Bibb. Although people are eating more fresh fruit, the composition of what is being consumed has changed. Consumers are eating more apples, grapes, bananas, and other noncitrus fruits and fewer citrus fruits such as grapefruit. Bananas remain the most popular fruit although more exotic fruits, such as kiwi fruit and mangoes, are increasing in popularity.

On the other hand, foods regarded as having high fat or cholesterol content have experienced declines in consumption. Veal and beef are notable examples.

While the content of each menu is unique to the targeted market of each individual restaurant, some national trends can be noted [2] to serve as the background to determine what items to put on the menu.

Appetizers

The median number of appetizers offered is seven, with seafood appetizers in general, and shrimp cocktail in particular, being the most popular. A number of restaurants include soup-and-salad selections as appetizers rather than each having its own section.

Soups

The median number of soups offered is two with one almost always being a soup du jour. Classics, such as vichyssoise and consomme, seem to be making an appearance again after an absence at the beginning of the 1990s.

Entrees

Restaurants offer a median of 15 entrees. Pasta, red meat, fish and shellfish remain popular items while customers are seeing more grains such as rice, risotto, polenta, couscous, quinoa, and bulgar. Beef remains the most popular meat product followed, in order, by chicken and pork. Consumption of fish and turkey, on a per-capita basis, is one-third that of pork. Slow growth in steak orders together with declines in other beef entrees have been offset by increases in roast beef/prime rib, burgers, and steak sandwiches. While satisfying customer demand for familiar dishes the number of menus offering ethnic dishes increased slightly in the 1990s.

Salads

More restaurants are offering salads as part of the menu—and customers report eating more of them. In fact, there are 12 million reported vegetarians in the United States alone. Restaurants are featuring more exotic greens in addition to

Ethnic foods are becoming more and more popular with consumers and operators. As consumers begin exploring foods from Japan and India, operators are attempting to cash in on the craze. Yet, many operators have found that it is important to remain consistent from day-to-day and unit-to-unit in order to satisfy customers. As a result, many restaurateurs are beginning to purchase branded items such as Uncle Ben's Oriental Stir-Fry and Sweet & Sour sauces.

One great way for chefs and operators to learn the authentic techniques and flavors of ethnic cuisines is to travel. However, it is not always possible due to time and/or financial restraints to travel the world, yet there are other ways to learn. In fact, one well-known chef from San Francisco is famous for his Asian cuisine, but he has never been to Asia; he has learned by exploring.

Ways to learn about ethnic foods and create menu authenticity include:

- Going to ethnic markets, buying exotic ingredients and experimenting with them. Often those working in the market can explain preparation of these items and offer suggestions for recipes.
- The Internet offers many sites that sell ingredients and provide free recipes.
- Cookbooks are an obvious source of information; however, it is important to determine whether they are reliable.
- Go to ethnic restaurants. Usually the best ideas originate from mom-and-pop restaurants.
- Food writers and educators are valuable sources of information and are usually happy to talk to an operator who is excited to tap their knowledge.
- Learn the functions of ingredients in cooking and flavoring.
- Ask suppliers for recipes.

Once an operator decides to add ethnic foods to the menu, it is important that the waitstaff has sampled and understands the dishes. The server should always know the ingredients, and should be able to describe the dish accurately and with excitement.

Source: "Engineering Menu Authenticity." *Brands in Foodservice: Supplement to Nation's Restaurant News,* April 26, 1999, v. 3, n. 1, pp. 27, 54.

other upscale items. Chicken and shellfish (most often shrimp) remain the most popular items atop a salad. Side-dish salads are harder to find, having moved to the first course part of the menu. Caesar salad is the most popular main-dish salad while Cobb and Nicoise salads also show up in many places.

quick bite 5.3
Vegetarian Cuisine

The reasons for choosing a vegetarian diet or meal, from health and ecology to ethics, are as varied as the type of vegetarians out there, from vegans and ovo- to lacto-. Regardless of the type or reason, vegetarianism is on the rise among consumers overall. Operators must consider this growing segment in order to be profitable. Vegetarian cuisine is growing more and more popular every day with everyone, not just vegetarians. Vegetarian dishes allow for creativity and inventiveness. Vegetarians value structure and balance, color and texture.

The rise in vegetarianism is not a temporary phenomenon. The American Dietary Association has found that positive correlations exist between a vegetarian diet and reduced risk for health conditions such as obesity, coronary artery disease, hypertension and diabetes. Furthermore, the American Cancer Society and the American Heart Association recommend increased consumption of fruits and vegetables. As a result, even seniors are becoming more interested in vegetarianism. One downside of vegetarian meals for operators is the amount of preparation time required. Vegetable handling is especially important; they need to be clean and cut. Storage and life span are also critical issues for vegetables.

Veggie Vocab

Vegans—eat no animal products or animal byproducts (including honey)
Ovo-vegetarians—eat no meat, fish or fowl, but will eat eggs
Lacto-vegetarians—eat no meat, fish or fowl, but will eat dairy products
Lacto-ovo-vegetarians—eat no meat, fish or fowl but will eat eggs
and dairy products
Pesco-vegetarians—eat no meat or fowl, but will eat fish
Pollo-vegetarians—eat no meat or fish, but will eat fowl

Vegetarian Don'ts

- Honey: a product of bees
- Refined cane sugar: sometimes processed with a filter made of cattle bones
- Egg products, such as mayonnaise
- Foods cooked in lard, bacon fat or chicken stock
- Pasta made with eggs
- Gelatin dishes

Source: McDaniel, Lynda. "Vegetarian Cuisine: Is in Bloom on Restaurant Menus." *Restaurants USA,* v. 19, no. 1, January 1999, p. 30.

Healthy dressings are increasing in popularity with vinaigrettes showing up more on mid-to-higher-check menus with the more traditional dressings being offered at casual-dining operations. Increased popoularity of locally grown produce is viewed as a customer vote for quality.

MENU PRICING

The pricing of items on the menu requires a knowledge of both marketing and accounting. From the marketing side, this means setting a price that will appeal to the market while being competitive; from the accounting side it involves establishing a price that will contribute to the profitability of the operation.

Pricing Philosophies

Before setting the prices of individual menu items, management should have determined what the pricing philosophy is to be. Three common approaches to pricing involve [3]:

1. Demand-oriented/perceived-value pricing
2. Competitive pricing
3. Cost-oriented pricing

Demand-Oriented/Perceived-Value Pricing

Demand-oriented or perceived-value pricing looks at the menu from the viewpoint of the customer and prices relative to what the item is worth to the customer—its perceived value. It is important to realize that it is the customer's reaction that is being sought rather than the manager's or employee's. Although an employee may consider the price charged exorbitant, a customer may perceive that the value gained is greater than the price charged.

The items being served are only part of the experience of the meal. The attention gained from having a special dessert flambèed table-side may be worth much to the customer in terms of prestige, and the value thus gained can offset the price charged. This approach prices menu items on the basis of what the customer will pay.

The perceived value in the mind of the customer has to do with more things than the items on the plate. Certainly, customers might be willing to pay extra for menu items advertised as prepared daily from scratch. People expect to pay more for dinner than for lunch; for more service than for self-service; for an inviting atmosphere rather than an austere environment. A brand-name fast-food chain may be perceived as delivering more value than an independently owned operation, whereas the reverse may be true of a fine-dining establishment. A number of things can be done to increase the perceived value of the meal experience (see Chapter 4), while, as we will see later, prices can be set in such a way that they appear less than they are.

Restaurant Management: Customers, Operations, and Employees

Two common approaches in demand-oriented pricing are market skimming and market penetration [4]. Conventional economics indicates that as prices rise, demand for the product falls. Total revenue is a combination of price charged and number of items purchased.

Market Skimming.   In the market skimming approach to pricing operators use a relatively high price to attract or skim a small segment of the market. This philosophy works best when there is a small percentage of a large potential market who can and will pay the higher prices; where the competition is unlikely to undercut the prices set for similar product offerings, and where customers perceive that the value given in the form of the restaurant experience is greater than the prices charged.

Market Penetration.   Market penetration, on the other hand, involves setting prices as low as possible while still contributing to profits. This approach sets out to attract as large a market as possible. Ideally, lower prices will create a loyal following, which will translate into greater sales volume and long-term profitability. This philosophy works best when demand is price elastic: that is, when changes in price result in a greater change in demand, and when lower prices will deter competition from invading the market.

Care must be taken when reducing prices in an attempt to increase sales revenue. An item priced at $12 and selling 120 portions produces $1440 in revenue. A reduction in price of 10 percent will bring the selling price down to $10.80. This will require that 134 portions be sold to produce a revenue of $1447.20. This is an 11.7 percent increase in the number of portions sold. In other words, a reduction in price requires a greater percentage increase in portions sold just to maintain total revenue.

Competitive Pricing

Competitive pricing establishes prices according to those set by the competition. Prices set are typically slightly below or above those of the competition. The major drawback to this pricing method is that it allows the competition to "control" the pricing of the operation. The competition may have a cost structure that is different and can afford to advertise lower prices.

It is not advisable to compete principally on the basis of price because price is a factor that can readily be met by a strong competitor. In such a situation the customer gains in the short run from the lower price until the weaker operation, unable to sustain profits based on the price charges, goes out of business.

However, the prices set must take the competition into account. It is unwise to offer essentially the same product as the competition but at a higher price. An increasingly value-conscious and educated consuming public will buy from the competition.

Cost-Oriented Pricing

Cost-oriented pricing is the oldest, and still the most commonly used, method of pricing in the industry. Prices are set on the basis of the costs incurred by the operation.

PRICING METHODS

A variety of quantitative or rational pricing methods are available to the restaurateur.

Factor, Cost-Multiplier, or Markup System

The factor, cost-multiplier, or markup system is very popular, because of its simplicity. In it, the raw food cost is multiplied by a pricing factor or divided by the desired food cost percentage to arrive at a selling price:

$$\text{selling price} = \text{raw food cost} \times \text{factor}$$

where

$$\text{factor} = \frac{100}{\text{desired food cost}}$$

or

$$\text{selling price} = \frac{\text{raw food cost}}{\text{desired food cost percentage}}$$

The raw food cost is obtained easily enough. This is the cost to the restaurant for the items in the dish. Standardized recipes and recipe cost sheets are essential to determine the actual food cost of every item served.

The factor is obtained by dividing the desired food cost into 100. For example, if a 30 percent food cost is desired (industry averages range from 28 to 34 percent of sales), the factor to be used will be

$$\frac{100}{30} = 3.33$$

The raw food cost is then multiplied by this factor to obtain the selling price. If the raw food cost on an item is $5.25, the selling price will be

$$\$5.25 \times 3.33 = \$17.50$$

The selling price can also be obtained by dividing the raw food cost by the desired food cost percentage. With a raw food cost of $5.25 and a desired food cost percentage of 30 percent, the selling price is

$$\frac{\$5.25}{30\%} = \$17.50$$

This method is simple to use. However, it should be noted that it is inexact because no costs other than food costs are used. When a combination of items prepared from scratch and convenience foods are being used, a high convenience food cost may be offset by a low labor cost to produce the item. Conversely, a low food cost for an item prepared from scratch may require costly amounts of time to prepare. Consider, for example, stew as a convenience product compared to stew prepared from scratch:

	Raw Cost	Labor Cost	Total Cost	Factor	Selling Price
Convenience	$2.25	$0.75	$3.00	3.333	$7.50
Scratch	1.10	1.90	3.00	3.333	3.67

While the total cost of preparing the dish is the same ($3), the higher food cost for the convenience item means that it would be priced higher than the stew made from scratch. Additionally, it disregards the fact that customers may be willing to pay extra for the perceived value of the item.

Prime Cost

The prime cost of a menu item is defined as its raw food cost plus the labor cost involved in preparing the item. The raw food cost of a dish is added to its labor cost.

The desired prime cost percentage is then divided into 100 (as above) to determine the factor. The prime cost is then multiplied by this factor to determine the desired selling price. For example, the prime cost of the beef stews above is $3. Assuming a prime cost percentage of 50 percent, the factor is

$$100/50 = 2$$

and the selling price is

$$\$3 \times \$2 = \$6$$

The cost of producing the item can be determined by means of a time-and-motion study. The actual time involved in preparing 100 portions of beef stew can be multiplied by the hourly rate of the person preparing the dish and divided by 100 to get a preparation cost per serving.

A variation breaks labor cost into unskilled, semiskilled, and skilled and assigns a dollar cost for each. A beef stew, 30 portions, might take 15 minutes of skilled time, 20 minutes of semiskilled time, and 30 minutes of unskilled time to prepare. If the pay rates for skilled, semiskilled, and unskilled labor were $12, $8, and $5, respectively, the labor cost to prepare the stew would be

$$\$12/4 + \$8/4 + \$5/3 = \$8.67$$

The labor cost per portion would be 28.9 cents ($8.67 divided by 30 portions).

A second method assigns an average labor cost to each item produced by dividing the number of meals prepared by the actual production labor cost. The drawback here is that the method assumes that all items take the same amount of time to prepare. Labor-intensive items will be underpriced, and vice versa.

Third, menu items can be designated as involving low, medium, and high labor costs and a dollar value assigned to each. It might be that low-cost items are defined as those requiring less than 10 minutes to prepare, medium-cost items those taking from 11 to 20 minutes, and high-cost dishes those requiring more than 20 minutes of labor time. A unit production cost can be determined by dividing labor cost by the number of low-, medium-, and high-cost meals produced. For example, assume that during a given period when production costs were $3145, 2000 meals were produced, of which 700 were low-cost meals, 800 were medium-cost meals, and 500 were high-cost meals. If we further assume that the medium-cost meal takes twice as long and the high-cost meal takes three times as long to prepare as the low-cost meal, the unit labor cost is

$$700(x) + 2(800x) + 3(500x) = \$3145$$
$$700x + \quad 160x + \quad 1500x = \$3145$$
$$3800x = \$3145$$
$$x = \quad 0.83$$

The cost of preparing a low-cost meal would be 83 cents; for a medium-cost meal, $1.66; and for a high-cost meal, $2.49.

The major drawbacks to this pricing method are that it ignores the other costs of preparing and serving the item in addition to the profit desired by management. The assumption is that desired profits will ensue as long as the prime cost percentage is not exceeded.

Actual Pricing or All-Costs-Plus-Profit

The actual pricing or all-costs-plus-profit method takes into account all the costs involved in running the business. In addition, the percentage of profit desired from each menu item is added before establishing a selling price.

Previously, we established a methodology for determining both raw food cost and preparation cost. Service and other costs can be divided by the number of covers served to get a cost per cover. This cost would then be added to the raw food and production costs to obtain the total costs for the dish. The desired profit percentage is subtracted from 100 and divided into the total costs to obtain the selling price.

If total costs are $9.50 and management wants a 15 percent profit,

$$\text{selling price} = \frac{9.5}{(100 - 15)\%}$$
$$= \$11.18$$

In this method all costs are accounted for, then profit is planned for and built into the price. The price of higher-cost entrees is reduced when compared to using other methods of pricing. In previous methods the factor used had to take into account both high- and low-cost items. The factor used is higher than reality for high-cost items and lower than reality for low-cost items. Thus high-cost items tend to be priced higher than they should be while low-cost items tend to be priced lower than they should be. Reducing the price of higher-cost entrees should lead to increased sales (and profits).

This method is more complicated than either of the first two, tends to increase the prices of lower-cost items (for the reverse of the reason cited above), and the determination of average cost may not be totally accurate. In addition, the desired profit percentage tends to be determined arbitrarily.

Gross Markup or Gross Profit

The gross markup or gross profit pricing method assumes that every customer should pay a specific amount to cover nonfood costs and profit. It can be used in situations where there is to be a narrow range of prices on the menu. The gross markup is determined by subtracting the cost of food sold from projected sales and dividing the result by the projected number of meals or covers.

For example, if $800,000 in annual sales is projected with a food cost of 30 percent, or $240,000, and an anticipated customer count of 120,000:

$$\text{gross markup} = \frac{\text{gross sales} - \text{cost of food sold}}{\text{forecasted customer count}}$$

$$= \frac{\$800,000 - 240,000}{120,000}$$

$$= \$4.67$$

This markup is then added to the raw food cost of each item to determine the selling price. This method is easy to use and, like the previous method, tends to reduce the price of higher-cost items. It is best used in operations that are not susceptible to changes and that have enough history to be able to accurately forecast sales, costs, and customers. Any change in any of these items makes this method inaccurate.

Base Price

The base price method identifies the desired selling price and works backward from that to determine how much can be spent for the raw food cost. Analyzing guest checks can identify the price range preferred by customers. It is necessary to know what the labor and other costs are in addition to the desired profit percentage. If the operator wants 15 percent profit and has a labor cost of 30 percent and a fixed cost per item of 20 percent, total costs will be 65 percent (15 + 30 + 20). This leaves 35 percent (100 − 65) for the raw food cost. If the customer is willing to pay $12 for a menu item, the amount that can be spent on the raw food cost for that item is $4.20 ($12 × 35 percent).

Alternatively, the selling price of the item can be multiplied by the desired food cost to identify the maximum amount that can be spent on the item. If, in the example above, a food cost of 33 percent is desired, the maximum that can be spent on food cost would be $3.96 ($12 × 33 percent). Some way would have to be found to produce the menu item for that amount. This method has the advantage of taking the customer's willingness to pay into account.

Texas Restaurant Association

The Texas Restaurant Association pricing method identifies actual costs incurred over a period of time and the sales associated with these costs, and adds the desired profit percentage to get the ideal or optimal food cost. If, over the course of a year, a restaurant has sales of $600,000, labor costs of $180,000 (30 percent of sales), other costs (excluding food costs) of $150,000 (25 percent of sales), and the owners want a 15 percent profit, the ideal food cost percentage is

$$600,000 - (180,000 + 50,000 + 90,000) = 180,000$$

$$100 - (30 + 25 + 15)\% = 30\%$$

This ideal food cost is divided into 100 to obtain a multiplier or factor, in this case 3.33. The raw food cost of the menu item is then multiplied by this factor to obtain the recommended selling price.

Recommended profit percentages will vary depending on the item. The common ranges are [5]:

Menu Category	Profit Markup Range (%)
Appetizers	20–50
Salads	10–40
Soups	100–500
Entrees	10–25
Vegetables	25–50
Beverages	10–20
Breads	10–20
à la carte	10–40
Desserts	15–35

Marginal Pricing

An operation's costs are either fixed or variable. Fixed costs do not vary as volume varies; variable costs vary proportionately with volume. After a restaurant has reached its break-even point, the fixed costs have been covered. At this point the only costs incurred by the restaurant are the variable or marginal costs, those extra costs incurred in serving another customer. Marginal pricing covers the marginal costs. Any revenue beyond this is profit. In this way, a facility, if it is sure that break-even will be reached, can offer special prices on slow nights.

Marginal pricing can be successful if it brings in business at the reduced price that would not come in at the full price. However, the operation must, at some point, account for covering fixed costs in pricing menu offerings.

Daily Pricing

When the cost of items varies from day to day (for example, fresh seafood) a menu offering may be listed as having a market price. This indicates that the price varies depending on the cost that day.

In Table 5.2, a comparison of menu prices using different methods, but assuming the same cost structure and desired profit level, is shown. Note that different selling prices and profit margins are obtained depending on the method used. Selection of an appropriate method should take costs, competition, and the desires of the customers into account.

Handling Price Increases

There is both a practical and a psychological side to handling an increase in prices. From the practical side, as costs increase, profits decline. Cost increase can come from such things as an increase in the minimum wage, in the cost of borrowing money, or higher wholesale prices charged for food and beverage items. Typically, an increase in costs is passed on to the customer in the form of higher prices. The key is to increase prices while maintaining customer counts such that sales volume is maintained.

Several strategies can be effective. Generally speaking, for minimum negative impact, price increases should be limited to 2 to 5 percent. Prices should also be kept stable during four to six customer visits. If an increase in the wholesale price of food is announced, the time to increase menu prices is when the an-

Table 5.2 Comparison of Menu Prices Using Various Methods

	Roast Rib of Beef Dinner		Stuffed Flounder Dinner	
	Menu Price	Profit Margin	Menu Price	Profit Margin
Factor method	$10.04	$6.53	$6.95	$4.52
Prime cost method	10.67	7.16	8.79	6.36
All-cost-plus-profit method	8.28	4.77	7.96	5.53
Gross markup method	8.16	4.65	7.08	4.65
Texas Restaurant Association method	9.86	6.35	6.83	4.40

Source: Robert D. Reid, *Foodservice and Restaurant Marketing* (Boston: CBI Publishing Company, 1983), p. 229.

nouncement is made public rather than when the increase in prices is passed on to the operator. The reason for this is psychological—the public is aware of increased prices and, as such, is more likely to accept it at that time rather than later, when the memory of the price increase has vanished from their minds.

Another approach, used by the fast-food chains, is to price the items à la carte, that is, individually. The price of the hamburger seems very economical to the customer. Most people will add french fries and a drink. This increases the average check, but in the mind of the customer, the meal price is acceptable because the price of the main item in the meal seems reasonable.

The key in keeping sales volume up is to ensure that the perceived value received by the customer is equal to or greater than the price charged. When prices are increased, one answer is to increase the value. Perhaps an additional accompaniment can be added to the entree at the time of the price increase to increase the value to the customer.

Listing Prices

Menu prices can be listed in a variety of ways [6]. The way the prices are presented should be part of the overall marketing plan for the operation. In the one-price or prix fixe method, a fixed price is set for all meals. Pricing is simplified. However, since the gross profit varies depending on the item chosen, the total gross profit may be reduced if too many higher-cost entrees are chosen. This can be avoided by having items on the menu that cost approximately the same to produce. Low-price operations offering few choices often choose this method of listing prices.

The à la carte menu was mentioned earlier. It is associated with upscale restaurants. The initial perception is that prices are low. "Sticker shock" may set in when the final bill is presented unless the perceived value is greater than the amount of the check. This approach appeals to customers who like to individualize their meal. It does complicate the pricing of checks for the employees. A version of the à la carte menu prices the entrees separately but includes potatoes and vegetables in the entree price.

A table d'hôte meal consists of a set number of courses at a set price. The price of the meal is determined by the price of the entree. It is assumed that all other courses cost about the same. Additional charges may be made for a special appetizer and/or dessert.

Finally, customers can be offered the choice of a platter or a complete dinner. Platters may appeal to those who wish to have a smaller meal. A modification involves serving a smaller portion of the entree at a lower price.

In selecting a method for listing menu prices, management should consider the overall impression they are seeking to give while attempting to produce satisfied customers and maximum revenue.

MEASURING MENU STRENGTH

A variety of ways exist to quantify the strength of the overall menu or of one item relative to another.

quick bite 5.6
Which Is Better?

Here are two ways of listing prices on a menu:

Auberge du Soleil (Rutherford, California) Menu Sampler

Hedgehog mushroom and asparagus soup
with marjoram cream $7

Thyme-roasted pheasant ravioli
with woodland mushrooms, lemon-maple glaze $12

Potato-crusted Chilean seabass
with caraway-Savoy cabbage, truffled beet relish $14.50

Hickory-smoked duck
with red lentil confit salad, bourbon-giblet gravy $25.50

Ginger-grilled New York strip steak
with sambal whipped potatoes,
mango-lemon grass sauce $30

Pear-walnut tart
with Maytag blue cheese cream,
Port reduction $7.50

Le Bernardin (New York) Menu Sampler
(Prix Fixe at $68)

First Course
Fish soup "Bernardin"

Lightly smoked salmon gravlax
with horseradish vinaigrette

Fricassee of mussels, clams, and oysters
in their broth, with sweet garlic
and tomato butter

Main Courses
Roast tournedoes of monkfish,
wild mushrooms, and a `jus de viande^

Crusted codfish on a bed of haricots vert,
fingerling potatoes, and diced tomato
with basil oil vinaigrette

Crispy Chinese spiced snapper with cepes,
aged port, and Jerez sherry vinegar reduction

Source: Alan Liddle, "Auberge du Soleil," and Milford Prewitt, "Le Bernardin," *Nation's Restaurant News*, Section Two, May 22, 1995.

Average Check

Operators will have determined that a specific average check—total sales divided by the number of customers—is necessary to ensure a particular level of profitability. The simplest method of evaluating menu prices is to compare the average check desired with the actual average check.

This method assumes that there will be a normal distribution of customers around the average, something that rarely occurs. For this reason, the average check method is not very useful.

Range

A better method is to establish menu ranges based on price—for example, $6 to $8; $8 to $10; $10 to $12—and track the number of actual sales in each of the ranges. The result is a frequency distribution graph. This will show the range of prices that customers are willing to pay. In addition, the graph can spotlight potential problem or opportunity areas. If the graph is skewed around the low-price end of the menu, it indicates that the items offered are outside the prices that customers are able or willing to pay. On the other hand, clustering toward the high end of the menu indicates that patrons are willing to spend more.

Menu Scoring

Menu scoring combines the profitability and popularity of menu items to arrive at a consensus score. The higher the score, the better the menu. An existing menu can be scored, then compared with a proposed new menu, after sales for the new menu have been estimated. Table 5.3 illustrates a menu scoring comparison for several items on a menu. After the initial menu score of 4.42 is developed, one or two items could be substituted for items on the list and another score developed. By comparing the two scores, a determination can be made as to which menu listing is better.

Menu Engineering

Menu engineering combines the concepts of menu mix percentage and dollar contribution margin to determine the relative strength of menu items. An item with a relatively low contribution margin percentage may still deliver a healthy dollar margin.

Table 5.4 and Figure 5.1 illustrate an analysis of a menu using menu engineering. The contribution margin of each menu item is determined and compared with the contribution margin for the menu as a whole. Similarly, the popularity of each item on the menu is compared with the average popularity of the items assuming an even distribution of purchases. Various authors have said that sales are acceptable if an item achieves anywhere from 70 to 90 percent of the average item sales per entree. If, for example, there were 10 items on a menu and sales were distributed evenly, each item would account for 10 percent of sales. Thus a sales percentage of 7 to 9 percent would be acceptable. This example uses 80 percent of sales as the acceptable figure.

Table 5.3 Menu Scoring

(1) Menu Item	(2) Number Sold	(3) Item Sales Price	(4) Food Cost Percentages	(5) Total Sales (2) × (3)	(6) Total Food Cost (4) × (5)
Chicken	65	$9.95	35	$646.75	$226.36
Beef	75	11.95	38	896.25	340.58
Turkey	90	10.25	31	922.50	285.98
Filet	55	12.95	45	712.25	320.51
Total	285			$3177.75	$1173.43

(7) Meal check average: (5) + (2)   = $11.15
(8) Gross profit: (5) − (6)   = $2004.32
(9) Gross profit percentage: (8) + (5)   =   63%
(10) Gross profit average per meal: (7) × (9)   = $7.02
(11) Total meals served: =   450
(12) Popularity of meals analyzed: (2) + (11) =   63%
(13) Menu score: (10) × (12) =   4.42

Source: Adapted from James Keiser, *Controlling and Analyzing Costs in Foodservice Operations,* 2nd ed. (New York: Macmillan Publishing Company, 1989), pp. 61–62.

The scores on both dimensions are combined and placed on a graph (Figure 5.1). Plowhorses are items that are relatively popular but have a low contribution margin. Items falling into this category can have their menu prices increased or the portion size cut in an attempt to increase the contribution margin. If the market does not resist the price increase, this action will move a plowhorse into the star category. If the market is price resistant, the items can be buried in an inconspicuous place on the menu in the knowledge that people will find these relative bargains anyway. Stars have both high popularity and high contribution margins. It may be possible to increase menu price and/or cut portion size to increase profits while maintaining volume. Puzzles have relatively low popularity and high margins. They need to be promoted more to stimulate sales. Dogs are low in popularity and contribution margin. They are prime candidates to be dropped from the menu. In the example used, chicken would be dropped from the menu, while the filet would be promoted more heavily. The prices on the beef and the turkey might be raised a little and these items featured visibly on the menu.

Menu engineering has been criticized because it uses the mean as the basis of comparison [7]. Using the mean will always put some menu items above the mean and some below. Thus, an item that was producing adequate sales and/or contribution margins becomes a problem if the sales and/or contribution margin of another menu item changes. It is suggested that a marginal analysis approach is better. Such an approach evaluates menu items individually based on the marginal, or extra, contribution gained from selling an additional menu item.

Table 5.4   Menu Engineering

(1)	(2)	(3)	(4)	(5) Total Sales (2) × (3)	(6) Total Food Cost (4) × (5)
Menu Item	Number Sold	Item Sales Price	Food Cost Percentages		
Chicken	65	$9.95	35	$646.75	$226.36
Beef	75	11.95	38	896.25	340.58
Turkey	90	10.25	31	922.50	285.98
Filet	55	12.95	45	712.25	320.51
Total	285			$3177.75	$1173.43

(7) Food cost percentage: (6) ÷ (5) =   36.93%

(8) Total contribution margin: (5) − (6) = $2004.32

(9) Average contribution margin/customer: (8) ÷ (2) = $7.03

(10) Contribution margin per menu item: $\dfrac{(5) - (6)}{(2)}$

$$\text{Chicken: } \frac{\$646.75 - 226.36}{65} = \$6.47$$

$$\text{Beef: } \frac{\$896.25 - 340.58}{75} = \$7.41$$

$$\text{Turkey: } \frac{\$922.50 - 285.98}{90} = \$7.07$$

$$\text{Filet: } \frac{\$712.75 - 320.51}{55} = \$7.12$$

(11) Average popularity:

80 percent of the average item sales per entree: 100 ÷ 4 × 80% = 20%

(12) Popularity of each menu item:

number of portions sold divided by total number of meals sold

Chicken: 65 ÷ 285 = 22.8%

Beef: 75 ÷ 285 = 26.3%

Turkey: 90 ÷ 285 = 31.6%

Filet: 55 ÷ 285 = 19.3%

Source: Adapted from James Keiser, *Controlling and Analyzing Costs in Foodservice Operations,* 2nd ed. (New York: Macmillan Publishing Company, 1989), pp. 61–62.

MENU DESIGN

The menu, to a large extent, determines what customers will order and how much they will spend [8]. A properly designed menu helps achieve the objectives of increasing the average check and promoting the sale of specialty items. This is done by presenting the product offerings of the restaurant in an attractive manner, describing them in a way that paints an attractive picture, and pricing them to give the impression of value.

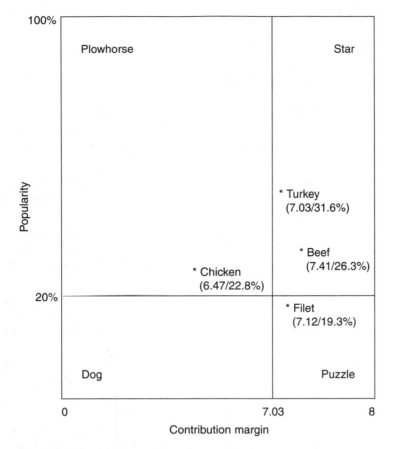

Figure 5.1 Menu engineering analysis.

Cover

The menu cover should be designed to complement the overall theme of the restaurant. Line graphics or photographs are often used to present an attractive first impression. Black-and-white photographs are easy to reproduce and less expensive than color.

The name of the restaurant is the only copy required on the cover. Additional information regarding the address, phone number, acceptance of credit cards, and so on, is best left to the inside or the back cover.

Size

The size of the menu will vary depending on the number of items being featured and the amount of copy used to describe them. Traditionally, one menu listed appetizers, soups, salads, side dishes, entrees, desserts, and beverages. A separate menu was common for breakfast, lunch, and dinner. Today, many of the

quick bite 5.7
Menu for Kids

Here are some ideas on how to design menus that appeal to children:

1. Let kids design the menu. At the Italian Oven, kids illustrate the menu. Inspired by Jurassic Park, the dinosaur concept was drawn by the 9-year-old son of the owners. The restaurant also features make-your-own pizza, pasta necklaces, and drawing on tabletops.
2. Don't think of it as one market. According to Banger Smith, vice president of Menu Workshops in Seattle, there are three markets: tykes (ages 1 to 7), "tweens" (ages 8 to 13), and teens (over 13).
3. Treat them with respect. Jim Gardner, president of Restaurant Concepts, which owns Bazooka Joe's Rock 'n' Roll Diner in Kearney, Nebraska, believes that letting kids order off their own menu says: "You kids are important to us."
4. Give them something to do. ZuZu Handmade Mexican Food revamped its children's menu to give the kids something to play with as well as to order from. It gives the kids something to do and helps take some pressure off the parents.
5. Give them familiar food. Kids like things they are familiar with. ZuZu is experimenting with a peanut-butter-and-jelly quesadilla. They found that kids don't like spicy foods. At the French Room the chef prepared macaroni and cheese by covering elbow macaroni with a creamy cheddar cheese sauce and a sprinkling of parsley. Parents loved it—kids said: "Where's the Kraft macaroni and cheese? Get that green stuff off of there."
6. Let the kids judge. At the Wyndham Anatole Hotel a panel of 8- to 12-year-olds decided what items should go on the menu.

Source: Crosby, Melanie A. "Menus That Speak (and Sell) to Kids," *Restaurants USA,* vol. 15, no. 5, May 1995, pp. 19–23.

rules have been broken. Separate menus can be created for children, wine, desserts, cocktails, and so on. The key is to design the menu in such a way that it effectively communicates with the customers. For example, many think that a separate dessert menu is more effective than listing them on the entree menu. They argue that this helps create the feeling that this is another separate occasion. Customers, in selecting an entree, may notice the price of desserts, add it to the price of the entree, and decide at that point not to order dessert because of the combined cost of entree and dessert. A separate dessert menu means that the decision to order dessert is more likely to be made on the basis of desire than of cost.

When presented with the entree menu for a dessert selection, diners may cast their eyes back to an item not ordered and wish that they had taken the chicken rather than the sole. A dessert menu says "forget the entree; this is different; this is separate; let's have dessert." As has been pointed out previously, a person can still have an appetite for dessert even though the taste for the entree has been satisfied. Presenting a separate menu reinforces that thought. The favored method of promoting desserts is to have the wait staff describe the desserts to customers.

Materials

The weight and quality of the paper on which the menu is printed adds to the impact. Heavier paper gives a feeling of quality. It also adds to the life of the menu. This has to be weighed against the menu price change cycle. When price changes are listed by stickers covering the previous price, the impression is not a good one. Similarly, menus that are torn or dirty give a very poor impression of the operation.

The life of the menu can be increased through the use of water-resistant paper or lamination. The latter is more appropriate for lower-priced operations. A compromise might be to have an expensive cover, which would not change, with a less expensive insert.

Placement

Menu Sequence. There are two schools of thought regarding the placement of items on a menu. Some believe that the sequence of dishes on the menu should follow the progression of a meal. Just as a meal moves from appetizers and soups through entrees to desserts, with side orders, salads, sandwiches, and beverages interspersed, so should the layout of the menu.

Focal Points. Others believe various focal points should be used on a menu. Customers' eyes are naturally drawn to specific points—focal points—when presented with a menu. The restaurateur should place menu items that he or she wants to push in the focal points of a menu.

The focal point varies with the type of menu. On a single-sheet menu, the eye initially focuses on the area just above the centerline. With a twofold menu the upper right part of the menu is the focal point.

On a threefold menu, the eye moves from the center to the upper right-hand corner, then to the upper left-hand corner, bottom left-hand corner, through the center to the upper right-hand corner, bottom right-hand corner, and back to the center. In all, the center is crossed three times. It makes sense to place in the center items that the restaurant wishes to push. In this regard it is not necessary to use the focal point to highlight items for which the restaurant is famous. Customers will search the menu for these items. Focal points are to be used to highlight items that the restaurateur wants to sell and that customers would not ordinarily search for.

A typical threefold menu lists appetizers in the left-hand column, entrees in the middle column, and desserts at the bottom of the right-hand column. However, the items that increase the average check are appetizers and desserts. One enterprising restaurant in Scotland features its appetizers in the center of the menu. Customers will not necessarily order an appetizer. However, they do see a listing of items that they might not generally search for.

Specials

There are various ways to draw attention to particular menu items. Specials can be listed in larger and bolder type than that used on the rest of the menu. They can also be given a longer description. The concept of closure indicates that peoples' eyes are drawn to whatever is enclosed by a box. By drawing a box around a menu description, attention is drawn to what is inside the box. In addition, color, illustration, and/or pictures can be used to draw attention to the restaurant's signature items.

Menu Descriptions

The objective in describing menu items is to present them in a way that will give customers an accurate picture of the dish, while increasing the likelihood of their sale.

Accuracy. Municipalities are becoming more vigilant about prosecuting restaurants for false statements on the menu. Typical errors deal with the grade, point of origin, size, weight, prepared form, preparation method, picture, price, or dietary or nutritional content of the product.

Government grades can and should be used accurately to describe fish. A USDA Choice piece of meat should be just that. Listing where the item came from can help sales. However, Lake Superior whitefish has to have come from Lake Superior. The precooked weight of menu offerings should be listed, as shrinkage during cooking can reduce the size and/or weight of an item. A great deal of controversy has arisen over the use of fresh or frozen on a menu. Fish that is frozen on the boat minutes after it is caught may actually taste fresher than "fresh" fish consumed two days after being caught. However, customers still seem to believe that fresh is better than frozen. The word fresh cannot be used to describe fish that has been frozen. A number of operations use pictures on the menu to help sell items. The dish being served should look like the one in the picture.

Many operations automatically include a 15 percent service charge on parties of six or more. If this is the case, it should be stated prominently on the menu. Additionally, it should be clear to the reader what is, and is not, included in the price of a meal. Finally, there is a great deal of confusion about the dietary and/or nutritional claims of certain dishes. A term such as low-calorie is too vague and should not be used. What does it mean? Low-calorie compared to what? Increased concern for health on the part of consumers is causing a number of operations to list nutritional information on the menu or, as in the case of the major fast-food chains, in prominent positions in stores. Organizations such as Healthmark certify certain menu items as being healthy choices.

Menu items should be described in such a way that customers can see them in their minds. This is important because we think in pictures, not in words.

Typeface

The typeface used must be large enough and legible enough to allow customers to read the descriptions. Type sizes are listed by point size, with 72 points to the inch. A type size of 12 or larger is recommended for menus.

The main styles used on menus are Roman, modern, and script. Most books and magazines are set in some version of a Roman typeface. Modern typefaces are newer, clean looking, and do not have the serifs or flourishes of the Roman typeface. Script imitates handwriting and should be used primarily for headings and subheadings, as it is difficult to read. Some upscale restaurants, however, use script for the entire menu, to give a handwritten look.

Typefaces can be set in uppercase or lowercase, regular or italics. It is easier to read letters that are set in regular lowercase. Italics and uppercase letters are tiring on the eyes and should be used sparingly for maximum impact.

Many feel that operators should stay away from unusual type styles, as they clutter a menu. This is an individual decision based on the image that is being portrayed.

Leading refers to the space between the lines of type. Three points of leading between lines is regarded as a minimum for a menu to ensure easier reading.

Type that is black and printed on white or light-tinted paper, such as tan, cream, ivory, or gray, is easy to read. Where colored inks are used, it is important that the shade be dark, to make it readable. Reverse type—white type on a black background—is very difficult to read and should be avoided.

Verbal Pictures

The words used to describe items on the menu should be chosen carefully to add to the sales appeal of the dish. The following questions can be used as a guide to writing compelling copy [9]:

1. What is it?
2. How is it prepared?
3. How is it served?
4. Does it have unusual taste and quality properties?
5. Where do the ingredients come from?

Menu descriptions should aim to excite the senses. People think in pictures. Consider the image given by the following:

new   moist   crisp   succulent

Certain words have been overused and have lost their effectiveness. These words do not excite the senses:

excellent   classic   special   the best

Consider the following:

BEEF TENDERLOIN

or

GOURMET SLICES OF BEEF TENDERLOIN

Generous slices of tenderloin, sauteed in butter and served with a sauce made with a delicate Madeira wine, shallots, and mushrooms.

The key is to praise the virtues of the dish while avoiding hyperbole; say it in words that are understandable to, and that will move, the customer while avoiding cutesy topical references that have a short shelf-life.

Menu Pricing

In a previous section we considered menu pricing in terms of profitability. In this section we deal with pricing as a marketing tool.

Odd-Cents Pricing.   The vast majority of menu prices end in either a "5" or a "9." There is psychology involved here. The real difference between $12.99 and $13.00 is one penny. However, psychologically, the former seems less expensive than the latter. The customer perceives that she or he is getting a "discount" from the higher price. This method of odd-cents pricing was actually instituted as a control method by R. H. Macy. By pricing items at $2.99, when a customer paid with three $1 bills, cashiers had to ring the item up on the cash register to give the penny change. This guaranteed that the sale was recorded.

First-Figure Dominance.   A price change from 25 cents to 29 cents seems less than one from 29 cents to 33 cents. The reason is that, in the first case, the dominant first figure remains at 2, whereas in the second situation, it increased from 2 to 3.

Length of the Price.   The length of the price is also important. A price increase from $9.95 to $10.25 is perceived as being more than an increase from $9.25 to $9.55. In the former case the length of the price has increased from three to four digits.

Price Rounding.   Price rounding also goes on in the mind of the customer. Within certain price bands, price increases have little negative impact on customers.

Price Spreads.   The price spread of a menu refers to the difference in price between the least expensive and most expensive item on a menu within a specific category. Excessive price spreads encourage the sale of lower-priced menu items. In general, the highest-priced item on the menu should be no more than twice the price of the lowest-priced menu item.

People tend to buy in the middle price range of a menu. By pricing new items slightly higher than the average guest check while lowering the price of the most expensive items and raising the prices of the lower-priced items, it may be possible to increase the size of the average check.

Restaurant Management: Customers, Operations, and Employees

quick bite 5.5
Creative Descriptions

Aroma	Garden Fresh	Old Fashioned
Assorted	Garnished	Original
	Generously	
Baked	Giant	Perfect(ion)
Blend	Golden-Brown	Piled-High
Broiled	Grilled	Piping-Hot
Carefully	Heap(ed)(ing)	Refreshing(ly)
Char-broiled	Hearty	Rich(ly)
Choice	Homemade	
Chunky	Hot	Sautéed
Classical	Huge	Secret(ly)
Colorful		Selected
Crisp	Iced	Sensational
Crunchy	In Season	Simmered
Crusty	Inch-Thick	Sizzling
Customized	Irresistible(ly)	Smothered
		Special(ly)
Delectable	Juicy	Stimulating(ly)
Delicate(ly)		Stuffed
Delight(ful)(ly)	Large	Succulent(ly)
Deluxe	Layers	
Designed	Legendary	Tangy
	Light	Tender(ly)
Enjoy	Lightly Breaded	Topped
Exotic	Lightly Seasoned	Treat
	Loaded	Tropical
Famous	Lovingly	
Favorite		Wrapped
Fancy	Meaty	
Filled	Mouth-Watering	Yummy
Finest		
Fluffy	Natural	Zesty
Fresh(ly)	New	100%

Source: Alliant Foodservice. "Restaurant Planning Manual: Creative Menu Descriptions." *Weekly 1999 Food Services Planner*, p. 48.

Placement.   Many customers read a menu from right to left. They look at the price first before considering the description of the dish. Consider the following:

Baked Chicken $8.99
Lemon Sole $11.99
Lamb Steak $12.99
Swordfish Steak $14.99

By using the same typeface for the prices as the menu items and listing them to the right in a straight line, attention is drawn to the price rather than to the dish. Compare that method with:

BAKED CHICKEN

Tender pieces of boneless breast of chicken served with stuffing $8.99

LEMON SOLE

Fresh filets of sole sauteed in a sweet lemon caper sauce $11.99

LAMB STEAK

Center cut of lamb steak served on a bed of rice with mint sauce $12.99

SWORDFISH STEAK

Charcoal grilled and served with a beurre blanc sauce $14.99

Packaging

One way to increase the sale of items not usually ordered is to include them with the entree and charge more for the package. If it is found that customers are not ordering appetizers, including an appetizer with the meal can increase the average check size. Similar strategies have been adopted by restaurants to sell soup-and-sandwich combinations.

Wine Menus

Wines can be described in a variety of formats. Some operations list suggested wines next to the entrees. If this approach is taken, two suggestions should be given for each entree: one in the low-to-moderate price range, the other in the moderate-to-high range. This gives customers a choice without the feeling that higher-priced wines are being pushed exclusively.

The most common thing for tableservice restaurants, however, is to have a separate wine list. A list of the more popular wines can be given to customers with a note that a more extensive list is available to the "connoisseur." This approach appeals to a customer seeking to impress a companion, be it a date or a business client. A short description is appropriate, indicating the relative sweetness or dryness of the wine and the types of dishes it will complement.

Serving Wine

Restaurants commonly have many oversights and missed opportunities when it comes to the sale and service of wine.

The following is a list of opportunities for operators to improve their wine offerings and service:

- Display more wine bottles and wine-related paraphernalia
- Rotate, clean and dust wine bottles that are on display
- Always provide a clean and complete wine list on each table
- Train all servers to open wine bottles, including sparkling wine
- Devise a system for handling out-of-stock situations so that no customer orders unavailable wine
- Train servers, captains and managers to pronounce each wine on the list properly
- Use stemware that matches the caliber of wines served and patron expectations
- Require bus persons to inspect wineglasses before bringing them to the table
- Encourage servers to offer or suggest wines after the initial greeting of customers
- Review the wine menu for misspellings, typos and errors
- Train servers to converse intelligently about wine with guests
- Have servers of legal drinking age to taste at least two different wines each week
- Provide descriptions and/or background information on unusual wines
- Do not assume that because the owner likes a particular wine, customers will too
- Select wines based on price, menu affinity, customer taste preferences, wine quality and availability, not on a reviewer's score
- Offer at least one wine of exceptional value, after markup, in the highest-volume section of the wine list.

Source: Wiegand, Ronn. "Prepare for the Millennium with a Restaurant-wine Wish List." *Nation's Restaurant News,* v. 33, no. 3, January 18, 1999, p. 39.

Restaurants commonly offer a house wine by the glass, half-liter, or liter. This offers good value, especially to the wine novice who might be intimidated by the thought of ordering a bottle of wine.

To appeal to the discriminating diner, an increasing number of restaurants are offering better-quality wines by the glass. Improvements in storage techniques allow them to keep opened bottles of wine fresher longer. Few half-bottles of wine are found on menus. It may well be that customers could be enticed to "trade up" from having a glass by effective merchandising of half-bottles of wine. Adults who drink alcoholic beverages away from home are more likely to order wine by the glass over wine by the carafe.

---

quick bite 5.8

Road to the Top: Elizabeth Blau, vice president of restaurant development

Elizabeth Blau has made her mark in the fine dining segment at an age where most people have yet to visit a fine dining establishment. As vice president of restaurant development for Mirage Resorts Inc., Blau is helping to change the fine dining environment in Las Vegas. Blau says that her love of fine food was developed by her world-traveling parents, whom took her and her sibling to quaint little inns and Michelin-rated restaurants.

Blau received her bachelor's degree in government from Georgetown University and her master's degree in restaurant marketing from Cornell University School of Hotel Administration. Blau has worked in positions varying from line cook to candy maker. Blau's early achievements, just two years out of Cornell, include helping New York restaurateur Sirio Maccioni open branches of their popular Le Cirque and Osteria del Circo concepts in Las Vegas' Bellagio Casino. Blau's thesis at Cornell consisted of the marketing plan for the first Osteria del Circo.

After the Bellagio project Blau assisted in the development of ten new restaurants at Beau Rivage, overseeing the creation or conversion of five restaurants at the Mirage and two at Treasure Island, in addition to beginning a preliminary concept in Atlantic City. Blau, in a way, represents a new breed of foodservice executive in Vegas, where themed resorts are struggling to grasp a competitive edge in the market.

According to Sirio Maccioni, one of Blau's greatest assets is her willingness to learn on the job. While many students come out of school believing that they are qualified managers, "Elizabeth knew she wanted to learn [on the job], and that's important." Maccioni believes that successful restaurateurs lead by example and find every activity in a restaurant, including menial tasks, is important, "I think Elizabeth learned that."

Source: Liddle, Alan. "Elizabeth Blau: Making Fine Dining a Sure Bet at Las Vegas' Mirage Resorts." *Nation's Restaurant News*, v. 33, no. 4, pp. 24–28.

Wine should always have a bin number listed on the menu. This prevents the guest from the embarrassment of mispronouncing the name. Most consumers feel comfortable ordering from a wine list although many do not feel well informed about wines. Wine glasses on the table are a subtle reminder that wine is appropriate.

A sommelier or wine steward can offer specialized knowledge to the customer while adding to the ambiance of the occasion. Care should be taken not to intimidate the customer with the mystique of wine: choosing the wine, feeling the cork, and tasting. The purpose is to sell the wine, not to impress the guest with one's wine knowledge. Whatever format is used, the wines offered should be those that appeal to the segments of the market being served.

Menu Alternatives

Restaurants can present their product offerings in a variety of ways. In keeping with the theme of the operation, some use chalkboards to announce the dishes. Items and prices can be changed with the swipe of an eraser. Menu cards placed strategically throughout is another alternative.

A hand-held menu is not practical for some segments of the industry, such as fast-food operations and institutional feeding. One such innovation won first place in 1991 in the Institutional Category of the National Restaurant Association's Great Menu Contest. Because the menu changes four times a day at the High Plains Inn facility at Malmstrom Air Force Base in Great Falls, Montana, employees had to take out the plastic strips listing the menu items and replace them with the new choices. This turned out to be labor-intensive and resulted in the strips being torn. The operation changed to an electronic menu that in addi-

---

 quick bite 5.9
Food and Menus in 2010

According to the National Restaurant Association the most likely developments regarding food and menus in 2010 are:

- Mid-scale restaurants will upgrade product quality and emphasize "fresh."
- There will be more demand for new items, for authentic items and flavor profiles.
- Menus will become more regionalized.
- More high quality bakery products, especially whole grain products, will be available.

Source: Restaurant Industry 2010: The Road Ahead (Washingon, D.C.: National Restaurant Association, 1999), p. 18.

---

tion to listing the menu items, could display graphics, messages, and digitalized photographs.

As mentioned earlier, wait staff are used when selling desserts. The use of the menu as a primary merchandising tool has eclipsed the traditional role of the employee in performing this function. It is a way for management to standardize the merchandising message—to have the menu "say" what management wants in a way that does not depend on the ability of the server. It also means that servers do not have to have the knowledge previously expected of someone required to recite the choices, methods of preparation, and ingredients of everything on the menu. A few operations do not present the customer with a menu but rely totally on employees to describe the items for sale. This can only be used when attempting to present an upscale image and where relatively few items are offered. Many table service restaurants use employees to describe the daily specials.

ENDNOTES

1. "Palatable Changes—Keeping Pace With Consumption Patterns," *Restaurants USA*, August 1996, pp. 43–45. "Foodservice Gets Fresh," Restaurants USA, August 1996, pp. 45–47.

2. 1997 Menus: Old and New Share the Plate," *Restaurants USA*, May 1998, pp. 39–40."Salad Selections Soar," *Restaurants USA*, August 1998, pp. 40–41. "Poultry Takes Flight," *Restaurants USA*, November 1998, pp. 39–40. "Healthy Portions," *Restaurants USA*, April 1998, pp. 39–40. "Beef: Is It Still What's For Dinner?" Restaurants USA, September 1997, pp. 41–42. "Foodservice Gets Fresh," *Restaurants USA*, August 1996, pp. 45–47.

3. Robert D. Reid, *Foodservice and Restaurant Marketing* (Boston: CBI Publishing Company, 1983), pp. 207–209.

4. Ibid., pp. 204–206.

5. James Keiser, *Controlling and Analyzing Costs in Foodservice Operations*, 2nd ed. (New York: Macmillan Publishing Company, 1989), p. 56; Reid, Foodservice and Restaurant Marketing, p. 228.

6. Keiser, pp. 49–50.

7. Bradley Beran, "Menu Sales Mix Analysis Revisited: An Economic Approach," *Hospitality Research Journal*, vol. 18, no.3/vol. 19, no. 1, 1995, pp. 125–142.

8. Albin G. Seaberg, *Menu Design: Merchandising and Marketing*, 4th ed. (New York: Van Nostrand Reinhold, 1991), p. vii.

9. Seaberg, *Menu Design*, p. 207.

CHAPTER SIX

DELIVERING HIGH-QUALITY SERVICE

learning objectives

By the end of this chapter you should be able to:

1. Identify the various features that make the service encounter unique.

2. Identify ways to determine service problems.

3. Specify the gaps that explain customer dissatisfaction with service and suggest ways to close these gaps.

4. Identify the various procedural and convivial dimensions of service.

5. Describe the principles of waiting.

6. Describe the duties and responsibilities of captain, server, and busperson in providing quality service.

Zagat's Diner's Bill of Rights

The right to courteous, hospitable, informative service, starting with reservations handling.

The right to clean, sanitary facilities and fresh, healthy food.

The right to make special dietary requests.

The right to send back any unsatisfactory food or beverage without charge.

(continued)

THE SERVICE ENCOUNTER

During restaurant service there is an encounter between customers and employees. It should not simply "occur." Management is responsible for ensuring that the encounter is planned, organized, and to the extent that it can be, controlled to ensure customer satisfaction.

Enduring Insights

Hollander has noted that a review of the historical literature on service uncovers certain features of the service encounter that persist [1]. Service encounters and purchases are considered important to the customer and routine to the service provider. Employees serve scores of customers a day. For the customer that meal out may be a once-a-week occurrence. It is difficult for the employee to generate the same level of enthusiasm for every customer that each customer has for the occasion.

Second, many service employees resent some or all of their customers. This may be because of one of a number of factors. For some employees there is the feeling that customers do not appreciate all the work that is necessary to provide good service. Others feel lower in status because they are serving the customer and may resent their job because of it. In some cases the difficult or rude behavior of customers generates negative feelings on the part of the employee.

Third, many customers want special treatment in a service situation. Perhaps they feel the need to throw their weight around or they feel that by demanding special treatment, they are accorded more status. This places the employees in a difficult situation. They probably resent the fact that everyone pays for equally good service, while some expect to receive more what everyone else is getting.

Fourth, customers have differing needs and wants regarding service. Some prefer an unobtrusive manner of service, while others revel in a fawning, attentive style. It is up to the employee to match the level of service expected to the service delivered.

Related to customer expectations is evidence that factors such as the age, gender, and dress of the employee affect customer perceptions of whether or not the service to be provided will be satisfactory. A customer in a first-class restau-

Jamba Juice

Jamba Juice was awarded a 1998 *Nation's Restaurant News* Hot Concepts award and continues it success by staying in touch with its customers and operators. Jamba Juice has gained in popularity as the nation's health craze continues; yet their ability to keep up with customers' want and needs is what keeps them going. Since their award in 1998, Jamba Juice has expanded to over 220 units across the country and 1999 sales are expected to reach $60 million. The company was able to acquire the Zuka Juice chain in February of 1999, which aided in their rapid expansion.

Jamba Juice has always focused on nutrition with their smoothies and juices. The company also focused on smoothies as their center-of-the-plate meal item. Yet customers, although happy with the smoothies, were not satisfied, they wanted something more, something they could chew on. According to Joe Vergara, director of research and development for Jamba Juice, they began looking for their "fries," so to say. And in that search, they found **Jambolas, Jamba Juice's healthy breadsticks**.

Customer behavior was really what led the company to introduce the new item. According to Vergara, "Many customers would come in, order a smoothie, and while it was being made, they'd go next door to pick up a bagel. We wanted to address that need." The Jambola became bundled with the smoothie and known as a "Power Meal," which has been very successful.

Vergara created the Jamba Juice concept after being raised on a traditional meat-and-potatoes diet in Santa Barbara, California. After his first visit to a health food store, he felt a connection to the health-food industry. Vergara was managing a juice bar in San Luis Obispo, California when he met Kirk Perron completely by chance behind the counter the grocery store. Perron later launched Jamba Juice in 1990. The company had a rocky start at first while they struggled for customer approval and word of mouth to spread. However, Jamba Juice made it through the though trial period and has been gaining in popularity ever since.

Source: "Jamba Juice: Jambola Bread Is on the Rise." *Nation's Restaurant News,* May 24, 1999, v. 33, n. 21, pp. 168.

rant may feel that "proper" service in such a setting would come from an older, male waiter. A younger, female waitress—no matter how skilled—may well set up negative initial reactions from the customer.

Finally, Hollander notes that many service encounters appear successful—or at least tolerable—because customers bring lowered expectations to the service encounter and employees develop coping strategies to deal with potential problems arising from the points made above.

Courtesy of Maggiano's Little Italy.

quick bite 6.2
Definition of Service

According to Bill Fisher, executive vice president of the National Restaurant Association, service means:

- <u>S</u>pirit of the employees who perform it
- <u>E</u>mpathy in placing oneself in the shoes of the customer
- <u>R</u>esponsiveness in taking timely and appropriate action to meet the needs of the customer
- <u>V</u>isibility to let customers know they are being served
- <u>I</u>nventiveness to do a little extra
- <u>C</u>ompetency on the part of service performers
- <u>E</u>nthusiasm to maximize the exchange value with the customer

Source: Fisher, William P. "S.E.R.V.I.C.E.," *Nation's Restaurant News,* v. 15, n. 3, March 1995, p. 39.

Courtesy of Jamba Juice.

Service Problems

What kinds of things can go wrong? A study by the National Restaurant Association [2] indicates that in the restaurant industry, complaints about service far exceed complaints about food or atmosphere. When asked to name their biggest complaint about tableservice restaurants speed of service and inattentive wait-staff are mentioned most often. The former is noted by about one out of every four customers while the latter is noted by one in six patrons. The level of customer satisfaction has not changed since the beginning of the 1990s even as the number of restaurants has increased. Customers indicate that servers are excellent or good at providing friendly service (81%), answering menu questions (80%), delivering an accurately totaled check (80%), provide timely service (70%), handling complaints (62%), and recommending appropriate menu items (61%). It might be argued, however, that these percentages are not very good.

A study of airline, hotel, and restaurant interactions between customers and employees by Nyquist et al. [3] indicated two major problem areas. Difficult interactions were caused when customer expectations were greater than could be delivered by the service system or when the performance of company or employee did not match up to the potential of the system.

In their study, difficulties regarding the former accounted for three out of every four problem encounters. Difficulties occurred for a variety of reasons:

- Demands by the customer that the industry typically does not or cannot offer
- Demands against company policies that are difficult or impossible to fulfill
- Unacceptable treatment of employees by customers
- Drunkenness of customers
- Breaking of societal norms by customers
- Customers with special needs

When performance did not match the capacity of the system, problems arose when services or products were unavailable, performance was slow, or where the service or product was unacceptable.

Assessing Customer Satisfaction

There are a number of ways in which restaurateurs can determine the extent to which customers are satisfied with the level of service they are being provided [4]. Probably the most commonly used method for collecting this information is through the use of comment cards. A card may be available on the table or it can be brought by the server at the conclusion of the meal. In either case, customers are asked to evaluate various aspects of the meal experience. The concern with comment cards is that they tend to be filled out either by people who have had a wonderful time or by those who have major complaints about the meal and/or the service. In either case those who respond are not typical of most customers.

quick bite 6.3
Common Customer Complaints

Here are some common customer complaints cited by Pat DiDomenico, as well as suggestions on how to avoid them.

1. "Where did our waiter go?" Many servers disappear after serving the entree. Servers can avoid this mistake by checking their entire section visually every time they enter the dining room area.

2. "We've been waiting for an hour!" Some tips: Give an honest estimate of the wait time; offer video games, television sets, contests; give restaurant pagers that allow customers to leave and be paged when their table is ready; offer free wine (at night) or coffee (in the morning).

3. "Our waiter was a little too friendly." Limit conversations to topics dealing with the food and the restaurant; act according to the type of service the customer wants.

4. "Is this a no-smoking section?" Avoid complaints by rotating the smoking section to avoid regulars getting stuck in the same seats; use natural barriers to help control smoke; install a good ventilation system; make both sections equally appealing.

5. "Our waiter had an attitude." Says Nick Nickolas, owner of Nick's Fish Market in Chicago: "A good waiter can save a bad meal, but a good meal can't bail out a bad waiter." Attitude cannot be trained—it has to be hired. Treat your employee the way you want them to treat the customers.

6. "Tell me the specials, not the whole menu." Tell people the price of each of the specials mentioned—they may be too embarrassed to ask. Limit the specials to three. If they are so special, why aren't they on the menu?

7. "Take my plate. No, don't take my plate." In more casual restaurants servers tend to remove a plate as soon as a person is finished; in more upscale operations, servers tend to wait until everyone at the table is done. According to Judith Martin, Miss Manners, the latter is preferable.

8. "I can't even hear myself think." Reduce the noise by installing windows to let the noise out, adding plants, tablecloths, tapestries, carpeting, acoustical ceiling tiles, and a separate bar area.

9. "Where's my waiter with the check?" According to Gen LaGreca, owner of Hospitality Industry Training in Lakewood, Colorado, at breakfast, bring the check with the meal; for lunch, deliver it with the coffee and dessert; at dinner present it as the coffee and dessert is being finished. Make sure, however, that customers do not feel that they are being rushed.

Source: DiDomenico, Pat. "Customer Complaints . . . and How to Avoid Them," *Restaurants USA*, v. 13, n. 10, November 1993, pp. 20–25.

How To Measure Customer Satisfaction

The service attribute matrix compares the importance of various items to customers with their satisfaction regarding how a restaurant performs in delivering on these items. Operators can use the results in developing a marketing strategy.

Customers are given a list of attributes and asked to identify how important each is to them. Using the same list, they are asked how satisfied they are with how the restaurant delivered on these attributes. A generic list of attributes can be taken from this list of the most frequent complaints and compliments in restaurants.

Complaints

1. Availability of parking
2. Traffic congestion in establishment
3. Quality of service
4. Price of drinks, meals, and other services
5. Noise level
6. Helpful attitude of employees
7. Food quality and method of preparation
8. Spaciousness of establishment
9. Hours of operation
10. Quantity of service

Compliments

1. Quality of service
2. Food quality and method of preparation
3. Helpful attitude of employees
4. Cleanliness of establishment
5. Neatness of establishment
6. Size of portions
7. Employee appearance
8. Quantity of service
9. Responsiveness to complaints
10. Price of drinks, meals, and other services

(*continued*)

How To Measure Customer Satisfaction (*continued*)

Scores are then plotted on the service attribute matrix and fall into one of four categories:

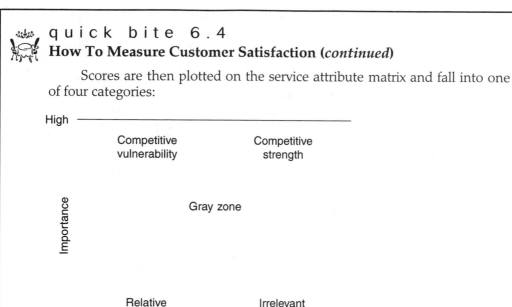

Items in the competitive vulnerability zone are those that customers consider important but where performance is not up to par. Performance on these items has to be improved. Attributes in the relative indifference area are not considered important by the customer. Neither is the performance of the restaurant. These should be ignored with a caution: If the importance of these items to the customer increases and the competition provides better quality in these areas, customers could be lost to the competition.

Items in the irrelevant superiority box are not important to the customer but the level of satisfaction is high. Unless the customer's need for these items can be increased, it is a waste of resources to provide them. Finally, attributes in the competitive strength area are those that customers consider important where the satisfaction is high. These are the items that should be marketed to potential customers.

Source: Almanza, Barbara A., William Jaffee, and Lingchun Lin, "Use of the Service Attribute Matrix to Measure Consumer Satisfaction," *Hospitality Research Journal,* v. 15, n. 2, 1992, pp. 63–75.

As such, this is a biased sample on which to make decisions about changing the service.

A similar comment can be made about customers who verbally complain or compliment the operation. Most people, if they have a mild complaint, will say nothing within the restaurant but will not return. Management does not hear from them and has no idea what caused the problem. Neither will management hear about experiences that were just "OK." The meal may have been adequate, but who wants to be "adequate"? In both situations management is unaware of potential problems.

One indirect measure of customer satisfaction is the percentage of repeat customers. If it is correct to assume that customers will not return to a place they are not satisfied with, this indicates potential problems with the operation.

Similarly, increasing sales indicate satisfied customers, while decreasing sales are a sign of problems. Care must be taken to measure sales changes in real terms, discounting sales increases by any change in menu prices. In addition to looking at sales trends, management can consider changes in market share. If the size of a market decreases but a restaurant's share of that market increases, sales overall may be down but the operation is more than holding its own. It is much more difficult to get a handle on the size of a particular market segment than on individual sales.

Finally, many companies use "mystery shoppers" to evaluate an operation anonymously. Since employees are unaware of the identity of the shopper, the report is a true indication of the physical and service aspects of the meal. Properly trained evaluators, oriented toward the unique aspects of a particular operation, can give very valuable feedback on potential problems.

SERVICE GAPS

Customers develop certain expectations about the service they are to receive based on such things as their own past experience, word of mouth from friends who have tried the restaurant, the advertisements of the restaurant itself, and their own needs and wants. During the restaurant visit they compare what they expected to get with what they perceive they got. The key word is perceive. The portion on the plate may be large. However, if the customer perceives the portion to be skimpy, it is skimpy. Perception, for the customer, is reality. The problem for the restaurant may be to change the image or perception of the customer rather than to increase portion size. However, a problem does exist.

If the perception of the service received is less than expected, the customer is dissatisfied; if the service received is perceived to be equal to or more than expected, the customer is satisfied. One Denver restaurant—now out of business—would advertise "Warm Beer, Lousy Food." By producing low expectations that are easily met, one would think that customers would be satisfied. However, expectations have to be raised to a level high enough that customers will want to eat out. The problem then becomes how to produce service good enough that their (raised) expectations are met.

Service problems occur because [5]:

- Management does not know what is important to customers.
- Management knows what is important to customers but does not translate that knowledge into service standards.
- Service standards are in place but employees do not practice them.
- Customers are promised a level of service that is not delivered.

Lack of Knowledge

The first gap in delivering service occurs when management's perceptions about what customers expect are different from the customer's expectations. Management may not be aware of what is really important to the customer for one or more of several reasons.

Marketing Research Orientation. The best way to find out what is important to customers is to ask the customer! As obvious as this seems, many people think that they know best when it comes to satisfying customers. Research should be conducted on an ongoing basis, both formally and informally, to understand the needs, motives, and expectations of existing and potential customers.

---

 quick bite 6.5
Value-Driven Customers

Patrons are increasingly value-conscious despite good economic times and conditions. Most operators feel that consumers are even more value-conscious than they were just two years ago.

Yet, patrons' expectations don't stop at value. As more and more "boomers" enter their peak earning years, they are growing more demanding about taste, plate presentation and the overall dining experience.

Because of increased customer expectations, operators need to improve their service throughout the entire dining experience. Consumers have raised the standards and heightened their expectations for food quality and service.

Percent of tableservice operators reporting increased customer expectations, by per-person check size.

	Less than $8	$8–$14.99	$15–$24.99	$25 or more
Service	47%	57%	69%	68%
Food Quality	46%	64%	73%	68%
Value for the Price	59%	64%	69%	58%
Food Safety	51%	71%	73%	61%
Nutrition	27%	51%	53%	53%

Source: "1999 Highlights." *Restaurants USA*, v. 18, n. 11, December 1998, p. F13.

Upward Communication.   Too often, communication is primarily downward from management to employee. Managers may think that they should know the answers to operational problems without having to ask employees. For others it is beneath them to seek guidance from their subordinates. Yet front-of-the-house employees have much more contact with customers than does management. They are in the best position to identify which features of the operation and menu please customers and which turn them off. To put such a system in place requires overt action on the part of the manager. Suggestions have to be encouraged from customer-contact employees. A system put in place to reward any idea about improving service will produce more ideas than a system to reward only good (in the eyes of management) ideas. Good ideas have to be rewarded and implemented if management wants the flow of ideas to continue.

The success of such a system will depend, to a large extent, on how management handles bad news—feedback about service problems. If the orientation is to find out who messed up and to punish the offender, employees will be reluctant to report bad news to management. On the other hand, if the emphasis is on finding out why the mistake happened and improving procedures to ensure that it does not happen again, employees will be more willing to share with management.

Levels of Management.   The further that decision-makers are from the customer, the greater is the likelihood that they will be out of touch with what is important to the customer. Many companies are flattening their organizational structure, getting rid of middle management, in a dual attempt to cut costs and get closer to the customer.

Lack of Standards

Appropriate service standards may not be set if management does not believe service quality to be a strategic goal, if management thinks that customer expectations cannot be met, if service cannot be standardized, or if standards are set based on management, rather than customer, expectations.

Management commitment.   As noted earlier, J. C. Penney has been credited with saying: "If you satisfy the customers but fail to get the profit, you'll soon be out of business; if you get the profit but fail to satisfy the customers, you'll soon be out of customers." The question is: Which comes first—profits or customers? Restaurants are in business to make money. Will the provision of quality service result in profitability? In *In Search of Excellence,* Peters and Waterman [6], compared the bottom-line profitability of companies that stressed financial goals—return on investment, net profit, and so on—with those that stressed nonfinancial goals—cleanliness, quality, and service, for example. They found that the companies that stressed nonfinancial goals actually produced better bottom-line results than companies that stressed financial goals. A major reason, they argued, was that employees could relate more to such things as quality and service than to return on investment and were more likely to support a program to improve these things than to get behind an effort to improve profit.

First, then, management has to set quality service as an important strategic goal. According to Zeithaml et al., there are five dimensions of service [7]:

1. Tangibles: appearance of physical facilities, equipment, personnel, and communication materials
2. Reliability: ability to perform the promised service dependably and accurately
3. Responsiveness: willingness to help customers and provide prompt service
4. Assurance: knowledge and courtesy of employees and their ability to convey trust and confidence
5. Empathy: caring, individualized attention provided customers

Tangibles in a restaurant setting might refer to the cleanliness of the rest rooms, the personal hygiene of employees, and the ease with which the bill can be understood. Reliability covers such things as a table being available at the time the customer was told it would be available, a steak being cooked as ordered, and the bill being free of errors. When employees correct problems immediately or when they show a willingness to answer customer questions about the menu, the company is demonstrating its responsiveness to the customer. Assurance comes from such things as employees demonstrating their knowledge and competence, being polite and friendly, and offering guarantees of satisfaction. Empathy is shown by how approachable employees are, talking to customers in language they can understand, and making an effort to understand the needs of the customer.

Surveys of customers of various service companies (which did not include the restaurant industry) indicated that of the five factors mentioned above, reliability was the most important factor, followed by responsiveness; tangibles was regarded as the least important of the five factors, although all five are regarded by customers as being critical.

Setting Service Standards

Martin suggests that service standards need to be developed in two areas: procedural and convivial [8].

Procedural Aspects.　The procedural part of service consists of what is involved in getting the products and services to the customer and consists of:

- Incremental flow of service
- Timeliness
- Accommodation
- Anticipation
- Communication
- Customer feedback
- Supervision

Incremental Flow of Service. This first aspect of the procedural dimension of service is concerned with ensuring that there are no bottlenecks in any part of the restaurant. A slowdown in service can occur because one part of the service system is overloaded. An inexperienced bartender may result in drink orders arriving long after the food has been served; overloading one server with too many tables in too short a time may mean slow service for his or her customers while other servers are underworked; it might also mean that in one station, all the tables are ready for their entrees at the same time. The result of any or all of these is poor service.

Standards can be set to help ensure that a breakdown in service does not occur. Customers can be seated in alternate sections, thereby ensuring an even spread of people throughout the restaurant. Within a particular section this will help ensure that each party is at a different stage of the meal: some being seated, others having appetizers, others enjoying entrees, with some relaxing over coffee.

Timeliness. Timeliness means giving customers the service they want when they are ready for it. This involves setting standards as relative to how long a customer should wait before being greeted, before being seated, and before a food and a beverage order is taken and delivered. Notations of the time made on the order pad can serve as a way of measuring whether or not standards are being met.

Accommodation. Accommodation implies that procedures are designed around the customer rather than around the restaurant or its employees. Often a customer will have a drink in the bar before dinner. The customer is then told that the bar charge cannot be transferred onto the dinner bill. It would be easier for the customer to pay one bill at the end of the night. The reason typically given is that the bar's computer system is different from that of the dining room. The obvious response from the customer's viewpoint might be: "Buy a system that is compatible and that makes it easy for the guest."

In many cases the real reason for this policy is to ensure that the bar server receives the tip for providing service in the bar. Here we have an example of a policy that is designed to accommodate the property and/or the employees rather than to serve the guest.

Another example is that of menu substitutions. Substitutions may either not be allowed or be actively discouraged because they make things more confusing for the server and cooks. The question needs to be asked: Who is most important—the customer or the employee?

An accommodating policy standard would be one that allows bar tabs to be transferred to the dining room, that allows menu substitutions, and that makes every effort to meet the needs of the customer.

Anticipation. Anticipation ensures that customers never have to ask for something—that service is provided before customers request it. Whenever customers have to ask for something, service is less than perfect. When customers arrive with little children, booster chairs should appear automatically. Servers should come by with something to keep the child occupied while the meal is being prepared. Customers should be asked about water and/or wine refills before a request is made, typically when the glass is one-fourth full. When a cus-

quick bite 6.6
To Team or Not to Team, That Is the Question

Many people feel that server teams can improve customer satisfaction by speeding up service. Under the team concept no one server is responsible for a customer—individual servers do what has to be done, irrespective of station. Here are some arguments both for and against the concept:

Pro:

1. Teams provide constant attention to customers: "Whoever gets to the guest first handles the request."
2. Service is more consistent: "All the tables around me will receive the same level of service."
3. There is more staff enthusiasm because teams are given more authority to deal with problems.
4. Absenteeism is less disruptive to service since everyone does everything.

Con:

1. More training is needed.
2. The team concept may confuse customers.
3. Tips have to be distributed differently. The most common approach is to collect and distribute tips from only one station, even if servers move outside their individual stations.
4. Teams can lead to too much service because no one server knows what has or has not been done.

Source: Liparulo, Robert. "Server Teams," *Restaurants USA,* v. 13, n. 2, February 1993, pp. 28–31.

tomer has to ask for something, the server has failed to anticipate the needs of the guest.

Communication. The provision of top-notch service requires effort on the parts of many people: servers, bussers, chefs, and management. Accurate, complete, and timely information is required between all parties to ensure customer satisfaction. Standards must be set to ensure, among other things, that servers are understood by customers, cooks can read the written orders of servers, and that customers receive exactly what they ordered.

Customer Feedback. To determine whether or not customers are satisfied with the level of service provided, it is necessary to get a reaction from them. At some point in the meal, every customer should be asked how it is and management should be made aware of any and every complaint. Often this is done in a perfunctory way. The first mouthful of food has barely been chewed when someone arrives to inquire about the food. A typical customer response is "fine" or "OK" and the employee leaves. This is not enough if the true intent of the question is to get customer feedback.

The natural tendency when there is a minor problem is to mumble "fine," continue with the meal, and never return. Don Smith of Washington State University suggests that employees should ask "Is everything FANTASTIC?" This question would probably elicit fewer noncommittal responses. A more subtle method would be for the employee to take note of the tone of voice and body language used by the customer in responding. A person given minimal training in nonverbal communication can tell whether or not an honest response is being given.

The truth is, however, that many employees do not want to hear about problems. If something is wrong, the employee will be expected to take care of it. This will slow down service for the other tables. Worse still, the manager may find out about the problem and blame the employee. This point is explored in more detail later.

Supervision. The six elements of service noted above will not happen smoothly unless the efforts of the staff are coordinated and monitored. This is the task of the dining room supervisor.

While an increasing number of companies are "empowering" their employees to handle any problems that arise, customers appreciate seeing and hearing from a "manager type" in the dining room. It is a mark of status to have a manager rather than an employee available. Where this is important to the level of service being provided or the type of customer being catered to, it may be desirable to have a supervisor check with each table at least once during the service.

As with all of the convivial elements of service, quantifiable standards are more difficult to develop than are procedural dimensions. The key is to identify, preferably with the help of employees and customers, the visible, measurable behaviors that are examples of the various factors.

Convivial Aspects. The convivial dimension of service is made up of:

- Attitude
- Body language
- Tone of voice
- Tact
- Naming names
- Attentiveness
- Guidance
- Suggestive selling
- Problem solving

Attitude. Attitude, the first element of the convivial dimension of service, refers to the way people act, think, and/or feel and is expressed through the way they act and the things they say. A smile is a visible manifestation of a positive

quick bite 6.7
Racism, a costly mistake

Customer service is a major issue for any operator. Yet, Denny's family-dining chain has learned that treating customers equally is as important if not more important as treating them well.

In an effort to promote racial harmony, Denny's devised an advertising campaign in an attempt to restore the chain's image that has been tarnished by discrimination lawsuits. The campaign cost approximately $2 million dollars and was scheduled to run for four months. Denny's campaign is just one diversity initiative that was implemented since paying almost $46 million to settle a discrimination lawsuit in 1994.

Denny's has a long way to go, however, in their effort to encourage racial diversity. Even after Denny's introduced the new campaign, claims of racism continued. A lawsuit filed by a group of Hispanic customers charged a Denny's outlet in San Jose, California of forcing them to wait while non-Hispanic patrons who arrived later than their party were seated first. Denny's subsequently issued a statement that it would not tolerate discrimination of any kind.

In an unrelated incident, two Muslims accused a Denny's in Billings, Montana of intentionally serving them pork after they requested their meals be prepared in a separate skillet to avoid contact with pork products. The Islam religion forbids the consumption of pork.

Unfortunately for Denny's, marketing experts predicted that the ad campaign would do little to stop discrimination complaints against the company or convince customers that the chain fosters racial diversity. Notwithstanding, Denny's has made efforts greater than the campaign to promote diversity. Almost half of Denny's employees are minorities, 35% of its franchise units are minority-operated and all 70,000 of its company and franchise employees have completed diversity training, earning recognition from the National Association for the Advancement for Colored People.

Source: Cebrzynski, Gregg. "Marketing experts predict few results from Denny's racial-diversity ads." *Nation's Restaurant News,* v. 33, n. 7, February 15, 1999, p. 18.

attitude. Thus a standard could be set that in all interactions with customers, employees should exhibit a smile before talking.

Body Language. People communicate much more through nonverbal communication than through the words that are used. Entire books have been written on the subject of body language. One point that is usually made is the desirability to maintain eye contact with the person being spoken to. This can be yet another standard of quality service.

Tone of Voice. The second most important way in which people communicate is through the inflections used in speaking. Although difficult to measure, standards can be set to ensure that servers communicate in an enthusiastic, friendly, and/or upbeat way, depending on the type of atmosphere desired by management.

Tact. Tact involves saying the correct thing at the right time. Standards can be set regarding proper etiquette for various situations. This will include the terms used to address people, how to respond to complaints and special orders, the avoidance of restaurant slang in front of customers, how to handle unruly customers, and so on.

Naming Names. We all like to think of ourselves as individuals. One way that service people can communicate individuality to customers is to call them by name. Standards can be set such that an individual is called by name when being seated by the host or hostess as well as when a credit card or check is being used to pay for the meal.

Attentiveness. Attentiveness implies that people are treated as individuals, not just numbers. It goes beyond calling people by name but means that service is adjusted to the special needs of the individual patron. Servers can be told to inquire, at the beginning of the meal, whether there are any particular restrictions on the party, such as requiring quick service to make the opening curtain of a play, or whether this is a special occasion. The latter situation is often self-evident, as when a large family group enters the restaurant with presents for the guest of honor. Management would want the server to follow up on the inquiry to make whatever adjustments were necessary to provide individualized treatment. In the former case, service would be speeded up; in the latter situation, a birthday treat might be provided on the house.

Guidance. When customers are perplexed about what to do or to order, the convivial server offers appropriate suggestions. To offer guidance, service personnel would have to be familiar with all the dishes on the menu, including the ingredients and the method of preparation and suggest items appropriate to the various perceived needs of the customers. This effort is hindered by management that refuses to allow servers to taste-test items—both food and wine—on the menu. The server, when asked what is good, is left to respond rather weakly: "Everything is" or (more truthfully) "I don't know; I haven't tasted anything."

Suggestive Selling. Some people think of selling as pushing unwanted choices on someone. The servers' job is, in part, to expose customers to items that might enhance the experience of the meal. Effective suggestive selling results in a higher check. What should be set as a standard, however, is that servers ask all customers if they would like appetizers, drinks, desserts, and other specialty items. Further, servers should describe the benefits of these choices in ways that paint a verbal picture of them. Not everyone who is asked will buy dessert. But no one will buy if they are not invited to.

Problem Solving. Finally, service providers are there to solve any problems that might arise. Rather than taking the attitude "I don't want to hear about any problems you are having with the meal," employees have an obligation to identify any problems that customers are having. This provides them with the opportunity to solve these problems and ensure a satisfied customer.

Problems will occur in any setting. The measure of excellent service is what happens after the problem is noted. Earlier we noted the desirability of identifying problems. At this point attention turns to the resolution of these problems. Standards can be set such that within the boundaries of reason and the law, every problem brought to the attention of an employee and/or management is dealt with to the satisfaction of the customer. Will this result in some customers taking advantage of the situation to get a discount or a free meal? Undoubtedly, yes. However, the cost involved will be small compared to the goodwill gained from attending to the real concerns of the restaurant patrons.

Feasibility. One reason that goals are not set is management's perception that customer expectations cannot be met. While customer expectations are seen as limitless, the resources of the company are not. Certainly, businesses have to make money. They do so by satisfying the customer. Too many managers use the idea of unlimited customer expectations as an excuse to maintain the status quo. If, in fact, satisfaction equals perception minus expectations [9], satisfaction is increased if expectations are lowered or perceptions are heightened.

The problem of attracting customers if expectations are lowered was noted earlier. It may, however, be possible to change the perception of the customers to increase satisfaction. Take as an example the problem of waiting. Given the fact that in a restaurant, supply is fixed in the short run and demand is variable, there will be times when there are more customers than tables available and a wait ensues. Management may take the view that nothing can be done to alleviate the situation.

Yet there are various principles of waiting that management can utilize to improve customer perceptions of service. Maister has identified eight such principles [10]. First, unoccupied time feels longer than occupied time. To reduce the perception of the wait, various strategies can be used. Menus can be handed out while customers are waiting for a table; the waiting area can be the bar, typically a scene of activity; and/or entertainment can be provided to occupy the time of the waiting patrons. The activity provided, according to Maister, should offer intrinsic benefit as well as being somehow related to the meal experience.

Second, the same amount of time after service has ended seems longer than that before service has begun, which, in turn, seems longer than that endured during service. In other words, a five-minute wait after the meal has ended and customers are waiting for the bill seems longer than a five-minute wait for a table which seems longer than a five-minute wait between courses.

Handing out menus as soon as people arrive gives the impression that the meal service has begun. Consequently, the wait appears shorter than it really is. Even when customers are seated, it is wise to bring water, menus, or, at least, acknowledge the customers' presence to let them know that they have not been forgotten.

Air travelers flying to an international destination are typically instructed to report to the airport two to three hours before takeoff. A series of activities helps to convince them that the "flight experience" has begun. Baggage is checked; they go through passport control; they are told to report to the international departure lounge; they go to shop duty free; they report to the gate. Each activity piece divides up a large block of time while attempting to give the impression that the "flight" has begun.

Third, anxiety makes the wait seem longer. Customers worry about such things as whether or not they have been forgotten, whether others are being seated out of turn before them, or whether they will still be able to eat and make the opening curtain of a play they intend to see after the meal. The idea is to be aware of the fact that customers have worries that are both rational and irrational, to identify them, and to seek to reassure the customer. Checking with people by name and giving them progress reports on the wait indicates that they have not been forgotten; asking if they have a deadline and indicating that they will have plenty of time to make it (if, in fact, that is the case) can also alleviate tension.

Fourth, uncertain waits are longer than known waits. When a customer makes a reservation for 7:30 P.M., the expectation is that a table will be ready at that time. The customer may arrive 30 minutes early, wait contentedly for the 30 minutes, but get very agitated at having to wait 10 minutes beyond the deadline. Yet restaurants may have parties who linger over a meal. They cannot be eased out. Some operations choose to handle this situation by refusing to take reservations. On the surface this seems fair. Yet the absence of a reservation system will be a turnoff for many, particularly if they travel a significant distance to the restaurant.

Another problem occurs when people who have made reservations do not show up, but the table is kept for them even as others wait. In taking reservations, a small number of operations ask for a credit card number and charge $10 per person against the card. The amount charged is credited to the bill for the meal. If the party does not show up, the $10 per person goes on their bill.

One thing that can be done is to let the customer know specifically how long the delay will be. "Your table will be ready in 10 minutes" is better than "your table will be ready in a few minutes."

Closely related to the principle noted above is the idea that unexplained waits are longer than explained waits. Not knowing why there is a delay creates a feeling of powerlessness. Customers are angry because employees do not share the reason for the delay. Respect the customer by sharing this information.

Sixth, unfair waits seem longer than equitable waits. In a restaurant situation there are two typical problem areas. The first occurs because restaurants have a limited number of tables for two, four, or more people. Customers are seated by matching the number in the party to the size of the table. From an operational viewpoint it does not make sense to seat a party of two at a table for six. Thus, even if the larger party came in later than the party of two, they would be seated before them. This seems unfair to the smaller group.

The second situation arises when a host or hostess is responsible for answering the phone in addition to seating people. Who has priority when the phone rings just as a table is about to be seated? The people who are there may resent the fact that a potential customer on the other end of the phone is receiving a higher priority than they—the actual customers—are receiving.

The point is that customers have a sense of equity that may be different from that of management. This has to be recognized and managed. In general this means matching the policy to the customer's feeling of equity or persuading the customer that the rules are fitting. In the examples given above the policy regarding seating can be explained to the customer. In the latter case the customer who is present should be given preference. This might involve having another employee who is nearby seat the customer while the host or hostess responds to the call or by putting the person phoning on hold or transferring the call while the party is seated.

The seventh principle indicates that the more valuable the service, the longer people will wait. Airlines segregate lines based on those with simple transactions—seat selection—and those who have more complex arrangements to make—ticket purchase. Supermarkets also have express checkout lines for people buying a limited number of items. In a restaurant situation a bar area may be set aside for snacks and light meals. Those wishing to spend a little can be seated immediately in the bar, while those desiring a larger meal will be willing to wait for a seat in the dining area.

Last, solo waits are longer than group waits. Although there is little that an operation can do in this regard, it is wise to note that people waiting alone will experience the wait to be longer than will those in groups, so more attention should be paid to alleviating their concerns.

Standardization. Some argue that because service is intangible and delivered individually, it cannot be standardized. Standards can be developed for a recipe, but how, it is argued, can a smile or a tone of voice be standardized?

Service standardization can occur with the use of hard or soft technology or with a combination [11]. Pizza Hut uses hard technology to improve its service. Instead of having order taking, baking, and delivery in all its stores, order taking is centralized and computerized in a customer-service center. With a database that shows what has been ordered in the past, an operator can take an order and verify directions to the house of the customer in an average of 17 seconds. The order is then delivered electronically to the store nearest the customer's house, from where it is baked and delivered usually in less than a half-hour from the order being phoned in.

Self-service salad bars exemplify the use of soft technology. By passing some of the service tasks to the customer, management diverts some of the responsibility for service from the operation and its employees to the customer.

Customer Requirements. The concept of a perceptual map was developed in Chapter 3. A perceptual map is drawn indicating what customers consider important when dining out and how they perceive the job the restaurant does in meeting these expectations. This approach ensures a focus on what the customers think is important rather than on what management thinks is important.

Goals should be set that are [12]:

- Designed to meet customer expectations
- Specific
- Accepted by employees
- Designed to cover the important dimensions of the job
- Measured and reviewed with appropriate feedback to the employee
- Challenging but realistic

Who should set the goals? In a customer-oriented operation, customers would be asked what they consider to be the main features of excellent service. They can then give examples of specific behaviors that employees would exhibit when giving excellent service. These behaviors can serve as the basis for setting standards for employee service.

Employee acceptance can come from involving them in setting quality service standards. Employees can also be asked to give examples of specific behaviors that would indicate, for example, that employees were displaying a positive service attitude toward customers. These behaviors, as identified by the employees themselves, become the standards by which quality service is provided.

Lack of Performance

Even when service standards have been determined, they may not be carried out by the employees whose task it is to deliver them. In fine dining establishments, service work is handled by one of four people: captain, front server, back server, or busser [13]. The positions of front and back servers are commonly combined into one job. Various operations will, in addition, combine the functions of their employees such that, for example, servers also bus tables or act as their own captains. This designation is useful, as it focuses attention on what has to be done in providing the highest level of service. Management can then tailor these functions to the level of service provided in their operations.

Busser.   The busser is responsible for [14]:

- Setup of the station
- Water, coffee, and tea service
- Bread and butter service
- Clearing of soiled dishes, glassware, and flatware from tables
- Resetting of tables

Server.   A server is responsible for three things [15]:

- Representing the operation to the customer
- Selling the dining experience, including food and beverage items, to the customer
- Delivering on that promise

Captain.   In an upscale restaurant the captain is in charge of a serving team consisting of several servers and bussers and a specific station consisting of a number of tables. The captain is responsible for ensuring that customers receive the level of service that is proper for the establishment. Captains coordinate the efforts of servers and bussers in providing the desired service.

The captain will:

- Take the order for food and beverages
- Use suggestive selling to increase the average check

Restaurant Management: Customers, Operations, and Employees

- Perform any tableside cooking necessary
- Stagger seating within the section to ensure that no server is overloaded

There are a number of potential reasons why employees will not produce the service expected by management [16]. Employees may lack the information and/or training to do the job; they may feel they cannot possibly satisfy all the demands placed on them by the variety of people they must please; the skills of the employee may be wrong for the job that he or she is in; employees may not have the tools to perform up to the standards set; the supervisory control system may reward actions inconsistent with the provision of excellent service; employees may feel that they have insufficient control over their ability to deliver service; and employees and management may not be pulling, as a team, in the same direction.

Information and Training. When employees do not know what management expects from them or how to go about satisfying management's expectations, they experience role ambiguity. Ambiguity is a result of the employees being given insufficient information and/or training to perform their jobs. Employees need to know what they are supposed to do, what parts of the job to focus on, how and for what they will be rewarded, and how well or how poorly they are performing. If skills are lacking, it is management's responsibility to train employees so that they can provide the level of service expected by management.

In the restaurant business there is a heavy reliance on on-the-job training. Many think this means following an experienced server around for a few days to observe what they do. Yet on-the-job training requires as much care in the planning as do more formal training methods. The design and implementation of an on-the-job training program are described in Chapter 13.

Satisfying Demands. The job of customer-contact employees is made more difficult by the fact that they have, at minimum, two bosses: the manager, who hired and can fire them; and the customer, who they are expected to please and who probably accounts for most of the employee's pay through tips.

When employees feel they cannot satisfy all the demands placed on them by the people—management and customers—they are responsible to, they experience role conflict. The expectations of management and customers may be very different (but they should not be!). Customers want service; management wants a higher average check. Customers want leisurely service; management wants turnover. Customers want more service; management, in an attempt to save money, has increased server station size to a point where personal attention is reduced.

Customers themselves are very different in their needs and wants. The term contact overload has been coined to refer to the emotional "work" that comes from having to deal with too many customers over a prolonged period of time. The result can be emotional burnout, resulting in emotionless employees. The problem is compounded by the fact that servers have to rely on other employees to provide excellent service. When items are held up in the kitchen or are cooked improperly, the result is a less than satisfactory experience for the customer through no fault of the employee.

Role conflict can be reduced by setting employee standards and behavior based on the expectations of customers rather than those of management. If employees know that given a conflict between what management wants and what customers want, the customer prevails, they can go about their work with less confusion. Take, for example, the customer who complains that a steak is not cooked to their satisfaction. If employees know that the customer is always right, neither server nor cook will attempt to argue with the customer. Servers will know that they can go back to the kitchen without getting an argument from the cook. Similarly, if in this situation, the server decides to make an adjustment in the customer's bill, they will know that they will be backed up by management rather than chided for "giving away something" and, thus increasing costs.

By actually involving employees in the setting of service standards, some believe that standards will be set that are higher than would have been set by management alone. In addition, employees are more committed to achieving these standards because they were involved in their setting. This point is made in Chapter 14 in a discussion of management by objectives (MBO). The basic premise behind MBO is that employees will work toward meeting objectives to which they are committed. The way to get that commitment is to involve employees in the setting of objectives.

Employee–Job Fit.   The basic skills used in any restaurant service are [17]:

- Loading and carrying a tray with food and/or beverages
- Loading and carrying a bus box or tray with soiled wares
- Handling serviceware
- Clearing a table during service

In more upscale settings, restaurant personnel will also be called upon to perform Russian or French service and to reset a table during service. Russian service consists of using a spoon and fork to serve from a platter, while in French service, a serving spoon and fork are used to serve a plate from a cart. Resetting a table during service includes changing the tablecloth with minimum disturbance.

In addition to the technical skills of service, dealing with the public requires certain skills not needed for employees in back-of-the-house positions [18]. Successful service providers possess interpersonal skills, demonstrate behavioral flexibility and adaptability, and show empathy.

Education in college programs and training on the job tend to focus more on providing technical skills than interpersonal skills. Yet successful service depends more on the latter than the former. Such skills can either be "bought" by hiring people who possess these skills or developed through training.

Servers who are successful are able to adapt their behavior to that of the guest and respond accordingly. So-called "flexible-focus" employees can be found through their scores on the Central Life Interest Measure [19]. Adaptable people would be low in dogmatism, high in tolerance for ambiguity, and/or high on self-monitoring. Simulations, assessment center techniques, and situational interviews are ways to determine the existence of all of these.

Finally, employees should demonstrate empathy—a temporary merging—with customers. Employees can demonstrate empathy through such techniques as repeating back to customers what they have heard and giving feedback that indicates an understanding of customer concerns.

Minor and Cichy suggest a number of open-ended questions suitable for identifying servers with service potential [20].

Question	Intent
How do you feel about working here?	How does the applicant feel about the company?
What is the most important responsibility of a server? Why?	What is the person's attitude about the job?
Who has more responsibility: a server or a cook?	Does the applicant appreciate the cook's job?
What are the most important qualifications of a server?	Does the applicant understand the responsibilities of the job?
Are servers usually fair to each other?	Can the applicant get along with people?
What would you do if a guest made insulting remarks to you?	Is the applicant easily upset?
Suppose the manager insists that you do a job a certain way when you know there is a better way to do it: What would you do?	What is the applicant's attitude toward authority? Toward supervisors? Is this person stubborn?
What do you think about servers who change jobs often?	Is this person a job hopper?
What is more important: courteous service or prompt service?	What is the applicant's attitude toward both?
What would you do if your tips were falling off?	Can you admit mistakes?

Personal hygiene for service people is also critical. This involves the following [21]:

- A daily bath or shower
- Daily use of an effective deodorant or antiperspirant
- Clean hair restrained above the shoulders
- Clear or natural nailpolish
- Clean fingernails
- One ring per hand
- Avoiding ornate jewelry and excessive cologne or perfume

- No gum chewing
- Moderate use of natural-looking makeup
- Clean uniform and well-polished shoes

Jobs that require customer contact tend to be rather low paying. This severely limits management in attracting highly skilled employees. Companies argue that because of low margins, they are unable to pay wages high enough to attract high-caliber employees. The result is that companies have to compromise in their hiring. For the customer that often means less than desirable service.

Companies are beginning to learn that they get, in employees, what they pay for. There is anecdotal evidence that paying premium wages will result in employees with better skills and lower turnover and absenteeism. Whether or not the bottom line improves is a matter open to debate.

Technology–Job Fit. Similarly, employees need the tools necessary to perform their jobs. Advances in technology have enabled servers to send customer orders to the kitchen by means of hand-held computers. As a result, servers are able to stay on the floor attending to customer needs and make fewer trips to the kitchen.

Supervisory Control. If companies wish to improve service, they need to set up a supervisory system that rewards employees who exhibit behaviors that are regarded as providing quality service. Employees are expected to engage in suggestive selling, describing a dish in such as way that the likelihood of the customer ordering that dish increases. An employee may engage in suggestive selling, painting a verbal picture of that dish while accurately describing its contents.

Suppose the customer is full and does not order the dish. Should the employee be rewarded? In many operations employees are rewarded solely on the basis of results, such as the number of desserts sold. Yet this employee has engaged in high-quality service behaviors. The employee who sells the dessert may have used tactics to get the order that leave the customer unhappy.

To be successful, employee recognition programs must set challenging standards, be accepted by employees, have the right number of rewards, and be long-lasting [22]. British Airways has identified for its middle managers 60 statements of behavior necessary for providing good-quality service. Their bonuses—worth 20 percent of their base pay—are determined half by their achievements and half by the behaviors used to get results.

Employee Control. Employees experience less stress in their jobs when they feel that they have control over situations that occur in their work. Customer satisfaction with the service depends on the efforts of several people: the host or hostess who receives the reservation and has a table ready at the appointed time, the busser who has set the table in the proper manner, the cook who prepares the order, and the server who delivers it. Yet if there is a problem, it is the server who is the recipient of the complaint. Giving the server—or, for that matter, any employee—the authority to resolve the complaint is an example of employee empowerment. Employee empowerment entails pushing authority down to the lowest level possible. Instead of getting a manager to hear a

Road to the Top

Joseph Bastianich, restaurateur

At a mere 30 years old, Joseph Bastianich has built an impressive resume that includes trading bonds on Wall Street, starting four restaurant concepts and branding his own Italian wines. One of the restaurateur's greatest skills may be the ability to handle multiple projects at once. Two of the four restaurants Bastianich runs opened within months of each other. Joseph was born into a family whose mainstay has been the foodservice industry, as the son of the well-known New York restaurateur, Lidia Bastianich. The mother-and-son duo has opened several successful restaurants together including Becco in New York's Times Square.

After working with his mother for several years, Bastianich decided to strike out on his own and created Babbo with a different partner. Despite its fledgling status, Babbo received a three-star rating for the *New York Times*, putting the restaurant in an elite few Northern Italian cuisine restaurants that have won the recognition. Bastianich has also expanded the family's vision into Kansas City opening Lidia's Kansas City. According to Bastianich, it is a dream of his to share his passion for Italian food and wine with diners across the country.

Although Bastianich's degree in political science and philosophy has little to do with the restaurant industry, he has been working in his parent's restaurants since he was a young child. After graduating, Bastianich deciding to leave the industry for Wall Street and a bond trader position with Merrill Lynch. Bastianich explains his return to the family business saying, "The work was interesting and rewarding, but at the same time it didn't offer the satisfaction that I got growing up in the restaurant environment. Working in the financial world, I felt a void without the interaction of making people happy through food and hospitality. So one day, I just up and left."

However, his mother didn't let him jump right in, she had him spend a year in Italy working in wineries and restaurants to learn about Italian food and service. According to Bastianich, that year in Italy solidified his decision to become a restaurateur. In Italy, he discovered his natural ability to understand and love wine and food and the culture of Italian hospitality. However, his experience on Wall Street and the financial knowledge he gained allowed Bastianich to marry finance and hospitality to achieve his success.

Source: Zuber, Amy. "Joe Bastianich: Lidia's Son Trades in Bonds for Pasta and Carves His Own Niche in the Restaurant Industry." *Nation's Restaurant News,* v. 33, n. 4, pp. 14–16.

Courtesy of Ruth's Chris Steak House.

complaint and to make a decision on how it should be resolved, the employee who gets the complaint owns that complaint and is responsible for solving it to the satisfaction of the customer. The result is a faster response to complaints and motivated employees who feel that they can control the delivery of high-quality service.

Teamwork. In the restaurant business there are a number of traditional rivalries: management and employees; kitchen staff and wait staff as a whole; dishwasher and busser as a specific. Quality service requires that everyone work together for the goal of good-quality service. Cooks may feel that their job is done when they cook the food even if the timing means that it is ready either before or after the customer is ready for it. Problems of timing? That is the concern of the server. Or consider the dining room that never seems to have enough silverware. Servers take to stashing a supply to take care of their individual stations.

The result of such practices is that employees feel they are working against one another instead of being united in a common goal. Management's task is to provide the climate for this unity to happen. Tom Peters has said that if employees are not serving the customer, they had better be serving someone who is. This type of attitude ensures that everyone realizes the importance of working together to serve the customer.

Hot Skills

Service 2000

As the year 2000 rolls around, service will become a top priority for managers. Not only will customers expect better service, but also they will be more diverse and will have needs that are more diverse. It will be essential for managers to get timely and accurate customer feedback.

Employee empowerment and training will need to be encouraged by managers in order to effectively cater to customer needs and desires. Employees must have the training and flexibility to immediately attend to customers' needs.

Managers are likely to spend more time than ever on customer relations in 2000. Managers will involve employees in setting standards for all employees in regards to customer satisfaction and their own performance. Managers will be spending more time on face-to-face interactions with customers.

The Top 10 Most Likely Developments for Managers in Service for 2000:

1. Service will be a competitive advantage
2. Employee empowerment for better service
3. Varying demands from an increasingly diverse customer base
4. Need for feedback from customers
5. More training required for customer service
6. Provide cost-effective, yet higher levels of service
7. Increased time spent on customer relations
8. Increased standards for employees when dealing with customers
9. Promoting good will through responsible alcohol service
10. Provide employees with immediate and constructive feedback regarding service

Source: Adapted from National Restaurant Association, *Foodservice Manager 2000* (Washington, DC: National Restaurant Association, 1992).

Promising Too Much

It was noted earlier that customer expectations have to be raised to a level high enough to motivate people to leave home for the restaurant. It is more difficult to sell a meal than a part for a car because if the part does not work, it can be returned and replaced. This is not true of a restaurant meal, which is consumed before the customer can determine whether or not it is all right.

This means that expectations have to be raised even higher for an intangible product such as food plus service than for a tangible good. This can lead to a tendency to promise too much in an attempt to get customers in the door. When customers come in with unrealistic expectations, employees may not be able to deliver, no matter how well they perform.

A second problem arises because of a lack of communication between those who sell the experience and those who are expected to deliver it. Employees who cook and serve the food must be involved in marketing decisions to provide a reality check on those who plan the advertising.

By the same token, employees should see what customers are being told in advertisements for the restaurant in order that they know what customers are being promised—promises they will be expected to deliver on.

Planned Attack

Where is the manager to begin? Closing all four gaps may require time, money, and effort. If all four gaps exist, management would be wise to begin with the fourth gap noted above, the tendency to promise too much.

It may not be possible to improve service immediately. In such a situation, the one thing that management can influence is customer expectations. It may, initially, be necessary to lower customer expectations to a level closer to the service provided. Care must be taken to ensure that the lowered expectations are high enough to induce patronage.

The other three gaps must be closed in order. Customer expectations have to be identified before standards can be set; appropriate standards must be set before they can be implemented.

ENDNOTES

1. Stanley C. Hollander, "A Historical Perspective on the Service Encounter," in John A. Czepiel, Michael R. Solomon, and Carol F. Surprenant (Eds.), *The Service Encounter: Managing Employee/Customer Interaction in Service Businesses* (Lexington, MA: DC Heath and Company, 1985), pp. 48–53.

2. "Rolling Out The Red Carpet: Restaurant Service Rates High With Diners," *Restaurants USA,* August 1997, pp. 39–41.

3. Jody D. Nyquist, Mary J. Bitner, and Bernard H. Booms, "Identifying Communication Difficulties in the Service Encounter: A Critical Incident Approach," in Czepiel et al., *The Service Encounter,* pp. 113–123.

4. Robert Reid, *Foodservice and Restaurant Marketing* (Boston: CBI Publishing Company, 1983), pp. 129–130.

5. Valarie A. Zeithaml, A. Parasuraman, and Leonard L. Berry, *Delivering Quality Service: Balancing Customer Perceptions and Expectations* (New York: Free Press, 1990), pp. 36–45.

6. Peters and Waterman, *In Search of Excellence.*

7. Zeithaml et al., *Delivering Quality Service,* pp. 21–22, 26.

8. William B. Martin, *Quality Service: The Restaurant Manager's Bible* (Ithaca, NY: Cornell University Press, 1986), pp. 79–81.

9. David H. Maister, "The Psychology of Waiting Lines," in Czepiel et al., *The Service Encounter,* p. 114.

10. Ibid., pp. 113–123.

11. Zeithaml et al., *Delivering Quality Service,* pp. 80–82.

12. Ibid., pp. 84–86.

13. Bruce H. Axler and Carol A. Litrides, *Food and Beverage Service* (New York: John Wiley & Sons, 1990), p. xiii.

14. Ibid., p. 1.

15. Ibid., p. 59.

16. David H. Maister, "The Psychology of Waiting Lines," in Czepiel et al., *The Service Encounter,* pp. 89–113.

17. Axler and Litrides, *Food and Beverage Service,* p. xv.

18. David E. Bowen and Benjamin Schneider, "Boundary-Spanning-Role Employees and the Service Encounter: Some Guidelines for Management and Research," in Czepiel et al., *The Service Encounter,* pp. 137–139.

19. Ibid., pp. 144–147.

20. Lewis J. Minor and Ronald Cichy, *Foodservice Systems Management* (Westport, CT: AVI Publishing Company, 1984), p. 148.

21. Ibid., p. 150.

22. Zeithaml et al., *Delivering Quality Service,* p. 103.

CHAPTER SEVEN

THE PHYSICAL FACILITY

learning objectives

By the end of this chapter you should be able to:

1. Identify the various elements of the immediate package and the external environment.

2. Show how elements of the immediate package can affect the psychological needs and behavior of customers.

3. Give examples of the ways that the size and shape of the room, seating arrangements, light, and color combine to influence customers.

4. Suggest procedures to improve existing layouts.

5. Develop more productive procedures for completing individual jobs.

---

*A restaurant tells you the minute you walk in the door what it's trying to do.
It's how they greet you. It's a feeling, like when you meet a new person. In a person,
it's body language. In a restaurant, there's a smell, there's an energy level.*
Elaine Tait, restaurant critic, quoted in *Dining Out.*

Source: Dornenburg, Andrew and Karen Page, *Dining Out* (New York, NY: John Wiley & Sons, Inc., 1998).

FRONT OF THE HOUSE: LAYOUT

The size of an operation will vary depending on the type of service to be provided and the extent of menu offerings: The more extensive the menu, the larger the operation tends to be. In the estimates given below, the higher-range figures refer to facilities with more extensive menus and that allow for more room. It is estimated that the total facility size for various types of foodservice facilities is as follows [1]:

Type of Operation	Total Area per Seat (square feet)	Dining Space per Seat[a] (square feet)
Table service	24–32	12–18
Counter service	18–24	16–20
Booth service	20–28	12–16
Cafeteria service	22–30	12–16
Banquet service		10–12

[a]Includes space for tables, chairs, aisles, and service stations but excludes waiting areas and rest rooms.

The amount of space required for the dining area depends on the number of people to be seated at any one time and the square feet of space per seat. The former is, in turn, a function of the total number of people to be served within a given period of time and the turnover. Turnover is a measure of how many times a seat will be occupied during a given meal period and is usually expressed on a per hour basis. It is, in essence, the average time a seat will be occupied during a particular time or meal period. If, for example, people stay an average of 30 minutes during lunch, the turnover is two times per hour. Turnover rates will vary depending on the time of day and the type of meal service. A dinner crowd will stay longer than a group of lunch people on a schedule. While turnover for the former might range from 1/2 to 1 (indicating an average stay of between 2 and 1 hours), regular table service tends to have an average turnover of 1 to 2 1/2. Cafeterias average higher turnover, anywhere from 1 1/2 to 2 1/2 for commercial cafeterias to 2 to 3 for industrial or school cafeterias.

Where a high turnover is desired, the concept can be built into the design by [2]:

- Using items that do not take long to prepare
- Using preprocessed items
- Using a high level of lighting and light colors in the serving area
- Arranging the tables close to each other
- Designing chairs that become uncomfortable after a short period of time
- Having enough employees to provide prompt service

quick bite 7.1
Hot Concepts: Kahunaville

Theme restaurants have not been doing well lately; however, Kahunaville is the exception to the rule. David Tuttleman, chairman of Adventure Dining Inc., the Wilmington, Delaware-based operator of the five Kahunavilles, sees opportunity to compete and earn a profit in the troubled segment. The tropical-themed restaurant features an extensive game-arcade complex and appears mainly in shopping malls. Tuttleman plans to expand the concept to malls across the country including seven new sites in 1999 and six in 2000. He predicts that the company will have approximately 26 stores in operation by 2003.

The concept started with one store in Wilmington, which featured an outdoor concert venue. Yet, chief operating officer Mark Green felt that they could expand the business to capture twelve solid months of business rather than the five "summer" months they had captured. The company adopted a tropical theme and called it an "oasis of food and fun." The restaurant is decorated with talking Tiki idols, abundant sound systems and sparkling waterfalls and fountains.

The Kahunaville menu features about 90 items including "Big Kahuna-sized" gourmet sandwiches and salads. The restaurant features entrees with American, Mexican, Cajun and Asian flavors. Many menu items are giant-sized and stacked including a "grilled portobello 'stack' sandwich, a seared ahi tuna stack appetizer and the Towering Sirloin Stack—the highest-priced menu item—combining grilled medallions of beef with layers of portobello mushrooms, grilled eggplant and garlic herb ricotta." Lunch checks average $9 per-person and dinner averages $16. Each unit has annual sales of approximately eight million dollars.

Many critics feel that the key to Kahunaville's success is their Disneyland-like culture. Tuttleman proclaims Walt Disney to be one of his idols. He calls the goal of providing customers with great food and quality service in a fun atmosphere to create a memorable experience, "The Pursuit of 'Wow.'" Extraordinary customer service is a major goal of the company. In one instance, when a waitress spilled a tray of drinks on a customer the general manager took the customer to a store in the mall and bought her a new outfit, then picked up the check for the entire table of eight. Managers are required to submit two stories a week recording one time where they improved the experience of a guest and one that details how they improved a co-worker's week.

Source: Rubinstein, Ed. "Kahunaville: Offering an Oasis of Food and Fun." *Nation's Restaurant News,* May 17, 1999, v. 33, n. 20, pp. 58–60.

The square feet per table is a function of the type of seating to be provided—the relative proportion of tables to booths to counters to banquettes—the table sizes and shapes that are preferred, how the tables will be arranged, the aisle space desired, and the number of serving stations required.

FRONT OF THE HOUSE: ATMOSPHERE

Atmosphere is the general mood or tone set by the restaurant. While excellent food and beverage items are crucial to the success of any operation, the surrounding atmosphere can significantly add to or detract from the diner's enjoyment of the experience of the meal. Research studies have consistently identified the top four reasons influencing a decision to return to a restaurant as:

- Quality of food
- Service
- Price
- Atmosphere

Courtesy of Kahunaville.

While food and beverage items are the basic product of a restaurant, they are "surrounded" by an immediate package that includes the table arrangements, furniture, and the provision of entertainment. This, in turn, is presented within an environment made up of the space, seating arrangements, lighting level, and the colors used. All elements have to come together to form a complete picture.

There is a difference between eating and dining. When customers go out to eat, their principal concern is the food and beverage items served, and their principal need is physiological. On the other hand, when people go out to dine, they want a complete meal experience and their needs are both physical and psychological. It is up to the atmosphere to cater to the psychological needs of the customer. This can be done in a variety of ways, by appealing to the guest through sight, touch, hearing, smell, temperature, and movement [3]. How people perceive and are affected by these elements make up, in their minds, the atmosphere of the restaurant.

It is also important that the elements that make up the atmosphere be designed in accordance with each other and that they bear in mind that customers will be present. The story is told of the modern Dutch painter, Mondrian, who was asked to design a stage set. Upon completing his work, he reportedly said, "The actors must read their lines from the wings: otherwise, they will spoil the set." An appropriately designed interior must include the presence of the customer as part of the final package.

Several elements of the immediate package are explored here: table arrangements, furniture, and entertainment.

Table Arrangements

The table top has been described as the center of the selling action—the silent sales promoter. The first impression for customers is visual and the first thing they see is the table setting. It is important to coordinate table settings to the mood of the restaurant: formal or informal; expensive or economical. The table arrangement should be an attractive blend of dinnerware, glassware, flatware, linens, and accessories.

Dinnerware. Many operators stick with simpler dinnerware patterns in order that they not detract from the food. There are four basic shapes for china: rolled edge, narrow rim, coupe, and scalloped edge. It is difficult to set specific rules for choosing china because of the variety of available colors and patterns. However, it is important that the china chosen fit the mood of the restaurant. For example, the narrow rim or coupe is preferable for a contemporary setting. Similarly, a formal atmosphere deserves softer, more delicate shades and a lighter weight than a family-style restaurant. On the other hand, heavier plates give customers the impression that they are getting a lot of food. This is the same rationale that bars have when they serve beer in heavy-bottomed beer mugs.

The average piece of restaurant china is used approximately 7,000 times and lasts about three years if handled properly. Operators should expect to replace 25 percent of their china every year due to breakage. In this regard, stock patterns of commercially made designs can be least expensive.

Department Stores

Nordstrom Inc. has redesigned their café concept to appeal to fast-paced customers who would like an alternative to the mall food court. The retailer has
created a food-lover's sanctuary to rival solo competitors. Nordstrom's cafés
feature a marketplace design with a variety of tactfully prepared food items
available at different food "stations" in order to keep up with their upscale
image. The design is an attempt to redesign Nordstrom's foodservice for the
new millennium.

Nordstrom's cafés have been in business for over 20 years and have
served a quick serve niche. The new concept provides a food-first style rather
than their traditional point-of-sale style service. Nordstrom's restaurant division manager, John Clem, claims that the new concept has been a raging success; customers have thronged to it.

When deciding upon the design for the new concept, Nordstrom used
several "root words" as the driving force for their new 4,000- and 5,000-
square-foot cafes. When Engstrom Design Group of San Francisco was hired,
they were given the words contemporary, fun, interactive, warm, casual,
fresh, attentive, quick and delicious to incorporate into the design.

According to the designers, creating the transition from an area where
retailing and clothing is the focus to an area where suddenly food is the priority was the biggest challenge for the design team. Previously, food in Nordstrom cafés was brought from the kitchen only after it was ordered by the
customer; however, the new design puts the food right out there where it is
merchandised much like the clothing is.

The café is designed so customers wander down the food line and examine all the offerings before they decide what to order. Stations include
gourmet sandwiches, soups, freshly tossed salads, pizza and panini, pasta,
and specialty items including roasted chicken, desserts and pastries, and specialty beverages. The variety of food is designed to fit the variety of moods
customers come in with.

Nordstrom designers went to great lengths avoid a cafeteria-like environment by arranging the space to avoid straight-line movement. The serving
lines actually snake around, forming L-shapes in order to keep it interesting.
In order to keep the upscale and sophisticated look of Nordstrom's no stainless steel surfaces are shown anywhere and all of the food equipment is custom millwork made of solid cherry wood to give the café a European
atmosphere. The Old World style is further augmented by forged metal, iron-
work detailing, granite countertops, cooper column tops and large, porcelain
pavers.

Source: Strauss, Karyn. "Nordstrom Develops In-store Concept 'for the Next Millennium.'"
Nation's Restaurant News, v. 33, no. 5, February 1, 1999, pp. 24, 27.

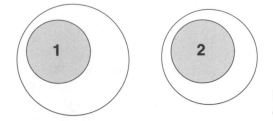

Figure 7.1 Effects of food on different-size plates.

It is important to consider the total effect of the food item and the plate. Overfilled plates look cluttered and are messy; sparsely filled plates give an impression of poor value. Perceptually, the size of the item compared to the size of the plate can make the item appear to be a better or worse value. Consider Figure 7.1. In reality, both inner circles are the same size. However, the inner circle on the right appears to be larger because it is surrounded by a smaller setting. Similarly, the same food item placed on a smaller plate will appear to be larger. A strip steak placed on an oval-shaped plate with mashed potatoes piped the length of the steak will tend to accentuate the length of the steak.

Specialty dishes for specialty items add value to the item. For example, soups can be served in small crockpots, fish on a fish-shaped platter, and desserts in a variety of differently shaped glasses.

Restaurants that cater to families with small children—for example, fast-food operations—will clear the table of most items, preferring to achieve the desired atmosphere through other means.

Glassware. Glassware is typically lime, or plain glass, and lead, or crystal glass. In selecting glassware two things should be considered: design and color. Design encompasses such things as heavy or light, simple or ornate, stemmed or unstemmed. Rustic or family operations might call for a heavier weight or heavy-bottomed glass; fine dining establishments would select a finer, lightweight stemmed glass. Unusually shaped glasses are ways to add interest to the table. However, the more different types of glasses used, the greater the storage space needed.

Wine glasses can suggest that this is the type of facility where wine with the meal is appropriate. Favorite colors for glass in restaurants are red, green, gold, and smoke blue. They can help give a totally coordinated look to the table.

Flatware. In selecting flatware—knives, forks and spoons—the basic decision comes down to a choice of silver plate or stainless steel. The latter is less expensive, although fine-dining establishments may feel that silver plate is more in keeping with the atmosphere provided. In this case, consideration will have to be given to periodic burnishing or polishing. This can be done by machine, in a soaking bin, or by hand, but it must be planned for in the warewashing area.

Today's stainless pieces can be delicately embossed and carved to give the look and feel of silverplate. The important consideration is to select the best-quality flatware consistent with the type of restaurant. Some experts suggest that a stainless steel mix with 18 percent chrome and 8 percent nickel gives excellent resistance to corrosion while giving off maximum luster.

Restaurant Management: Customers, Operations, and Employees

Linen. Linens add to the feeling of quality within an operation. They come in a variety of colors that can be chosen to blend with the mood of the operation. Special attention should be given to flame retardancy, resistance to stains, colorfastness, and texture. Linen, polyester, cotton, or cotton–polyester blended napkins all feel different. Operators have to determine what feels right for their facility. Resistance to stains is important because of the constant wear and tear inflicted on napkins. Linked to this is the colorfastness of the napery. If linens start out deep red and, after a few washings, the color fades, the combination of deep-red new napkins and faded-red older napkins will create a negative impression.

The cost of laundering can be greatly reduced by having a full table covering that remains during the meal period and a smaller piece overlaying this that can be changed after each party on an as needed basis. Inexpensive or family restaurants prefer no table covering, utilizing placemats for a touch of color.

The use of warm and inviting colors for place settings in institutions can take the edge off the sterile dining environment. A cloth or doily lining on a tray can also create a warm feeling.

In cafeteria dining it is possible to use Formica tops, such as imitation marble patterns, which tend not to show stains.

Accessories. Many restaurants insist on covering the table with a variety of table tents advertising special menu items. Operators need to consider carefully whether or not these items produce increased sales or a cluttered image in the minds of the guest. Most texts advise against having too many table decorations. According to them, a flower vase, a candle or lamp, and an ashtray (if the table is in a smoking section) are the only "decorations" that should be on the table. On the other hand, a small bowl of nuts on the table can be a useful way of getting people to order drinks before a meal.

In addition, small touches to the table can add to the mood of the meal. Bringing a hot loaf of bread on a cutting board to the table accomplishes several things: It allows guests to participate in the meal; it keeps them busy during waits before the meal or between courses; and by allowing them to cut slices as thin or as thick as they wish, it gives some degree of freedom over part of the meal. At the same time, the smell of hot bread can act as a stimulant to the appetite.

Furniture

The selection and placement of chairs, tables, and banquettes has a physical and a psychological dimension. The physical dimension involves having enough room to be comfortable; the psychological dimension involves the feeling the furniture gives the customer.

Chairs. Chair or banquette seats of breathable vinyl are practical, durable, and allow for easy maintenance. Placing fabric on the inside and outside back where there is less wear adds an attractive touch. Fabrics can be treated with either vinyl or acrylic coatings to make them more soil resistant and to last longer.

Particular attention should be paid to firm construction in the legs and backs of chairs, as these factors influence how comfortable it feels to customers.

Some restaurants specialize in the "15-minute chair"—so named because after 15 minutes it becomes uncomfortable and the customer is "reminded" that it is time to go. The idea for this chair came from Henning Larsen, who built it after consultation with Copenhagen cafe owners distressed that their customers loitered too long over their coffee. Conrad Hilton noticed that in the lobby of the Waldorf-Astoria, the comfortable divans were utilized every day by the same people. Although well-dressed and well-mannered, they were not spending money in the hotel. His solution was to move the comfortable divans into the nearest food and drink area of the hotel.

Chairs with arms make it easier to rise from the table. People can get up from a sitting position by pushing upward and outward until the body's center of gravity is moved forward to a position over the feet. This takes the strain off the leg muscles.

Traditional seating will appeal to a discerning clientele. Business travelers, who may walk on hard floors or pavements all day, will appreciate big plush chairs; hard plastic chairs and Formica tables will move people in and out very quickly.

Chairs should be selected in combination with the tables chosen. It is important, for example, that, if armchairs are purchased, the arms fit under the tabletop. Although more comfortable, armchairs take up more space.

Tables.   The most important characteristic of a table is that it should be sturdy. Tops should be a minimum of one-inch thick. Most tables are made of flakeboard with a topping of a material such as Formica. While durable and practical, it tends to look "cheap" if left uncovered. If linens are not to be used, the only alternative is a solid wood top.

The shape of the table is also important. Round tables, because they offer more opportunity for eye contact with others around the table, promote more communication. This tends to slow down turnover but increases the check average. Rectangular tables do the opposite.

Many people prefer booths as seating. A booth will offer a feeling of privacy, something that may be important for sensitive business meetings or romantic meals. By extending the back of each booth to come behind the customer's head, the guest, when seated, cannot see into the other booths. A feeling of privacy is created.

Entertainment

Providing the right kind of entertainment can influence customer enjoyment and customer behavior. In a dining situation the entertainment should complement the overall atmosphere in the operation. In some types of facilities the entertainment may be a major reason why people come in.

Cost.   The cost of providing entertainment must be justifiable from a profit standpoint. The objective behind the provision of entertainment is that the cost involved will result in greater profits for the operation. This can come about in one of four ways. Customers who would not come in except for the entertainment can be drawn into the lounge and/or the restaurant; customers stay longer; they eat and/or drink more; or they come back again.

Music

Music can contribute significantly to a restaurant's revenue. It has the ability to create an atmosphere that encourages customers to enjoy their dining experience. Operators must select music and playback equipment that preserves consistency with menu, décor, lighting and all of the other marketing elements. There are several options when selecting music for a restaurant; some of these are listed below:

Foreground or background

One consideration when selecting music is whether or not it will be in the foreground (clearly audible) or in the background (heard distantly). Venues that choose foreground music may do so in order to reinforce the theme of the restaurant. For example, a Tex-Mex restaurant could play trendy salsa or upbeat jazz selections at fairly loud levels to establish an exciting rhythm for patrons. On the other hand, a fine-dining establishment may select background music, typically light classical or jazz to create a more refined environment. Once an operator chooses between background or foreground music, a sound processing system must be chosen that meets the restaurant's volume and power requirements.

Programmed music services

Programmed music is often referred to as "canned" music. These types of services are transmitted through either standard cable radio signals or direct broadcast satellites in which either a small receptive dish on the roof or a receiver is plugged into an existing sound system. Advantages to a music service is that signals are clear and free from distortion, and managers can instantly make selections from numerous types of professional music.

Priority-disks

Most operators choose programmed music services; however, others find that "priority disks" provide a reasonable alternative. The priority disks are customized with musical selections produced by a programming service. These disks are then played at the restaurant using a special compact disk player. Priority disks are higher in price than music services, but they allow operators to customize selections while still retaining control.

CDs and jukeboxes

For operations that do not find the "canned" approach suitable and for whom the priority disks are too expensive, similar results can be obtained with a programmable CD player. A CD player allows managers to suit the local atmosphere.

(continued)

The cost of entertainment must produce a revenue increase greater than that cost. Consider the following example:

Before entertainment:

150 customers buy, on average, three drinks at $1.75 each.

Revenue produced each night =	$ 787.50
	× 6 nights
	4725.00
Subtract cost of goods sold	1181.25
(assume 25%)	3543.75
Subtract payroll and related expenses	350.00
Gross operating profit	$3193.75

After entertainment:

182 customers buy, on average, three drinks at $1.75 each.

Revenue produced each night =	$ 955.50
	× 6 nights
	5733.00
Subtract cost of goods sold	1433.25
(assume 25%)	4299.75
Subtract payroll and related expenses	350.00
Subtract cost of entertainment	750.00
Gross operating profit	$3199.75

Note that approximately $1,000 in additional revenue must be generated in order to pay for the $750 in entertainment costs. This can be done by attracting more customers (as above), charging higher drink prices during the entertainment, charging a cover charge to offset the entertainment cost, realizing an increase in beverage revenue because people stay longer and/or drink more, or having an increase in restaurant food sales because of increased business in the lounge.

Programmed Music. In lounge settings offering dancing, proper programming of the entertainment can encourage and control alcohol consumption by alternately encouraging patrons to the dance floor and sending them back to their seats for a thirst-quenching drink.

Programmed music with a disk jockey can cost 50 to 60 percent of the cost of providing live music and, depending on the skill of the disk jockey, can be easier to program relative to the needs of customers. This involves playing a type of music in the first set that will appeal to a majority of the crowd. The second set would have music appropriate to the next largest audience, followed by a set of music that would have limited appeal. This may satisfy a small number of customers, while sending the majority back to their seats for rest and refreshment. A fourth set of slow music provides a contrast to the faster earlier sets. The format should be adjusted to changing demographics as the programmer notices what music keeps people on the floor and what sends them back to the bar. In nightclubs, where customers are more homogeneous, the same kind of music tends to be played most of the night.

Effect on behavior.   The provision of background music has been shown to affect customer behavior in restaurants. In one experiment [4] the effects of slow-tempo background music (72 or fewer beats per minute) were contrasted with fast-tempo background music (92 or more beats per minute). It was found that:

- Customers eating with slow-tempo background music took longer to finish their meals than did customers eating with fast-tempo background music—56 compared with 45 minutes.
- When fast-tempo music was being played, the waiting time per group was reduced from the 47 minutes usual when slow-tempo music was played to 34 minutes as a result of the diners eating faster.
- The tempo of the music had no impact on the decision to wait for a table.
- The tempo of the background music did not significantly affect the speed with which customers and orders were handled by employees. (The increased time came from the time it took the customers to eat rather than the time it took them to be served.)
- While the tempo of the background music had no impact on food sales, it did affect bar sales. Slow-tempo music increased bar sales. (This has been verified in studies that show increased drinking in bars featuring slow country music.) Because the gross margin (the difference between selling price and food or beverage cost) is greater for drinks than for food, this had the effect of significantly increasing gross margins for the restaurant.

Space

Early concepts of layout have given way to a field of study known as environmental psychology which looks at the influence of the physical environment on people's behavior. Four concepts are of particular importance: privacy, personal space, territoriality, and overcrowding [5].

---

quick bite 7.4
Determining Equipment and Space

Many operations have been built using age-old industry standards that determine necessary equipment and space. However, economics have caused many operators to question industry rules-of-thumb for front- and back-of-house equipment and space needs. At this time in the market floor plans and unit costs need to be reduced in order to stay competitive.

As a result of the need to use less space, many restaurateurs are beginning to "right-size" their facilities. One way to determine the right size for an operation is by using tools developed in other industries. Retailers use margin analysis to evaluate the paybacks from their investments in space and equipment for each product category they offer including selling costs. This type of margin analysis has lead many retailers to discontinue the sale of toys and large appliances.

Operators can prepare a similar margin analysis by menu segment, which will result in suitable space allocation and equipment expenditures for each menu item. The analysis should go beyond food and labor costs and include all the equipment and space needed to store, prepare, and serve the item.

A margin analysis should be used when considering high-cost investments such as a wood-fired pizza oven, a rotisserie or a grill. Many of these items require separate ventilation systems. However, the margin analysis should not be used solely to make a decision, many items need to be there in order to meet customer expectations.

The industry rule-of-thumb is to allocate 8- to 12-square feet per seat, or 35 to 40 percent of the dining area, for back-of-house functions in a typical "eat-in dining" restaurant. Yet, determining the size of a kitchen based upon the number of meals served per day gives a more relevant idea of space and equipment requirements. Using number of meals served versus the industry rule factors in the increased storage and preparation space that is needed for a restaurant open 18 hours a day as opposed to one open for breakfast and lunch only.

Source: Frable, Jr., Foster. "Rethinking Old Assumptions and Rules about Equipment and Space." *Nation's Restaurant News,* April 26, 1999, v. 33, n. 17, pp. 20, 26.

Privacy.   The more people are afforded privacy, the more control they feel over their behavior. Little is known of the effects of privacy on such things as turnover, conversation levels, and so on.

Personal Space.   There are four zones within the concept of personal space. Intimate distance extends 18 inches around a person. If others enter this space, people back off to establish a more comfortable distance between themselves and others. Personal distance goes from 18 inches to about 4 feet and allows an exchange of conversation. Social distance extends from 4 to 12 feet, while public space involves anything beyond that. The amount of personal space and personal distance that people feel comfortable with varies by culture. The British have a larger comfort zone than that of Americans, who in turn, feel more comfortable farther apart than the space preferred by Latin Americans.

Forcing people together, as in a nightclub, induces conversation between them. On the other hand, a wide table introduces a more formal space between parties and indicates more formal behavior is appropriate.

Territoriality.   Territoriality refers to the need to control a defined space. When space is restricted, people move objects to define boundaries. In British restaurants it is common for two parties of two to be seated at a four-top (a table set for four people). This would not be tolerated in American restaurants, where "having one's own territory" means not sharing a table with others. More work needs to be done to identify how much space people need compared to how much is provided.

Crowding.   Crowding refers to the feeling of being one of a large number of people in a small space. The perception of crowds, whether real or not, may influence a person's decision to leave one restaurant for another.

The space allocated to diners may range from 8 square feet in a cocktail lounge or bistro to 18 square feet in an upscale establishment.

Lighting

The cost of lighting ranges from a low of 10 percent of total energy consumption for a fine dining restaurant to 25 percent of the total for a fast-food operation.

Lighting serves four basic purposes. It helps set the mood of a restaurant; it should make both the food and the customers look good; it has to be bright enough to allow employees to complete their work; and in places, it helps provide for the safety and security for the guests.

Five factors must be considered in selecting the type of lighting in a restaurant: time, size, contrast, brightness, and sound [6].

Time.   The lighting level should be selected in accordance with the amount of time a customer has to enjoy a meal. Low lighting levels mean that customers have to take longer to read the menu. It also encourages them to linger over the meal. High levels of lighting help provide an atmosphere that encourages people to leave. Low lighting permits greater intimacy between couples, thereby increasing seating capacity.

Size.   As with colors, careful selection of lighting systems can affect people's perceptions of the physical facility. A low ceiling, brightly lit, will appear

quick bite 7.5
Food Facility Planning

A major principle in foodservice design is that the menu drives design. But, while the menu is significant, its primary influence is on preparation and cooking equipment required. Designing a facility based only upon the needs of the menu is a huge mistake for an operator. Planning should take into consideration the operating style and philosophy into order to ensure that the facility will meet the restaurateur's needs and expectations.

When planning the design of a facility, the owner or operator is responsible to provide the designer or consultant with a deep understanding of the organization and its individual culture. A good consultant or designer of both front- and back-of-the-house areas will probe for and request information about the organizational culture in an effort to satisfy their client.

Food facilities planning includes several variables:

- Purchasing style: takes into consideration number of distributors, number of weekly deliveries, and number of sources which impact the amount of dry and refrigerated storage required.
- Inventory control: takes into consideration the size of the operation, number of storerooms desired, locations needed. Three operating styles exist: 1) all purchases received into a central store room and then issued to individual departments; 2) food and beverages delivered directly to individual points of service and 3) separate dry and refrigerated storage for each operating unit, called independent business units or IBUs.
- Food preparation style: scratch, speed scratch or convenience: takes into consideration the preparation style that has such a significant impact on the size and cost of a restaurant. With an understanding of the operating style, a consultant can decide whether an operator requires a 20- or 30-quart mixer.
- Cook to order or cooking to inventory: the first requires high output/ high temperature cooking equipment, while the second requires food warming and holding equipment. Layout and equipment requirements can be very different for the two.
- POS systems and other management controls: takes into consideration the importance of the location of the "nervous" system (Point of Sale) as it can have a major effect on the layout and configuration of workstations as well as customer flow.
- Service volume projections: takes into consideration the number and length of service periods for the operation. Facilities with extended hours should be designed to operate with a minimum number of employees.

(continued)

higher; high ceilings, dimly lit, will look lower; a narrow room will appear narrower if the long walls are lit. Bright lights will give an impression of speed, thereby increasing turnover. Similarly, trash cans in white or bright colors will appear lighter weight than those in dark colors.

Contrast. Contrast is the perceived difference between the detail of an object and its background. Use can be made of direct, indirect, or spotlighting. Direct lighting is stronger, indirect lighting is softer, and spotlighting can be used to focus attention on particular features or objects.

Courtesy of Vicorp Restaurants, Inc.

An important consideration is the reflective difference level of the task at hand and the surrounding area. Strange as it may sound, a brightly lit area against dimly lit surroundings make the former more difficult to see. For example, a cash register keyboard can be made easier for the cashier to read by increasing the lighting of the immediate surrounding area to a point where there is only a 10 percent difference between the reflective level of the cash register—reflecting back 50 to 60 percent of the light—and the immediate surrounding area—reflecting back 40 to 50 percent of the light. In short, the correct levels of lighting can improve employee productivity and reduce errors.

Brightness. Of the two types of lighting systems—incandescent lights and mercury vapor lights—mercury vapor or fluorescent lights produce up to 4 1/2 times the light and have 9 to 10 times the life of standard incandescent lamps but have lower aesthetic appeal. Incandescent lights, on the other hand, enhance reds and are easier to control; they can be turned down with a dimmer. In addition, food looks best and more natural under this system of lighting.

Because fluorescent lights pick up most of the color spectrum, blues and greens dominate reds and oranges, causing skin to look pasty and food to look gray. Green fluorescent light makes roast beef appear greenish gray, a red pear becomes purple, shrimp cocktail is grayish pink, and coffee becomes muddy green.

Candlelight, with its reddish flame, gives off a light that is flattering to both food and people. Additionally, it gives a romantic feeling of intimacy.

To be as kind to the customer as possible, lights should be placed at or slightly below eye level. Having high-angle lighting produces glare while enhancing shadows and wrinkles on the face. This effect can be reduced by having light-colored tablecloths which reflect light onto the unlighted portion of people's faces.

In bars there seems to be a connection between lighting, noise level, and duration of stay. As the lighting level increases, so does the noise level, and both reduce the amount of time customers stay. The lighting levels in bars should be 20 to 30 percent brighter than in the dining area.

In dance clubs, lighting and sound are combined to give a total effect. In the early days of discotheque clubs—the 1960s—the sound budget was often 90 percent of the budget. Because people are more visually oriented, today's budgets tend to be closer to 80 to 90 percent on lighting and 10 to 20 percent on sound. The dance floor will take up 50 to 60 percent of the total lighting budget, depending on how important it is in attracting customers.

In selecting the appropriate type of lighting, an order should be maintained: The light must be selected before the bulb and the bulb must be chosen before the fixture. One way to prolong the life of the bulb is to stipulate higher-wattage lamps than required for the space, and keep them dimmed by using lower-wattage bulbs. For example, operators might request 150-watt lamps from the designer for a particular location, but use only 75-watt bulbs. The bulbs will last much longer. This is particularly important if the location of the lamp makes it difficult to replace the bulb. The ease with which bulbs can be replaced is yet another factor that must be considered.

Color

Colors are classified as either primary, secondary, or intermediary. The primary colors—so-called because other colors are obtained from them—are red, yellow, and blue.

Secondary colors are made by mixing two of the primary colors. Green is made by mixing blue and yellow; orange from red and yellow; violet from blue and red. Intermediary colors are a combination of a primary and a secondary color—such as red-violet and yellow-orange. The color wheel is shown in Figure 7.2.

Colors are referred to as either warm or cool. The warm colors, so-called because they give off a feeling of warmth, are red, yellow, and orange. The cool colors, which are relaxing and cooling, are blue, green, and violet.

Harmony. Colors should be selected that are harmonious together. Five harmonic principles are useful in the selection of colors: monochromatic, analogous, complementary, split complementary, and triad.

Monochromatic harmony involves the use of a single color as either the pure color itself, as a tint (that is, mixed with white) of the pure color, as a shade (mixed with black) of the pure color, or as a tone (mixed with both black and white) of the pure color.

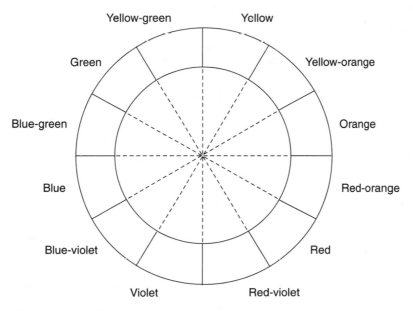

Figure 7.2 Color wheel.

Analogous harmony comes from the use of any three or four consecutive colors on the color wheel. Blue-violet, blue, and blue-green would be an example of analogous harmony.

Complementary harmony is obtained by using any two colors directly opposite each other on the color wheel. Blue-violet and yellow-orange or red-violet and yellow-green are examples of this.

Split or near complementary colors come from the use of three colors. One of the two complementary colors is used in combination with the two colors adjacent to the other complementary color. For example, blue and orange are complementary colors. A split complementary would be blue, yellow-orange, and red-orange; or orange, blue-green, and blue-violet.

Triad complementarity involves the use of three colors. Every fourth color on the color wheel is selected.

Once the colors are selected, a decision must be made as to the tint, shade, or tone to be used. As noted above, a color is tinted when white is added to it; a shade comes from the addition of black; and a tone comes from adding both white and black to the color.

Contrast. One of the most important elements in dealing with color is the idea of contrast. One color cannot operate alone. The guidelines for dealing with contrast are [7]:

- Use a light form (pink) with a darker form (red) of the same color.
- Use a weak version (pale blue) with a stronger version (royal blue) of the same color.
- Use a warm color (red) with a cool color (blue).
- Use complementary colors, such as peach and gray-blue.

Contrasts in colors can have a safety effect by making obstructions and exits stand out.

Effects. We can now turn to the overall effect of color on the room, the food, and the customers. Colors should be selected under the type of lighting in which they will be used, as they will look different under fluorescent lighting than under incandescent lighting. Care should be taken in selecting a color from a small sample, as it will appear brighter in a larger area than on the small sample.

Colors can give a feeling of spaciousness or of intimacy. Light colors make a small room look larger, while dark colors make high ceilings appear lower. In general, dark colors will make objects appear smaller; light colors make them appear larger. Similarly, the use of dark colors to emphasize horizontal lines will make the ceiling appear lower, while using dark colors to emphasize vertical lines will make the ceiling appear higher. The ceiling can also be "lowered" by carrying a wall color over to the ceiling.

Long, narrow rooms can be made to feel squarer by using colors on the end walls that are warmer or deeper than those on the other walls.

Another factor to consider is the location of the restaurant. It has been found, for example, that, in the northern states, people will stay longer if warm colors—reds, oranges, yellows—are used, while in the warmer south, greens and blues encourage longer stays.

The location of different rooms in the facility must also be taken into account. Rooms with a northern or eastern exposure will tend to be cool in the afternoon. Muted warm colors will offer a counterbalance. Rooms with a southern exposure will already be pleasantly warm and can benefit from the coolness of green, blue, and turquoise. The natural light in rooms with a western exposure will be tinted by the sun and, in the evening, the sunset. Earth tones—brown, tan, yellow, burnt orange, and copper—will complement the natural light.

Food looks better under warm colors such as red, brown, yellow, gold, and orange. People like food in the red-yellow spectrum: roast beef, brown rolls, french fries, red apples, strawberries, cherries, oranges, and so on. Yellow-greens, apart from the green of salads, peas, broccoli, and spinach, are not highly regarded. Blue, purple, and pink have much less appetite appeal.

Another important consideration is not only how the food looks but how the customers look. Greens and grays tend to make people look pale and is most unflattering. The combined effect of color and light is important. Green lights tend to show up wrinkles, while pink lighting pales lipstick colors, and amber lights wash out colors.

Some researchers argue that colors affect a person's mood, while others feel that the intensity is the key. Red is perceived as exciting, intense, and stimulating; orange is jovial, exhilarating, and energetic; yellow is cheerful, inspiring, and boosts morale; green is quieting, refreshing, and peaceful; blue is subduing and melancholic; purple is gracious, elegant, and dignified; brown relaxes; white is pure and clean; black is depressing and ominous.

There is some research to indicate that older people have more trouble distinguishing between blues and greens than among the warmer reds and oranges. In general, they prefer brighter primary, secondary, or tertiary colors to pale pastels.

High turnover can be encouraged by having bold colors and high-intensity lighting. The closer to the primary colors of yellow, blue and green, the bolder the effect. Fast food operations, in their early development, utilized bright yellows and reds for this reason.

BACK OF THE HOUSE: SPACE REQUIREMENTS

The following rules of thumb regarding the amount of production space for various foodservice facilities should be taken as general guides only. These recommendations should be adapted to the special needs of particular projects.

The amount of production or back-of-the-house space required will vary depending on the type of service. Tableservice restaurants will require 8 to 12 square feet per seat; counter service, 4 to 6 square feet; booth service, 6 to 10 square feet; and cafeteria service, 8 to 12 square feet [8].

Once the amount of space required has been determined, the amount for each of the functional areas must be calculated. The top-down method allocates certain percentages of the total space to each of the functional areas. One suggestion is as follows [9]:

Functional Area	Space Allocation (percent)
Receiving	5
Food storage	20
Preparation	14
Cooking	8
Baking	10
Warewashing	5
Traffic aisles	16
Trash storage	5
Employee facilities	15
Miscellaneous	2

 quick bite 7.6
Making the Most of Space Available

Here are some tips on how to make the most of available kitchen space:

1. Design the kitchen according to the menu. The Top o' the Cove restaurant, a 95-seat dining room and 90-seat cafe in La Jolla, California, has a menu that features sauteed items. To make the most of the 925 square feet available, designers got rid of the "traditional" stock pots and back burners found in most kitchens. Says owner Ron Zappardino, "You can't saute on a back burner." When Rhys Lewis, executive chef at the American Club in Kohler, Wisconsin, changed the menu at Cucina to serve lesser-priced pastas and gourmet pizzas, he realized that "pasta makes the kitchen a little faster. There is less time between courses." He concentrated on selecting equipment that saved time and labor. A dough cutter was purchased to reduce the preparation time of the pizzas, while the pizza oven is also used to prepare the sandwiches on the lunch menu. The $15,000 cost of redoing the kitchen was saved in the first four months through increased sales and lower labor costs.

2. Design the kitchen according to the shape of the kitchen. The Riveranda is a cruise ship equipped with a 700-square foot kitchen used to serve four-course dinners to 275 passengers. Two of the bulkhead walls taper in toward each other. Designer Tony Mazurkiewicz built shelves into the bulkhead, thereby freeing up floor space. Refrigerators were custom built to the shape of the ship's hull. Tony believes the kitchen uses 95 percent of the usable space available.

(continued)

BACK OF THE HOUSE: WORKPLACE DESIGN

A bottom-up approach to determining space requirements involves designing individual workplaces and assembling them into functional areas.

The workplace is where people perform their jobs. The amount of space made available at each workstation and the way it is laid out can aid or hinder employee productivity.

Systematic Approach

A systematic approach to workplace design begins with an analysis of the menu. Each item on the menu should be identified, together with the portion size, the estimated total number of portions per meal period, the materials, utensils, or hand tools and process required to prepare the item, together with the type of work surface needed [10]. A similar process will determine the area needed for other nonfood functions.

Work Aisle Space.   Work aisle space is the term used for the floor space needed by an employee to perform a task. Traffic aisles, on the other hand, refer to areas where there is foot traffic. Work aisles and traffic aisles should be kept separate wherever possible to avoid hindrances to employees as they work. A single-person work aisle requires a space of between 24 and 36 inches, depending on the tasks to be done. To allow for employee bending or oven door opening, the larger space is needed. For two employees working back to back a minimum of 42 inches is required; more—6 to 12 inches more—if equipment projects into the work space.

Traffic Aisles.   Traffic aisles are used to move people and materials. They should be kept separate from work aisles. Traffic aisles are not productive space and should be kept to a minimum while allowing easy movement. It may be possible to have one aisle serve two or more functional areas. They should not be placed along perimeters, as this allows access to only one working area. An aisle width of 30 inches will permit one person to walk without a problem. When carts are being pushed or containers carried down an aisle, 24 inches plus the width of the equipment is necessary to allow two people to pass. If a work aisle is combined with a traffic aisle, a minimum of 42 inches is required to allow one person to pass someone who is working. Where two people are working back to back, 48 inches is needed to allow someone else to pass between them. The less movement within the operation, the less aisle space is required.

Work Surface Space.   The space required for work surfaces depends on the materials to be used and the hand and arm movements required to perform the task. Normal and maximum hand and arm movements can be identified for the "typical" employee and the work area built to allow employees to perform their jobs within these areas. The normal work area for a work surface is defined as "the space enclosed within the arc scribed by pivoting the forearm in a horizontal plane at the elbow" [11]. For most people this is 14 to 16 inches. Cutting, slicing, mixing, and assembling are best done within this area.

To determine the maximum work area, the entire arm is pivoted at the shoulder. When a task has to be performed outside this area, the employee must bend his or her body. The result will be a less productive worker. Most food facility jobs can be performed within an area 2 feet deep by 4 feet wide.

Workstation Height.   The height of a workstation depends on the task to be performed there. Lightweight tasks can be done at a surface height 2 inches below the employee's elbow. The larger or heavier the materials used, the lower the work surface should be. For light tasks the preferred height should be 37 to 41 inches; heavy jobs should be 34 to 36 inches off the ground, depending on the height of the employee.

Storage.   Tools and utensils should be close to where they will be used and readily accessible to employees.

Equipment.   Equipment is either mounted or freestanding. The feeding and working height should be appropriate to the employees who will use them. Freestanding equipment can be moved from one location to another. This makes it easier to clean under and behind the equipment. In addition, changes in layout can be made to accommodate more efficient layout when changes occur in the menu.

Workplace Environment.   Productivity is affected by the physical conditions under which employees must work. A temperature between 65 and 70° F in winter or between 69 and 73° F in summer with a relative humidity between

40 and 60 percent is comfortable for most people. The heat and moisture generated in a kitchen can be contained by purchasing equipment that is well insulated.

Despite some research which indicates that kitchen workers are up to 25 percent more productive in the summer if kitchens are air conditioned, most people consider it economically unfeasible to air-condition this part of the operation. There are some measures, however, that can be taken to reduce kitchen temperatures [12].

- Steam and water pipes and equipment that emits heat can be heavily insulted, as can the entire building.
- Hot-water heaters, refrigerator compressors, and condensers can be placed away from the kitchen.

---

quick bite 7.7
Kitchen Temperature

Operators often look for areas in which they can cut costs in order to increase their margins. One area that restaurateurs often attempt to cut costs in is temperature control in the kitchen. Often the importance of maintaining proper temperature is neglected, yet a comfortable temperature can improve productivity. Although conditioned and properly distributed supply air was often ignored in past kitchen designs; new regulations and codes require operators and designers to consider both supply air systems and distribution.

New building codes legislate indoor air quality require operators to increase air volume in both front- and back-of-the-house areas. Air quality is not just a consideration for employees. The regulation was actually passed in the interest of food safety. Even newly manufactured refrigerators can't maintain the 41° temperatures mandated by new health code requirements in kitchens where the ambient temperatures exceed 85°.

When designing supply air systems, operators must be careful that air is properly regulated. Improperly designed systems create severe drafts in both the front- and back-of-the-house areas. These drafts can cause hot food in warmers or waiting for server pickup to rapidly cool down.

Not only does proper makeup air movement and temperature allow operators to comply with code and preserve the serving temperature of food, but also has a dramatic effect on the comfort and productivity of employees. "It may be easy to recite Harry S. Truman's maxim, 'If you can't stand the heat, get out of the kitchen,' but do you really want to take that approach with the limited labor market today?"

Source: Frable, Jr., Foster. "Proper Temperature and Makeup Air Movement Affect Productivity, Comfort." *Nation's Restaurant News,* v. 33, no. 5, February 1, 1999, pp. 21, 26.

- Equipment can be preheated for the minimum amount of time necessary.
- Sun-reflecting windows can be used to reduce sun heating.
- Whenever feasible, heat-emitting equipment can be covered during pre-heating and after use.
- Lower temperatures can be used to cook food.
- Gas flames should be adjusted so that they do not come up around the sides of pots.
- The building can be aired out at night.

The amount of lighting required depends on the job to be done. Lighting levels in a kitchen range from 15 to 20 footcandles in nonwork areas to 30 to 40 footcandles for most kitchen tasks. General white fluorescent lights tend to distort food color and are not recommended. Incandescent or color-improved fluorescent lighting should be used for work areas. The latter is more expensive to install but cheaper to operate.

There are two other considerations related to lighting: the brightness ratio and glare. The brightness ratio—the relative brightness between a lit and nonlit area—should not exceed 3:1 where the work area is the brighter area. Direct glare occurs when light sources are placed near the line of sight. Both direct and reflected glare tires employees and is an annoyance. The latter tends to come from the large number of stainless steel tables and amount of equipment used in kitchens.

Three aspects of color are important in the workplace: contrast, actual color used, and color coding. Objects are easier to see and the eye is less tired when there is a color contrast between two areas. This can be achieved in one of several ways [13]. A light color can be used with a darker version of the same color; a warm color can be combined with a cool color; a color can be used with its complementary color. The level of contrast in the workplace should be at a moderate level, as too much contrast can be just as bad for the eyes. Warm colors—reds and oranges—tire the eyes easily. Blues and greens are much more restful. In a similar fashion, pure colors, as distinct from tones, strain the eyes after a short period. Pure white is usually not recommended for a work area because it reflects light too much, again tiring the eyes. Colors can be used to color-code various pieces of equipment. Green tends to be used for first-aid equipment; red signifies danger; steps coded with yellow can serve as a signal to be careful.

Exposure to noise levels above 50 decibels for a prolonged period can lead to contentious employees. Silencing enclosures can be placed around equipment, acoustical materials can be utilized on ceilings, walls, and floors, and sound-absorbing materials can be used to construct work surfaces.

Music has been shown to boost employee morale. It is particularly useful for workers performing physical tasks. Most workers are productive for the first 2 to 2 1/2 hours after they begin work. Their work performance then declines and holds steady at the lower level until shortly before a meal break, when it improves. Upbeat music during the lull in performance can help a worker perform more productively.

Because of the type of work performed in the kitchen, ventilation is important to remove odors, moisture, and the smell of grease, but air conditioning creates special problems in the kitchen. When food is cooked, the work area becomes hot. Air conditioning aims to cool the work area down. The control system used is very important to ensure that the working conditions are comfortable for the employees without causing the cooked food to cool before it is taken into the dining room.

Safety in the Workplace. Unsafe workplaces increase costs for the employer by increasing insurance coverage and reducing productivity. Accidents in the kitchen can occur for a number of reasons [14]. Falling results from slippery floors, floors that are highly polished, and stairways that are too steep. Nonskid flooring or carpeting can help with floors that are wet and/or greasy. Accidents from cuts happen because moving edges are not sufficiently guarded or employees are not using hand tools properly. These can be reduced by guarding cutting edges and ensuring that workers are trained in the safe and proper use of their tools.

Burns can be caused by hot grease, steam, hot water, or hot pipes. Steam and hot-water lines should be insulated and/or placed out of the way of employees, who should be trained in the proper use of equipment.

Electrical shocks in the kitchen are the result of frayed wires, poor insulation on wires, or improper grounding of equipment or machines. Built-in ground wires with three-pronged plugs can be used with portable equipment and grounding outlets provided. Heavy-duty waterproof wiring is recommended.

When hands are sweaty or greasy or when fingers are stiff due to exposure to the cold, there is a tendency to drop things. Keeping hands dry and using gloves when picking up hot or cold items over a long period of time will reduce such accidents.

Layout of Functional Areas

By identifying the functions within the kitchen and the order in which they are undertaken, management gets a feel for the flow of activities within the operation. Boxes of canned goods are received, the boxes are unpacked, the cans are checked for quantity and quality, the boxes are discarded, and the cans are placed on shelves. The order in which activities occur is referred to as flow. The idea is to minimize the amount of movement of both people and goods.

Layout Principles. The layout process consists of two steps [15]: arranging individual pieces of equipment into a functional area (for example, salad preparation) and arranging the functional areas into the entire operation. Both steps tend to occur at somewhat the same time in the designer's mind.

Industrial engineers have developed various principles of layout that serve as a guide to this process. The more important of these tend to stress such things as designing the layout to make the production process as easy and as flexible to change as possible, allowing for ease of access for such things as maintenance and the taking of inventory, protecting the equipment from damage, providing a safe and productive environment for employees, and minimizing movement of both materials and employees.

Principles of Flow.   A flow diagram showing the flow of employees, customers, and primary materials helps determine where areas should be, relative to one another. For example, after being received, items are separated into either dry or refrigerated storage, from where they go to either baking, meat, or vegetable preparation. From vegetable preparation items go to salad preparation; items from meat preparation go to final cooking and then either to salad preparation or to serving, then to the dining room, and finally, to dish washing. Silverware and flatware from the dishwashing area go back into the serving area. The pot wash area receives items from both baking and cooking.

In a station manned by one employee, a flow diagram is best accomplished by surveying the employee's movements between various pieces of equipment and placing pieces involving most movement between them next to each other.

Where employees are engaged in tasks that do not require them to move much, as in dishwashing, where employees scrape dirty dishes prior to loading them into the dishwasher, the most important consideration would be the flow of materials rather than the analysis of employee movements.

Generally speaking, when material flow is minimized, employee movement is minimized. Whichever criterion is used, the following principles are important [16]:

- Flow should be along straight-line paths as much as possible. This principle is particularly important, as it results in minimum movements. Various layouts can be charted and the one giving the best straight-line pattern selected.
- Cross-traffic results in bottlenecks and congestion. The amount of cross-flow or cross-traffic should be minimized. This can be done by locating aisles, passageways, and doors such that traffic flows do not cross.
- When people move back to where a particular activity occurred, they are guilty of backtracking. This should be minimized.
- Bypassing should also be minimized. This occurs when material or people pass one or more pieces of equipment to get to the next part of the process.

Configurations.   Five basic layout patterns are common (see Figure 7.3). The single straight-line arrangement consists of pieces of equipment laid out next to each other in a straight line. They may be laid out along a wall or in an island. It is simple but the layout options are very limited.

An L-shaped arrangement places equipment on two legs that are perpendicular to each other. It is a useful arrangement where linear space is restricted. Different types of equipment can be separated by using one leg for each type.

U-shaped arrangements are particularly useful for confined areas where only one employee is working. A problem is that this layout does not allow for straight-line movement through the area.

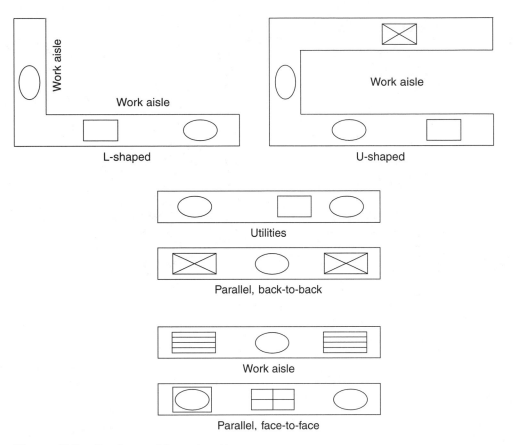

Figure 7.3 Equipment layout patterns.

Parallel, back-to-back arrangements consists of two parallel lines of equipment placed next to each other back-to-back. In this way the utility line for each line can be centralized between them.

Parallel, face-to-face arrangements utilize two lines of equipment with a work aisle between them. Very commonly used, this arrangement requires separate utility lines for each line of equipment.

Arranging Functional Areas

As noted above, the layout process consists of arranging individual pieces of equipment into a functional area and arranging the functional areas into the entire operation. A relationship chart is useful for this second step. A relationship chart shows the desired physical relationship between various functional areas. Such a chart is shown in Figure 7.4. Departments involving a great deal of movement between them are located in relative closeness to each other.

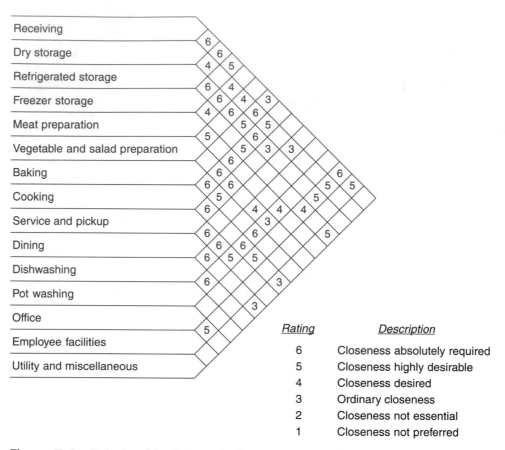

	Rating	Description
	6	Closeness absolutely required
	5	Closeness highly desirable
	4	Closeness desired
	3	Ordinary closeness
	2	Closeness not essential
	1	Closeness not preferred

Figure 7.4 Relationship chart with closeness ratings for a typical foodservice facility. *Source:* Edward A. Kazarian, *Foodservice Facilities Planning,* 3rd ed. (New York: Van Nostrand Reinhold, 1989), p. 283

Comparing Systems

Boger examined four different systems to evaluate their efficiency [17]—the scramble, production-line, mall, and airport. In the scramble system, employees "scrambled" to prepare, gather, and deliver the food items to the customer. In the production-line system employees were in stationary positions. The customer traveled from the cashier station to the expediter station where they received their food items and continued on to the self-service drink station. Under the mall system, employees recorded the orders, then gathered the food items for delivery to the customers. Order and pick-up stations were separated by several feet to allow other orders to be recorded. The airport system allowed customers to travel along the serving line, selecting food items from self-serving units. They paid for these items at the end of the line, preparing their own drinks at a self-service station. The cashier was the only employee to interact with the customers.

Each system is appropriate for different volume levels. The scramble system is designed for high volume, the production line for medium to high volume, and the mall and airport systems for low volume. All but the mall system recorded similar total service times. However, they each use various methods to achieve this. The scramble system makes up for an inefficient design by using more employees. Fewer employees are used in the production-line system through the utilization of customer flow and keeping employees in fixed positions. The mall system, unlike the other three, has a limited and scattered volume of business. Also unlike the other systems, self-service units carried limited inventory to prevent waste. This slows down service time considerably as items are made after the food order is placed.

Each system offers unique advantages and disadvantages. The scramble system can serve up to four customers at the same time and can handle high volumes. However, it is difficult for the production area to catch up if they fall behind during peak periods. The production-line utilizes customers as a part of the process by having them prepare their own drink items. This is liable to reduce labor costs. On the other hand, congestion at the drink station can interfere with customer flow. The airport system allows customers to select items from self-service units while also allowing them to fix their own drinks. The system can only handle low volume and tends to offer only a limited menu selection. The mall offers food either made from scratch or assembled after the order is placed while being able to serve low volume.

It may be that a hybrid system could be designed utilizing the best features from each of the four listed above.

IMPROVING EXISTING LAYOUTS

The layout of existing operations is improved if the flow between various workplaces can be reduced. Travel charts can be used to evaluate the flow involved in a kitchen layout.

Two methods are used. The first looks at the movement of individuals between workplaces; the second considers the flow of materials between workplaces. Whichever method is used, the objective is the same, to minimize movement of both people and materials.

Individual Movements

When the weight or volume of materials involved in a process is not great, analyzing the movements of individuals is the best method of evaluating equipment layout.

When using individual movements, the most common form of travel charting involves analyzing workplaces that are in a straight line and where workplaces next to each other are equal or can be assumed to be equal. A workplace may be a sink, piece of equipment, worktable, or counter. Watching employees as they work, the sequence and frequency of movements between workplaces can be determined.

A chart can then be constructed showing the number of times an employee moves from workplace to workplace. A travel chart is shown in Figure 7.5. The numbers in each cell represent the number of movements from one workplace to

| | From: | | | | |
To:	A	B	C	D	E
A		5	2	3	6
B	3		4	0	2
C	3	4		1	4
D	1	2	4		3
E	2	4	3	5	

Figure 7.5 Travel chart for five workstations showing frequency of movements. *Source:* Idea adapted from Edward A. Kazarian, *Foodservice Facilities Planning,* 3rd ed. (New York: Van Nostrand Reinhold, 1989), p. 298.

another. For example, the employee moves from C to B twice, while there are four movements from B to C. The cells below the diagonal show forward movements; those above show backward movements. The farther the cells are from the diagonal, the greater will be the number of workplaces that have been bypassed. For example, there are four movements from D to A. This represents backward movement that bypasses three workplaces.

Those movements next to the diagonal—for example, from A to B—indicate that no bypassing takes place.

If it is assumed that the distance between workplaces is equal, the total distance covered can be determined by adding both forward and backward movements and multiplying the totals by a factor of 1 plus the number of workplaces bypassed.

Referring to Figure 7.5 we find the following values:

	Total Movements		Bypass Factor		
No bypassing:					
3 + 4 + 4 + 5 + 3 + 1 + 4 + 5 =	29	×	1	=	29
Bypassing one workplace:					
3 + 2 + 3 + 4 + 0 + 2 =	14	×	2	=	28
Bypassing two workplaces:					
1 + 4 + 2 + 3 =	10	×	3	=	30
Bypassing three workplaces:					
2 + 6 =	8	×	4	=	32
					119

This index of 119 provides a base against which other arrangements can be compared. One way of improving the index is to get the larger numbers as close to the diagonal as possible while getting the smaller numbers as far from the diagonal as possible.

Another possibility is to reduce backward movements. The objective would be to get more numbers above the diagonal and fewer numbers below it. The percentage distance moved forward is the index for forward distances divided by the total distance moved. In our example the calculations would be:

	Forward Movements		Bypass Factor		Backward Movements	Bypass Factor
No bypassing	16	×	1	=	16:13	1 = 13
Bypassing one workplace	8	×	2	=	16: 6	2 = 12
Bypassing two workplaces	5	×	3	=	15: 5	3 = 15
Bypassing three workplaces	2	×	4	=	8: 6	4 = 24
					55	64

So the percentage distance moved forward is

$$\frac{55}{55 + 64} = 46 \text{ percent}$$

When the distances between various workplaces vary, a simple adjustment can be made to construct a travel chart. In such a case the number of movements from one workplace to another is multiplied by the distance from the midpoint of one to the midpoint of another to give the total distance traveled. For example, if A is 6 feet wide and is placed next to B, which is 2 feet wide, the distance from A to B is 4 feet (6 + 2 ÷ 2). If there are three movements from A to B, the total distance traveled is 12 feet. In this way a travel chart can be constructed using the same methodology as suggested above and different configurations tried to reduce the distance that employees move.

Product Flow

Where large quantities of heavy material are moved, it is better to construct a travel chart based on product movement. The methodology is similar to that described above except that the amount of weight multiplied by the distance covered is used instead of the number of feet traveled by an employee.

A travel chart is constructed by multiplying the distance traveled between two workplaces by the amount of material moved. If, for example, A and C are 4 feet apart and 300 pounds of material travels from A to C, the travel chart would indicate the index from A to C to be 1,200. The amount of product flow for a given arrangement of workplaces is found by totaling the sums of each column. Various workplace arrangements can then be tried to find the one that minimizes product movement. Product movement can be minimized by locating workplaces involving large quantities of material close together.

TASK PLANNING

Task planning involves the "analysis of specific actions involved in carrying out a job, in order to establish a more productive procedure for completing that job" [18].

The task to be analyzed is chosen and the various factors affecting it determined. The accessibility and storage of the raw materials used in performing the job is one such factor. Since handling materials does not add to their value, such handling should be kept to a minimum. How far an employee has to walk to get the raw food items prior to preparation will affect the amount of time and effort taken to complete the job.

Figure 7.6 illustrates what can be achieved. Prior to analysis a cook had to walk 235 steps to prepare a batch of macaroni. The process involved:

- Ten steps to the pot-and-pan rack to get the pan
- Thirty steps to the sink to add the water
- Fifteen steps to the range carrying the pan and the water
- Fifty steps to the storeroom while the water is heating, to get the macaroni
- Fifty steps back to the range
- Ten steps to the drawer in the salad table for a spoon
- Ten steps back to the range
- Fifteen steps to the cabinet for salt
- Fifteen steps back to the range
- Fifteen steps to the sink for a little more water
- Fifteen steps back to the range

Storing the macaroni in the lower cabinet, using the steam-jacketed kettle instead of the range, locating the spoon on a rack above the table, having a hot-water faucet above the kettle, and remembering to get the salt and the macaroni at the same time reduces the procedure to 50 steps. The cook begins at the baker's table, walks 10 steps to the steam-jacketed table, turns on the hot-water faucet located above it, fills the kettle, and turns on the heat, walks 20 steps to the cabinet for the macaroni and salt, walks back to the kettle, and adds the macaroni and salt with a spoon that is located on a rack over the kettle.

Next, the process used in completing the task is identified. In the kitchen this means identifying every item on the menu and its proposed preparation method. The desired quality level and the quantity to be produced must also be determined, as both will have an impact on the process to be used. For example, hamburger patties can be prepared in different ways depending on the quantity to be produced. Large quantities can be readied by spreading the meat evenly in a rectangular baking pan, covering the pan with waxed paper, flattening with a rolling pin, and cutting into squares prior to cooking. This method presupposes that a square burger is acceptable to the customer. Small quantities can be shaped by hand.

The task itself is also affected by the amount of space employees have to work in, the availability of the right kind of equipment, the number and type of employee, how long it takes to perform the task, and when it has to be done relative to the completion of other tasks. Certain menu items require that several tasks be done at the same time. Of necessity, more than

Figure 7.6a Steps involved in preparing macaroni.

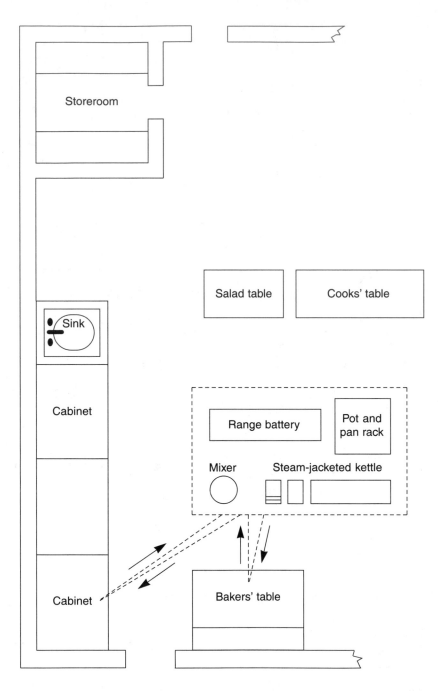

Figure 7.6b Steps involved in preparing macaroni—simplified.

quick bite 7.8
Road to the Top: Larry Zwain

Senior Vice President of Marketing

Newly appointed senior vice president of marketing for McDonalds USA has promised to solicit information from and really listen to McDonalds owners-operators in an effort to strengthen the chain's marketing programs in order to carry on and encourage the company's sales and profit boost of 1998. Zwain says that he will work to grow sales and gives credence to a well-balanced approach to manage, support and preserve the McDonalds brand. The idea is to build frequency and provide patrons with a reason to desire us more.

Zwain was promoted to senior vice president from regional Northeast Division manager for McDonalds. Zwain began his career at McD's after leaving his position as president and chief executive at Boston Market. Zwain has also held the position of president and chief operating officer for PepsiCo Restaurants International, which then included Pizza Hut, KFC and Taco Bell. Zwain's combination of operations and marketing skills made him a prime choice for McDonalds. McDonalds obtained its strongest market share ever at the end of 1998. The 1998 market share outpaced the 1997 market share, which came in at 42.2 percent of the hamburger market.

One of Zwain major goals is to "build on the momentum that the marketing team and ad agencies have created." McDonalds hopes that Zwain's promotion will bring stability to McD's marketing department that was recently realigned to do more strategic planning and support the launch of the chain's "Made for You" food-production system. Zwain reports directly to the president of McDonalds USA and is responsible for an estimated $600 million media budget. McD's USA is comprised of more than 12,000 restaurants.

Source: Cebrzynski, Gregg. "New McD Marketing Chief Zwain Appeals to Franchisees." *Nation's Restaurant News,* v. 33, n. 5, February 1, 1999, pp. 3, 83.

---

one employee will have to be involved. On the other hand, in certain situations, some activities can be completed ahead of service and finished at the last moment.

Procedures can now be established to get the job done as effectively and efficiently as possible. Several questions help in this process.

- Can it be eliminated? The purchase of a potato-peeling machine eliminates the need to peel potatoes by hand.
- Can it be combined? Can one employee perform several different jobs? Can employees work with both hands at the same time?
- Are there unnecessary delays? Are insufficient supplies causing slowdowns in service? One bar the author worked with was experiencing service delays

quick bite 7.9
Restaurant Facilities in 2010

According to the National Restaurant Association the most likely developments regarding restaurant facilities in 2010 are:

- The most prominent design themes will continue to be casual and comfortable.
- More dual concepts will share the same site.
- Smaller pad sites will be available for takeout concepts.
- Standard design plans, taking into account local demographics, will be available from chains.

Source: Restaurant Industry 2010: The Road Ahead (Washington, D.C.: National Restaurant Association, 1999), p. 10.

because management, in an attempt to save on inventory costs, stocked only 12 highball glasses behind the bar. When the bar got busy, servers would have to clear the tables of glasses and have them washed and dried before drinks could be served to additional customers.

- Is there misdirected effort? Can a conveyor belt be used to move food, supplies, and/or dishes? Can wheels be put on equipment to roll rather than carry it?
- Are employees doing too many unrelated tasks? Have a $5-an-hour employee perform a $5-an-hour task.
- Is work spread evenly? At one hotel, 500 room-service breakfasts were served between 7:00 and 11:00 A.M. In the dining room, service was busiest between 8:30 and 9:00 A.M. Although most of the soiled dishes did not reach the dishwashing area until 10:00 A.M., the entire dishwashing crew was on duty from 7:00 A.M. Upon analysis of the situation, they were brought in at 9:00 A.M.

ENDNOTES

1. Edward A. Kazarian, *Foodservice Facilities Planning,* 3rd ed. (New York: Van Nostrand Reinhold, 1989), pp. 239, 242.

2. Ibid., p. 240.

3. Ibid., pp. 116–119.

4. Ronald E. Millman, "The Hidden Influence," *N.R.A. News,* vol. 6, no. 5, May 1986, pp. 28–29.

5. Carolyn U. Lambert, "Environmental Design," *Cornell Hotel and Restaurant Administration Quarterly,* May 1981, pp. 62–68.

6. Richard E. Hopkins, "Light," *The Consultant,* vol. XVI, no. 4, Fall 1983, pp. 34–37.

7. Marilynn Motto "Profit by Design," *Cornell Hotel and Restaurant Administration Quarterly,* May 1970, pp. 113–116.

8. Kazarian, *Foodservice Facilities Planning,* 3rd ed. p. 401.

9. Ibid., pp. 246–247.

10. Ibid., pp. 393–398.

11. Arthur C. Avery, *A Modern Guide to Foodservice Equipment* (Boston: CBI Publishing Company, 1980), pp. 18–19.

12. Ibid., p. 142.

13. Ibid., p. 150.

14. Ibid., pp. 159–161.

15. Kazarian, *Foodservice Facilities Planning,* p. 272.

16. Ibid., p. 275.

17. Boger, Carl A., "A Comparison Between Different Delivery Systems of Quick Service Food Facilities," *Hospitality Research Journal,* vol. 18, no. 3/vol. 19, no. 1, 1995, pp. 111–124.

18. Robert Christie Mill, *Managing for Productivity in the Hospitality Industry* (New York: Van Nostrand Reinhold, 1989), p. 65.

CHAPTER EIGHT

FOOD AND BEVERAGE: FROM SUPPLIER TO CUSTOMER

learning objectives

By the end of this chapter you should be able to:

1. Develop procedures for the effective purchasing, receiving, storing, and issuing of items used in the operation.

2. Compare and contrast the various production and service systems.

3. Illustrate the importance and use of purchase specifications, yield, standardized recipes, and portion control in implementing a system of cost control.

The commandments of nouvelle cuisine

1. *Avoid unnecessary complications*
2. *Shorten cooking times*
3. *Shop regularly at the market*
4. *Don't hang or marinate game*
5. *Avoid too-rich sauces*
6. *Return to regional cooking*
7. *Investigate the latest techniques*
8. *Consider diet and health*
9. *Invent constantly*
   Gault-Millau, quoted in *Dining Out*.

Source: Dornenburg, Andrew and Karen Page, *Dining Out* (New York, NY: John Wiley & Sons, Inc., 1998).

STEPS IN THE PROCESS

The process by which food and beverage items find their way to the customer consists of several steps:

- Purchasing. Items are ordered from vendors.
- Receiving. Items are delivered by vendors and accepted at the restaurant.
- Storage. Items are kept in a secured area until needed by the kitchen staff.
- Issuing. Items are released from storage to the kitchen staff.
- Preparation. Items are prepared for cooking.
- Cooking. Items are prepared for customers.
- Service. Items are served to the customer.

After service there is a need to wash dirty dishes, pots, and pans and dispose of waste. At each stage there are specific procedures to be put into place to ensure that costs are controlled while quality is maintained.

PURCHASING

Importance

According to Khan, "The primary function of any type of foodservice operation is to convert raw food into cooked products" [1]. Profits come from converting and serving the food as efficiently as possible. High-quality dishes come from high-quality

Courtesy of King's Fish House.

University Restaurant Group, located in Southern California, changed its name to King's Seafood Co. after sealing a sweet deal with Santa Monica Seafood Co. that allows King's Fish House locations to operate at lower costs and improve kitchen efficiency. The name change reflects the owners' commitment to seafood, according to Sam King, president and chief executive. The company operates three King's Fish House locations, all of which house a dual-concept including the exciting King Crab Lounge and the capacious King's Fish House tableservice dining room.

The contract King's entered into with Santa Monica Seafood Co. allows King's a competitive advantage over the competition like the McCormick & Schmick's chain that operates out of Portland, Oregon. King's units currently average $1 million more in annual unit sales than McCormick & Schmick's locations. The two chains will face head-on competition in 2001 when McCormick & Schmick's Long Beach location opens.

King's Seafood Co. actually got its start in 1983 with a steak-house restaurant in Long Beach, California. The company operates a total of nine restaurants. The first King's Fish House featured a "classic neighborhood" style dining room and a King Crab Lounge, which is designed to look like a Louisiana crab shack. The restaurants feature a huge selection of oysters and forty-eight different appetizers and almost four dozen grilled, broiled, sautéed and fried seafood entrees.

Part of King's success, other than the wild and fun environment, is the strategic alliance they have created with the Santa Monica Seafood Co., which is now King's only supplier. Under the terms of the contract, King's has two full-time seafood cutters inside one of Santa Monica's Seafood Co.'s facilities who select and cut fish for King's units as it is delivered. King's employees are allotted 2,000 square feet of space. The cutters place the ready-to-cook fish into containers that fit directly into the restaurant's reach-in refrigerators.

The seafood distributor also dedicates a delivery truck to King's locations and has a dedicated phone and fax line linked directly to King's Seafood Co. The deal benefits King's in many ways including increasing purchasing volume, lowering food and labor costs and appropriate temperature control from the prep area to storage, right until the fish reaches the cooking line. According to King controlling seafood cost and quality is key to the concept's success.

Source: "King's Fish House," *Nation's Restaurant News*, May 17, 1999, v. 33, n. 20, pp. 58–60.

ingredients—thus the importance of purchasing. The objective is "to obtain the right quality and quantity at the right time and price and from the right source" [2].

Process

Forecast. Once the menu is set, the number of servings of each item needed for each meal period must be forecast. This serves as the basis for the quantities of each item to be ordered. The easiest forecasting method, and the one used most often, is to use the average number of dishes ordered in the past. Poor forecasting results in too many or too few items ordered. If too many items are ordered, there is increased waste; too few items mean that the restaurant will run out of specific items and customers will be dissatisfied. Restaurants are increasingly using computer systems to improve their forecasts.

Quantities Needed. A standard procedure for identifying how much needs to be purchased involves five steps [3]:

1. Determine, from the recipe, the factor to be used to determine the number of servings. If the recipe is for 50 and the number of servings needed is 150, the factor will be 150 divided by 50, or 3.
2. Multiply all the ingredients in the recipe by the factor. This will give the edible portion (EP) weight of each item. The "as purchased" (AP) amount of each item is found by dividing the EP by the percent yield (see above).
3. Select the wholesale purchase unit (case, box, carton, etc.) nearest to the AP weight.
4. Complete the calculations for every item on the menu for that day.
5. Calculate the amounts needed for the delivery. The amount ordered will depend on such things as how much inventory is on hand, the storage space available, seasonal availability, and the time between deliveries. The latter will vary by operation depending on the kind of service given by the suppliers. It is better for an operation to have the supplier maintain inventory rather than having the restaurant keep too many supplies on hand. An order form can then be filled out and the order processed.

Buying Methods

Informal. Purchasing may be done formally or informally. Informal buying usually occurs over the telephone. Several vendors may be called for a price quotation and the order placed with the lowest bidder. This method is ideal for a small operation, as there is little paperwork and the buying can be done quickly. It may be possible to take advantage of lower costs in the marketplace. However, because prices have not been agreed upon ahead of time, price increases will result in higher costs.

Buying can be done on a cash basis at markets or after getting quotations from various vendors. A quotation-and-order sheet would be made out, listing specifications for the various items needed. Several vendors would then be called

quick bite 8.2
Finding a Distributor

The distributor that serves a restaurant can often make or break that facility. If deliveries are constantly late or wrong, it can spell disaster for a restaurateur. A distributor must be a real business partner; the right distributor can contribute a great deal to an operator. An effective distributor can promote effective supply chain management, low delivery costs, technological advantages and value-added services. The following items should be considered when choosing a foodservice distributor.

Does Size Matter?

The food distribution business is one where bigger is better. Only a large company can support an efficient nationwide system. Smaller regional companies often have to sub-contract with a distributor not hired by the restaurant just to reach it. This can cost an operator money and time. A huge distributor can also provide lower prices due to their leverage and buying power. Small savings of just pennies per product can cumulatively save a distributor's customers millions of dollars per year.

What Else Can They Do?

Providing food is almost secondary when it comes to choosing a foodservice distributor. The real differentiation between distribution companies is how they impact a restaurant's operations. Do they provide value-added service? Do they improve the unit's efficiency, convenience and cost structure? Distributors can add value in freight and inventory management, logistics services, and order processing and new product/promotions support.

Are They Technically Superior?

As in most industries, food distribution companies can use technology to eliminate redundant tasks, improve communications, reduce confusion and greatly increase efficiency and productivity. A distributor, in order to be really effective, should have system capabilities that give an operator a competitive advantage. Examples of technical improvements include computerized ordering systems and automated routing systems.

Are They Fair and Honest?

When comparing the prices between different distributors, it is important that an operator look for hidden costs. Many distributors will quote extremely low per case costs, only to tack on freight costs or charge up-front payments in addition to other elusive costs. It is important to realize, however, that the distributor needs to make a profit as well. Prices that are too good to be true probably are. The cheapest distributor does not typically have the best service.

Source: Marshall, Raymond. "Issues to Consider in Hiring a Distributor." *Nation's Restaurant News,* November 3, 1997 v. 31, n. 41, p. 64.

and asked to quote prices for these items. Space would be available on the form to write down the various prices. The cost of items purchased should be lower because prices are being compared. However, more time is needed to compare the quotes of the vendors.

Under the blank-check method, certain vendors are given authority to deliver various items and bill the restaurant without quoting prices beforehand. This would be done on a very limited basis with vendors who have shown they can be trusted and for items that are in short supply. It is advisable to set a range of prices beyond which the vendor must communicate with the restaurateur.

For items whose price varies erratically, the cost-plus or fixed-markup method ensures that the supplier will have a guaranteed profit, negotiated ahead of time and typically 10 to 30 percent over cost.

Formal. There are also a variety of formal buying methods. The most common formal method of buying is the competitive-bid method under which vendors submit written quotes based on specifications sent out by the restaurateur. Bidding is competitive, so a good and fair price can be negotiated. Because everything is done in writing, the process takes longer but provides written safeguards should disputes arise.

In another form, prices may be negotiated with vendors before the formal written bid. Prices are usually set for a relatively long period. Under the standing-order method, vendors send items at predetermined intervals. Milk and bakery items are usually purchased in this way. Once the vendor has been chosen and the quantities set, time savings result because the decision does not have to be revisited every time an order is needed. The quantities ordered should be checked periodically to ensure that the amounts bought are appropriate to the needs of the business.

Prices, but not quantities, are determined under a future-contract method. For a specified amount of time, prices of specific items are guaranteed.

Finally, under the buy-and-hold method, the restaurateur buys large quantities of an item at a good price and the vendor is responsible for storing the item until it is needed by the operation. In this way the restaurateur can take advantage of cost savings even if he or she does not have large storage space.

Standards

The following items indicate specific guidelines for purchasing food items.

Fresh Fruits and Vegetables
1. Specific standards can be obtained from the United States Department of Agriculture (USDA).
2. Because these items are perishable, specify the grade desired at the time of delivery rather than the time of shipping.
3. Look for "bright, attractive colors, good shape and appearance, good proportion of weight and size, and absence of any mechanical damage or signs of decay" [4].
4. Specify size, especially for fruit. Smaller sizes tend to have more flavor, while larger sizes are important for display.

Processed Fruits and Vegetables

1. As specified by the USDA, processed fruits and vegetables come in the following grades:

Fruits	Vegetables
U.S. Grade A or U.S. Fancy	U.S. Grade A or U.S. Fancy
U.S. Grade B or U.S. Choice	U.S. Grade B or U.S. Extra-Standard
U.S. Grade C or U.S. Standard	U.S. Grade C or U.S. Standard

U.S. Grade A items are "practically perfect" and score between 85 and 100 points; U.S. Grade B items are "reasonably perfect" and score between 75 and 84 points; U.S. Grade C items are "fairly perfect" and score between 60 and 74 points. For items where there are only two grades, A and B, the specifications for A are as above, while for B they must be "fairly perfect" and score between 70 and 84 points.

2. Specify minimum drained weight needed, as this is a better indicator of yield.
3. Syrup density is important because the heavier the syrup, the less chance the product will break up. Also, for dietetic menus, the sugar content of the syrup is important.

Frozen Vegetables.   As above, with the following notes:

1. They may be packed in sugar or syrup.
2. They may be treated with an antioxidant to prevent browning.
3. Salt may have been added as a preservative.

Meats and Meat Products

1. Meats are graded on the basis of quality and yield.
2. The various grades are U.S. Prime (highest grade), U.S. Choice, U.S. Good (lacks juiciness, relatively tender), U.S. Standard (tender), U.S. Commercial (lacks tenderness, more waste), U.S. Utility, U.S. Cutter, and U.S. Canner (for processed meat products).

Poultry and Eggs

1. Available grades are U.S. Grade A, U.S. Grade B, U.S. Grade C, U.S. Procurement Grade I, and U.S. Procurement Grade II.
2. Order poultry as follows: breasts, breasts with ribs, wishbones, legs, wings, drumsticks, thighs, halves, quarters, and backs.
3. Eggs are graded by size and most are packed in 30-dozen cases. The grades most often used in restaurants are large and medium. Medium eggs are a better buy if they are 12 percent or more cheaper than large eggs, while small eggs are a better buy if they are 24 percent or more cheaper than large eggs [5].

Size	Weight (oz) per Dozen	Weight (lb) per 30-Dozen Case
Jumbo	30	56
Extra large	27	50.5
Large	24	45
Medium	21	39.5
Small	18	34
Peewee	15	28

Milk and Milk Products

1. Specify the type of product, grade, milk fat content, and type of packaging.
2. Pasteurization is done to destroy bacteria; homogenization is done to prevent the formation of cream and results in an enhanced flavor.

Fish and Shellfish

1. Items are available as U.S. Grade A (top quality), U.S. Grade B (good quality), and U.S. Grade C (fairly good quality).
2. Specify whether or not the skin should be left on and whether the item should be fresh, chilled, or frozen.
3. Fish may be whole (just as they came from the water), drawn (entrails removed), dressed (cleaned with head on), chunks, steaks, or fillets.

Control

Within the purchase function two important aspects of control are the need for purchase specifications and an understanding of yield.

Purchase Specifications. Specifications are "the description of a particular commodity in terms of its size, quality, or condition" [6]. Using specifications lets the vendors know exactly what is required. Specifications ("specs") should be detailed, in writing, and cover the following [7]:

1. Common, trade, or brand name of the product
2. Amount to be purchased in the most commonly used units
3. Recognized trade, federal, or local grade
4. Name and size of the basic container
5. Count and size of the items or units within the basic container
6. Ranges in weight, thickness, or size
7. Minimum and maximum trims, or fat content percentages
8. Degree of maturity or stage of ripening
9. Type of processing required (for example, freeze-dried)
10. Type of packaging desired

Yields. The yield percentage must be known before ordering. The yield percentage indicates how much usable food will be obtained from a particular purchased item. Standardized recipes will indicate the number of portions from a specific item. The number should take waste and shrinkage into account. If this has not been done, the yield can be calculated as follows [8]:

$$\text{percentage of yield} = \frac{\text{weight after cooking}}{\text{weight before cooking}} \times 100$$

The yield percentage will vary depending on such things as the cooking temperature and type of oven and percentage of fat in the item. Cooking at lower temperatures, for example, will result in less shrinkage or waste.

Food can be purchased in one of two ways. Food as purchased (AP) refers to items bought without prepreparation. Edible portion (EP) indicates that the item has been processed and is ready for cooking. The EP to be ordered is calculated as follows [9]:

$$EP = AP - \text{shrinkage (or preparation losses)}$$

$$\text{percentage shrinkage or preparation losses} = \frac{\text{losses due to shrinkage or preparation (wt)}}{AP \text{ (wt)}} \times 100$$

$$= \frac{AP \text{ (wt)} - EP \text{ (wt)}}{AP \text{ (wt)}}$$

RECEIVING

The objective in the receiving function is to ensure that the items delivered are exactly what was ordered. Ideally, for quantity and quality verification, the person who ordered the item should receive it. In large operations this is not feasible.

Methods

There are three methods that can be set up for receiving goods: invoice, blind, and partially blind [10]. Under the invoice method, the delivery is accompanied by an invoice prepared by the supplier and listing the quantities, prices, and specifications for the order. The order is compared against the invoice by someone at the restaurant. This method is simple and fast. It works only if the person receiving the delivery takes the time to thoroughly compare the physical order to the invoice.

Under a blind receiving method the invoice accompanying the order is blank or, at most, lists only the items being delivered. The receiving clerk is forced to physically count the number of items being delivered and judge their quality to complete the invoice. A separate and fully completed invoice is sent directly from the supplier to the person in charge of purchasing. This supplier-supplied invoice is compared to the one filled out by the receiving clerk and any discrepancies reported to the vendor. While this method is very accurate, it is also very time consuming.

The partially blind receiving method attempts to combine the primary advantages of the previous methods. The delivery comes with an invoice that contains all relevant information about the order except the quantities delivered. The receiving clerk is forced to physically count the number of items received and input those data on the invoice that comes with the order. This invoice is then compared with the order and a later invoice sent by the vendor.

Space Requirements

The following tasks are involved in receiving [11]: examining, moving, receiving, unpacking, and verifying. The amount of space required for receiving depends on the number, type, and size of deliveries. If deliveries are accepted only between certain restricted hours, for example, the receiving area will be larger than if deliveries are spread out over a longer period.

Large deliveries might require specialized equipment for handling the goods as they come in. This might range from a cart to a moving conveyor belt system.

Getting the distributor to make smaller, more frequent deliveries will mean that the restaurant will require less moving equipment and storage space for both perishable and nonperishable items. If moving equipment is required, some provision will have to be made for its storage. In addition, space must be available to verify the order and dispose of packing materials.

Practices

Good receiving practices involve several steps [12]:

1. An invoice or delivery sheet should be used to verify each delivery.
2. All deliveries should be checked in the following ways:
   - Each container should be inspected for signs of external damage.
   - Each item should be weighed and/or counted, checked, and noted on the receiving invoice.
   - When appropriate (as for eggs), convert the weight of the item into the relevant quantity. Conversion tables should be readily available.
   - Remove all packing before weighing items.
   - Tag all wholesale cuts of meat. Meat tags consist of two parts; one stays on the meat while the other goes to accounting. The tag identifies the supplier, cut, weight, and unit price and is used for control purposes as well as to ensure the first in, first out (FIFO) system of inventory control.
3. Verify the quality of the items delivered. This can be done by random inspection using the specification guidelines developed by the restaurant and/or standard USDA criteria. Date all items in order that the operation use a FIFO inventory method. Expiration dates should be identified on cans

quick bite 8.3
Ethnic Menu Items

Foodservice operators are continually looking for ways to appeal to customers, differentiate their operation and increase profits. As a result, many restaurateurs have added ethnic items to their menus to accomplish all of the above. Ethnic items meet consumer demand, increase menu variety and can have low food costs. More than two-thirds of all chains including casual, family and fine-dining, high-volume independent operations and non-commercial operators offer at least one ethnic item on their menus and two-thirds of those plan on adding more.

A survey conducted by Strategic Foodservice Solutions for *Nation's Restaurant News* revealed that more than 90 percent of operators say that ethnic cuisine is popular with their customers. The majority also feels that offering ethnic items enhances customers' perception of the operation overall. Another 80 percent feel that ethnic foods make their stores look "cutting edge." And two-thirds agree that ethnic foods increase patronage and distinguish their chain from their competitors'.

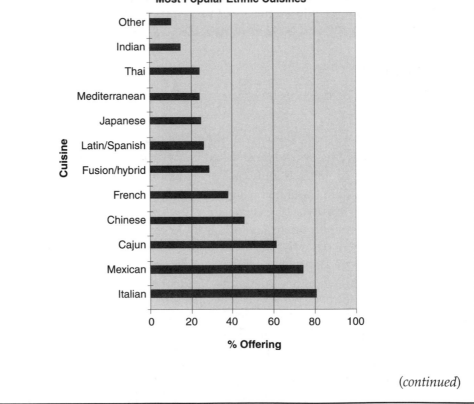

Most Popular Ethnic Cuisines

(*continued*)

Restaurant Management: Customers, Operations, and Employees

and packages and cans specifically checked for bulging and leakage. Inspection stamps should be verified on meat items.

4. Checking temperatures is particularly important for frozen or refrigerated items. Recommended standards are [13]:
   - Frozen foods, 0 to 20°F
   - Dairy products, 38 to 46°F
   - Meat and poultry, 33 to 38°F
   - Fish and shellfish, 23 to 30°F

5. Any shortages or other discrepancies should be noted and the invoice signed, dated, and stamped. One copy is kept at receiving, another sent to management, and a third given to the delivery person.

6. All items should be sent immediately to the appropriate storage area.

7. Invoices would then be filed.

STORAGE

Storage will be needed for dry, refrigerated, and frozen goods in addition to beverages and nonfood supplies. The objective is to have enough items on hand so that the restaurant does not run out while minimizing loss caused by spoilage and/or theft. Spoilage comes from holding items for too long. Excessive amounts of various food and beverage items tie up money and space.

In storage the following tasks are common [14]: inspecting, inventorying, issuing, rotating, and storing.

Space Requirements

The number of days of storage to be provided determines how large this area must be. An isolated resort community that gets deliveries once a week will require more storage space than a restaurant that can demand daily deliveries.

Since buying in bulk will costs less, it is desirable to analyze the reduced costs of buying in bulk against the cost of providing additional space.

The following rules of thumb can be used to estimate the storage space required [15]:

- Two to four weeks' supply for dry storage goods
- A weight per meal of 1/4 to 1/2 pound
- An average density of 45 pounds per cubic foot

If an operation plans on serving 400 meals a day and wishes a two-week supply of dry goods, the space requirements can be estimated as follows:

Required storage will be for 400 meals × 14 days	= 5600 meals
Total weight (1/2 pound per meal)	= 2800 pounds
Total volume (45 pounds per cubic foot)	= 62.2 cubic feet
Shelving required (at a height of 1.5 feet) (62.2 ÷ 1.5 feet)	= 41.5 square feet
Length of shelving required if shelving is 9 inches wide = 53.3 feet (41.5 ÷ 0.75 foot)	

Convenience and accessibility are the principles upon which storage areas are laid out. They should be designed such that heavy and/or bulky materials are moved as little and as easily as possible. Many operations will find that a central storage area combined with smaller storage spaces scattered throughout the facility will cut down on the movement of people and goods. For example, a hotel with several restaurants will benefit from one major store serving all restaurants, each of which has space for storing small amounts of frequently used products. A combination of one walk-in and several reach-in refrigerators spread throughout the operation can reduce the walking employees would have to do to get required items. A restaurant serving over 300 to 400 meals a day should have a walk-in refrigerator.

It should be noted, however, that more storage areas will lead to increased inventory and greater control challenges. Combination walk-in and reach-in storage facilities greatly assist in increasing access to and within storage areas. Cleaning of walk-in storage areas is made easier by having items stored at least 8 inches off the floor. Mobile bins and containers also achieve this objective. All chemical items and cleaning supplies should be stored separately from foods because of the contamination risk.

Dry Storage. Dry storage for food items requires a temperature between 50 and 70°F and a relative humidity of 50 percent. As such, heat-generating equipment should not be located in these areas. Similarly, pipes carrying hot water should be insulated to prevent temperatures from rising beyond the highs noted above.

Refrigeration. Fresh meats, vegetables, fruits, dairy products, beverages, and leftover items require refrigeration at temperatures between 32 and

37°F. Items should not be in direct contact with the floor, walls, and/or ceiling. In addition, air circulation is needed to help eliminate odors and remove moisture.

Calculations similar to those above can be made for refrigerator and freezer storage. The weight per meal of refrigerator and freezer items will vary from 0.75 to 1 pound. The average density of refrigerator and freezer items is approximately 30 and 40 pounds per cubic foot, respectively. With refrigerated areas, temperature control is vital. Periodic checks should be made of the temperature at various points in the storage area. As with dry storage areas, items should not be in direct contact with floors, ceilings, and/or walls. Refrigerated areas can also be used to store cooked food items. It is imperative that cooked and raw items not come into contact with each other. Additionally, hot, cooked items should not be placed in the refrigerator as, in cooling down, they will increase the temperature of the surrounding area.

Frozen Foods. If frozen foods are used, thawing facilities, sufficient for one day's production, will have to be provided. Frozen foods should be stored at 210 to 215°F. It is possible, and highly desirable, to have a layout wherein walk-in freezers open into walk-in refrigerators [16]. Thawed food items should never be refrozen. As above, raw food items should never come into contact with items that have been cooked and then frozen.

ISSUING

For control purposes it is advisable that as few people as possible have access to the storage and issuing areas. Some type of requisition form, signed by someone in authority, is needed before food and beverage items can be released from storage. Such forms aid in inventory control and analyzing menu costs. The objective is to ensure that only authorized personnel are allowed to requisition food and beverage items.

Control

A system of inventory management helps ensure cost control. The inventory refers to the items available in storage. Commonly, two types of inventory are kept: physical and perpetual [17]. A physical inventory refers to the actual number of each item on hand. It is typically taken on the last day of each month.

Perpetual inventories are continuous records of what is bought and issued. While time consuming, especially if manual records are kept, the perpetual inventory will alert management to what must be reordered when, as well as to items that are overstocked.

Food and beverage costs are calculated on the basis of the value of the inventory as follows: cost of food (beverage) for a specific period = value of opening inventory + food (beverage) purchases after opening inventory − value of closing inventory.

PREPARATION

Function

In the production area, functions tend to be divided into meat/fish/poultry preparation, vegetable preparation, salad preparation, and sandwich preparation. In smaller operations the salad and sandwich and/or the vegetable and salad functions are often combined. The objective is to prepare items to predetermined quality levels in sufficient quantities to meet customer demands while minimizing waste.

The preparation area is where items are made ready for final cooking. Operations that purchase preportioned items—a growing trend—will have minimal need of such facilities for the preparation of meat, poultry, and fish. Similarly,

WOLLENSKY'S GRILL

Soup	4.50
Mixed Green Salad	5.50
Shrimp Cocktail	12.50
Fried Zucchini & Onion Rings	6.75
Fresh Lump Crabmeat	12.50

Our Cruvinet Has 7 Vintage Cabernets By the Glass

The Grill Sirloin	25.75
English Cut Prime Rib	22.50
Roast Beef Hash	16.50
Wollensky's Burger	9.75
Memphis Ribs	18.50
Lamb Chops	19.75
Grilled Chicken Club	15.75
Filet Mignon	24.50
Veal Chop	22.50
Filet Tips	18.50

Lemon Pepper Chicken	18.75

Chef's Salad	16.75
Cobb Salad	17.75
Stone Crabs	- -
Sea Scallops	17.75
Capt. Kissane's Catch of the Day	18.75
Wollensky's Steamed Lobster	19.50

Smith & Wollensky's Menu Available

Cheesecake	5.50
Chocolate Cake	6.50
Melon or Ice Cream	4.50
Apple Betty	5.50
Chocolate Basket	7.50
Fresh Fruit	6.75
Pecan Pie	6.50
Napoleon	6.50
Apple Strudel	6.50

We are open every day from 11:30 A.M. to 2 A.M.

Our classic Smith & Wollensky steak knife is available for purchase.
49th Street Off of 3rd Ave., N.Y. 10017, Telephone: 753-0444

Wollensky's Grill—a classic! Courtesy of Wollensky's Grill, New York City using preprocessed and/or frozen vegetables has reduced the need for space to perform the traditional functions of washing, cutting, and chopping.

Space Requirements

Equipment layout in this area can be arranged in a straight line because the tasks involved in preparing food occur in a logical sequence. Vegetables are trimmed, washed, and reduced in size, in that order. A worktable for trimming can be placed next to a sink for washing and draining, which, in turn, can be placed next to the area where vegetables are cut, diced, or chopped.

Because vegetables come from the storage area and go on to the main cooking or salad preparation area, the trimming table is located close to the stor-

---

quick bite 8.4
Healthy Dining

More and more people want healthy meal options. Here is how to deliver:

1. Use egg substitutes, flavored with herbs. The Inn at Twin Linden in Churchtown, Pennsylvania, makes a light eggs benedict with grilled portobello mushroom instead of bacon, and a tomato confit instead of hollandaise.
2. Go lean with the protein—use poultry sausage, marinated chicken breasts, and fish. The Shelburne Inn in Seaview, Washington, has a smoked seafood hash with smoked oysters, salmon, sturgeon, and onions.
3. Use whole-grain and multigrain items. IHOP offers a harvest-grain pancake made with whole grains.
4. Offer hot cereals—try oatmeal with raisins, cinnamon, low-fat or non-fat milk, honey, and yogurt. The Greenbrier serves oatmeal with sour cherries.
5. Serve fruit—baked apples, grapefruit soaked in Grand Marnier.
6. Serve bagels, muffins, and breads. The bread at the Firehook Bakery and Coffee House in Alexandria, Virginia, is naturally leavened, made with organic flour and baked in a wood-burning stove.
7. Offer breakfast shakes with powdered milk, yogurt, and fruit.
8. Offer sugar-free condiments.
9. Serve juices—pear and pineapple, carrot, and apple.

Source: Somerville, Sylvia. "Getting Diners Off to a Healthy Start," *Restaurants USA*, v. 15, n. 1, January 1995, pp. 32–36.

---

age area and vegetables are chopped near the cooking and salad preparation areas.

Vegetables will have to be stored temporarily prior to processing and a waste disposal area will also have to be included. Similar considerations are necessary for a salad preparation area.

COOKING

Service Systems

Minor and Cichy have identified four major foodservice systems based on the extent to which processed foods are used [18]. Many operations use a combination of systems. The four systems are:

- Convenience systems (maximum use of processed foods)
- Conventional systems
- Ready-food systems
- Commissary systems (minimum use of processed foods)

In convenience or assembly–serve systems, foods are purchased completely prepared and assembly, consisting of heating and/or minor preparation, is done in the operation. Although food cost is high and selections limited, only unskilled, low-cost labor is needed at the service point. Less preparation equipment and energy are required, but more storage space, particularly frozen storage, is needed.

There is some concern over product quality and customer acceptance of various convenience items. Foods are available in bulk, preportioned, and preplated form. Bulk convenience foods are portioned either before or after heating; preportioned items require only assembly and heating, while preplated foods need only be heated before serving.

A conventional system is one in which dishes are prepared from raw ingredients in the restaurant itself. Yet compromises, because of increased labor costs, are being made. Few operations have their own bakery or butcher shop on the premises. More employees, equipment, energy, and space are needed in a conventional system compared to one relying on convenience items.

In a ready-food system the food is prepared on-premises, then chilled (cook–chill) or frozen (cook–freeze) for service later. Chilled items are usually held for 1 to 3 days; frozen foods for 30 to 60 days. This system is more complex than the previous two because of the need to package, distribute, and store the food. Management has more control over the handling, quality, and cost of the food because the items are prepared ahead of time. Consequently, there is less of a pressure atmosphere than when cooking items to order. These systems are best suited for large operations such as hospitals, airlines, banquets, and schools.

In a commissary or satellite system, food is prepared in large quantities at a central source and distributed to various service outlets. Economies of scale are possible in purchasing and production, and quality assurance is made easier.

Distributing the food to the various satellite units is a major part of the system. Care must be taken to ensure that food safety is assured as the items are moved from the central facility to the outlying units.

Space Requirements

The design of the cooking area is dependent on the type and amount of items to be prepared. A market analysis should determine what items will go on the menu; a market forecast will predict the amounts to be cooked at any time. From this estimate the type and size of equipment needed and the relationship of one piece to another can be determined.

The amount of space required for baking will depend on whether or not the restaurant prepares its baked goods from scratch. Most operations use either basic mixes or prepared unbaked goods requiring thawing and baking rather than the full line of baking functions.

Goods come into the cooking area from storage and preparation areas; utensils and cooking containers come from the pot-and-pan-washing locations. Food goes out to the service, salad, and sandwich preparation areas.

Equipment that produces heat and/or moisture must either be located under ventilating hoods or have their own ventilating systems. Equipment that uses steam to cook the food must be installed carefully using curbs or in depressed areas of the floor.

Vents and grill openings that are required for equipment that needs air for ventilation or cooling must not be blocked. The location of the air conditioning for the main kitchen is extremely important in order that the air be kept reasonably cool while the food and cooking equipment remains reasonably hot.

If a great deal of baking is done, the cooking and baking areas can be placed close together in order that they can share kettles, ovens and mixers. Both should be located close to the pot-washing area.

Where cooks and bakers expect to use the same equipment extensively, employee work times can be staggered to ensure full utilization of equipment without employees getting into each other's way. Bakers, for example, might work at night preparing the following day's pastries and breads.

A well-thought-out layout would have a proof box, an oven, and a landing table next to each other to handle the baking of bread. Baker's tables tend to be centrally located to permit easy access to storage areas and frequently used equipment. Space has to be available for storage of baking supplies and finished items. Perishable items will have to be refrigerated prior to being moved to the serving area.

Principles of Cooking

Moist-Heat Cooking.   Cooking is done by one of two methods: moist-heat or dry-heat cooking. Meat contains collagen, a fibrous matter that makes it tough. A similar tissue in vegetables is cellulose. Moist heat dissolves both to render the meat and vegetable tender. This is the reason that tougher cuts of meat are cooked in liquid.

The liquid used might be water, milk, tomato juice, wine, broth, or stock [19]. The most common cooking methods using liquid are boiling, blanching, braising, poaching, simmering, steaming, and stewing.

Boiling involves immersing the item in water at a temperature of 212°F (100°C). Boiling tends to take valuable nutrients out of the food being cooked. They remain in the water, which can be used for soup, stock, or a sauce. Foods tend to be boiled for a short period of time. Vegetables may be undercooked by boiling and transferred to a steam table, where the cooking process is completed as they wait to be served. Meats are simmered rather than boiled, while the process is not recommended for eggs, poultry, or fish because of the harm boiling does to the nutrients contained in these items.

Blanching or scalding involves exposing the food to boiling water for a very short period. Some items are blanched to remove some of their strong flavor, while others are blanched to dislodge external membranes. Blanching makes it easier to remove the skin from some fruits and vegetables. The term blanching also refers to the cooking of vegetables in deep oil, almost to the point of doneness, prior to finishing just before service. Parboiling involves keeping the food in the water longer and is used to cook the item partially before finishing it with another form of cooking. Squash, for example, may be parboiled before baking.

The appearance and taste of cooked vegetables and fruits are influenced by the alkalinity or acidity of the liquid in which they are cooked. Thus green vegetables turn drab in an acidic liquid, while the color is intensified in an alkaline medium. The latter type of liquid, however, may negatively affect the structure and presence of vitamins in the vegetables. To maintain as many nutrients as possible, cooking should be kept to a minimum.

In braising, meat is cooked in a small amount of fat in a covered container. Meat may be browned before stewing—called brun—to give it color. Blond braising involves no searing. Searing the food, according to a number of studies, does not help seal in the juices. The juices in which the meat is stewed add to its flavor. Less tender cuts of meat can be made tender by simmering in a liquid for a long time at a low temperature. Stewing is closely related to braising. Whereas braising involves cooking whole or sliced foods, stewing involves chopped or cubed foods. Stewing uses more liquid compared to braising, the liquid covering the entire item being cooked. A heavy pot is used to ensure even cooking. Dishes may be browned (brun) first or not (blond). Thicker stews result from cooking without a lid over the pot.

Poaching is the term given to cooking in a liquid at a temperature below the boiling point of water. It is useful for foods that require gentle handling and low-temperature cooking, such as eggs and fish. Poultry, particularly bigger birds, are moister, more tender, and more flavorful when poached than when roasted.

Simmering involves cooking in a liquid whose temperature is between 185 and 205°F. When meat is placed in cold water and brought to a simmer, it has more flavor than when added to hot water and cooked. Chefs call simmering "let the liquid smile, not laugh out loud" [20].

Restaurant Management: Customers, Operations, and Employees

Steaming food in the vapor of boiling-hot water is an excellent method for retaining nutrients in the food being cooked. Shrinkage is reduced and flavor maintained. Cereal products are typically steamed or boiled. Salt and a little oil can be added to the water for best results.

Dry-Heat Cooking.   Dry-heat cooking is used for the more tender foods and includes baking, barbecuing, broiling, grilling, ovenizing, roasting, and frying. Traditional barbecuing means roasting food in a covered pit, usually at a low temperature. The term now includes cooking over a grill or broiler and higher temperatures.

---

quick bite 8.5
Beef

As Americans continue to improve their lifestyles through diet many consumers have begun to question whether beef is a brand or a commodity. Many have abandoned red meat altogether. According to the National Cattlemen's Beef Association, beef consumption in the U.S. fell from 72 pounds (boneless) per person in 1980 to 63 pounds in 1997.

In response to reduced consumption, many companies have begun producing value-added beef products. This move to provide the best quality beef to health-conscious customers has helped to increase consumption and improve image. The entire beef industry has worked to become a brand rather than a commodity.

The industry serves both operators and consumers. For operators, beef suppliers are supplying value-added products like pre-marinated strips, fully prepared pot roast and meatloaf, oven-ready roast beef and portion-controlled sizes of cuts. The demand for branded beef products has risen dramatically from 1979 to 1998 from a few million pounds to over 480 million pounds. The industry expects over $1 billion in sales by 2003.

Beef suppliers are also beginning to add value to their service to operators. Some restaurateurs are able to place orders on one day and pick up the meat at a local airport as little as two days later. Many fine restaurants are beginning to acquire Niman Ranch meats produced by 30 ranchers who raise, process and distribute natural, organic beef. These restaurants purchase Niman beef in order to satisfy customers who seek the highest quality natural, organic foods. According to Robert Chopak of the Vinegar Factory, the Niman beef attracts many additional patrons.

Often the cost of branded beef can be higher than that from a traditional supplier, but it usually depends on the cut and the value added. However, when better meats are served, chefs often restrain from using expensive sauces and most operators feel that any incremental costs are negligible.

Source: "Beef: A Commodity or a Brand?" *Brands in Foodservice: Supplement to Nation's Restaurant News,* April 26, 1999, v. 3, n. 1, pp. 12, 54.

Broiling is usually reserved for the best cuts of meat. Thick pieces of meat will produce uniformly cooked meat with minimum shrinkage. Food is dipped in or brushed with oil to prevent it from sticking to the cooking surface. Meats are cooked on both sides for best results. Temperature is best between 300 and 350°F. The internal temperature should be 140°F for rare, 160°F for medium, and 170°F for well-done. Grilling is similar to broiling and is usually reserved for steaks and hamburgers.

In ovenizing, food is placed on greased pans and fat dribbled over it frequently while it bakes in the oven. The finished product resembles fried or sautéed food.

Ideally, roasting is done at lower temperatures (250 to 350°F). In this way, shrinkage is reduced while flavor is enhanced. Because roasts continue to cook after removal from the oven, they should be taken out before the desired internal temperature (the best guide to doneness) is reached. The roast should then "rest" for 15 to 20 minutes before it is sliced. This makes slicing easier.

Foods are fried when they are cooked in fat or oil. The result is a pleasant, nutty flavor. Sautéed items are shallow fried; deep frying involves complete immersion of the food into the fat or oil. In the latter case it is important to ensure that grease does not penetrate the item being cooked. This is accomplished in one of two ways: Either the food is coated with a protective covering or the food is cooked at a temperature high enough that the food emits a barrier of steam to prevent the fat from penetrating the food.

The major ingredients used in baking are:

- Flour. All-purpose flour consists of 20 percent soft wheat flour and 80 percent bread flour. Soft, weak, or pastry flour should be used for making pastries; hard-wheat flour is used for making bread.
- Shortening. Hydrogenated fats, oils, butter, and lard are used as shortening to produce a tender finished product.
- Leavening agents. Air, steam, and baking powder are examples of leavening agents, all used to add texture and volume. Heat helps in the process.
- Yeast. Added to water before being stirred with other ingredients, yeast gives off carbon dioxide and alcohol in the baking process.
- Eggs. Eggs can be added for flavor, color, or to act as a binding agent.

Salads.   Salads consist of a base, body, garnishes, and dressings [21]. The base typically consists of salad greens, is used for visual effect, and is usually not eaten. The body of the salad consists of the items that make up the salad. Garnishes are also added for eye appeal and include such things as croutons, nuts, and fish. Finally, garnishes add flavor and help keep the salad moist. It is difficult to maintain consistent quality because fresh vegetables are used in salads. They are also labor intensive and difficult to keep for extended periods. However, they are easy to make, the ingredients can be changed at the last minute, depending on what is available, they are nutritious, and they add a different taste and texture to other items on the menu.

Restaurant Management: Customers, Operations, and Employees

Salads should be made up shortly before serving, as they are highly perishable. Stainless steel equipment is required for their preparation. Fruits such as apples and bananas will brown when exposed to the air. This can be prevented by dipping the fruits in lemon juice.

Control

One important key to controlling costs is to use standardized recipes. Standardized recipes ensure that "when the specified conditions are followed in them, the result is always a product which is similar in all respects" [22]. Standardized recipes should contain "(1) the name of the menu item; (2) the pan size; (3) the temperature; (4) the yield; (5) the portion size; (6) the portion utensil; (7) the cooking time; (8) a sequential list of ingredients; (9) the quality of each ingredient; (10) the method; and (11) the special equipment needed" [23].

To prepare a standardized recipe, the following steps should be followed [24]:

1. Prepare the recipe according to the original source and evaluate according to acceptability for the operation.
2. Multiply the recipe to meet the number of portions needed and evaluate again as to acceptability, making any adjustments necessary to improve the dish. For example, the amount of seasonings required is not a simple multiple of the recipe.
3. Prepare the enlarged recipe and have it evaluated by a taste panel for suitability.
4. Prepare the recipe a minimum of three additional times, testing the popularity, preparation cost, and yield.
5. Standardize the recipe relative to ingredients and preparation methods and list all relevant information on a recipe card.

SERVICE

Service Styles

Over the years a variety of service styles have evolved, some more formal than others. Good service is more than following various rules of service. Good service is that which pleases the customer, which adds to the customer's enjoyment of the meal. Where the choice is between slavishly following rules and pleasing the customer, the choice should be the latter.

Family-Style Service.   In family-style service, sometimes called English service, food is brought to the table in bowls or on platters and placed before the host. Traditionally, the host plates the food and, if necessary, carves the meat and hands it to the server, who lays the plate before the guest. Less formally, guests may help themselves from the serving dishes placed on the table. This style of service requires fewer servers and is particularly useful for serving large numbers of people in a short period of time, as at a banquet.

Plate Service.   Plate or American service involves plating the food in the kitchen and serving it in the dining room. Solids are served from the left and

The Hamburger

The hamburger has always been and will continue to be an all-time favorite. McDonalds claims that the amount of ketchup sold in a year could fill Lake Michigan and the burgers could stretch to Mars and back many times.

Hamburgers are a perfect topic for creative statistics. A 1973 *Time* magazine cover story claimed that the 12 billion hamburgers McDonalds had sold at that time could "form a pyramid 783 times the size of the one erected by Snefu." "Hamburger numerology manages to be impressive, fabulous and utterly meaningless, all at the same time."

A 1997 *Economist* article reported that the average American eats three hamburgers a week, all together equaling about 40 billion burgers annually. The National Cattlemen's Beef Association (NCBA) lists the popularity of ingredients on burgers as:

1) 38% include ketchup
2) 30% include mustard
3) 28% include cheese
4) 21% include onion
5) 20% include mayo or salad dressing
6) 20% include tomatoes
7) 19% include lettuce
8) 17% include pickles
9) 4% include relish
10) 2% include BBQ sauce

Other statistics gathered by the NCBA include:

- 1/3 of all Americans have eaten a hamburger or some form of ground beef in the past 24 hours.
- Hamburgers appear on 73% of all foodservice menus.
- Hamburgers and cheeseburgers make up 76.5% of all beef consumed away from home. Prime rib only accounts for 2.9%.

Source: Graulich, David. "'Companion' Tome Dishes up Beef on the Hamburger du Jour." *Nation's Restaurant News*, April 19, 1999, v. 33, n. 16, p. 60.

beverages from the right. Designed to be quick and efficient, this service allows for close control of portions.

Table-Side Service. Table-side or French service requires a *chef de rang* (waiter) and a *commis de rang* (assistant). Food is plated and served in the dining room from a *gueridon* (rolling cart). Final cooking may also be done on the gueridon by means of a small stove warmer or *rechaud*. The waiter takes the order, which is delivered to the kitchen by the assistant. The assistant will bring the food from the kitchen to the gueridon, where it is finished and plated by the chef de rang. The assistant serves the plates to the customers. The waiter is responsible for serving drinks and presenting the check.

In French service everything is served from the customer's right except for bread, butter, and salads, which are served from the left. Finger bowls, containing warm water with rose petals or lemon slices, are often provided for rinsing fingers.

Because side tables are required for this style of service, fewer dining tables can be located in a given area. This limits the revenue-producing ability of the restaurant. Due to the heavy use of employees and equipment, table-side service

---

quick bite 8.7
Food Trends—Tableside Foods

Tableside food preparation is making a comeback in restaurants across the country. One reason for the resurgence in popularity is growing competition in the industry, which causes restaurateurs to search for a competitive edge. Classic food items that are regaining popularity such as steak Diane and baked Alaska are encouraging the trend.

Tableside preparation intrigues younger patrons because they have never experienced such personal service and it stirs up feelings of nostalgia and fond memories for older patrons. While meager efforts at tableside service such as tossed-to-order Caesar salads and table-mashed guacamole have been popular for years, a resurgence of hot tableside foods is appearing in a variety of venues, from moderate-priced multi-unit chains to top-dollar restaurants.

Tableside service has many benefits; one in particular is that it involves customers in the food. Preparation also challenges the staff and keeps them interested. However, training is essential, and at a maximum, only one or two items should be featured. An operator should take into consideration the ability of the staff, available space, style of cuisine and a restaurant's volume before deciding whether or not to offer tableside service. Tableside service does not require a large investment in service carts or cooking classes for servers. Tableside service can be as simple as garnishing soup in a creative fashion.

Source: Liddle, Alan. "At Your Service: Tableside Foods Make a Resurgence." *Nation's Restaurant News*, v. 33, no. 11, March 15, 1999, p. 41.

---

is the most costly of all service styles and therefore tends to be used in restaurants that can command a high average check. It is very dramatic and personal.

Platter Service.   In platter, sometimes called Russian, service the food is prepared and portioned in the kitchen, where it is placed on platters. Plates are placed in front of each customer from the right of the guest and the food served from the platter to the plate by the server, serving from the customer's left and working counterclockwise around the table. Plates are removed from the right.

---

quick bite 8.8
Road to the Top: Neil Kleinberg

Executive Chef/Culinary-arts Training Manager

Neil Kleinberg is not your ordinary executive chef; in fact, he works in a place that doesn't even need an executive chef. As culinary-arts training manager at Ezekial's Café, a very small, 12-seat, takeout café operated by Convenant House, a shelter for runaway teens in New York City, Kleinberg never wakes up and says "I don't want to go to work today." Kleinberg says that he wants to go to work every day just to see what happens and even just to see who shows up. Kleinberg's job includes being a father, mother, brother, counselor, teacher and adviser as well as a demanding boss to the 17- to 21-year-old trainees who work with him.

Kleinberg worked in many successful restaurants after earning his associate degree in hotel and restaurant management from New York City Technical College in Brooklyn. Some of Kleinberg's career highlights include opening Simon's with partner John Simon; working with Rick Moonen and other top chefs at The Water Club and reopening Lundy's, a Brooklyn legend that was closed for 20 years, with its original recipes and menu.

According to Kleinberg, despite his title, his real job is teaching. By 1997, after building an impressive resume, Kleinberg wanted to teach. The job at Convenant was perfect for Kleinberg who also wanted to continue cooking. Ezekial's Café was opened to give the kids at Convenant House hands-on training in the foodservice industry so that they can obtain good jobs. But, since these kids are mostly troubled with difficult pasts, they need as much life training as they do skills training.

One of Kleinberg's favorite aspects of the job is that there is no typical day. However, although he says he shouldn't, Kleinberg cannot help but get emotionally involved with the kids he works with, which can make it difficult to teach them skills, hygiene and sanitation, food prep and convince them that they have to show up on time and behave. Yet, his students come back to tell him that he was right, it is tough out there.

Source: Blake, Kathy. "Neil Kleinberg: Molding Troubled Kids into Future Chefs." *Nation's Restaurant News*, v. 33, no. 6, February 8, 1999, p. 33.

Buffet Service.   In buffet service customers choose their meals from items laid out on a serving table. They either plate their own dishes or are served by employees standing behind the table. Silverware can be provided either on the buffet table or at the individual eating tables.

Space Requirements

Table-service operations need pickup areas next to the cooking area to hold items prior to service. Salads, beverages, and desserts are picked up separately from cooked items. Rolls, bread, butter, and water are stored at server stations throughout the dining area.

In self-serve operations a variety of serving-line configurations are possible. Straight-line arrangements allow for easy access and a clearly defined flow of traffic. However, this layout limits the number of people who can be served within a set period of time. The greater the amount of linear space available for serving food, the greater the capacity of the system.

For most table-service restaurants, space requirements for serving areas are estimated as part of the main cooking area. Cafeterias, however, are different, in that separate areas are needed for serving. Space is required for the serving counter, for customers, and for servers. The amount of space needed depends on the number of customers to be served and the time allotted for service. Straight-line cafeteria counters can serve anywhere from 2 to 10 people a minute, depending on the number of choices and the number of servers. The more choices and the fewer the servers, the lower the number of customers who can be served per minute.

In recent years the traditional straight-line cafeteria counter has given way to island counters that are accessible to customers from all sides. These so-called shopping-center arrangements can accommodate up to 20 customers per minute.

Straight-line counters require 10 to 15 square feet of floor space for each linear foot of counter. The linear length of the counter depends on the number of items to be displayed. Shopping-center counters require 18 to 20 square feet of floor space per linear foot of counter. In both cases this space takes into account the counters, customer aisles, room for servers, and back-bar equipment.

The size of the serving area for cafeterias should be based on the dining room capacity. Ideally, the rate of people entering the dining room from the serving area—the flow rate—should equal the rate of people leaving the dining room having completed their meals. The number of usable seats needed in the dining room can be determined as follows:

$$N_d = \frac{N_m + N_{sa}}{(T_m/T_d) - 1}$$

where N_d is the number of persons in the dining room or the number of usable seats, N_m the total number of persons to be fed, N_{sa} the number of persons in the serving area, T_m the meal period, and T_d the time a person spends in the dining area.

Cafeteria counters are placed as close to the cooking area as possible. This allows for speedy replacement of food items as they become depleted. Desserts and salads are placed at the beginning of the line; hot foods are located at the end of the line. This minimizes cooling of the hot items while increasing the sales of cold items. Having loaded up with an entree, a customer may be reluctant to add a dessert. If the dessert is located before the entree, however, the customer may be more inclined to select it.

The flow of many cafeteria lines breaks down as customers leave the line to pay. Additional cashier stations may be required to take care of this problem.

---

quick bite 8.9
Food and Beverage 2000

As consumers becoming increasingly health conscious, managers will need increased understanding of health and dietary issues including ingredient and nutritional content. Managers will also be expected to be responsible for quality control and consistency.

The financial impact of purchasing decisions will play a bigger role on the bottom line in 2000. Inventory control will also become an essential part of the manager's role. Industry experts feel that a manager's ability to promote items that do well will increase, thereby affecting profitability.

Video training is likely to become an important tool in the food and beverage quality standards training of employees. Managers will concentrate on producing the highest possible quality product preparation.

The Top 10 Most Likely Developments for Managers in Food and Beverage for 2000:

1. Consumers more concerned about nutrition
2. Need to be more aware of health and dietary issues
3. Responsibility for quality control and product consistency
4. Greater knowledge of ingredient and nutritional content needed
5. Video becomes important food-quality training tool
6. Menu items adapted to regional tastes
7. Inventory control becomes a top concern
8. Awareness of the impact of purchasing decisions
9. Increased role in the distribution of nutritional information
10. Increased diversity of menu items

Adapted from: National Restaurant Association, *Foodservice Manager 2000.* (Washington, D.C. National Restaurant Association, 1992.)

Restaurant Management: Customers, Operations, and Employees

Portion Control

The last step in the control process is to ensure effective portion control. The easiest way to ensure this is to use standard utensils when measuring and/or serving food. This can be done using such things as standard-sized pans, ladles, serving spoons, scoops, portion scales, cutting markers, meat slicers, egg slicers, and individually weighed, measured, and packed items (for example, sandwiches) [25].

DISHWASHING

Dishwashing facilities are typically separated from other functions in an area that requires high levels of ventilation and illumination. Acoustical tile is useful in reducing the high noise level associated with this activity. Machines can be purchased appropriate to the number of dishes to be washed.

Often, separate facilities are used for washing glasses. Satisfactory results can be obtained with the use of additives or by washing glasses shortly after the water has been changed.

Design of this area depends on how much has to be washed and the time available for this function. Some operators carry a large inventory of flatware and store the dirty dishes, washing them over a longer period of time, taking advantage of off-peak energy rates while spreading employee workload. In other situations, management reduces inventory cost but requires that soiled dishes be washed immediately and put right back into service during the course of a meal period.

The sequence of tasks during dishwashing is sorting, scraping or preflushing, stacking, loading, removal, and unloading. Equipment should be arranged accordingly. Consideration has to be given to the movement of dishes in and out of the dishwashing area. Commonly, bussers bring dirty dishes into the area in bins. Clean dishes will either go to the kitchen, where the cooked food will be plated, or the dining room, where tables will be reset. Mobile plate and cup racks can be provided to move dishes to these areas.

Pot and Pan Washing

The amount and type of space required for pot and pan washing will depend on the volume to be washed and when it is to be done. Where the same person washes dishes as well as pots, storage space for the pots will be required, as the dishes will have a higher time priority. Larger facilities may use machines rather than the typical sink for this purpose.

WASTE DISPOSAL

Waste disposal requirements depend on the total relative amounts of paper, plastic, and cans generated, the cost of removal, and the prevailing laws regarding disposal.

Various disposal options are compaction, incineration, grinding, and pulping [26]. Compactors are useful when handling large amounts of waste. They reduce large volumes of waste into smaller amounts. Both volume and weight are concentrated. Care must be taken that the resulting package can be handled easily. Incineration involves burning the waste. Local pollution regulations may make this option cost prohibitive.

While most municipalities allow grinding as a way of disposing of waste, some communities have experienced problems with non-biodegradable materials and have placed restrictions on the use of this method. In waste-pulping a liquefied waste is produced through the use of heavy-duty rotary grinders using recirculating water. The water is extracted and the resulting semidry pulp is stored in bins prior to removal. This system cannot accommodate glass or metal.

ENDNOTES

1. Mahmood Khan, *Foodservice Operations* (Westport, CT: AVI Publishing Company, 1987), pp. 254–257.

2. Lewis J. Minor and Ronald F. Cichy, *Foodservice Systems Management* (Westport, CT: AVI Publishing Company, 1984), p. 100.

3. Khan, *Foodservice Operations*, pp. 148–149.

4. Ibid., p. 175.

5. Ibid., p. 197.

6. Ibid., p. 163.

7. Ibid., pp. 164–165.

8. Ibid., p. 148.

9. Ibid., p. 148.

10. Ibid., pp. 209–211.

11. Edward A. Kazarian, *Foodservice Facilities Planning*, 3rd ed. (New York: Van Nostrand Reinhold, 1989), p. 11.

12. Khan, *Foodservice Operations*, pp. 211–215.

13. Ibid., p. 214.

14. Kazarian, *Foodservice Facilities Planning*, p. 12.

15. Ibid., p. 13.

16. Khan, *Foodservice Operations*, p. 218.

17. Ibid., p. 220.

18. Minor and Cichy, *Foodservice Systems Management*, p. 33.

19. John B. Knight and Lendal H. Kotschevar, *Quantity Food Production, Planning, and Management*, 2nd ed. (New York:Van Nostrand Reinhold, 1989), p. 173.

20. Ibid., p. 275.

21. Khan, *Foodservice Operations*, p. 267.

22. Ibid., pp. 252–253.

23. Minor and Cichy, *Foodservice Systems Management*, p. 130.

24. Khan, *Foodservice Operations*, pp. 254–257.

25. Ibid., p. 283.

26. Kazarian, *Foodservice Facilities Planning*, p. 17.

CHAPTER NINE

KITCHEN EQUIPMENT AND INTERIORS: SELECTION, MAINTENANCE, AND ENERGY MANAGEMENT

learning objectives

By the end of this chapter you should be able to:

1. Identify the considerations involved in the selection of kitchen equipment.

2. Identify the basic types of equipment found in kitchens.

3. Compare and contrast the relative advantages of the various materials used in kitchen interiors and equipment construction.

4. Identify the most important concepts in cleaning and maintaining kitchen equipment.

5. Design a comprehensive energy management program.

We always strive to bring some excitement to the customer. The drive is different today because chefs are restaurateurs, whereas before more restaurateurs didn't have such a dedication to food. The front of the house used to sort of hold a place together, but now it's the back of the house. It's a big difference because nobody is more dedicated to food than the people who cook it.
Daniel Boulard, quoted in *Dining Out*

Source: Dornenburg, Andrew and Karen Page, *Dining Out* (New York, NY: John Wiley & Sons, Inc., 1998).

EQUIPMENT SELECTION

Basic Considerations

Several basic considerations are involved in the selection of kitchen equipment [1]. Management should consider capacity, need, cost, functional attributes, and sanitation and safety.

Capacity. Determining the capacity of each type of equipment to be used in an operation is critical before deciding how many pieces of which equipment to purchase. If the capacity calculation is too low, bottlenecks and slowdowns occur; if it is too high, the restaurant spends too much money on equipment that will not be used to its capacity.

Required equipment capacity can be determined as follows [2]:

1. Analyze each food item on the menu to estimate the number of portions to be prepared for every meal period. If menus are changed daily, it will be necessary to use a sample of dishes to be served.
2. The portion size for every menu item is then determined.
3. Multiplying the projected number of portions by the portion size will give the total volume of food to be prepared at each meal period.
4. The method of preparation and production is selected next for each item on the menu. Depending on the style of operation, items may be prepared individually to order, in small batches prior to the order, in large batches prior to service, or partially prepared in batches and finished when an order is received. The processing time has to be taken into account, together with when the preparation can be done. It may, for example, be possible to use the same piece of equipment at different times during the day to prepare more than one item.
5. The batch size is then determined for those items to be prepared in batches. The smaller and more frequently prepared the batches, the less equipment capacity is needed and the fresher the end product.
6. For items prepared to order, the number of portions to be prepared at any one time is estimated based on the projected number of customers, which items they are likely to order, and their arrival patterns.
7. Equipment catalogs can then be consulted to determine the number of pieces of equipment to be ordered. Some types of equipment are selected on the basis of the number of pans they can hold. In this case it is necessary to divide the number of portions to be prepared by how many can fit into a standard-size pan to get the capacity of the equipment in "number of pans required." For example, ovens hold bake pans that are 18 by 26 inches. Identifying how many portions can fit into a pan 18 by 26 inches and dividing that into the number of portions required will give the number of pans required and, consequently, an estimate of the size of the oven needed.

Need. Equipment should not be bought or leased unless it is needed. But what, exactly, does this mean? A piece of equipment is "needed" if it improves

quick bite 9.1
Hot Concepts: Mars 2112, Tinseltown Studios

Despite declining sales at theme restaurants, two new players are entering the market. These two start-up theme restaurants do not expect that customer satisfaction or frequency will present problems for them. According to the founders of Mars 2112 and Tinseltown Studios, an interactive experience is the way they create repeat business.

Mars 2112, the $15 million, 35,000-square-foot, 425-seat restaurant in Manhattan, imitates what it might be like on a space flight to Mars and a dinner below the Martian surface. Patrons enter the restaurant by taking a five-minute motion-simulator "ride" to "Mars." Two space shuttles "transport" guests to the Red Planet rather than having them line up outside.

The $16 million dollar Tinseltown Studios project is a 44,000-square-foot dinner-theater restaurant located in Anaheim, California and was opened by Ogden Entertainment. Patrons at Tinseltown play characters as superstars attending an event similar to the Academy Awards ceremony. Many guests in a night will be digitally inserted into real "big-time" movies in an actor's part. Clips are shown during the mock broadcast. The winners are called up on stage in order to make acceptance speeches and receive their "Oggie" award.

Paschal Phelan, a resourceful entrepreneur in Killkenny, Ireland founded Mars 2112 and acts as its chairman. Phelan realized that customers were dissatisfied with the available options in theme restaurants and hired Deloitte & Touche to research what customers don't like about the segment through surveys in New York, Philadelphia and London. The firm discovered three key issues:

- Customers don't like to wait in line outside.
- The dining experience was usually a letdown.
- The experience didn't live up to the promise.

People didn't like eating a mediocre meal and looking at things hanging on the wall. One respondent even said that it's like eating in a museum.

The name Mars 2112 comes from the year in which NASA believes colonization of Mars will begin. The concept corrects all three of patron's concerns. There is no line. Customers travel to Mars in a 22-vibrating-seat space ship that simulates space flight. A large lounge, the Star Bar, and a game room, Cyber Street, are available if no tables are immediately available. Tinseltown Studios is like nothing else in the restaurant industry.

Source: "Mars 2112, Tinseltown Studios Aim for 'Interactive' Success." *Nation's Restaurant News,* v. 32, no. 51, December 21, 1998, p. 36.

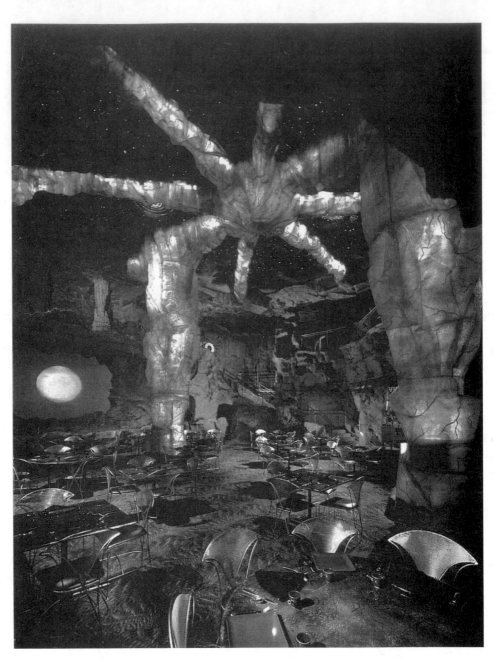

Courtesy of Mars 2112.

Restaurant Management: Customers, Operations, and Employees

quick bite 9.2
New or Used?—You Decide

Here are some considerations involved in purchasing used equipment:

1. In renovating an existing operation, check to see whether kitchen equipment was purchased new and was well maintained. It may only need a good cleaning to keep it operating efficiently.
2. Using old equipment is risky if it must be moved to a new location. Without the original packing, pieces may break loose.
3. It is risky to rely totally on used equipment.
4. There is less risk when purchasing used nonmechanical equipment. However, check for the NSF logo and make sure that it meets local codes. Georgia, for example, requires four-compartment pot sinks.
5. Buy new if the equipment is "menu critical," if the food items need critical temperatures or finish, if there is any question of employee safety, if the equipment is mechanically or electronically complex, if you don't have someone you trust to check it out beforehand, or if the manufacturer is out of business.
6. Used refrigeration equipment should be priced at no more than 10 to 20 percent of the cost of new equipment.

Source: Frable, Jr., Foster. "Is Purchasing Used Equipment a Wise Decision?" *Nation's Restaurant News,* October 3, 1994. v. 28, n. 37, p. 36.

the quality of the food being prepared, produces product and/or labor cost savings; results in increased quantity of finished product, and/or contributes to the profitability of the operation [3].

The need for a particular piece of equipment should be classified as either essential, high utility, or basic [4]. In this way, priorities can be established in the event of a cash shortage.

Cost.   Various costs are involved in the purchase of a piece of equipment [5]. In addition to the initial purchase price, the equipment must be installed, insured, maintained and repaired, financed, and operated.

Part of the cost analysis involves inclusion of the labor costs involved in preparation. The cost of buying preprocessed vegetables should be compared with the cost of a vegetable peeler plus the labor cost of peeling the items in-house.

Khan suggests the following formula as a method of calculating the value of a piece of equipment [6]:

$$H = \frac{L(A + B)}{C + L\,(D + E + F) - G}$$

where H is the calculated value; L the expected life of the equipment in years; A the savings in labor per year; B the savings in material per year; C the cost of the equipment, including installation; D the cost of utilities per year; E the cost of maintenance and repair of the equipment per year; F the annual projected interest on the money in C, if invested elsewhere for the life of the equipment; and G the turn-in value at the end of the life of the equipment.

If H is greater than 1.0, the equipment should be purchased. The higher the value of H, the more attractive the purchase becomes. This equation requires an estimate of the expected life of the equipment. The normal life of kitchen equipment varies from 9 to 15 years.

Functional Attributes. It is important that equipment do what it is intended to do. Performance relative to cost and compared to the performance of other equipment should be examined carefully. Consideration should also be given to likely changes in the menu that may render an expensive piece of equipment obsolete. Quietness of operation, availability of parts, and ease of maintenance are also important. Finally, the type of energy used must be noted as part of the cost consideration.

Sanitation and Safety. The National Sanitation Foundation (NSF) certifies equipment that meets the sanitary standards required for foodservice operations. NSF-approved equipment should be a consideration in making equipment purchases.

Safety is also an important consideration. All materials used should be nontoxic. Parts should be easily disassembled for easy cleaning, moving and sharp parts need to be protected, and safety locks are desirable on all equipment.

Materials Used

The cost of a piece of equipment is directly related to the type of material used to construct it. The following are the most common materials used in constructing kitchen equipment.

Wood. The disadvantages of wood-constructed items outweigh the advantages. Because wood absorbs moisture it tends to crack, thereby making it unsafe from the viewpoint of sanitation. It is, however, light in weight, can be designed into various shapes, cushions noise, is attractive, and is relatively inexpensive. Today, its use is limited to areas where there will be no contact with food.

Metals. Although a variety of metals are used in foodservice equipment, the most common metals in use are alloys. An alloy is a combination of one or more metals, commonly stainless steel (iron and carbon), brass (copper, zinc, and other metals), and Monel (nickel and copper). Pure copper is almost never used because it needs constant polishing, is heavy, and reacts with some food items.

Stainless steel is easily cleaned, is attractive, resists rust and stain formation, and can, because its surfaces show dirt easily, be kept sanitary. Two important considerations in purchasing stainless steel are thickness and finish. Thickness is important because stainless steel is fairly expensive. Selection is

Digital Drive-thru

Customers are hearing new tunes in the drive thru as restaurants like A&W encourage them to change their FM stations to a "ham" radio frequency. The quickserve restaurant posts signs in the drive-up lane asking patrons to tune in to 95.9—WA&W. The A&W chain and other quick serve operators are using low-signal radios to broadcast food and beverage specials directly to customers' car radios, seeking to create sales opportunities, boost check averages, and enhance customer loyalty.

A&W tested the concept last December in Michigan at a large free-standing unit near Dearborn. The store's managers would record and air daily specials, which are available only to customers who tune in to the station. As a result of the specials being aired, promoted items are selling 20 to 30 times more per day.

The radio units measure the size of a large clock radio and feature a continuous digital loop of up to three minutes of recording. Restaurant operators and managers can connect to the system through the use of a remote telephone modem interface. Digital audio files can be updated from computer generated WAV formatted disks.

Irving Titre, a McDonalds franchisee, installed the radios in two of his restaurants labeling it "McRadio." As a result drive thru sales increased five to six percent. One other McDonalds operator claims a 19 percent increase in drive thru average checks since installing the low-frequency radio. Since the radios don't transmit over 300 feet they do not have to be licensed by the Federal Communications Commission. According to Mark Burris, a recruiting officer for a 71-unit burger franchisee, the radios not only provide advanced marketing opportunities, but also recruiting opportunities. The radios are used by Burris to announce hourly job openings and even unit-level managers. The system only costs about $1,800 and provides more results than most job fairs, newspapers, and bonuses.

The radios available are expected to have the capability of downloading the messages produced by ad agencies. Operators can broadcast promotional tie-ins with suppliers and other local businesses. The radios also provide a restaurateur the opportunity to air public service announcements for local charities.

Source: Rubinstein, Ed. "A Sound Strategy: Operators Use Digital Radios to Get Customers to Brake." *Nation's Restaurant News*, April 12, 1999, v. 33, n. 15, pp. 51–52.

done through gauge numbers, which indicate the thickness of the steel. The thicker the steel, the lower the gauge. Gauges 8, 10, and 12 are good supports; 12 and 14 can be used for tabletops. Cost is also a function of the amount of polishing desired. The more polishing required, the higher the cost. The amount of polishing done on the equipment is a function of the finish number; the higher the number, the more polishing was done and the higher the cost. In production areas, finish 4 is common. In serving areas, a higher number would be appropriate.

Nickel is often found on equipment trim, railings, and counters. Aluminum is popular for utensils, equipment both inside and out, and steam-jacketed kettles. It is light, is a good conductor of heat and electricity, does not corrode easily, and is durable.

Cast iron is used in places that do not come into contact with food, such as stands and equipment supports. Iron is used in pots, pans, griddles, and gas burners, while brass is favored in faucets and shutoff valves.

Steel ovens, range interiors, frames, and supports are common. When steel and iron are treated with acid, they are galvanized. Galvanized steel and iron are common in dishwashing machines, sinks, and equipment legs.

Plastics. Various plastics are being used increasingly in foodservice operations. They are very versatile, durable, and capable of being molded into different shapes. Acrylics are used in food covers; melamine can be used for dishes and glassware; fiberglass trays are common; nylons are used for mobile parts; storage bowls and containers are made of polyethylene; dishwashing racks are commonly made of polypropylene; polystyrene is used in cups and covers.

Coatings. Coatings are placed on the interior surfaces of equipment to give it additional properties. For example, silicone makes a nonsticking surface; Teflon® aids in the release of food from a pan. For surfaces that come into contact with food, the coating should be smooth, corrosion resistant, nonabsorbent, as heat resistant as possible, and easily cleanable. There should be no interaction between the food and the coating such that the taste, color, or smell of the food is changed.

Energy Sources

Because of the rising cost of energy, the source used to power the equipment is becoming an increasingly important consideration in selecting equipment. Electricity, gas, steam, and oil are all used as energy sources in kitchens.

In foodservice operations the form of energy used most commonly is electricity. Two voltage systems are used; 110–120 volts and 220–240 volts, the latter being more powerful. It is important that the correct voltage be available for a particular piece of equipment.

Fuses are used to prevent the entire electrical system from "blowing." The fuses used must be appropriate to the task. A simple equation is useful in determining the type of fuse required [7]:

$$W = V \times I$$

where W is the measure of electricity in watts, V the force behind the electrical current, and I the amount of electricity flowing.

For 2,000 watts of electricity on a 110-volt line, the amount flowing, I, is W divided by V, or 2,000 divided by 110, or 18.2 amperes. Adding in a 25 percent safety factor means that this circuit should be protected by a 25-ampere fuse. Electricity costs are expressed as a certain number of cents per kilowatt-hour, the cost of 1,000 watts of electricity running for 1 hour.

Specifications

It is vital that exact specifications be used when purchasing equipment. These should include [8]:

1. The title or name of the piece of equipment
2. The scope or intended use
3. Classification: the type, model, size, and style
4. Specific requirements to include such things as:
   - Dimensions and temperature ranges
   - Materials used in construction and finish
   - Electrical requirements
   - Control regulations and displays
   - Performance criteria
   - Certification by various agencies [such as the Underwriters' Laboratories (UL), National Sanitation Foundation (NSF), National Electric Manufacturers Association (NEMA), American Gas Association (AGA), and the American Society of Mechanical Engineers (ASME) for steam equipment]
   - Types of warranties
   - Parts and labor numbers and costs for maintenance and repair
   - Number of manuals required
5. Quality assurance: inspection and performance tests
6. Delivery and installation dates
7. Payment terms and dates
8. Drawings and illustrations
9. The name of the contact

EQUIPMENT TYPES

Dry-Heat Cooking Equipment

Ranges.   Ranges, either gas or electric, are the most basic piece of cooking equipment for most foodservice operations. Generally, they are mounted on the floor, with the cooking done in pots directly on the range top. A heavy frame is preferred because of the heavy use that ranges receive. Ideally, they should have reflectors and removable drip pans for ease of cleaning. While the number of

quick bite 9.4
Purchasing New Equipment

When deciding whether or not to buy that shiny piece of new equipment, operators often ignore important maintenance issues. Often restaurateurs are impressed by equipment that seems to do everything they ever desired. However, promises made by manufacturers and sales people aren't always delivered. Restaurants and other foodservice outlets place heavy demands on equipment very seldom found in other businesses. Products that provide excellent value and service in some businesses can fail in restaurant or other on-site foodservice outlets.

Oftentimes the newest products are too complex and need a higher level of maintenance than older equipment does. Usually the skills of managers and employees do not match those necessary for today's high-tech equipment. For example, a large hospital kitchen in Florida installed an advanced-technology fryer with continuous filtration, yet the only two people capable of operating the equipment were the executive chef and the foodservice director. As a result, the fryer was out of service several times, not because it broke down, but because none of the employees could figure out how to change the filter mechanism.

In order to get the most out of any piece of equipment an operator must be willing to ensure proper disassembly and cleaning. Many pieces of equipment including automated espresso machines, coffee grinders and brewers, frozen yogurt and ice-cream makers and waste pulping and extracting systems require daily cleaning for smooth operating. It is essential that the operator personally take the time to learn how to care for the equipment or assign a designated individual often called a "key operator" to learn and teach others.

In order to avoid the burden of equipment that requires more care and maintenance than expected, an owner should:

- Read a copy of the operating manual to get a good idea of the in-house maintenance required and the supplies and cleaning required for the equipment.
- Figure out the daily or annual cost for supplies needed and any necessary service contracts. Find out if supplies are only available from the equipment manufacturer or a single vendor.
- Get a list of references (other operators who have used the equipment for a period of time). Call references that operate similar facilities for their opinion on the equipment.

Source: Frable, Jr., Foster. "If You Cannot Maintain a Product or Finish, Do Not Purchase It." *Nation's Restaurant News*, v. 33, no. 3, January 18, 1999, pp. 29, 58.

ranges required will vary depending on the type of menu served, the following guidelines can be used as a guide [9]. For a restaurant serving fewer than 300 meals a day, one range would be sufficient, two ranges would be needed to cook between 300 and 400 meals a day, three could handle 400 to 500, while four could cope with 500 to 1,000 meals daily.

Hot tops require from 20 to 30 percent more energy than open burners because the heating plate must be heated before the pan is heated. While burners are limited to one pan each, hot tops offer more flexibility by providing an area for several pots and pans.

It is important that grease traps be easily removable for both cleaning and maintenance.

Conventional Ovens. Because conventional ovens are used a great deal, durability is important. The ease of cleaning and energy conservation should also be considered. Four to five inches of insulation (fiberglass, rockwool, or vitreous fiber) is desirable to help cut energy losses. Ovens may be stacked one on top of the other to cut down on space needs. The same guidelines for range requirements can be used to estimate oven needs. A more sophisticated formula is [10]:

$$\text{required no. ovens} \ = \ \frac{\text{no. servings}}{\begin{array}{ccc} \text{no. servings} & \times & \text{no. pans} & \times & \text{no. batches} \\ \text{per pan} & & \text{per oven} & & \text{per hour} \end{array}}$$

Convection Ovens. Placement of the heating element(s) in a conventional oven does not allow for the consistent distribution of heat inside the oven. Convectional ovens are designed to eliminate this problem. The forced-air model uses a fan to distribute heat in a uniform manner, thus allowing more internal space to be used.

In the roll-in type, carts or racks can be rolled into a large oven, thereby allowing heat to reach all the racks equally. Another model, the pulse-type, alternates hot and cold air. The hot air cooks the food; the cold air prevents overcooking.

In general, convection ovens require less labor, space, and energy, cook at lower temperatures, and enhance quality by allowing for an even distribution of heat. On the other hand, soft foods or batters may suffer visually from the circulation of air in the oven.

Infrared Ovens. The relatively new infrared ovens take up less space than conventional ovens while using less energy because they cook at higher temperatures for relatively short periods.

Mechanical and Pizza Ovens. The major differences between conventional and mechanical ovens are that the latter are larger and have mechanical parts inside that help move the food while inside the oven. A reel oven has trays that move vertically in the oven. Glass doors allow for inspection of the food as it is being cooked. Rotary ovens, on the other hand, have circular shelves that rotate horizontally around a central axis. Traveling tray ovens are large ovens that allow food items to travel through the oven on trays. Pizza ovens are deeper than the other types and allow for the horizontal placement of pizzas.

Microwave Ovens.   Microwave ovens use radiation to cook food. Because of this, food is cooked faster and the surrounding air is not heated. These ovens are particularly useful for reheating items and thawing meats. They cannot handle large quantities of food nor can they brown food items. To eliminate the latter problem, a combination convection/microwave oven has been developed.

Deck Ovens.   Deck ovens are decked or stacked to save on floor space. They may be either roasting or baking ovens. Capacity can be estimated by identifying the number of batches per hour that can be handled. Roasting times vary from 15 to 18 minutes per pound for a cooked ham to 30 to 50 minutes per pound for fresh pork. Baking times vary from 15 to 20 minutes for rolls to 50 to 60 minutes for fruit pies.

The two-deck arrangement is the maximum height for safety in a deck oven. In a three-deck arrangement the top oven is too high while the lower deck puts a strain on workers' backs because of the bending that is required for loading and unloading.

Broilers.   Broiling produces a charred or smoked flavor to meats by cooking the meat on a grid, which allows the fat to drip down and partially burn, thereby imparting the smoked flavor.

Broilers are commonly included into the range area in one of three ways [11]. Either the broiler is at the same height as the range top, or it is purchased as a central component with an overhead oven heated by the burners in the broiling compartment, or it is mounted on a conventional range-type oven with or without an overhead oven.

A small broiler—a salamander—can be mounted on top of a heavy-duty range for smaller operations that do not require much broiling. Broiler capacity is a function of the size of the broiler grid and the type of food to be cooked. For example, a 1-inch steak will take 15 minutes to be cooked rare, while a half-chicken will require 30 minutes of cooking. The number of portions to be prepared at any one time will determine the number and size of broilers needed.

Griddles.   A griddle offers a heated surface particularly useful for short-order cooking. For example, the cooking time for various items on a griddle will range from 1 to 2 minutes for a grilled cheese sandwich to 8 to 10 minutes for a ham steak. Space should be provided near the griddle to hold supplies and other equipment necessary for its operation. Griddle capacity is determined as suggested above for broilers.

Steam Equipment

Steam-Jacketed Kettles.   Steam-jacketed kettles are indispensable in most restaurant kitchens. They are excellent for foods that do not require high temperatures. The steam in the jacket heats the metal, which, in turn, heats the food inside the kettle—the steam does not come into contact with the food, so the nutritional loss is low. If there is no steam supply, a special generator must be purchased, adding to the cost of the equipment. A water faucet over and a drainage line near the bottom of the kettle are important considerations.

The capacity of the kettle needed is calculated as follows [12]:

$$\begin{array}{c} \text{capacity of kettle} \\ \text{(in gallons or liters)} \end{array} = \frac{\text{no. servings} \times \text{portion size} \times \% \text{ headspace}}{128 \text{ oz (1 gal) 3 no. batches}} \\ \text{[or 1000 ml (1 liter)]}$$

Fifteen percent is usually allowed for the headspace to prevent overflow, spillage, and/or spattering.

Steamers. Steamers are capable of cooking large quantities of food quickly while retaining nutrients and maintaining quality. Once food is placed in the steamer, even from a frozen state, it can be left alone. Although useful for vegetables, rice, pasta, and special desserts such as custard, other types of food cannot be successfully steamed. In addition, adjustments are necessary to get the food quality to where it should be.

Fryers

Deep-Fat Fryers. In purchasing deep-fat fryers it is important that they be made of noncorrosive material and that the temperature controls be placed such that they can be reached safely without exposure to spattered fat. A convenient system should be in place to drain the fat and a mechanism should be in place for removing food particles from the fat.

The capacity of a fryer depends on the pounds of fat in the fry kettle, the heat input, and the cooking time required. Typically, fryers are designed on a fat-to-food ratio of 6:1, indicating that 6 pounds of fat is required in the kettle for each pound of food to be fried. Conventional fryer capacity ranges from 15 to 130 pounds. A useful rule of thumb is that a fryer can prepare 1.5 to 2 times its weight of fat per hour. Thus a 130-pound-capacity fryer can cook from 195 to 260 pounds of food per hour.

Pressure fryers have lids that can be sealed, thus allowing frying under pressure. As a result, cooking time is shorter and at a lower temperature. Because of this the fat does not break down so quickly. In addition, there is less moisture loss, resulting in food that is crispy on the outside and juicy on the inside.

The continuous-type fryer moves food continuously through the fat on a conveyer belt. An automatic basket-lift or a timer bell allows cooks to attend to other tasks while frying food without the danger of it being overcooked.

Tilting Skillets. A tilting skillet or tilting fry pan is fastened to the floor by brackets. Its versatility makes it very desirable: It can substitute as a griddle, deep-fat fryer, poacher, or holder of food.

Small Equipment

Food Cutters. Able to handle meats, vegetables, and fruits, food cutters can cut, dice, and shred. Food is placed in a bowl that rotates and exposes the food to high-speed rotating blades.

The capacity of the machine is a function of the size of the bowl and the amount of food that can be processed per minute. Cutters can be either bench or floor models.

Slicer.   The essential elements of a food slicer are a circular knife blade and a carriage that passes under the blade. These allow for strict control of the thickness of slices of food.

Mixer.   Every kitchen needs some blenders and mixers. The major purchasing consideration is the horsepower of the motor. It is preferable to purchase a larger model over a smaller one that requires several batches. The variety of attachments available make mixers very versatile pieces of equipment.

Through the use of a variety of attachments, a mixer can do much more than mix food. Adapters are available to allow chopping, dicing, shredding, and juice extraction. The smaller bench model comes in sizes from 5 to 20 quarts, while the larger models are sized from 30 to 400 quarts.

Vertical Cutter/Mixer.   Consisting of a stationary bowl with high-speed horizontal blades, the vertical cutter/mixer has a greater capacity than that of other food cutters.

Vegetable Peelers.   Vegetable peelers consist of a cylindrical tank that has a revolving disk in the bottom. There is an opening above the disk for loading the vegetables and one below for removing the peels. As the disk revolves, the vegetables are peeled by being thrown against the abrasive-coated walls.

Dishwashers

Dishwashers come in a variety of types. The most common are the immersion dishwasher, which submerges racks of dishes; the single-tank, stationary-type dishwasher, which wash racks of dishes with jets of water within a single tank; the conveyer-rack machine, which carries racks of dishes on a conveyer belt through the dishwasher; the flight-type dishwasher, which has a continuous rack conveyer on which dishes are placed on pegs or bars for transportation through the machine; and the carousel-type dishwasher, which features a closed-circuit conveyer for loading and unloading dishes.

Dishwasher capacity is stated as the number of pieces that can be washed per hour or the number of meals to be served per meal period. A single-tank dishwasher can handle from 50 to 600 meals per meal period; two-tank machines are capable of handling from 1500 to 2000 meals per meal period; three-tank machines are suitable for 2500 meals per meal period.

Refrigeration Equipment

Refrigerating equipment may be either mobile or fixed reach-ins, specialized units, or ice-making equipment [13].

Reach-ins.   Reach-in units may be of either refrigerated or low-temperature type. Whether the door opens to the left or right is an important consideration when considering traffic flow throughout the kitchen. Doors, which may be full- or half-length, should have strong catches. Adjustable shelving allows maximum storage flexibility.

Low-temperature reach-ins may be either upright or chest type. The former cost a little more and will lose more refrigerated air than the latter, but they are easier to defrost, require less floor space, and allow for easier storage and removal of items.

Specialized Equipment. Specialized equipment consists of such items as fountains, salad or cold pans, display refrigerators, and walk-ins.

Because fountains must provide for different refrigeration needs, two or more condensing units may be required. For example, drinking and carbonated water, whipped cream, and other foods should be kept at about 40°F, while ice cream must be slightly colder than 10°F for dishing.

Salad pans or cold pans are commonly used in cafeteria counters for display of salads and other cold items. Some are designed to be flooded with water, which is then frozen and the display items placed on the ice.

Walk-ins are used to store large quantities of food in central storage areas. Typically, a large operation uses three walk-ins: one for fruits and vegetables, one for meats, poultry, and fish, and one for dairy products.

Ice-Making Equipment. Electricity, cold water, and drainage facilities are necessary for ice-making equipment. Ice can be made in blocks, cubes, or crushed/flake form. Flake machines produce more ice per day than do cube machines. Block ice can be sculpted into decoration pieces. Cubes can be from 1/4 to 1 inch. Cube ice lasts longer in drinks and is, therefore, used in takeout and for drinks to be held before being consumed. Flake ice, on the other hand, cools the drink faster but melts faster as well. Small cubes or flakes make a drink look larger in the glass than do large cubes.

INTERIOR SURFACES

Materials

Selection of materials for interior walls, floors, and ceilings has to take into account not only attractiveness to customers, but also such things as ease of cleaning, ease of maintenance, and safety.

Flooring. The most important factors to consider when selecting floor coverings are the resiliency and porosity of the material. Resiliency refers to the ability of the material to withstand shock. Asphalt, linoleum, vinyl, and sealed wood are examples of resilient floors.

Porosity identifies the extent to which the material can be penetrated by liquids. Absorption of liquids can damage a floor, in addition to making it difficult to get rid of microorganisms on or below the surface.

A variety of materials can be used for floor coverings [14]. Asphalt is tough, inexpensive, and resistant to water and acids. However, it tends to buckle under heavy weight and does not wear well under exposure to grease or soap.

Good carpeting holds its shape. It absorbs both sound and shock and has a good appearance. It should not be used in food preparation areas because of the difficulty in keeping it clean and hygienic in an area where spills are common.

Ceramic tiles are nonabsorbent. They are useful for walls but are much too slippery for use on floors. Concrete, a mixture of cement, sand, and gravel, is inexpensive. However, because it is porous, it should not be used in food preparation areas.

Although it retains its shape, linoleum is nonabsorbent and is unable to withstand weight. Marble has a good appearance, is nonresilient, nonabsorbent, expensive, and slippery. Plastic is the most resilient of all the materials listed. It is, however, nonabsorbent and cannot be exposed to alkalines or solvents.

Rubber helps prevent slips and is resilient. It can be slippery when wet unless an abrasive is added. Although resilient and resistant to water, grease, and oil, water seepage can cause vinyl tiles to lift, causing a safety and sanitation hazard.

Terrazzo, a mixture of marble chips and cement, offers a good appearance if sealed properly. However, it is nonresilient and nonabsorbent, and it is slippery when wet. Additionally, the installed cost is approximately six times that of vinyl. However, because of its longer lifespan, over a 40-year period the cost of terrazzo is only 12 percent higher than that of vinyl.

Wood is absorbent, can be fairly inexpensive, and offers a good appearance. It should not be used in food preparation areas, as it offers a breeding place for dust and insects. Properly sealed, wood can be used in serving areas.

Kitchen floors need to be nonslip, sanitary, and able to handle spills and constant cleaning. Preferred materials are marble, terrazzo, natural quarry tile, asphalt tile, or sealed wood. Poured seamless concrete can be used if it has been sealed adequately.

Carpeting can only be used in serving areas. Carpets that are closely woven are easier to clean. Medium to dark colors with patterns tend not to show spots. They do, however, require vacuuming on a daily basis in addition to periodic shampooing. Because bar areas suffer from dropped cigarettes and spilled drinks, they can use marble or tile to advantage.

Coving is a useful technique that improves sanitation by providing a curved sealed edge between floor and wall. Sharp corners or gaps that would be difficult to clean are thus eliminated.

Walls and Ceilings.   In selecting wall and ceiling materials, four things are particularly important: cleanability, location, noise reduction, and color. Often materials are chosen without regard to future maintenance time and costs. For example, ceramic tile, which is a popular wall covering, should have its grouting smooth, waterproof, and sealed to help in keeping it clean.

Stainless steel is a favorite material for kitchen locations because it is durable and moisture resistant. This is important in an area such as a kitchen, which involves a great deal of traffic and has a high humidity level. On the other hand, painted plaster or cinder-block walls, if selected properly, can be used successfully in dry areas. They would not, however, be suitable in areas where food or grease could splash on the wall.

Older people tend to touch the wall for support, especially on stairs and in corridors. Wall surfaces in these areas should be easy to clean. Smooth sealed plastic, plastic-laminated panels, and plastic-coated tiles are excellent ceiling choices for their ability to spread light and absorb sound.

In food preparation areas it is desirable to have light-colored walls and ceilings to help distribute light and to make dirt easier to see (and, therefore, to clean).

EQUIPMENT MAINTENANCE

The cost of equipment maintenance, which is largely a function of labor, should be determined when purchasing equipment. Planning the maintenance function will help assure lower operating costs through reduced maintenance while ensuring continued high sanitation standards throughout the life of the equipment.

The following are the most important concepts involved in cleaning and maintenance [15].

1. Minimize soil, dirt, and food buildup.
2. Remove buildup immediately.
3. Avoid as many soil-collecting surfaces and recesses as possible.
4. Select smooth, nonporous surfaces.
5. Provide easy access to areas that have to be cleaned frequently.
6. Streamline electrical, gas, and plumbing connections.
7. Use coved corners on equipment and building surfaces.
8. Provide adequate drains and cleanouts.
9. Use automated cleaning and sanitizing systems.

Stainless Steel Surfaces

Stainless steel surfaces are subject to staining. It requires contact with air to keep the layer of oxide that gives it its shine, and thus it must be cleaned regularly. On a routine basis the surface should be cleaned with a hot detergent solution, rinsed, and wiped dry with a soft clean cloth. Periodic deep cleaning consists of a paste of water and a nonabrasive scouring powder. The paste is rubbed in the direction of the polish lines to prevent scratches. The surface is then rinsed and dried.

Stainless steel, wood, or plastic scrapers—but not steel wool, steel scrapers, or knives—can be used to remove heavy deposits of food and/or soil. A vinegar and water solution, followed by rinsing and drying, is appropriate for removing hard water deposits.

Equipment

Broilers. Broiler grates and other movable parts should be cleaned daily. With gas broilers it is important to check the flame. A yellow-tipped flame indicates insufficient air. The burners can be adjusted to give a blue flame. Gas ports should be kept clean. With electric broilers heating elements can be replaced when they burn out.

An energy management program would ensure that [16]:

1. Burner orifices are checked and cleaned.
2. Pilot lights are cleaned and adjusted.
3. Air shutters are checked to ensure that the air–gas mixture is correct.
4. Ceramic and metal radiant units are checked for deterioration and replaced with new chips if blackened or cracked.

quick bite 9.5
A Green Makeover

Typical profit margins for operators typically range between 3 and 9 percent. With such narrow margins, restaurateurs are continually searching for ways to increase profits. There are ways to increase profits by about one-third and reduce operating costs without sacrificing quality or customer satisfaction. In fact, many of these methods actually increase customer satisfaction.

Increasing a business' energy efficiency will reduce costs and attract customers who seek out "green" products and services. Some simple changes in lighting and air conditioning can increase patrons' comfort and encourage repeat business while yielding up to a thirty-percent return on investment.

One way for restaurateurs to discover ways to save on energy costs is to employ an energy specialist who will determine methods to improve energy efficiency and reduce costs. A professional will present an operator with a report that assesses opportunities and payback period for the investments. Operators can also perform their own assessments using the ENERGY STAR Small Business Program provided by the Environmental Protection Agency. Using the EPA's ENERGY STAR Small Business Program can provide an operator with free advertising as a "green" place of business that will attract customers.

Possible improvements and upgrades include:

Lighting Upgrades

- T-8 fluorescent lamps with electronic ballasts will lower electric costs and improve the coloring and quality of lighting, which customers will appreciate.
- Replacing incandescent parking lot lights with high-pressure sodium or metal halide lights will reduce costs, improve lighting level and parking lot safety.

Heating and Air-Conditioning Systems

- Replacing older model furnaces and air-conditioners with high-efficiency programmable models can save a restaurant up to $1,500 per year.

Other Methods

- Replacing current ventilation systems with customized exhaust hoods can save up to $2,000 per year.
- Reducing number of coolers needed and using high-efficiency refrigerators help to save money as well.
- Replacing an old dishwasher with an insulated one can save operators up to $1,200 per year.

Source: Smith, Robert. "A 'Green' Makeover Can Improve Your Image And Your Profit Margin." *Nation's Restaurant News,* March 29, 1999, v. 33, n. 13, pp. 26, 82.

Coffee Urns.   Two problems with coffee urns can ruin the taste of the coffee. First, minerals in the water can be deposited. Second, deposits will accumulate on surfaces that are exposed to brewed coffee or coffee vapors.

The solution is to clean the urn after making every batch of coffee. This is done by rinsing the urn out to remove any remaining coffee and deposits, adding a gallon or so of hot water, and brushing the interior of the urn, then rinsing the urn. Twice a week the urn can be cleaned with a manufacturer-recommended product to remove stubborn deposits.

Thermostats should be checked periodically to ensure that the correct serving temperature is being maintained. Weekly checks for leaks should also be made.

Dishwashers.   The power should be turned off before cleaning a dishwasher. Tanks have to be drained and cleaned, wash arms removed, and lime or hard-water deposits eliminated from the rinse jets.

The exterior can be cleaned with a detergent solution, rinsed, and dried. Periodic checks are necessary for leaks, and belts and conveyors are examined for wear and lubricated.

On a regular basis [17]:

1. Spray nozzles, tanks, and heater coils are cleaned with a wire when lime deposits are detected.
2. The temperature of the final rinse is checked to ensure that it is at 180°F on high-temperature machines and at 140°F on low-temperature machines.
3. Feed and drain valves and pumps are checked for water leakage.
4. Speed reducers on conveyor-type washers are examined to ensure proper lubrication.
5. The insulation of water lines in the recirculation loop is noted.
6. The power rinse is examined to ensure that it turns off automatically.
7. Thermometers are checked and adjusted.

Fryers.   Fryers should be cleaned daily or at least twice weekly, depending on use. The fat must be removed and the interior wiped out and filled with water and a fryer cleaner solution. The interior is then rinsed and dried after removal of the cleaning solution.

Tilting fry pans should be cleaned daily. Food residue is scraped from the surfaces, which are then washed down with warm water and the pan rinsed.

An energy program would ensure that [18]:

1. Fat containers are inspected for grease leaks.
2. Thermostats are calibrated.
3. Gas burners and pilot lights are cleaned and adjusted.
4. Flues are examined for possible obstructions.
5. Gas valves are lubricated.

quick bite 9.6
Avoiding Disaster

Kitchen fires and flood- or weather-related disasters can destroy a business. The impacts of a disaster are long-lived; they can cause stress and reduce profits. Not only does it impact profits, but it also emotionally affects the owner(s) and employees. According to the National Archives and Records Administration in Washington DC, only 43% of businesses that experience a disaster recover well enough to continue business. Even of businesses that do reopen only 29% are still in operation two years after. Restaurants should prepare disaster plans and prepare to survive and recover during and after a disaster.

Some ways to protect a restaurant and reduce losses include:

- Check the lease to make sure that rent is not charged if the property is not accessible.
- Create a videotape of the restaurant's assets periodically and store it off-site in a bank vault.
- Store a copy of all insurance policies off-site as well.
- All important computer files should be backed up on disk and stored off-site.
- Keep the employee roster current and make sure all managers have a copy.
- Keep a list of suppliers and customers to keep in contact with during a disaster.
- Make a list of disaster restoration agencies and services.
- Make sure that the restaurant is boarded-up and secure after a disaster to prevent looting.
- Retain the services of a certified restorer immediately after the incident.

Source: Griggs, C.R., "Avoid the Shoulda, Woulda, Coulda Woes with a Well-Considered Disaster Plan." *Nation's Restaurant News*, April 12, 1999, v. 33, n. 15, pp. 26, 69.

Fat is the most costly part of the frying process. During frying the food absorbs fat, which must constantly be replaced. Fat should be strained daily and 15 to 20 percent of the kettle capacity added as fresh fat.

Fat breakdown can be minimized by [19]:

1. Switching the fryer to "standby" during slack periods.
2. Never adding seasonings to foods during frying.
3. Keeping all metal components in contact with the fat free of carbon, food crumbs, soap, and moisture.

4. Ensuring that the fat level not be topped up with lard, meat drippings, or other fatty substances.

Griddles. At a minimum, griddles should be cleaned once a day. A griddle stone rather than steel wool should be used on the griddle surface, always rubbing with the grain of the surface. The surface is then seasoned prior to the next use.

It is also important that [20]:

1. Thermostats are calibrated.
2. Pilot lights are adjusted to the lowest possible flame.
3. The air–gas mixture is checked to ensure a blue flame. Cold spots should be checked for on a periodic basis.

Ovens. Similar maintenance procedures for griddles should be evident in the operation of ovens. On a daily basis, burned-on particles of food should be removed from the decks and the interior of the oven brushed out. Hardened food can be removed by sprinkling with salt and running the oven at 500°F for half an hour. The charred food is then removed with a spatula.

Ovens and oven racks need to be level for even cooking. Door crevices need to be kept clean to ensure proper closure, which keeps the heat in.

The interior of convection ovens may be porcelain, stainless steel, aluminized steel, or Teflon®-coated and should be cleaned following the recommendations of the manufacturer. Clean doors help ensure minimum heat loss. Fan blades that are dirty reduce airflow and can be cleaned with a detergent solution.

Microwave ovens require less maintenance than do other types. As before, special attention should be paid to the door to ensure a tight fit.

After cleaning ranges a light coating of cooking oil is applied to help prevent rusting.

Food Cutters, Choppers, and Slicers. Choppers and cutters should be rinsed after each use. They should be unplugged before cleaning. Special care must be taken with slicer blades, which should be sanitized and allowed to dry after cleaning.

Mixers. As above, mixers should be cleaned right after use.

Tables. Tabletops can be scrubbed with a hot detergent solution before being rinsed, sanitized, and allowed to dry. Drawers should be emptied and washed weekly.

Refrigerators. The inside of reach-in refrigerators should be cleaned once a week. Shelves are removed and cleaned at the pot sink or run throughout the dishwasher.

Condenser coils need to be watched for dirt buildup, which cuts down on the transfer of heat and causes the unit to run excessively. Coils are dusted or wiped free of dust and dirt.

Walk-ins should be cleaned at most once a month, depending on use, following the procedures outlined above. A comprehensive program would ensure that [21]:

1. Worn or damaged compressor belts are replaced.
2. The refrigerant level is checked if a short cycle or loss of temperature control is noticed.
3. The fan, condenser fins, plates, and blower coils are cleaned.
4. Gaskets, seals, and hinges on doors are checked for a tight fit.
5. Defrosting is done monthly.
6. Thermostats are properly calibrated.
7. Hinges and latches are lubricated with food-grade oil.
8. Outside walls are felt for cold spots that would indicate insulation failure.
9. The defrost cycle is set such that freezers will defrost during off-peak hours.
10. Compressors are checked for leaks and refrigerant levels.
11. The condenser is brush cleaned.
12. Coils are examined to ensure that they are not clogged with dirt or grease.
13. All service motors are inspected regularly.

Steam Equipment.   Steam-jacketed kettles are cleaned after the steam is turned off and they have been allowed to cool. The kettle is flushed, filled with a detergent solution, and soaked for 30 to 60 minutes. The kettle is then drained, rinsed, and sanitized.

Ventilating Hoods.   Filters should be cleaned at least once a week. Clogged filters reduce airflow and significantly reduce the efficiency of the ventilation system. As a result, droplets can fall onto food that is being prepared. A more serious danger is that posed by the threat of fire due to grease buildup.

ENERGY MANAGEMENT

It is estimated that a comprehensive energy management program can save the average foodservice company 20 percent of its energy bill. One of the major problems in controlling energy costs is that a significant part of the cost is fixed. Refrigerators and fans are in operation regardless of sales volume, and most appliances are designed for high-volume operation. A reduction in number of meals prepared will not result in a corresponding reduction in energy costs. To get costs under control it might be possible to plan less energy-intensive meals—prepared foods and salad plates—during low-business periods.

Comprehensive Program

A comprehensive approach to handling energy costs involves several steps [22].

Top Management Commitment.   Employees pay attention to what management pays attention to. Getting the support of top management is an essential first step in a successful program. Top management's responsibilities are to define the goals and standards for the program. Basic goals might include [23]:

quick bite 9.7
How to Cut Utility Costs

According to Edison Electric Institute, restaurants consume twice as much energy per square foot than does any other business. Here are some ideas on how to cut utility costs:

1. Turn off unneeded equipment during slower periods.
2. Perform routine maintenance to cut up to 10 percent from energy bills.
3. Turn employees on to conservation.
4. Take advantage of the time-of-use rate. Under this option energy used during off-peak hours (evenings and on weekends) is much cheaper than energy used during peak times.
5. Have someone devote 100 percent of her time to energy issues.
6. Switch to energy-efficient equipment if it is right for your menu and you can get it repaired locally.
7. Monitor your energy use monthly.
8. Purchase insulated cooking equipment.
9. Preheat cooking equipment no longer than the manufacturer's guidelines.
10. Use cooking equipment to capacity.
11. Change heating, ventilation, and air-conditioning filters quarterly.

Source: Winchester, Sarah Hart. "Putting Energy into Cutting Utility Costs," *Restaurants USA,* vol. 15, no. 5, May 1995, pp. 12–14.

- Reduce the consumption and cost of energy and water utilities by 20 percent per year.
- Improve the quality of the operation such that guest satisfaction is increased.

Standard methods to track and summarize energy consumption must also be developed to monitor the program. A base level should be established to serve as a measure of progress made. Usually, this figure is developed from the 12-month period prior to the implementation of the program.

Base measures should be established for each month. The total water consumption in gallons and water consumption per customer should be noted.

For electricity, gas, and other energy sources the various units of energy, as reported on utility bills, must be converted into a standard measure, usually the British thermal unit (BTU). The following factors are used to convert energy use into a BTU value [24]:

Source	Measure	BTU
Electricity	kWh (kilowatthour)	3,413
Natural gas	Cubic foot	1,000
Oil	Gallon	140,000
Steam	Pound	1,000

quick bite 9.8
Road to the Top: Niki Leondakis

Vice President of Restaurant Operations

A good management style can get you everywhere in life if you apply it well, just ask vice president of restaurant operations for Kimpton Hotel & Restaurant Group, Niki Leondakis. According to Kimpton's former chef and GM, David Machado, it is Leondakis's blend of the old with the new that makes her so successful. Leondakis has a strong work ethic that leads her to put in fourteen-hour days if necessary.

However, Leondakis's management style is no way reflected by her "old school" work ethic. She embraces some very modern self-awareness tools including personality typing and industrial psychologists in her management technique. Leondakis has gone so far in embracing the company's concept that a psychologist helps to screen for desirable qualities in Kimpton's candidates.

According to Leondakis, "It's our belief that by understanding yourself, you are better able to lead others—if someone is rigidly opposed to self-awareness and improvement, it is probably better that they run away from us." She uses this philosophy in her management of 21 contemporary full-service restaurants of varying ethnic and conceptual flavors.

Leondakis first majored in art at University of Massachusetts before switching to a hotel and restaurant management and travel administration program. She first began her foodservice management career at Marriott before moving to Ritz Carlton. Leondakis then joined Kimpton in 1993 to oversee three restaurants and was promoted to her current position in 1995.

Leondakis's co-workers have been known to call her focused, diligent, and driven. She has a very direct management style and considers hiring good people the most difficult part of her job. "I like to be challenged and challenge other people," she acknowledges, "I don't think I'm insensitive, but I do feel that I have the inner strength to handle adversity and differences of opinion."

Source: Liddle, Anne. "Niki Leondakis: Cultivating Success through Self-awareness Tools and a Strong Work Ethic." *Nation's Restaurant News*, v. 33, no. 4, pp. 142–144.

From these sources total annual water and energy use can be determined, broken down by month and per meal served. This will serve as a base for comparing consumption before and after the program is implemented.

Energy Coordinating Committee.   Management will not, however, have the time to oversee every detail of the program. Responsibility must be placed in the hands of someone to ensure accountability. The committee should be made up of a representative from each major department. This committee is responsible for tracking energy consumption and implementing improvements.

Energy Audit.   Once a base level has been established the coordinating committee can conduct an audit to determine where energy waste is occurring.

---

quick bite 9.9
Facility Maintenance 2000

At the turn of the century, even more emphasis will be placed on foodservice waste management and recycling and managers will be required to take the lead. Managers will need to train and supervise back-of-the-house employees in proper sorting and recycling of materials. It is also likely that local, state, and federal government will create new laws regarding this issue and managers will need to ensure compliance.

In order to reduce costs, it is likely that managers will begin to take a closer look at security and safety issues. Managers will be responsible for developing safety committees with employee input. And through these committees, managers will be responsible for developing safety plans to prevent both employee and customer incidents.

Managers will need to become more adept at developing preventive maintenance plans. Because repairs and maintenance can be costly, they are an important part of profitability. The maintenance of both the facility and equipment will become a priority and managers will likely rely heavily on outside expertise.

*The Top Five Most Likely Developments for Managers
in Facility Maintenance for 2000:*

1. Increased responsibility for waste management and recycling
2. Increased emphasis on safety and security
3. New technologies for facilities management including energy management systems
4. Growing emphasis on preventative maintenance
5. Development of safety committees and plans

Source: Foodservice Manager 2000 (Washington, D.C.: National Restaurant Association, 1992).

Revise Operating Procedures. The audit should have revealed areas for improvement. Based on the findings of the audit, the committee can develop revised operating procedures for presentation to management. A new procedure might require ovens to be turned on 30 minutes prior to use rather than at the beginning of the shift.

A list of operating procedures can be developed and new policies implemented and explained to employees. Employees may need to be trained in the new procedures, and incentives may have to be developed to ensure compliance.

Analyze Alternatives. Some energy-saving suggestions will require the modification of existing or the purchase of new equipment. Detailed analysis will be required to determine the costs and benefits of a suggestion. The following recommendations can assist in reducing energy consumption [25].

Lighting
1. Wash walls and ceilings to help maximize light reflection.
2. Remove decorative lighting in the dining room.
3. Clean all lamps and light fixtures.
4. Replace several small-wattage light bulbs with one large one.
5. Remove all unnecessary light bulbs.
6. Change extended-life lamps to standard-life lamps; reflector floor lights to parabolic floodlights; and older-model fluorescent lights to high-efficiency fluorescent lights.
7. Replace lamps installed more than two years previously because of the decrease in light output.

Water
1. Replace washers immediately in dripping faucets.
2. Drain and flush hot water tanks every three to six months.
3. Check the steam trap on steam water heaters regularly.
4. Check insulation on water heaters by feeling for hot spots.
5. Have burners adjusted if the exhaust is smoky or high in CO_2 emissions, or if the stack is extremely hot.
6. Insulate all hot-water pipes.
7. Use a lower water temperature for nonsanitizing areas.
8. Reduce water pressure at the intake valve.

Heating, Ventilation, and Air-Conditioning (HVAC) System
1. Turn off the heating and cooling in seldom-used spaces.
2. Remove obstructions from heating and cooling vents.
3. Replace caulking and weatherstripping around doors, windows, and ventilating units.
4. Clean or replace all filters in exhaust hoods and the HVAC system.

quick bite 9.10

Restaurant Operations in 2010

According to the National Restaurant Association the most likely developments regarding restaurant operations in 2010 are:

- Equipment will be on wheels for ease of movement.
- Quick disconnect systems on equipment will allow for easy cleaning and flexible layouts.
- Inventory management will become more automated.
- Equipment will have to monitor and record critical control points (HACCP) electronically.
- Food handling at the restaurant will be reduced as more items will be pre-made by commissaries or manufacturers.

Source: Restaurant Industry 2010: The Road Ahead (Washington, D.C.: National Restaurant Association, 1999), p. 10.

5. Check heating and cooling ducts and exhaust hoods for cleanliness, insulation, and leaks.
6. Use natural gas rather than electricity as the energy source for the booster heater for dishwashers.

ENDNOTES

1. Mahmood Khan, *Foodservice Operations* (Westport, CT: AVI Publishing Company, 1987), pp. 112–116.

2. Ibid., pp. 164–166.

3. Ibid., p. 112.

4. Lendal H. Kotschevar and Margaret E. Terrell, *Foodservice Planning: Layout and Equipment,* 3rd ed. (New York: John Wiley & Sons, 1985), p. 330.

5. Khan, *Foodservice Operations,* pp. 112–113.

6. Ibid., p. 113.

7. Ibid., p. 119.

8. Ibid., p. 138.

9. Ibid., p. 126.

10. Ibid., p. 126.

11. Edward A. Kazarian, *Foodservice Facilities Planning,* 3rd ed. (New York: Van Nostrand Reinhold, 1989), p. 171.

12. Khan, *Foodservice Operations,* p. 113.

13. Kotschevar and Terrell, *Foodservice Planning: Layout and Equipment,* 3rd ed. (New York: John Wiley & Sons, 1985), p. 447.

14. Kazarian, *Foodservice Facilities Planning,* pp. 112–113.

15. Kazarian, *Foodservice Facilities Planning,* p. 219.

16. Lewis J. Minor and Ronald F. Cichy, *Foodservice Systems Management* (Westport, CT: AVI Publishing Company, 1984), p. 242.

17. Ibid., p. 242.

18. Ibid., p. 241.

19. Kazarian, *Foodservice Facilities Planning,* pp. 223–224.

20. Minor and Cichy, *Foodservice Systems Management,* p. 241.

21. Ibid., p. 242.

22. Robert E. Aulbach, *Energy and Water Resource Management,* 2nd ed. (East Lansing, MI: The Educational Institute of the American Hotel and Motel Association, 1988), p. 99.

23. Ibid., p. 101.

24. Judy Ford Stokes, *Cost Effective Quality Food Service: An Institutional Guide* (Rockville, MD: Aspen Systems Corporation, 1985), p. 258.

25. Minor and Cichy, *Foodservice Systems Management,* pp. 243–244.

CHAPTER TEN

SANITATION
AND FOOD SAFETY

learning objectives

By the end of this chapter you should be able to:

1. Identify the role of the restaurant manager in sanitation.

2. Identify the major sanitation problems in a restaurant.

3. Show how to establish proactive sanitation and safety programs.

4. Develop procedures for preventing foodborne diseases.

5. Build effective employee hygiene habits.

---

*Food poisoning is an occupational hazard. I had campylobacter, which is
in the family of salmonella. It was truly a work-related injury,
but it wasn't seen that way.*
Penelope Corcoran, food critic for *The Arizona Republic,* quoted in *Dining Out.*

Source: Dornenburg, Andrew and Karen Page, *Dining Out* (New York, NY: John Wiley & Sons,
Inc., 1998).

ROLE OF THE MANAGER

Management is responsible for serving food that is nutritious, appeals to the senses, and is safe to eat [1]. According to the National Assessment Institute, a restaurant manager is responsible for [2]:

- Identifying health hazards in the daily operation of the restaurant.
- Developing and implementing policies, procedures, and standards to prevent foodborne illnesses.
- Coordinating training, supervision, and direction of food handling and preparation while taking corrective action as required to protect the health of customers and employees.
- Inspecting the operation periodically to ensure that policies and procedures are being followed correctly.

To assist them in taking a proactive stance in assuring sanitary procedures, managers should have some knowledge of the following [3]:

1. Properties of food: the amount of available moisture and the pH level that strengthens or represses the growth of bacteria together with a list of potentially dangerous foods.
2. Food processing/preparation: processes the food will undergo.

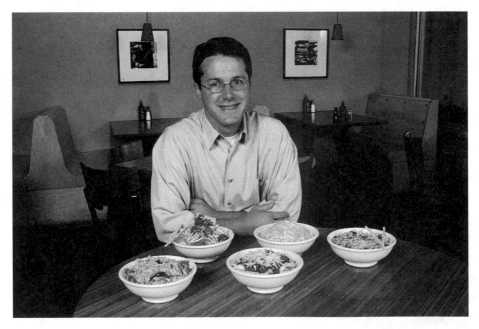

Courtesy of Noodles & Company.

quick bite 10.1

Hot Concepts: Noodles & Company

Noodles & Company's first store opened in 1996. Aaron Kennedy, the restaurant's founder, plans to open 30 restaurants within seven years. The company, which calls itself "a global noodle shop," recently opened two metro-Denver area restaurants. The second market that Noodles caters to with two restaurants and a third planned for September 1999 is Madison, Wisconsin, where Kennedy went to graduate school. The chain's expansion is funded by a recent private stock offering at $2.50 per share. The offering earned Noodles $1,000,000. Noodles' product is low-cost and provides customers with a good value meal and Noodles with acceptable margins.

The restaurant's main dish is noodles, which are served with any one of a variety of sauces from cuisines around the globe. Kennedy describes Noodles' fare as "comfort food from around the world." Varieties include Japanese pan noodles, pesto linguini, Indonesian peanut sauté, Thai noodles and Wisconsin mac and cheese. Each bowl of noodles cost approximately $5 with an additional charge for beef, chicken, tofu or shrimp. Each bowl is cooked to order and forty percent of the restaurant's business is take-out.

Kennedy comes from a strong marketing background. He worked as a brand manager for Pepsi and was involved in many of Pepsi's national campaigns. Kennedy got his idea for Noodles when he moved to Boulder, Colorado, due to his wife's job change, giving him the opportunity to start a new career. Kennedy and the company are evaluating markets with populations of 500,000 to 1.5 million to build new stores. Kennedy said that he does not plan to franchise his concept, but to continue growth of the company-owned stores through more private stock offerings.

Source: Parker, Penny. "Entrepreneur Uses His Noodle." *The Denver Post,* Feb. 16, 1999, Sec. C, pp. 1C & 7C.

3. Volume of food prepared: the larger the quantity of food to be fixed, the greater the potential danger.
4. Type of customer: acknowledging the fact that certain people (the very old, very young, infirm, and those who are sick) are more susceptible to foodborne illness than the rest of the population.

MAJOR SANITATION PROBLEMS

Foodborne Illnesses

According to the Centers for Disease Control (CDC), foodborne illnesses occur because of [4]:

1. Inadequate cooling and cold holding (63 percent). Storing food in large containers more than 4 inches deep means that the food in the center of the container will not cool fast enough to prevent bacterial growth. Putting tight lids on containers in which hot foods are stored will slow cooling when the product is refrigerated. Similarly, stacking food containers one on top of the other and arranging cooler racks such that air is prevented from flowing freely around all surfaces of the containers will also slow down the cooling process.

2. Preparing food ahead of planned service (29 percent). Food should not be prepared more than a day ahead of time.

3. Inadequate hot holding (27 percent). Contaminated food will come from holding food at temperatures between 70 and 120°F for more than 4 hours; using hot-holding units for uses other than intended; improper operation of hot-holding units, such as turning the thermostat too low or failing to turn on the fan; and combining new and old food items.

4. Poor personal hygiene/infected persons (26 percent). Inadequate hand-washing and food contact with employees who have infectious diseases are major problems in this area.

5. Inadequate reheating (25 percent). It is important that temperatures be brought to 165°F and kept there for a time sufficient to kill any micro-organisms.

6. Inadequate cleaning of equipment (9 percent). It is especially important to sanitize sinks and cutting boards, ensure that water temperature is above the safe level, and that sanitizing agents are strong enough to re-duce bacteria.

7. Cross-contamination (6 percent). Cross-contamination can come from such things as touching raw foods, then handling cooked foods before washing hands, inadequate cleaning of raw food items, and improper sani-tizing of surfaces and utensils between use with cooked and raw food items.

8. Inadequate cooking or heat processing (5 percent). Of particular concern would be the undercooking of poultry, pork, and eggs. Checking the inter-nal temperature of food is essential to ensure adequate cooking.

9. Contaminated raw materials (2 percent). Serving food raw means that there is no chance to reduce the level of microorganisms once the initial prepara-tion has occurred.

10. Unsafe sources (1 percent). It is vital that approved suppliers be used and that fish be certified as having come from clean waters.

(Note: Figures add up to more than 100 percent because more than one factor is usually involved in an outbreak.)

Foodborne illnesses occur from one of three sources [5]: biological, chemi-cal, and physical.

Biological Sources

Bacteria. Biological contamination can come from bacteria, viruses, and parasites. Most foodborne illnesses are caused by microorganisms, the most significant group of which are bacteria. Bacteria are transmitted by wind, moisture, dust, and direct contact with other living things. They reproduce two to three times an hour, depending on the available moisture, pH, temperature, oxygen, and food levels present. Bacteria prefer high-protein food products. Thus items with high protein—poultry, meat, gravy, eggs, salads, fish, and so on—are particularly susceptible to bacterial growth. They also require a certain amount of moisture. Dry products such as cereals, flour, rice, and sugar do not contain enough moisture for bacteria to multiply.

The U.S. Public Health Service defines the temperature danger zone as being between 45 and 140°F. Most bacterial growth occurs within this range. The amount of time that food products remain within this temperature range should be minimized. Certain bacteria actually prefer cold temperatures as low as 19°F and can even reproduce in refrigerated storage. Freezing or drying foods will delay the growth of but not kill organisms.

Some bacteria require oxygen to reproduce, while others can multiply even without it. Neutral pH is 7.0. As the pH value moves closer to zero, food becomes more acidic and the conditions for bacterial growth lessen. The preferred range for bacterial growth is 6.5 to 7.5.

The best way to limit bacterial growth is to control time and temperature—the time that foods are within the temperature danger zone. It is impossible to eliminate all bacteria; it is only possible to limit the growth of harmful bacteria to levels considered safe.

Viruses. Viruses are spread to food by employees infected with the virus. This can occur through such means as failing to wash hands after going to the bathroom, coughing, sneezing, or wiping a runny nose with a hand. Hepatitis A is one common illness transmitted by a virus. The most likely foods to cause illness through viral transfer are those which are not heated after handling: salads, cold sandwiches, raw or uncooked oysters, and so on.

Parasites. Parasites live within or feed off another organism. Parasites and their eggs can be contained in such foods as pork and fish. Parasites can be destroyed by cooking the food to at least 140°F. Trichinosis and dysentery are the result of parasites in pork and water, respectively.

Fungi—molds, yeasts, and mushrooms—can be poisonous. Certain molds can produce toxins that have been associated with foodborne illness. Freezing will retard the growth of molds but will have no effect on those already present. Molds will be destroyed by heating to 140°F for 10 minutes, but heat will not get rid of any toxins already present. Cooking at the correct temperature is the best way to prevent fungi growth.

While yeasts are not known to cause illness, they will cause certain foods and beverages to spoil. They can be killed by heating items to 136°F for 15 minutes and controlled with cleaning and sanitizing.

Chemical Contamination

Chemical contamination occurs when substances such as cleaning compounds or pesticides get into food. Food additives and preservatives are used to enhance food flavor and keep the product fresh longer. Some, however—such as nitrites, sulfites, and MSG—can be harmful. Although the use of sulfites is prohibited by restaurants, it is allowed in food processing under tight regulations.

Pesticides, used to control insect damage on crops, can lead to poisoning if the residue is not removed completely. Chemical contamination can also come from toxic metals such as copper, brass, cadmium, lead, and zinc. Zinc-galvanized containers can make acidic foods such as fruit juice and pickles poisonous. Care should also be taken that items used for cleaning purposes be stored properly in a manner that will not bring them into contact with food.

Physical Contamination

Physical contamination occurs when hair, dirt, and similar items come into contact with food. Poor ventilation and maintenance can contribute to objects or moisture coming into contact with food.

Cross-contamination occurs when there is contact between safe and contaminated foods: for example, when raw food comes into contact with food that has been cooked. Cleaning and sanitizing of equipment should occur between use with different foods and between the same cooked and raw foods. As an example, raw chicken might be trimmed on a cutting board and then cooked. The cooked chicken should not be placed back on the cutting board until the board has been cleaned and sanitized.

The symptoms of bacterial food infection are nausea, vomiting, diarrhea, and intestinal cramps.

TAKING A PROACTIVE STANCE: HACCP

The objectives of a food sanitation program are to protect food from contaminating substances and to minimize the effects of any contamination that does occur [6]. The Hazard Analysis Critical Control Points (HACCP) system, developed in the 1960s to ensure the safety of food prepared for astronauts, is set up to maximize food safety. The system combines three elements—principles of food microbiology, quality control, and risk assessment—and emphasizes a movement away from the inspection of facilities to one that centers on the process of preparing and serving safe food [7].

The HACCP system consists of six steps [8]:

1. Identify hazards and assess their severity and risks. This involves examining the menu and recipes to identify potentially hazardous foods. Reducing the number of steps involved in preparing menu items will reduce the risk of contamination [9].

2. Determine critical control points. Four important control points are good personal hygiene, avoidance of cross-contamination, cooking, and cooling [10].

3. Implement control measures and establish criteria to assure control. Procedures must be observable and measurable. For example, the directions for fixing a baked chicken breast should include: 1. washing hands; 2. washing, rinsing, and sanitizing the cutting board and knife that are used for slicing the chicken breast; and 3. maintaining the actual product temperature of 160°F (73.9°C) [11].

4. Monitor crucial control points and record data. After receiving turkey and checking that the temperature is lower than 45°F, it is important to check that after storing it, the temperature in the refrigerator is 40°F or lower and that the raw turkey is not stored above cooked food.

5. Take appropriate action when control criteria are not met. You might find, for example, that the chef is preparing turkey breasts all at one time. The turkey is within the temperature danger zone for longer than it should be. Corrective action is required that will reduce the amount of time the turkey is within the danger zone. New procedures have to be developed such that turkey breasts are prepared in smaller batches and returned to the cooler immediately upon completion.

6. Confirm that the system is working as planned. For each step in the process of receiving through reheating for service, four areas are determined: the critical control point, the potential hazard, appropriate standards, and whatever corrective action is needed if the standards are not met. For example, the first control point is in receiving beef and vegetables. Contamination and spoilage are potential hazards in both cases. Receiving standards should be set such that the temperature of the beef is at 45°F or lower, packaging on both products is intact, there is no odor, stickiness, or cross-contamination from other foods on the truck, and there are no signs of insect or rodent activity. If any of these conditions are present, the proper corrective action is to refuse delivery. A similar procedure is spelled out for each step in the process.

PREVENTIVE PROCEDURES

Purchasing

The key to effective procedures in purchasing is to use reliable suppliers.

Receiving

Deliveries should be scheduled during slow periods so that time can be devoted to careful inspection. Check the condition of the delivery truck for signs of improper storage during transit. Temperatures should be checked to make sure that refrigerated foods are below 45°F and frozen foods are below 0°F. Cartons that are damaged should be rejected.

Glass thermometers or those filled with mercury should not be used, as they can break. Select thermometers at least 5 inches long and insert at least 2 inches into food when taking a reading. The thermometers should then be cleaned and sanitized after every use.

Meat products must be inspected by a federal or state regulatory program. If they pass the inspection, they are given a circular identification stamp indicating where the meat was processed. Suppliers can be asked for written confirmation that individual cuts have been inspected. Check the appearance and smell—aged meat will be darker in appearance than fresh; slimy, sticky, or dry meat should be rejected, as should products with a sour smell.

Poultry must also be inspected under a federal or state program. Operators should use only Grade A poultry. Signs of aging are purple or greenish color, bad smell, darkened wing tips, and soft, flabby, and sticky flesh.

Since there is no mandated inspection program for seafood, it is particularly important to buy from suppliers you trust. Fresh fish should be delivered in crushed ice at a temperature between 32 and 45°F. Fish is safe if it has bright skin, moist, red gills, eyes that are clear and bulging, and scales that are firmly attached. The flesh should be firm and elastic to the touch and should not separate easily from the bone.

Fluid or frozen liquids in cartons of frozen foods or large ice crystals in the product itself are indications that it has been thawed and refrozen. Such items are not acceptable.

Carefully check the expiration date on milk and dairy products. All products must be Grade A pasteurized. Once milk has been taken from a container, it should never be returned to that container.

Eggs can be spot-checked by breaking one or two open to check that the temperature is below 45°F, there is no noticeable odor, the yolk is firm, and the white clings to the yolk.

It is now possible to purchase certain items in packaging from which air has been removed. Gases may be added to help preserve the item. Vacuum-packed foods must be kept at temperatures below 45°F, fish below 38°F. *Sous vide* refers to products that are vacuum packed and then fully or partially cooked. Products must be stored at temperatures from 32 to 38°F. Plants that sell *sous vide* products must be certified by the Federal Drug Administration (FDA).

Storage

The six most significant reasons for food spoilage are [12]:

1. Incorrect storage temperatures
2. Excessive storage time
3. Inadequate ventilation in storage areas
4. Failure to segregate foods in storage
5. Unacceptable sanitation standards
6. Excessive delays between receiving and storing functions

Table 10.1 Recommended Conditions for Storage

Storage Area	Temperature (°F)	Relative Humidity (%)
Dry storage	50–70	50–60
Refrigerated storage		
Dairy products and eggs	38–40	75–85
Red meats and poultry	32–40	75–85
Fresh fish	30–34	75–85
Live shellfish	35–45	75–85
Fresh vegetables and fruit	40–45	85–95
Frozen storage	< 0	

Source: Applied Foodservice Sanitation, 4th ed. (New York: John Wiley & Sons, 1992), p. 121.

The National Restaurant Association recommendations for storing food are shown in Table 10.1. Food products should be used in the order in which they have been received. This concept is known as FIFO: first in, first out. Items should be dated and newer stock placed behind older stock to help ensure the integrity of the process. Ideally, purchases will be kept in their original containers. If not, care must be taken that the items are kept in containers that are clean and nonabsorbent. Metal containers can be dangerous when they come into contact with foods with a high acidic content.

Different types of meat should be kept separate from each other, as should raw and cooked items. Items should be stored at least 6 inches off the floor and away from pipes that might drip onto the food. Allow for air circulation around all surfaces between packages. Before opening cans, wipe them with a clean cloth to prevent contamination from the outside of the cans. Cleaning supplies should be stored separately from food items.

We can see that the potential hazards are due to cross-contamination and bacterial growth and spoilage. Appropriate standards would be to store raw beef on a lower shelf with vegetables above it, label, date, and use FIFO rotation, and ensure that the beef temperature remains under 45°F. Corrective action would involve moving the beef to a lower shelf and discarding either beef or vegetables if they have been kept longer than they should have.

Preparation and Serving

The highest risk for contamination is when food is being prepared and served. There are three concerns [13]: employee hygiene, time and temperature control, and the cleaning and sanitizing of utensils, equipment, and surfaces with which food comes into contact. Employee hygiene is dealt with later. As far as time and temperature are concerned, the major goal is that the time that a product is in the danger zone, between 45 and 140°F, be minimized. One particular problem for operators is the procedure for thawing frozen food. To minimize time in the danger zone, frozen food should never be thawed at room temperature but can, instead, be thawed under refrigeration, by cooking as a continuous process, in a microwave oven, or under water at about 70°F for a maximum of two hours.

Cross-contamination becomes a potential problem during preparation. As noted earlier, cross-contamination occurs when cooked food comes into contact

---

quick bite 10.2
FDA Food Code, 1993

The Federal Drug Administration has released a 400-page food code. This is not a federal law or regulation; however, local authorities can choose to adopt all or part of it.

Here are some of the changes from prior codes:

1. Standards for time and temperature.
   - Poultry: 165°F for 15 seconds
   - Pork: 150°F for 60 seconds or 145°F for 3 minutes
   - Ground beef: 155°F for 15 seconds
   - Cold holding: 41°F
2. Provides a two-step cooling process (140°F to 70°F in 2 hours and 70°F to 41°F in 4 hours) for potentially hazardous foods.
3. Requires that employees wash their hands twice and use a nailbrush after each rest room use.
4. Requires food workers to use gloves when handling ready-to-eat foods.
5. Requires that consumers who order raw or partially cooked foods of animal origin must be informed of the increased risk to especially vulnerable populations.
6. Requires that the person in charge demonstrate to the regulatory authority a knowledge of foodborne disease prevention and the requirements of the 1993 code.
7. The definition of "potentially hazardous food" is expanded to include cut melons and garlic–oil mixtures.

The full report can be ordered through the National Technical Information Service at (703) 487-4650. It costs $23 for a spiral-bound copy and $17 for a diskette.

Source: Austin, Kim. "FDA Releases New Food Code," *Restaurants USA,* v. 14, n. 4, April 1994, p. 7.

with raw food. Similarly, surfaces that have had contact with raw food must be sanitized before coming into contact with cooked food.

In cooking, it is especially critical that the internal temperature of food items be checked in several places to ensure that cooking is complete. As noted before, thermometers with stainless steel stems should be used. They should be sanitized between uses and allowed to return to room temperature before being used again. The following minimum temperatures are recommended [14]:

- 45°F or below: steak tartare
- 130°F: beef
- 145°F: potentially hazardous foods
- 150°F: pork and pork products
- 155°F: ground beef
- 165°F: poultry and meat containing stuffing
- 165°F: all foods previously served and cooled that are reheated
- 170°F: pork and pork products cooked in a microwave

Holding equipment should never be used to heat food. The equipment itself should be able to maintain a temperature of at least 140°F and hold the food at the required temperature at all times. A food thermometer will be necessary to check that temperatures are maintained. Chances for contamination can be reduced if holding time is kept to a minimum, if foods are stirred periodically, and if covers are used over containers.

Milk, eggs, and egg products should be stored at temperatures below 45°F. After cooking, eggs should be held at a minimum of 140°F.

Ice should be treated and handled with the same care as for food. Using hands, cups, or glasses to handle ice is to be avoided; hands carry germs, and glasses can break in the ice bin.

In self-service areas, customers, who probably have less sanitation background, are the people who come into contact with the food. The key is to set up the system such that contact with food is minimized. This will mean such things as providing individually wrapped portions wherever possible, supplying food or "sneeze" guards, furnishing enough utensils so that each dish has its own utensil and changing them periodically for fresh, sanitized items, and constantly monitoring the temperatures of the various items.

Reheating

If food has been cooked and held under sanitary conditions, it can be reused. Great care must be taken that it has not been exposed to contamination. It is estimated that up to 20 percent of usable food in the United States is thrown out. Various agencies have been set up to collect restaurant leftovers and distribute them to the needy. The major rule of thumb, however, is: If in doubt, throw it out [15].

If the decision is made to keep leftovers, the food must be chilled to reach an internal temperature of 45°F as quickly as possible. This can be done by dividing large quantities of food into smaller portions prior to chilling, placing food in containers with a depth no greater than two inches, stirring the contents of the container; giving the containers an ice-water bath (placing them in larger containers filled with ice), and using specially designed refrigeration units.

Stored leftovers should be covered and sealed, stored above raw foods, and labeled clearly. Reheated foods must reach an internal temperature of 165°F.

Bars

The National Restaurant Association has published a list of 12 effective bar sanitation tips [16].

1. Wash glasses in a high-temperature dishwasher with a chemical sanitizer.
2. Air-dry all glasses.
3. When using the three-sink method, have the first sink filled with a detergent solution at a temperature of at least 110°F; the second sink filled with clean water at a temperature of 120°F, and the third sink filled with water at 170°F, in which the glasses are sanitized for at least 30 seconds.
4. Have employees use racks or baskets when using the three-sink method, to avoid burning themselves.
5. As a sanitizing alternative to hot water, use a chemical sanitizer at a temperature of at least 75°F.
6. Test the sanitizing water with a test kit.
7. Store glasses upside down.
8. Store bar utensils such that they will be picked up by their handles.
9. Check local regulations on the frequency of cleaning of beer lines; it may have to be done once a week.
10. Use different cloths for wiping down bottles and wiping down the bar.
11. Do not use scented or oxygen bleaches as sanitizers. The label will say whether or not it is registered with the Environmental Protection Agency (EPA).
12. Store glasses a minimum of 6 inches from the ground and protect from soil and condensation.

Equipment

Various equipment manufacturers have developed standards for equipment designed for sanitation. Operators should look on equipment for designations from Underwriters' Laboratories (UL) or NSF International, for assistance in purchasing.

Cleaning. To reduce bacteria to safe levels, kitchen equipment must be sanitized. Sanitizing equipment means going beyond cleaning with detergent and hot water; it means using heat and chemical agents after cleaning.

A variety of factors must be considered before cleaning begins [17]:

- Type and condition of soil. Soil can be protein-based (for example, blood or egg), grease or oil, dissolved in water (for example, flour), and acid or alkaline. Whether it is fresh, ground-in, soft, dried, or baked-on will influence how easy it is to remove.
- Type of water. Hard water makes cleaning more difficult and leaves a scale or lime deposit on equipment.
- Temperature of water. The higher the temperature, the faster the cleaning.
- Surface being cleaned. Aluminum can darken in highly alkaline or chlorinated cleaners; abrasive cleaners may be needed for hard, baked-on soils.
- Type of cleaning agent. Soap can leave a film; abrasives can scratch the surface being cleaned; acid cleaners may be needed from time to time to remove lime buildup from equipment.

quick bite 10.4
Sanitation Checklist

Often food safety is the main concern of operators, which is essential. However, opportunities for food contamination and accidents happen throughout the facilities. The following is a checklist of building safety items.

Condition of Building

- Walls and ceiling are clean and in good repair.
- Floors are watertight where required, properly pitched and drained.
- Ventilation system is operating properly and is adequate. Fume hoods, ducts, and fans are free of grease, dust and dirt.
- Adequate lighting is provided and food is sheltered from light bulb breakage.

Garbage and Vermin

- There are no signs of active rodents and/or insects; effective extermination measures are taken when necessary and premises are protected against rodent entry.
- Sufficient watertight and tightly closed garbage containers are available.
- Garbage storage areas are properly located and clean.

Plumbing Facilities

- Suitable bathrooms are provided, completely enclosed, ventilated, properly located and maintained.
- Handwashing facilities with hot and cold running water, soap and hand-drying facilities are provided with "wash hands" signage.
- Water supply is protected against contamination (no cross-connection or submerged inlets; protects against back siphonage).
- Food and prep areas are protected from contamination from soil lines.
- Potable water pressure is accurate, supply system is in good repair, and waste plumbing is in good repair.
- Gas burners and lines are clean and working properly.

Cleanliness of Equipment and Dishes

- Utensils and equipment are of sanitary design and construction and kept clean.
- There is adequate utility-sink space for cleaning utensils and equipment.

(continued)

quick bite 10.4
Sanitation Checklist (*continued*)

- Clean linen is properly stored and kept away from soiled linen.
- Ice cream serving scoops are immersed in running water.
- Single service equipment is used once and disposed of.
- Manual dishwashing is done in a clean 3-compartment sink and immersion baskets are used for final rinse. Mechanical dishwashers are properly designed and working properly with an adequate supply of hot (170°F) wash water.
- Procedures and test kit for chemical sanitizing of glasses is adequate.
- Plates, glassware and silverware ready for use are clean, uncracked, and properly stored and handled.

Source: Alliant Foodservice. "Restaurant Planning Manual: Sanitation Checklist." *Weekly 1999 Food Services Planner*, pp. 8–9.

- Agitation or pressure to be applied. The more agitation, the more effective and faster the cleaning.
- Length of treatment. The longer the cleaning agent is exposed to the object, the more effective the cleaning.

There are three main types of cleaning products [18]: detergents, acid cleaners, and abrasive cleaners. Detergents are used with water to loosen dirt. They are very effective, inexpensive, and can be used on food-contact surfaces. Acid cleaners are used on dirt that alkaline-based detergents cannot remove. Used incorrectly, they can damage surfaces and cause chemical burns on the skin. Abrasive cleaners work by using finely ground minerals that scour the surface to remove soil that is crusted on. Soft plastic surfaces can be easily scratched, thereby making them less effective to bacteria prevention. After using abrasive cleaners, care must be taken to rinse away any residue.

Sanitizing occurs after cleaning and rinsing to kill bacteria. It involves the use of hot water or chemical compounds. Sanitizing should occur after every use. To sanitize using hot water, equipment and utensils must remain under water at a minimum temperature of 170°F for at least 30 seconds.

Chemical sanitizers are used more often than hot water for the purpose of destroying microorganisms. They include chlorine, iodine, and quaternary ammonium. Chlorine compounds work well in either hard or soft water and do not irritate when used properly. However, they can cause damage to metal equipment. Water should be used to thoroughly rinse away any trace of detergents prior to the use of the chlorine compound, which should be at a temperature of 75°F. Iodine compounds work well in hard water and, being less corrosive than chlorine, do not irritate the skin or harm metal or rubber surfaces. Water temperature should be between 75 and 120°F. Quaternary ammonium compounds (quats) are skin safe and do not damage equipment, but their effectiveness can be reduced in very hard water. At a temperature of 75°F they work well in both acid and alkaline solutions.

Combination detergent–sanitizers are available. They must be used twice, once to clean and a second time to sanitize. Equipment and utensils should not be rinsed after sanitizing. The cycle is wash–rinse–sanitize.

Rodent and Insect Control

The most frequent pest problems in a restaurant come from rats, mice, flies, and cockroaches. A good pest control program uses both environmental sanitation and chemical or blockage control [19]. Control for rats and mice begins with disposing garbage in a sanitary manner. Rodents must have access to food. Removing the trash and keeping storage areas clean will eliminate hiding places. Rodents can be killed with poison—mice are more susceptible—or trapped. Slow-killing poisons are best because they allow rodents to leave the premises before they die. Rodent-proofing the building consists of ensuring that doors are tight-fitting, with the bases flashed with metal; screening all windows less than 3 feet from the ground with hardware cloth screening; having concrete rather than wooden basement and ground floors; and closing all holes in foundations.

Control of flies begins with eliminating potential breeding places. This entails not allowing food to accrue and spoil and removing garbage quickly. Screens help keep flies out. Sprays, insecticides, and poisons eliminate flies, but their use should be monitored carefully to ensure that food is not affected by them. An electric fly catcher draws flies to an electric element, which kills them.

Cockroaches need moisture to survive. Most commonly, they enter an operation from deliveries. Hence crates and boxes should be inspected and disposed of as soon as possible. Frequent cleaning will reduce the number of new cockroaches. Once their hiding places are known, a qualified exterminator can lay poison to kill them.

In general, the following practices will help prevent problems [20]:

- Use a reputable supplier.
- Dispose of garbage properly and promptly.
- Store recycleables as far away from the premises as is allowed.
- Store all foods and supplies properly.
- Dispose of mop and cleaning water properly, mopping up spilled water at once.
- Clean and sanitize the operation thoroughly.

Crisis Management

Crisis management is "the organized and systematic effort of an operation to prevent, react to, and learn from crises" [21]. The development of a crisis management plan is one mark of proactive rather than reactive management. Three steps are involved in such an effort: preparation, management, and evaluation [22]. In the first stage a crisis team is formed. This team develops procedures and policies to be undertaken in case of a crisis. It is important that one and only one spokesperson be appointed to speak for the operation.

To manage the plan, a standardized complaint form should be developed and used to get information from complaining customers. Once it has been determined that the complaint is justified, the company decides whether to deal with the situation internally or whether outside help is needed. If the problem is small—the food was served cold—it can be settled in-house with a refund or small gift. Bigger problems, such as food poisoning, require outside assistance. It is important to communicate effectively with regulators, the public, employees, and the media.

Afterward, evaluation begins. Whatever caused the problem has to be identified and corrected. Employees should be involved in giving their reaction to what happened, how it was handled, and how it can be prevented in the future. Finally, a copy of the complaint should be kept.

EMPLOYEE HABITS

Employee Health

Employees who have symptoms that suggest they are susceptible to passing along bacteria should not be allowed near food. If they have a fever or are sneezing, coughing, or have oozing burns or cuts, they are prime candidates for spreading harmful bacteria. Blood contaminates food and any surface with which it comes into contact. If food is exposed to an employee's blood, it must be discarded immediately. Employees who have cuts can continue to work as long as the cut is protected. Water-resistant bandages, changed often and covered with water-resistant material or plastic gloves, will serve as protection. The same procedures should be followed for burns.

The HIV microorganism that causes the AIDS virus is not spread by food. Service workers infected with AIDS can safely work around food unless they are cut or have other infections or illnesses.

Employee hygiene is very important. *Source:* Robert Christie Mill.

quick bite 10.5
Employees and Hygiene

The National Restaurant Association has unveiled a comprehensive program designed to develop hygiene-conscious employees: SERVSAFE. Foodservice units whose managers and supervisors have been trained, tested, and certified in the SERVSAFE program in the past five years can become participants in the Industry Council on Food Safety. Participants receive:

1. A recognition plaque that is to be posted in a prominent place in the restaurant
2. A window decal
3. A council logo sticker that can be used on letterheads or menus
4. A sample press release suitable for sending to the consumer press
5. A slick sheet of consumer food-safety tips than can be printed on fliers or takeout boxes for customers
6. Crisis-management steps to take in the event of an outbreak

Source: "Food Safety," *Restaurants USA*, v. 14, n. 4, April 1994, pp. 11–15.

Personal Hygiene. The first step to staying healthy is to practice good health habits. This involves:

- Bathing daily with soap and water
- Covering one's mouth when coughing or sneezing, then washing hands immediately afterward
- Avoiding such things as scratching the head or touching the mouth or nose
- Not eating, drinking, chewing gum, or smoking when food is being prepared or cleaned
- Avoiding the dropping of sweat onto food or equipment
- Using disposable towels to wipe away sweat and washing the hands before working with food
- Using hair restraints
- Keeping nails short and clean

Hand Washing. Bacterial contamination occurs primarily when microorganisms are spread to food from the hands of employees. For this reason the best way to prevent contamination is effective hand washing. Hand sinks should be readily accessible and be used exclusively for this purpose. Warm water, soap, and disposable towels or an air-drying machine are required for effective hand washing. Hands must be washed after any act that might cause contamination—

using the toilet, eating or drinking, handling raw food, and so on. Similarly, hands should not be dried or wiped on aprons.

Clothing. Employee changing rooms should be kept separate from food preparation areas. Uniforms should also be clean and changed when necessary to prevent contamination.

Safety and Accident Prevention

The Industrial Commission of Ohio's Division of Safety and Hygiene identifies six acts that often result in accidents [23]:

1. Failing to look where one is going
2. Failing to observe surroundings
3. Failing to handle knives and tools with care

---

 quick bite 10.6
Proactive Procedures

It is generally agreed that effective safety programs require that operators analyze past accidents to identify areas of concern, inspect the facility to identify problem spots, and develop a plan to make employees more aware of the problem.

Here are some specific steps to take:

1. Give someone the responsibility to oversee the implementation of safety procedures. When Southwest Cafe, Inc. hired Randy Conner as director of risk management, he instituted procedures that saved the company $250,000 in the first six months of the program.
2. Get free or low-cost advice from insurance companies, many of whom have a loss-prevention service. Liberty Mutual conducts safety audits of Red Lobster and Olive Garden restaurants to advise on safety.
3. Check internal claims records and get accident-loss records from insurance carriers. When Godfather's Pizza found out that the leading cause of workers' compensation claims was "cuts," they had employees use a cut-resistant glove, reducing cuts by 68 percent and claims from $246 to $141.
4. Utilize free or inexpensive training methods. The local fire department will teach fire-extinguishing techniques and the Heimlich maneuver, and the American Red Cross covers basic first aid.

Source: Somerville, Sylvia R. "Safety Is No Accident," *Restaurants USA,* v. 12, n. 7, August 1992, pp. 14–18.

---

quick bite 10.7
Kitchen Safety

The lost productivity, ruined food, sick time and workman's compensation resulting from kitchen accidents cost hundreds of millions of dollars. Although employee mistakes and/or mishaps cause many of these accidents, too many are caused by facility design or equipment placement errors.

Slips and falls, which are the most common kitchen injuries, mainly result from poor finish on the floor or spilled water or grease. Prevention of these injuries is simple, merely placing a slip-resistant diamond tread, raised rib-quarry tile or industrial sheet-vinyl safety floor can stop the majority of these injuries. Most chains and independents use one of these floor coverings, making them the industry standard. If an employee is injured without one of these safeguards in place, an operator is most likely going to face a lawsuit.

Regardless of what type of flooring is used, operators and/or facility designers should take the following steps to prevent slips and falls and other injuries:

- Place mop sinks near all workstations to allow for fast cleanup of all spills.
- Install floor troughs and/or drain in front of ice machines to avoid fallen ice hazards.
- Conduct an audit of all equipment in the facility in order to search out extended handles, trim and sharp edges.
- Make sure pipes, sprinklers and other hanging items are raised or relocated to a height of at least 6 feet 4 inches.
- Plan layouts carefully to avoid equipment attachments from extending into walkways.
- Make sure replacement equipment has approximately the same dimensions as the original equipment.
- Make sure placement of drain troughs in bulk-cooking areas can accommodate a full-pour path of a tilting kettle or braising pan.
- Consider drain troughs for all wet areas of the kitchen.
- Make sure all drain trough grates have a nonslip or filed finish; new fiberglass grates with slip-resistant aggregate cast on the finish are very popular.
- Create a recess in the concrete slab of a walk-in cooler or freezer to prevent raised floors from insulation.
- Install ground-fault receptacles for any electrical outlet near a wet area.

(continued)

quick bite 10.7
Kitchen Safety (*continued*)

- Allow all equipment to be unplugged from the wall outlet for cleaning or repairs.
- Any equipment that starts automatically, such as refrigerators and compressors, should have safety switches.
- Make sure there is a 16-inch separation or side shield between any deep-fat fryers and open flame cooking devices (including electric charbroilers) to prevent flash fires and burns.
- Plan for ease of movement in the kitchen; any back-to-back work areas should be at least 4 feet wide.
- Walk-in doors should not open into walkways; new lightweight sliding doors are available.
- Limit need for stools to reach items on shelves.
- Provide proper lighting (30 foot-candles).

Source: Frable, Jr., Foster. "Planning Kitchen Safety in Restaurants Should Never Happen by Accident." *Nation's Restaurant News,* v. 33, n. 1, January 4, 1999, pp. 23, 28.

4. Reaching too high or too low; lifting a weight that is too heavy, or lifting incorrectly
5. Failing to pay attention when using knives, grinders, or other cutting tools
6. Failing to protect hands from hot pans, pots, and plates

Restaurant employees are particularly susceptible to falls, burns, cuts, and improper lifting. Falls can be minimized by keeping floors dry and in good repair, wiping up spills immediately; rinsing after cleaning to remove any detergent or grease film; using slip-resistant shoes and floor coverings; and using signs indicating when a floor has just been cleaned.

Burns can be prevented by removing lids slowly to let steam escape; by using dry, flameproof potholders; by turning pot handles inward on the range; and by keeping stove tops and hoods free from grease.

Cuts can be avoided by keeping knives sharp, always cutting away from the body, having knives with built-in guards or shaped handles, and storing knives in a rack or knife holder.

Improper lifting accounts for 25 percent of lost-time accidents [24]. Most injuries occur when putting down objects rather than picking things up. People should lift with their feet rather than with their back. This means [25]:

- Getting a good footing
- Placing the feet shoulder-width apart

- Bending the knees before grasping the weight
- Keeping the back straight
- Getting a firm hold
- Lifting gradually by straightening the legs

---

quick bite 10.8
Road to the Top: Patrick McDonnell

Vice President, Research & Development

Patrick McDonnell, vice president of research and development at Aramark, may be one of the least-known and most famous chefs in the country. During his employment at ConAgra Foods Inc., McDonnell developed one of the most successful retail lines of healthful foods in the U.S., Healthy Choice.

Possibly attracted to behind-the-scenes roles, McDonnell took on a position at Aramark Corp., the country's second largest food-management firm. Through his position at Aramark, McDonnell will again be influencing the tastes of millions of consumers. However, his goal at Aramark is internal organization.

McDonnell attributes much of his success to the team that was already in place at Aramark. "I didn't come into the company to change it overnight," he notes. "Everything was already in place here; there is incredible talent in this company. But there was nothing to link it all together. It had minimized value out in the field." McDonnell wants to bring together communications between the culinary side of the operation and various divisions including Human Resources, Purchasing and the Design Solutions Group.

McDonnell feels that partnerships are important both internally and externally. He has arranged negotiations with several manufacturers including General Foods, Pillsbury and Rich Products Corp. to develop menu items together in order to keep food costs down. McDonnell's business savvy is impressive and was gained on the job—including three years' management training at Savoy Hotel Group in London—after McDonnell refused to go to college regardless of his father's prodding. He instead joined the Savoy Hotel Group where he fell in love with the kitchen.

McDonnell began his career in the U.S. by opening his own restaurant, the Sarabande in Baltimore, then he moved to the executive chef position at the Rainbow Room and then began an R&D position with General Foods. After starting a consulting business, McDonnell began his job at ConAgra. However, one of McDonnell's fondest career moments came when he worked as the chef of the U.S. Ski Team both at their training facility and during the Olympics in Nagano, Japan.

Source: King, Paul. "Patrick McDonnell: Working Behind the Scenes at Aramark to Influence the Future of Foodservice." *Nation's Restaurant News,* v. 33, n. 4, pp. 156–158.

q u i c k   b i t e   1 0 . 9
Hot Skills

Sanitation and Food Safety 2000

Industry experts predict that in the near future managers will be required to have a food sanitation certificate for which they must pass government mandated testing to receive. Managers are also likely to be required to attend continuing education classes after receiving their certification.

Managers will need to develop a better understanding and more thorough knowledge of sanitation and food safety. They will also need the ability to stress the importance of safety and sanitation to their staff. Many of these staff members may also require limited training in the area.

Pesticides and cleaners will be more heavily regulated at the end of the millennium. Environmental concerns will contribute to more restrictions on these products and will lead to the development of natural products. Managers will need to purchase these natural products or create them in-house.

The Top 5 Most Likely Developments for Managers in Sanitation and Food Safety for 2000:

1. Food sanitation certification requirement
2. Must pass mandated testing
3. Increased regulations for food handling
4. Need for continuing education classes
5. Alternative pesticide and cleaning products

Source: Foodservice Manager 2000 (Washington, D.C.: National Restaurant Association, 1992).

---

q u i c k   b i t e   1 0 . 1 0
Food Technology in 2010

According to the National Restaurant Association the most likely developments regarding food technology in 2010 are:

- Higher customer expectations will lead to improved food handling and sanitation.
- Better microbial detection/reduction processes will be used.
- More exacting product portioning and costing techniques will be used.
- Corporate quality assurance inspection programs will be the norm.
- Improved preservation technologies will reduce spoilage and the risk of foodborne illnesses.

Source: Restaurant Industry 2010: The Road Ahead (Washington, D.C.: National Restaurant Association, 1999), p. 11.

The Occupational Safety and Health Act (OSHA) was passed in 1970 to assure safe and healthy conditions in the workplace. It lays out guidelines for the work environment and inspects facilities to ensure that businesses are in compliance. OSHA checklists can be used as a guide to whether or not the restaurant is safe for employees. A comprehensive program involves four things: inspecting all equipment and physical facilities, examining the physical fitness of employees to perform their jobs safely, reviewing operational practices and personnel activities as they do their jobs, and checking compliance with safety and health regulations.

ENDNOTES

1. Lewis J. Minor and Ronald F. Cichy, *Foodservice Systems Management* (Westport, CT: AVI Publishing Company, 1984), p. 161.

2. National Assessment Institute, *Handbook for Safe Food Service Management* (Upper Saddle River, NJ: Regents/Prentice Hall, 1994), p. 8.

3. Ibid., p. 42.

4. Ibid., pp. 11, 39–41.

5. Mahmood A. Khan, *Concepts of Foodservice and Management,* 2nd ed. (New York: Van Nostrand Reinhold, 1991), p. 208.

6. Minor and Cichy, *Foodservice Systems Management,* p. 162.

7. National Assessment Institute, *Handbook for Safe Food Service Management,* p. 35.

8. Ibid., p. 37.

9. National Institute for Food Service Industry, *Applied Foodservice Sanitation,* 4th ed. (New York: John Wiley & Sons, 1992), p. 86.

10. Ibid., p. 87.

11. Ibid., p. 89.

12. Minor and Cichy, *Foodservice Systems Management,* p. 181.

13. *Applied Foodservice Sanitation,* p. 67.

14. Ibid., p. 135.

15. Ibid., p. 176.

16. "Top Twelve Bar Sanitation Tips," *F&B Business,* December 1989, p. 55.

17. *Applied Foodservice Sanitation,* pp. 188–189.

18. National Assessment Institute, *Handbook for Safe Food Service Management,* p. 96.

19. John Knight, p. 47.

20. *Applied Foodservice Sanitation,* pp. 228–229.

21. Ibid., p. 279.

22. Ibid., p. 280.

23. Knight, p. 52.

24. Ibid., p. 51.

25. Ibid., p. 53.

CHAPTER ELEVEN

CONTROLLING COSTS

learning objectives

By the end of this chapter you should be able to:

1. Identify the four types of financial ratios used by management.

2. Describe a systematic way of analyzing an income statement.

3. Identify the appropriate ratios to calculate when analyzing sales, expenses, and profit.

4. Identify the appropriate ratios to calculate when analyzing the balance sheet.

5. Determine the break-even point for a business, given the appropriate sales and expense figures.

Citing the restaurant's ability to deliver low labor costs, he speculated that the operation was producing a profit of close to 28 percent of sales. . . . Dave delivered his "books" which were papers of all kinds stuffed in a peach basket. . . . He simply threw in his sales records, checkbook, and various invoices representing the purchase of his equipment, preopening expenses, and miscellaneous expenses he had incurred in opening and operating the business. . . . Not only was he not making 28 percent profit on sales . . . he had actually lost 56 percent on the sales he had been generating up to that point.
James McLamore, co-founder of Burger King, quoted in *The Burger King.*

Source: McLamore, James W., *The Burger King* (New York, NY: McGraw-Hill, 1998).

---

quick bite 11.1
Hot Concepts: Oscar's

The privately-held Oscar's cashed in on over $27 million in sales at just seven locations in 1998, which earned it the title of one of the fastest-growing companies in San Diego. The restaurants have grown immensely in popularity due to their scratch-cooked specialties, limited-tableservice format and casual-dining environment. Oscar and Pat Sarkisian began the chain with one 1,200-square-foot takeout shop in the early '90s. Their company, S&C Co., now employs 750 people.

According to chief executive officer and the owner's son, John Sarkisian, they plan to open a minimum of 15 new units in the next five years. The company has already been named the 16th-fastest-growing business by the *San Diego Business Journal.* John Sarkisian has had over fifteen years' experience in real estate, which helped him to select the restaurants' locations.

The concept is a hybrid fast-food/casual-dining restaurant that focuses on family. The menu revolves around the restaurant chain's signature breadsticks and made-from-scratch foods. Some of Oscar's specialties include lemon chicken wings, ribs, designer pizzas, pocket sandwiches, rigatoni and Greek salads. Locations feature "Dinners for Two+" and "Family Feasts." These dinner specials are served in family-style portions that customers split between themselves.

Even with the large variety of foods Oscar's offers, the breadsticks and eight varieties of salads make up 40 percent of annual sales. Sales are evenly divided between dine-in and take-out/catering orders. Average lunch checks for the chain are $10 and dinner checks average $15. Breadsticks are the main marketing tool of the company. The sticks are chewy, yeast-raised, golden-baked, garlic-butter coated and have attracted customers since the opening of the first store. A prime tactic is to distribute a basket of the breadsticks to local businesses when a unit first opens. The sticks are also passed out to customers in line on busy nights. The company has developed "Breadstick University" to train employees and "High Rollers" awards to employees who have rolled over one million breadsticks.

The chain also offers a Starbucks-brand all-you-can-drink coffee station for convenience with a high-end atmosphere. The idea of bringing in Starbucks and maintaining a 28% average food cost results from the Sarkisian family's lack of restaurant experience. But according to John Sarkisian, it can benefit the company to spend money on quality products: "What we miss in pricing we make up in volume."

Source: Spector, Amy. "Oscar's Turns Breadstick Recipe into Hybrid Fast-Casual-Catering Success." *Nation's Restaurant News,* May 10, 1999, v. 33, n. 19, pp. 5, 135.

FINANCIAL STATEMENTS

An understanding of financial statements is necessary for preparing tax forms, negotiating loans, and—the topic of this chapter—determining the financial condition of the business. Management looks at four types of ratios. Liquidity ratios determine the extent to which a business can meet short-term obligations as and when they become due. As we will see later, this includes such ratios as the current ratio and the acid test or quick ratio. Solvency ratios, on the other hand, look at the ability of the operation to meet its long-term obligations. Both types of ratios are generated from the balance sheet.

Activity and profitability ratios take information from both the balance sheet and statement of income. Activity ratios show how well management is using the assets of the operation in generating income. Profitability or rate of return ratios show how profitable the business is. Finally, operating ratios deal with the efficiency of management in actually operating a business.

The two fundamental accounting statements are the statement of income and the balance sheet. The former indicates the profitability of the business over a period of time. The various costs of operating the business are subtracted from the revenue generated to show either a profit, if the revenue is greater than the costs, or a loss, if the costs are greater than the revenue. The balance sheet indicates the financial condition or value of the business at a particular point in time. Typically, December 31 is used as that point.

Statement of Income

A representation of where the average restaurant dollar comes from and goes to is shown in Table 11.1. Following the standard format for an income statement, averages are shown for three types of restaurant: full-service restaurants where the average check per person is less than $10.00; full-service restaurants where the average check per person is $10.00 and above; and limited-service fast food restaurants.

Revenue and other income for the period are listed. All expenses incurred during the period in question are then subtracted from total revenue to determine the profit (if any) before taxes.

The Uniform System of Accounts for Restaurants has been developed by the accounting firm of Laventhol and Horwath and accepted by the National Restaurant Association as a blueprint for categorizing revenues and costs and laying out a statement of income. By following this guide, individual operations can compare their operating figures with those of similar restaurants in the industry. Annual figures and ratios for this purpose are produced by both the National Restaurant Association and Deloitte & Touche. In analyzing statements of income it is useful to consider not only the dollar figures but also the amounts as a percentage of revenue. Such a procedure allows for a more reliable comparison of, for example, management's effectiveness in controlling labor costs relative to the volume of sales.

Revenue. Revenue is primarily from sales of food and sales of beverages. Other revenues—for example, from room rental—would be shown later as other

Table 11.1   Statement of Income

	A	B	C
Sales			
Food sales	97.0%	78.4%	100.0%
Beverage sales (alcoholic)	5.6	21.9	0.0
Total sales	100	100	100
Cost of sales			
Food cost	33.6	34.6	32.3
Beverage cost	30.0	30.0	0.0
Total cost of sales	33.3	33.5	32.3
Gross profit	66.7	66.5	67.7
Operating expenses			
Salaries and wages	30.4	28.3	26.9
Employee benefits	3.4	4.1	2.2
Direct operating expenses	5.2	5.5	5.2
Music and entertainment	0.0	0.1	0.0
Marketing	1.6	2.1	3.9
Utility services	3.6	2.9	2.9
Restaurant occupancy costs	4.7	5.3	6.6
Administrative and general	2.3	3.8	2.1
Repairs and maintenance	1.6	1.7	1.4
Total operating expenses	60.9	61.0	60.1
Interest expense	Insufficient data		0.5
Income before income taxes	4.7	3.6	5.7

Source: *Restaurant Industry Operations Report, 1998* (Washington, DC: Deloitte & Touche and the National Restaurant Association, 1998), pp. 25, 55, 85. Note: (1) All figures are medians based on 1997 data. (2) All ratios are based on a percentage of total sales except food and beverage costs, which are based on their respective sales. A, full-service restaurants, average check per person under $10.00; B, full-service restaurants, average check per person $10.00 and over; C, limited-service fast food restaurants.

income. The relative proportions of food to beverage revenue is important because the cost of sales for beverages is less than the cost of sales for food. An operation with a high percentage of beverage to food revenue is thus typically good for bottom-line profit.

Cost of Sales. Cost of sales is the cost of the food and beverage items that have been sold. To determine the food and/or beverage cost for an operation, beginning and ending inventories must be made. The ending inventory for period 1 becomes the beginning inventory for period 2. Because inventories can vary from day to day, a physical inventory should always be taken on the same day of the week. If an operation deliberately avoided ordering food until the day after a physical inventory was taken, the food cost would be uncharacteristically low; similarly, an unusually high inventory would increase the cost of food and a corresponding lower profit. Inventories are normally taken once a month.

The cost of food sales is calculated as follows:

inventory of food

at beginning of period (dollars) + purchases of food during the period

= total value of available food − inventory of food at end of period

= value of food used during the period

A similar calculation is made to determine the cost of beverage sales. Food and beverage cost percentages will be different. It is, therefore, desirable to compare the cost of food to food revenue and the cost of beverage to beverage revenue and express them as percentages.

Gross Profit.   Gross profit is the profit after taking the cost of sales—food and beverage—from total revenue.

Other Income.   As noted above, the principal sources of revenue for a restaurant will come from sales of food and beverages. Other income would cover any other revenue taken in the sale of nonfood and nonbeverage items, such as candy, room rental, and concessions.

Controllable Expenses.   Management has direct responsibility for and can influence controllable expenses. They include such things as:

- Salaries and wages: employee payroll
- Employee benefits: employee meals, Social Security taxes, medical insurance costs, workers' compensation insurance, etc.
- Direct operating expenses: costs involved in the operation of the business, such as uniforms, laundry, and decorations
- Music/entertainment: live or canned music
- Marketing: promotion, advertising, etc.
- Energy and utility service: cost of fuel, water, waste removal, etc.
- Administrative and general: overhead costs not directly connected with providing customer service, such as telephone, postage, and office supplies
- Repairs and maintenance: cost of repairing and maintaining the building and equipment

Total Controllable Expenses.   Managers have control over both the controllable expenses listed above and the food and beverage costs noted earlier. Any costs listed later are fixed in the short run and usually cannot be influenced by the unit manager.

Income before Rent and Other Occupation Costs.   This figure is obtained by subtracting total controllable expenses from total income. Companies often use this figure as the basis for determining management bonuses.

Rent and Other Occupational Costs.   These costs are those associated with getting the property operating and include rent, real estate taxes, and property insurance. This overhead is fixed and cannot be changed in the short run. These figures depend on the agreement negotiated and will be in effect for the term of the agreement.

Depreciation. Depreciation is a noncash, tax-deductible expense. Since the building, equipment, and other assets wear out, an allowance is given to indicate the cost involved as the assets are used. Various methods can be used to depreciate assets in accordance with guidelines as to how long the assets are expected to last. The expense reduces taxes due and is available as positive cash flow to the operation.

Interest. When bank loans are used to finance a business, the cost of borrowing the money is charged as interest. Depending on how a building is financed, the operation may have rent costs (if the building is leased) or interest costs (if it is purchased).

Income Tax. Businesses pay taxes on their profits just as individuals pay taxes on their income. Net income is what is left after taxes have been subtracted.

Balance Sheet

The balance sheet shows the financial situation for the business at a particular point in time, usually December 31. The fundamental equation is

$$assets = liabilities + equity$$

The assets are what the business owns; the liabilities are what is owed by the business; the difference is the net worth or equity of the business.

Assets. Assets are either short-term or fixed. Short-term assets are those that can be or are liquidated within a year. This includes cash on hand, accounts receivable (money owed to the operation), inventories of food, beverage, and other items (china, cutlery, etc.), and any expenses that have been prepaid.

Fixed assets are those items that have a life longer than a year. This includes such things as land, building, and equipment and uniforms. If the building is leased and the operator has made improvements, the improvements would be listed here as leasehold improvements. Note that although the value of the building and furniture and fixtures is reduced by the amount depreciated, the value of the land (although it can change in value) is not changed by depreciation.

Liabilities. Current liabilities are those payable within the year. Most of this is made up of accounts payable, bills owed by the operation to various people. Long-term liabilities are those that will be paid off over several years. The total amount of the outstanding mortgage (less the current portion, which is included under current liabilities) tends to be the largest part of this item.

Shareholder's Equity. As noted above, the difference between assets and liabilities is the equity or what the business is worth. Profits are either distributed to the owners as dividends or kept in the business. The latter are referred to as retained earnings.

ANALYZING FINANCIAL STATEMENTS: STATEMENT OF INCOME

Financial statements will be analyzed by various people for different reasons [1]. Bankers will look at the numbers in evaluating a loan proposal to determine the likelihood of repayment; an investor will use the statements to estimate a return on the investment; a supplier may look at the books before deciding whether or not to extend credit; management analyzes the numbers to determine the profitability or efficiency of the operation.

The figures mean little unless they are compared to something. Statements of income may be compared to forecasted or budgeted figures, to industry averages, or to previous results of the operation. Similarly, with the income statement, the dollar figures are not as meaningful as when they are expressed as a percentage of sales. A large operation will have food costs, in dollars, much higher than those of a smaller operation. For people evaluating the operation, the key is how well the costs have been controlled compared to sales. Looking at percentages allows an analyst to compare one operation to another.

Systematic Approach

A systematic way to analyze the statement of income is to begin with the bottom line, working upward in an attempt to zero in on problem areas. In this approach, the first step is to compare net income as a percentage of total revenue to a standard. As noted above, that standard may be a forecast, the previous year's figures, or an industry average. If the ratio is acceptable, management will presumably be pleased. This is not to say that the way the business is run cannot be improved; it merely indicates that the operation is "on target."

If, however, the bottom-line ratio is not acceptable, the second step is to move to the next major level, total controllable expenses. Here again, the approach is to compare the ratio of total controllable expenses to total revenue. If this figure is "acceptable" but the bottom-line figure is not, the problem lies somewhere in between the two ratios, in this case with the uncontrollable fixed costs, such as rent, interest, and other occupation costs. We have an indication that management is able to keep the controllable expenses in line but is still not having an acceptable bottom line. The problem in this case is that total revenue is not sufficient to produce enough income before rent and other charges to cover the fixed uncontrollable expenses. The task for management is to increase sales volume while continuing to control costs, thereby generating enough income to cover the fixed costs.

If the ratio of total controllable expenses is not acceptable to management, the problem is somewhere above this line on the statement of income.

This, in essence, is the systematic method of analyzing the statement of income:

1. Compare ratios at two levels.
2. If the lower level (closest to the bottom line) is acceptable and the higher one is not, the problem is with some figures in between the two.
3. If the ratio at a particular level is not acceptable, the problem is with one or more of the figures above this level.

Continuing this analysis, let us assume that the ratio of total controllable expenses to total revenue is not acceptable. As noted above, the problem lies somewhere above this line. We would then go to the next major level on the statement of income—total income—in an attempt to isolate the problem. If this ratio of total income to total revenue is acceptable, the problem lies somewhere in between total income and total controllable expenses. Each line under controllable expenses would be analyzed to determine which figures are over budget or out of line with competing ratios.

The analysis would continue using the method outlined above. Using this method management can isolate problem areas systematically.

Three-Part Method

According to Keiser [2], a statement of income can be divided into three parts: sales, expenses, and profit. He recommends analyzing each part separately.

Sales.   In looking at sales, management basically wants to know three things:

1. Are sales increasing or decreasing?
2. Why is this happening?
3. Is the level of sales appropriate to the value of the business, the size of the operation, and/or the amount invested in it?

To answer these questions it may be necessary to break sales figures down by product category and/or by meal period. The former is germane to profitability, as the profit potential on beverages is greater than that on food. In making comparisons it is important to ensure that the comparison base is the same. Figures can be compared for the same month or week of the year compared to previous years as well as year-to-date.

Since revenue is a product of the number of covers (customers) times the average price of a meal, an increase in sales is due to one or both of these factors. A sales increase might reflect an increase in menu prices. This may, in fact, camouflage a reduction in the number of covers served. It is important that the average cost of a meal cover, at a minimum, any cost increase the business incurs. If the cost of doing business increases by 8 percent, for example, the average price of a meal should be at least 8 percent more.

The laws of supply and demand indicate that other things being equal, as price goes up, the number of customers will go down. A price increase that results in fewer customers may actually generate less revenue, than previously. This concept is known as elasticity of demand. A menu item is price elastic if an increase in price produces less revenue because of reduced demand. Similarly, a price reduction will result in more demand and more revenue. Price elasticity means that the demand is sensitive to changes in price.

The item is price inelastic if the price increase generates more revenue. In this case the market is less sensitive to changes in price. An increase in price has not caused sufficient customers to stop ordering the item such that total revenue—the product of price times number of customers—increases. Similarly, a price cut will not generate enough additional customers to generate more total revenue in a price-inelastic situation.

To fully understand the reasons for a decrease in sales, each meal period, and each menu item, should be analyzed separately. It is only by doing this that management can pinpoint the meal period and/or menu item(s) causing the problem.

Several ratios are important when analyzing sales:

1. Average check $= \dfrac{\text{revenue}}{\text{number of customers}}$

If the average check is less than "normal," prices may have to be increased or promotions put into effect to "push" the sale of more expensive items or to package appetizers and/or desserts with entree items to increase the average amount spent.

For full-service restaurants where the average check is less than $10.00, the median check (the middle value of all amounts) was $7.50 in 1997. [All figures quoted in this section are taken from *Restaurant Industry Operations Report, 1998* by Deloitte & Touche and the National Restaurant Association (Washington, DC, 1998).] This figure was greater for establishments that served alcohol, served lunch and dinner only, and had sales volume of $2 million plus.

The median check for full-service restaurants where the average check is $10.00 and above was $15.00 in 1997. This amount was greatest for operations that are located in office buildings, served dinner only, had a French/Continental theme and had sales volume of $2 million and above.

The median check for limited-service fast food restaurants in 1997 was $5.00. There are no appreciable differences in this figure based on characteristics of the business.

$$2. \text{ Seat turnover} = \frac{\text{number of customers}}{\text{number of seats}}$$

This ratio demonstrates how well the facility is being utilized. A low turnover indicates poor utilization—more customers can be accommodated; a high turnover may be a sign to expand.

Average daily seat turnover for full-service restaurants with an average check under $10.00 was 2.1. This figure was greater for those operations that only served food, were located in a shopping center or mall, and had an average check of less than $5 with a hamburger menu theme.

The median daily seat turnover for full-service restaurants with an average check of $10.00 and above was 1.0 and was significantly less for establishments located in hotels or clubs, serving dinner only with a French/Continental menu theme.

For limited-service fast food restaurants the median figure of 4.7 was greatest when operations were open for breakfast, lunch and dinner with a hamburger menu theme, that were multi-unit franchise operated and sales volume was high.

$$3. \text{ Sales per square foot} = \frac{\text{sales}}{\text{number of square feet}}$$

This ratio is useful when comparing alternative uses for a particular space. What, for example, would the sales per square foot be for sit-down versus take-out service?

Full-service restaurants with an average check of less than $10.00 reported median sales per square foot of $170.33. This figure is greatest for those serving food only and having high sales volume.

The median figure of $179.33 for full-service operations with an average check of $10.00 and above is greater when food only is served featuring an American theme, with an average check of more than $15.00, located in a shopping center or mall and annual sales volume of more than $2 million.

For limited-service fast food operations, with a median figure of $289.82, there are no appreciable differences in restaurant characteristics.

Expenses. Expenses are either variable, semivariable, or fixed. Variable expenses are those that vary proportionately with volume. Food and beverage costs fall into this category. If selling one hamburger costs 35 cents in product cost, selling two will cost 70 cents.

Semivariable expenses contain both a fixed and a variable component. They will change with volume but not directly. Employee wages is a good example. As volume increases the number of employees needed will increase and the wage bill will go up. An operation must be staffed in advance of customers coming in and a certain minimum number of employees must be present. As volume increases, the number of employees can be increased. However, sales forecasting is very difficult and there will be times when there is an imbalance between the number of customers and the number of employees needed to cook for and serve them.

Fixed expenses are those that do not vary as volume varies. The rent must be paid whether one customer or 1,000 customers are served. According to Keiser, "The more variable the expense, the more significant its percentage figure as related to sales" [3].

The three most important, because they are the largest, controllable ratios comprise the prime cost. They are:

1. Cost of food sales $= \dfrac{\text{cost of food sold}}{\text{food sales}}$

2. Cost of beverage sales $= \dfrac{\text{cost of beverage sold}}{\text{beverage sales}}$

3. Labor cost (%) $= \dfrac{\text{cost of labor}}{\text{total revenue}}$

It should be noted that an operation can offset a high cost in one area with a low cost in another. For example, a restaurant that uses convenience products will have a higher food cost than one that prepares items from scratch. The latter, however, will have higher labor costs.

For full-service restaurants with an average check of less than $10.00 the median prime cost is 67.5 percent of sales. Operations with a Mexican menu theme and those that are multi-unit franchise operated are better able to control food and labor costs. Restaurants open 24 hours have lower food and beverage costs but higher labor costs. This latter is due to having to be staffed during times when sales are low. Labor costs are essentially the same whether or not alcoholic beverages are sold though cost of sales is less, reflecting the lower cost of beverage sales.

Multi-unit company-operated units have higher labor costs but lower cost of food and beverage compared to single-unit independents.

In general, the higher the sales volume generated, the better the food and beverage cost percentages. Labor cost percentages, however, increase until sales volume goes past $2 million a year.

The median prime cost for full-service restaurants with an average check of $10.00 or higher is 67.1 percent and is lowest for those places operating in an office building and highest for clubs. Operations serving food only are better able to control payroll costs. Multi-unit franchise operations are better able than independents and multi-unit company operated stores to control food and beverage costs.

For limited-service fast food restaurants the median prime cost is 62.2 percent of sales. For operations specializing in sandwiches, subs, and deli items, food cost is higher though labor cost is lower. Once again, multi-unit franchise operations do the best job of controlling food costs.

Although the three items noted above are the most important—or prime—costs, every controllable expense should be tracked on a regular basis. It is also vital when comparing ratios that the same type of restaurant be used. The ratios for a fast food unit will be much different from those for a full-service operation. Figures can also be compared on a cost-per-seat or cost-per-meal basis.

Profit. How much is "enough" profit? In the final analysis the profit generated must be sufficient to keep the owner(s) pleased with the investment. A restaurant may produce profit, but if the owners feel they could get a better return on their investment from another investment, the level of profit generated may not be enough to keep the operation open.

Three ratios are particularly important:

$$1. \text{ Operating ratio} \quad = \quad \frac{\text{net income before taxes}}{\text{net sales}}$$

This ratio is also referred to as net profit to net sales, earnings ratio, operating margin, or profit ratio. Obviously, the higher that ratio, the better.

In full-service operations with an average check less than $10.00 the median operating ratio is greater for units serving food only (5.4 percent) compared to those also serving alcohol (4.4 percent). Franchise-operated multiunits produce more (10.3 percent) than either company-operated multiunits (5.8 percent) or independents (3.7 percent). Operating profit increases as sales volume increases.

For full-service restaurants with an average check of $10.00 and above, the operating ratio is better for stores serving food and alcohol compared to those only serving food. Multiunit company-operated restaurants have a greater median operating profit (5.4 percent) than independents (2.8 percent). Insufficient data exists on multi-unit franchises to compare. As above, operating ratios increase as sales volume goes up.

For limited-service fast food operations the operating ratio is more for company-owned chains (7.4%) than either chain franchises (6.5%) or independents (3.6%). As before, operating ratios increase with increasing sales volume.

$$2. \text{ Net profit to net equity} \quad = \quad \frac{\text{net profit after taxes}}{\text{net equity}}$$

Some businesses—for example, fast food units—make a relatively small profit on each item sold. However, they rely on a large volume with a relatively small investment compared to sales to produce a modest operating ratio but a good net profit to net equity.

$$3. \text{ Management proficiency ratio} \quad = \quad \frac{\text{net profit after taxes}}{\text{total assets}}$$

This ratio indicates what management does with the assets it has. The higher the ratio, the better job that management is doing.

quick bite 11.4
Increasing Profitability

The immediate reaction to decreasing profitability in the restaurant industry is promotion, less leader menu items, or expense advertising to boost sales. However, these methods may increase sales, but they will also increase costs. Operators can often implement several small efforts in order to boost the bottom line. Some of these efforts include:

- **Analyze the Income Statement.** A well-designed Income Statement (IS) will offer ideas about where an operation can save money. Often a restaurant's IS does not contain the necessary detail to find these money-saving clues. Operators should create (or hire someone to create) an extremely detailed IS before the business even opens. A good IS will show exactly where money flows out of the business and where it comes into the business, allowing an operator to discover areas for improvement.

- **Create a "strategic mix of costs."** Essential for profitability in the restaurant business is effectively balancing food and labor costs. However, it is essential that an operator's decisions are based on the expectations of customers. Many industry experts suggest daily tracking of purchases to help a manager stay on budget rather than tracking inventory. This also helps to eliminate waste. Analyzing labor needs is simple according to one industry executive, "If you have people standing around, you have too many people. If you have people running around, you don't have enough."

- **Profitable equipment.** Often spending more on equipment at the forefront helps to save a great deal of money in the long run. One way to ensure that cost-reducing equipment is selected is by giving a copy of the menu to the restaurant's supplier. Then the supplier can select the equipment that is necessary for the business.

- **Training for profit.** In order to create profit, sales are necessary. And, the trick to increasing sales is training employees despite the cost. But, in order to sell dishes, desserts and appetizers, servers "must have confidence in their knowledge of the dishes, confidence in their ability to explain them, and confidence in the kitchen staff." When servers are able to boost check averages by $3 or $4 through suggestive selling of dessert, a restaurant's profitability can skyrocket.

(continued)

quick bite 11.4

Increasing Profitability (*continued*)

12 simple ways to boost profitability include:

1. Design a detailed Income Statement.
2. Hire an accountant with foodservice experience.
3. Monitor daily purchases.
4. Buy only cost-saving equipment.
5. Base equipment purchases on menu items.
6. Plan one week in advance to prevent unexpected events.
7. Shop for lower insurance quotes.
8. Train and test servers on menu knowledge.
9. Design menus and table tents that promote profitable menu items.
10. Keep the menu exciting.
11. Offer merchandise sales (i.e., t-shirts, caps, etc.).
12. Use entertainment as a profit stream.

Source: "Profit by the Inch." *Nation's Restaurant News,* v. 82, n. 11, pp. 52–62.

ANALYZING FINANCIAL STATEMENTS: BALANCE SHEET

Current Assets

As noted above, current assets are those that can easily be liquidated.

Cash. Sufficient cash must be available to meet current expenses. Any remaining cash can generate interest from a bank. Cash is kept on hand for change and petty cash, and is also maintained in a bank account to pay expenses.

Accounts Receivable. Accounts receivable are what customers owe. A business that is strictly cash will have no accounts receivable. On the other hand, an operation that has a large banquet business and bills customers after the event may have a substantial accounts receivable.

The time between providing the service and being paid for it represents the restaurant "allowing" the customer use of the restaurant's money. Thus the shorter the average collection period or the greater the turnover, the better for the operation. At the same time, extending credit may be necessary to attract the customer. The important point to note is that there is a cost involved in providing credit.

1. Accounts receivable turnover $= \dfrac{\text{total sales}}{\text{average accounts receivable}}$

2. Average collection period $= \dfrac{365 \text{ days}}{\text{accounts receivable turnover}}$

$$3.\ \text{Number of days tied up}\ =\ \frac{\text{accounts receivable}}{\text{daily sales}}$$

The third ratio shows how many days' sales are tied up in accounts receivable. The figure should be as low as possible.

Inventories. Inventory turnover will vary depending on the type of operation and will vary from twice a week for fast food units to three to five times a month for full-service operations.

The restaurant must balance the need for it to have sufficient supplies on hand so that it will not run out of items with the fact that inventory costs money. The more items on hand for a period of time, the more money the restaurant ties up. Slow turnover indicates that inventory levels are too high. In addition to the money tied up, the longer items are kept, the greater the chance of spoilage.

On the other hand, a particularly high turnover may indicate that the business is, in essence, using the cash from day 1 to purchase supplies for day 2. Some balance must be found.

$$\text{Food inventory turnover}\ =\ \frac{\text{value of the food inventory}}{\text{cost of food sold}}$$

$$\text{Beverage inventory turnover}\ =\ \frac{\text{value of the beverage inventory}}{\text{cost of beverage sold}}$$

Current Ratio. The current ratio measures how strong the business is in its ability to pay off short-term debts. Suppliers need assurance that they will be paid on schedule.

$$\text{Current ratio}\ =\ \frac{\text{current assets}}{\text{current liabilities}}$$

Analysts want to see a ratio approaching 2:1 ($2 of assets for every $1 in liabilities), although in the restaurant business, the ratio is closer to 1:1. This is attributed to three factors [4]: a lack of accounts receivable, small inventories, and fast inventory turnover.

$$\text{Quick ratio}\ =\ \frac{\text{cash + marketable securities + accounts receivable}}{\text{current liabilities}}$$

The quick ratio or acid test is a better measure of bankruptcy risk than is the current ratio because it does not assume that inventory can be sold quickly. A quick ratio below one is cause for concern.

The difference between current assets and current liabilities is working capital. There should be enough working capital to allow the business to get through a financial crisis.

Fixed Assets

Comparing operations on the basis of fixed assets is difficult because of the variety of ways in which operations can be financed. One useful technique is to use a "cost per seat" figure as the basis for determining how much can be spent on the operation.

Liabilities

The major short-term liabilities are employee wages and payments to suppliers. The average monthly payment to suppliers can be determined by dividing cost of goods sold by 12. An accounts payable figure much higher than this average indicates an operation that is slow to pay.

Liabilities are often looked at relative to the net worth of the operation. Creditors will feel more secure when the ratio of debt to equity is low. Such a ratio indicates that the owners are heavily involved financially in the business compared to the amount of outside or debt financing. Lenders feel that the more owners are involved in the business financially, the greater their commitment to the business. A low ratio will increase the chances that the operation will get more credit.

Solvency Ratios

Solvency ratios measure the ability to repay debts. The debt-to-equity ratio looks at the proportion of assets financed through debt or, alternatively, the amount financed through owner's equity. A debt-to-equity ratio of less than one is regarded as desirable. However, if it is too low, it may indicate that an operation is not taking advantage of its situation to expand the business.

COST–VOLUME–PROFIT ANALYSIS

Cost–volume–profit or break-even analysis is a graphical representation of the relationship between sales volume, fixed and variable costs, and profit. Management can determine what sales volume is required to show a profit as well as determining the level of costs and profit or loss at specific levels of sales.

Break-Even Chart

The horizontal axis of a break-even chart (see Figure 11.1) consists of the number of meals sold or customers served; the vertical axis represents both sales volume and costs in dollars.

Sales. A sales volume line can be drawn by multiplying the number of meals served by the average price of a meal. Thus if the average check is $9, $6,300 in sales volume will result when 700 meals or customers are served. This is represented by point A on the chart.

Costs. For the purpose of break-even analysis, costs must be defined as either fixed or variable. Fixed costs are those that do not vary as volume varies.

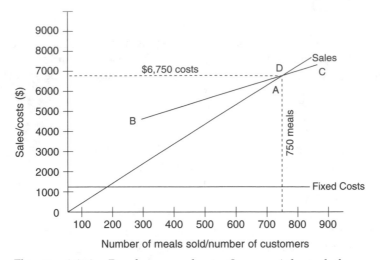

Figure 11.1 Break-even chart. *Source:* Adapted from James Keiser, *Controlling and Analyzing Costs in Foodservice Operations,* 2nd ed. (New York: Macmillan Publishing Company, 1989), pp. 410–411.

The amount of interest to be paid is the same whether one meal is served or 1,000 meals are served.

Thus fixed costs can be represented by a line parallel to the horizontal axis. Variable costs are those that, by definition, vary proportionately with volume. That is, if sales volume doubles, variable costs double. The obvious variable costs are food and beverage costs.

Many costs are semivariable. Labor costs are a good example. A certain number of employees are necessary to open the doors for business. If sales volume increased by 30 percent, the operation would need more employees but labor costs would probably not increase by 30 percent. Existing employees could pick up some of the slack by producing more.

Three methods for breaking costs into their fixed and variable components are [5]:

1. Maximum/minimum calculation
2. Multipoint graph
3. Regression analysis

Using the labor cost as an example, it is necessary to identify the sales volume in terms of meals sold or dollar sales volume together with the appropriate labor cost by month. In the maximum/minimum method the months with the lowest and highest labor costs are separated out and the lower labor cost is subtracted from the higher labor cost.

For example, assume that the highest and lowest sales volumes were in July and February, respectively.

Restaurant Management: Customers, Operations, and Employees

	Sales Volume	**Labor Cost**
July	$40,000	$12,500
February	15,000	8,000
Differences	$25,000	$ 4,500

The variable cost per unit is obtained by dividing the wage difference by the difference in sales volume. In the example above, $4,500 is divided by $25,000 to give 0.18, the variable cost per dollar of revenue. At $40,000 sales volume the labor variable cost is $40,000 × 0.18, or $7,200. This figure is then subtracted from total costs to obtain the level of fixed costs. Monthly fixed costs are $12,500 minus $7,200, or $5,300.

The same type of analysis can be plotted on a graph. Assume the following daily figures for a restaurant [6]:

Number of meals sold	300	900
Average check	$9.00	$9.00

Revenue	$2700	$8100
Fixed costs	$1000	$1000

(Determined by dividing the fixed costs of the operation for the year by 365)

Administrative and general	$ 850	$1320
Labor cost	1750	2350
Food costs	945	2835
Profit or (loss)	$(1845)	$ 595

It can be seen that if 500 meals are sold a day, the restaurant will lose $1,845 per day and will have a profit of $595 if 900 meals are served. Plotting these figures on a chart will show the profit or loss at various levels of sales volume.

The daily fixed costs of $1,000 are represented by the horizontal line FC in Figure 11.1. At a volume of 300 meals the remaining costs—administrative and general, labor, and food—of $3,545 is added to the fixed costs and charted

---

quick bite 11.6
How to Cut Costs

Here are some ways to cut costs:

1. Maintain tight inventory control. Ronald Allcorn, owner of the Hilltop Cafe & Pizzeria in Pittsburgh, found that one of his cooks was putting an extra pinch of cheese on every pizza. That one pinch was costing the operation $30 a day, which, Allcorn pointed out, "was $30 I wouldn't be able to put toward a raise for him."

2. Check various suppliers' prices once a month. George Lamb, general manager of the Greystone Restaurant in Edmond, Oklahoma, recommends talking to four different suppliers.

3. Make prepared items in-house. Jacqueline Canter, manager of Canter's in Los Angeles, finds that it is cheaper and the food is fresher.

4. Reduce staff expense. Stephen Jais, co-owner of Sweetwaters Grille & Bar in Hyannis, Massachusetts, has a three- rather than four-person prep line by cross-training employees. Staggering the times at which employees work can also save on costs.

5. Watch energy costs. Jais uses low-cost fluorescent bulbs and double doors in the entry so that cold air doesn't come in.

6. Lease rather than buy. Lamb finds it cheaper to lease three ice machines than to own one and pay maintenance on it.

Source: Winchester, Sarah Hart. "Cutting Costs without Cutting Quality," *Restaurants USA*, v. 15, n. 3, March 1995, pp. 11–13.

(point B). At a volume of 900 meals a day, the variable and semivariable costs of $6,085 are added to the fixed costs and plotted (point C). A line is then drawn joining points B and C. The break-even point is where total revenue equals total costs (point D). By extending lines to both the horizontal and vertical axes we can see that this restaurant breaks even when 750 meals are sold. The resulting sales volume of $6,750 (750 × the average check of $9) will exactly equal the costs incurred. When fewer than 750 meals are served, costs are higher than revenue and a loss will result; when more than 750 meals are served, revenue is greater than costs and the result is a profit.

Similar charts can be prepared to show the impact of changes in price on profit. If, for example, a 5 percent increase in price is being considered, the impact on the number of meals served can be forecast and a new chart prepared to determine the impact on profit. Of course, the analysis is only as good as the impact forecast.

Because this method requires only two sets of figures it is simple to use. However, these two sets of figures may not be representative of sales volume and labor costs levels.

A multipoint graph improves on this by plotting on a graph monthly figures for an entire year. The horizontal axis would be the sales volume and the vertical axis would be the labor cost. The result is called a scatter graph: "a number of points scattered around a line that has been drawn through them" [7]. The resulting line is the one that seems to be the best fit through all the monthly points. The spot at which the line hits the vertical axis represents the level of fixed labor costs.

Regression analysis takes this process one step further by using an equation to determine fixed costs. For each month of the year four figures are listed: the sales volume or number of meals served, the appropriate level of labor cost, the product of these previous columns, and the sales volume or number of meals served squared:

$$\text{fixed costs} = \frac{(\Sigma Y)\,(\Sigma X^2) - (\Sigma X)(\Sigma XY)}{n(\Sigma X^2) - (\Sigma X)^2}$$

where ΣY is the sum of the monthly labor costs, ΣX is the sum of the monthly sales volumes, ΣXY is the sum of the monthly (X times Y) columns, and n is the number of periods (12 months).

Break-Even Point. The break-even point can also be arrived at arithmetically. When a customer orders a meal for $9, the variable costs associated with producing that meal are subtracted immediately. The remainder contributes toward paying off the fixed costs. When all of the fixed costs have been paid off, the restaurant breaks even. (Remember that variable costs are paid after every sale.) Thus the contribution margin is the selling price of a meal minus the variable costs associated with its production.

Once the break-even point has been reached, the contribution margin becomes profit. Thus if the variable costs associated with the $9 meal are $5.50, each time a meal is served the restaurant takes in $9, pays out $5.50 in variable costs,

quick bite 11.7

Find the Break-Even Point

Given the following information, find the daily break-even point for Bubbles restaurant.

1. Forecasted annual sales: $178,500
2. Number of days of operation per year: 255
3. Projected annual costs:

Fixed	
Labor	$36,720
Payroll tax	3,672
Insurance	700
Rent	8,400
Accounting	500
Bank service charge	180
Utilities	6,000
Telephone	1,200
Interest	812
Advertising	900
Dues/subscriptions	120
Business personal property tax	280
Cleaning expenses	480
Donations	200
Depreciation	1,800
Miscellaneous	1,000
Variable	
Food and paper products	71,400

Solution

1. Separate fixed and variable costs.
   - Total fixed costs: $62,964
   - Total variable costs: $71,400
2. Divide total variable costs by total sales: 40%
3. Subtract total variable costs as a percent of sales from 1:
   $1 - 0.40 = 0.60$
4. Divide the result into total fixed costs:
   $$\frac{\$62,964}{0.60} = \$106,940$$

(continued)

and "contributes" $3.50 toward paying off the fixed costs. Once they have been paid off, the restaurant gets $3.50 profit for each meal sold beyond that point.

The break-even point can be determined by dividing fixed costs by the contribution margin:

$$\text{break-even point} = \frac{\text{fixed costs}}{\text{contribution margin}}$$

where the contribution margin is the unit selling price minus the unit variable cost, or

$$\text{break-even point} = \frac{\text{fixed costs}}{\text{contribution margin ratio}}$$

where the contribution margin ratio is contribution margin/sales volume.

Earlier we noted that many costs are semivariable. In calculating the break-even point, some authors recommend that costs be classified as either fixed or variable. If we revisit the example above, the drawbacks of allocating costs in this manner can be seen.

The only "true" variable cost in the example above is food cost, which is 35 percent of revenue. The contribution margin ratio would, therefore, be 65 percent of revenue. The remaining costs when serving 300 and 900 meals are $3,600 and $4,670, respectively. If these are classified as fixed costs, it is obvious that different break-even points will result.

Using the cost structure for 300 meals, we find that

$$\text{break-even point} = \frac{\text{fixed costs}}{\text{contribution margin ratio}}$$

$$= \frac{\$3600}{0.65} = \$5539 \quad \text{or} \quad 616 \text{ meals}$$

This is the sales volume necessary to break even. The number of meals that must be sold to break even is this figure divided by the average check of

$9, or 616. (All figures are rounded up.) Using the cost structure for 900 meals yields

$$\text{break-even point} = \frac{\text{fixed costs}}{\text{contribution margin ratio}}$$

$$= \frac{\$4670}{0.65} = \$7185 \quad \text{or} \quad 799 \text{ meals}$$

To get more precise it is necessary to attempt to classify how much of any one cost is fixed and how much is variable. Working with historical data, it would be possible to derive graphs plotting the various categories of cost against volumes and extrapolate the line back to determine the fixed component of that cost.

Referring to Figure 11.1 and extrapolating line BC back to the vertical axis, it can be seen that at zero volume $3,050 is incurred in costs. This, then, becomes the "true" level of fixed costs. Using the previous example:

Number of meals sold	300	900
Average check	$9.00	$9.00
Revenue	$2700	$8100
Fixed costs	$3050	$3050
Variable costs	550	1620
(administrative and general and labor)		
Food costs	$ 945	$2835
Total variable costs	$1495	$4455
Contribution margin	$1205	$3645
(revenue minus variable costs)		
Contribution margin ratio	45%	45%
(contribution margin divided by revenue)		
Break-even point (dollars)	$6778	$6778
(fixed costs divided by contribution margin ratio)		
Break-even point in meals	753	753
[break-even (dollars) divided by average check]		

The sales volume necessary to produce a given level of profit can be calculated as follows:

$$\text{sales revenue required} = \frac{\text{fixed costs plus desired profit}}{\text{contribution margin ratio}}$$

Useful as they are, break-even charts can be only a rough approximation of profit. This is, in part, because assumptions must be made regarding allocation of costs. In Figure 11.1 we assumed that the line CB could be extrapolated back. Cost allocations are good only over short ranges of sales volume. When they are extrapolated beyond that range, the analysis is less exact. In addition, this analysis works best when there is only one product. In a restaurant where there are many items on the menu, markups will vary and an average will have to be used. This limits the accuracy of the analysis.

CAPITAL BUDGETING

Capital budgeting is defined as "the planning of expenditures whose returns are expected to extend beyond one year" [8]. Funds can come from depreciation, retained earnings or profit, additional debt, or additional equity from investors and are used for the replacement of existing equipment or facilities or expansion of the operation.

Determining Priorities

Typically, the amount of funds available is not enough to meet the number of projects available. Some method or methods are necessary to allocate scarce resources (money) to desirable projects. Four methods can be used [9]:

1. Economy study: a financial analysis comparing two or more proposals
2. Rate of return: a comparison of the savings or additional income generated to the amount invested
3. Net present value (NPV): the value in the present of future returns, discounted at the cost of capital less the cost of the investment
4. Internal rate of return: a rate of return that equalizes the present value of the return and the investment

Economy Study. An economy study might be used to compare the long-term costs and returns on the purchase of a new piece of equipment compared to keeping and maintaining existing equipment.

Future costs, both fixed and variable, need to be forecast and become part of the analysis. The annual fixed expenses would include such things as interest, depreciation, and taxes and insurance.

There are several methods to calculate depreciation. The simplest method estimates the salvage value of the equipment at the end of its useful life, subtracts this amount from the initial cost of the equipment, and divides this by the number of years the equipment is expected to be in operation. For example, if an oven were to cost $20,000 and have an expected life of eight years, at which time it could be sold for $1,000, the annual depreciation expense would be

$$\frac{20,000 - 1000}{8} = \$2375$$

Annual operating expenses would include labor, power, supplies, and repairs and maintenance.

Many firms will use the amount of time it will take for the expenditure to pay for itself to judge whether to make the capital expenditure. The shorter the payback period, the better. Payback periods can range from a matter of three years for a small piece of equipment to much longer for a building. The formula for estimating the payback period is [10]

$$\text{payback period} = \frac{\text{cash outlay for project}}{\text{annual net income or savings before depreciation but after taxes}}$$

Although it is fairly easy to estimate future costs, it is much more difficult to calculate changes in sales brought about by capital expenditures. Redecorating the dining room may be justified if the project will bring in more business. A reliable estimate of the new business due entirely to the redecoration is difficult at best.

Rate of Return. The rate of return on a project is the average additional income of savings after taxes and depreciation divided by the average investment in the project.

The rate of return can be determined annually as well as over the lifetime of the equipment. Annual savings of $500 on an investment of $4,000 will give an anticipated rate of return of $500/$4,000, or 12.5 percent.

The average value of the equipment is the initial investment minus the salvage value divided by 2. If we assume for this example that there is no salvage value and the equipment will last five years, the average value is $2000. The rate of return on the average value of the equipment over its lifetime is $500/$2,000, or 25 percent.

Net Present Value. One problem with the methods described above is that they do not take into account the fact that the value of a dollar today is greater than its value in the future.

The desired rate of return on the investment must be determined and an analysis carried out over the life of the project to determine cost savings in present value terms. A piece of equipment might cost $3,000 today and will result in annual savings of $1,000 for four years.

Net present value calculates the present value of a return in the future. The formula is

$$PV = \frac{FV}{(1+i)\,n}$$

where *PV* is the present value of a future return, *FV* the amount received at the end of *n* years, *i* the desired return on the investment, and *n* the number of years before the future return will be received.

Tables have been formulated to indicate the net present value of money at specified interest rates. Using the figures above, the cash savings would be calculated as follows:

Year 1	$1000	×	0.893	=	893
Year 2	$1000	×	0.797	=	797
Year 3	$1000	×	0.712	=	712
Year 4	$1000	×	0.636	=	636
Year 5	$1000	×	0.567	=	567
Total					3605

Thus, over five years, the cash savings in present terms would be $3,605. Proceeds from the sale of the piece of equipment to be replaced and any tax ad-

---

quick bite 11.8
Road to the Top: Peter Niemitz

President

Peter Niemitz takes a unique view of the restaurant industry, a designer's view. Niemitz's design firm, the Niemitz Design Group, holds an impressive client list including Legal Sea Foods, Capital Grille and Walt Disney. Niemitz spearheaded the project to design nine American-themed restaurants in Paris's EuroDisney. Clients claimed that Niemitz's biggest talent as a designer is taking the time to understand restaurant concepts.

According to Ned Grace, founder and former president of the Capital Grille and Bugaboo Creek steak-house chains, design is extremely important in today's competitive market and Niemitz's talent has helped his concept gain a competitive advantage. However, talent is not all that attracts operators to Niemitz; according to Grace, he is also fun to work with and will always figure out a way to get things done.

Niemitz's ideas for design always focus on the concept of a restaurant. "Our most basic fundamental philosophy is that the design has to fit the concept." He does not believe that the design should ever upstage the concept or the food. Although Niemitz has a unique understanding of restaurant design, it was not his focus during his studies, which earned him a bachelor's degree in fine arts and architecture from the Rhode Island School of Design in Providence.

Through his work designing a variety of businesses, Niemitz found that he really truly enjoyed restaurant design. "They were a lot more fun to open than card shops or dentists' offices." However, in his early days, Niemitz often had difficulty convincing operators that design could drive profits. But, in today's competitive market, he doesn't have to do too much convincing.

Source: Zuber, Amy. "Peter Niemitz: Solving the Challenge of Restaurant Design from the Ground Up." *Nation's Restaurant News,* v. 33, no. 4, pp. 164–166.

vantages resulting from a loss from that sale would also be considered as part of the cash inflow to be compared to the cash outflow of $3,000.

Internal Rate of Return. The discounted or internal rate of return considers the time value of money and determines the rate of return that would result when the present value of the return equals the initial investment. Management could then determine whether or not this rate of return was acceptable to them in making a decision on the project.

quick bite 11.10
Operations Budget in 2010

According to the National Restaurant Association the most likely developments regarding the operations budget in 2010 are:

- Technology will allow operators to monitor profit and loss on a daily basis.
- Real estate costs will rise rapidly.
- More money will be spent on employee training, particularly in the areas of food safety and accident prevention.
- Waste disposal costs will increase.
- Wage costs will increase dramatically, leading to the acquisition of more labor-saving equipment.
- As childcare, leave, and maternity/paternity benefits become more common, benefit costs as a percentage of sales will increase.

Source: Restaurant Industry 2010: The Road Ahead (Washington, D.C.: National Restaurant Association, 1999), p. 9.

When the cash savings are the same per year, the net investment can be divided by the annual savings to give a factor that can be compared to figures in tables of net present value to give the internal rate of return. Such tables can be found in capital budgeting texts.

Using the figures above—a $3,000 initial outlay with nothing from the sale of the old equipment and no resulting tax savings—and such a table, the internal rate of return is 19 percent.

ENDNOTES

1. James Keiser, *Controlling and Analyzing Costs in Foodservice Operations*, 2nd ed. (New York: Macmillan Publishing Company, 1989), p. 335.

2. Ibid., pp. 335–347.

3. Ibid., p. 339.

4. Ibid., p. 349.

5. Michael M. Coltman, *Cost Control for the Hospitality Industry* (Boston: CBI Publishing Company, 1980), pp. 16–25.

6. Keiser, *Controlling and Analyzing Costs in Foodservice Operations*, p. 410.

7. Coltman, *Cost Control for the Hospitality Industry*, p. 21.

8. Keiser, *Controlling and Analyzing Costs in Foodservice Operations*, p. 381.

9. Ibid., p. 410.

10. Ibid., p. 385.

CHAPTER TWELVE

EMPLOYEE SELECTION

learning objectives

By the end of this chapter you should be able to:

1. Identify the work groups that management will increasingly turn to for employees in the next decade.

2. Discuss the major laws and regulations affecting employee hiring.

3. Identify the steps involved in staffing the operation, outlining important principles at each stage of the process.

4. Develop guidelines on how to conduct a hiring interview.

Prospective employees should be 1) extremely nice, 2) intelligent, 3) infused with an extraordinary work ethic, 4) empathetic, and 5) emotionally self-aware.
Danny Meyer in *Dining Out*

Source: Dornenburg, Andrew and Karen Page, *Dining Out* (New York, NY: John Wiley & Sons, Inc., 1998).

SUPPLY OF LABOR: THE CHANGING PICTURE

The "typical" employee in a foodservice operation is [1]:

- female (56 percent)
- under 30 years of age (59 percent)

- a high school graduate or less (70 percent)
- single (71 percent)
- a part-timer working an average of 25.3 hours per week
- someone with a relatively short job tenure

---

quick bite 12.1
Hot Concepts: Razzoo's Cajun Café

"A poor schmo who succeeds in spite of himself" is a "razzoo" in Louisiana's Cajun country. A razzoo is also known as a winner at dominoes or marbles and a seven-unit restaurant chain based in Irving, Texas. Razzoo's Cajun Café is an appropriate name for the growing Gulf Coast seafood chain according to Mike Leatherwood, president and chief executive.

Leatherwood and his investors started the first Razzoo's in the Dallas suburb of Richardson for $120,000 cash. The location has already held four failed restaurants and Razzoo's barely hung on by a string at first. According to Leatherwood, many of their first customers only returned to the restaurant because they saw how hard he was trying to make it work. Razzoo's Inc. is doing much more than barely hanging on now, with an average of $3.8 million in annual sales at each of the seven units. The average per person check is $10.25. The company plans to open two additional stores this summer and would like to open four to six more in each of the next five years.

The restaurants can be called eccentric; the company focuses on interior décor and marketing. One industry expert describes the restaurants as a less expensive version of a Joe's Crab Shack. According to James Scurlock, Dallas-based publisher of the *Restaurant Investor Newsletter*, Razzoo's extends a very casual atmosphere and "outstanding" value. "It's taking the Cajun niche and doing a very, very, good job with food quality and terrific people."

Leatherwood explains the atmosphere as "casual, upbeat and a bit crazy." The menu includes items such as fried seafood, coleslaw, hush puppies and fries. One Dallas restaurant critic describes Razzoo's décor as "swamp-gaudy," but gives the menu high praises for its diversity. Top selling items include "rat-toes," which are fried jalapenos stuffed with crab and shrimp with dipping sauce, $5.79; fried alligator tail, $5.79; and the fried seafood combo platters, including one with crawfish for $10.99.

The locations use an unusual route to customer satisfaction by lowering expectations when they come in with specials like "Crawfish hollandaise or whatever with a caulking gun served with a side of veggie whatever" and then exceed expectations during the meal. And the tactic works. A great many customers leave proclaiming that they received much more than expected.

Source: Ruggless, Ron. "Razzoo's Cajun Café: Playing for All the Marbles." *Nation's Restaurant News,* May 17, 1999, v. 33, n. 20, pp. 68–71.

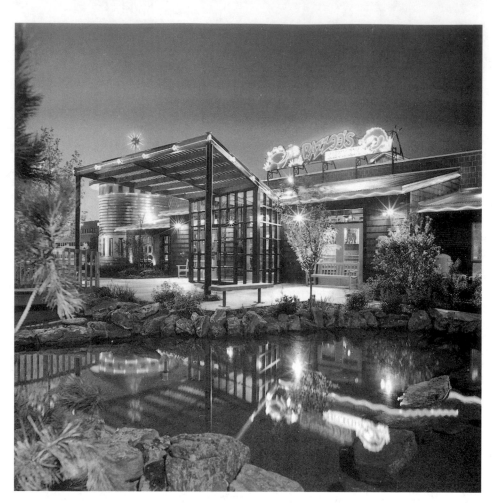

Razzoo's Cajun Café

The biggest challenge facing restaurant operators today is a lack of employees who are both qualified and motivated to work [2]. During the early 1990s the pool of potential employees restaurants primarily draw on—16 to 24 year olds—fell 3 percent. At the same time the number of restaurant locations increased substantially. As a result there has been a steady decline in the number of qualified applicants for hourly positions in the restaurant industry. In response, operators worked to improve productivity amongst existing employees while turning to other groups, such as seniors and immigrants. Since the mid-1990s the 16- to 24-year-old segment has bottomed out and is forecast to increase more than 18 percent through 2010. An examination of major demographic trends identifies the hiring environment in which management will operate.

To meet their needs, operators will continue to turn increasingly to sources of employees they have previously not considered.

Restaurant Management: Customers, Operations, and Employees

Women

The proportion of women working in foodservice occupations fell from 62 percent in 1987 to 57 percent in 1997. However, the proportion of management positions held by women in foodservice and lodging establishments increased from 41 percent in 1992 to 45 percent in 1997 [3].

To attract and keep female employees, companies may have to develop more "female-friendly" policies. Flexible work schedules, assistance with day care, and medical benefits aimed at women are some of the ways that companies can demonstrate their interest in attracting and keeping female employees.

A female-friendly atmosphere is one that does not tolerate discrimination or sexual harassment. Discrimination on the grounds of sex has been prohibited since 1968. Sexual harassment—increasingly regarded as a form of sexual discrimination—is an area of increasing importance to employers. The Equal Employment Opportunity Commission defines sexual harassment as:

> Unwelcome sexual advances, requests for sexual favors, and other verbal or physical conduct of a sexual nature constitute sexual harassment when (a) submission to such conduct is made either explicitly or implicitly a term or condition of an individual's employment, (b) submission to or rejection of such conduct by an individual is used as the basis for employment decisions affecting such individual, or (c) such conduct has the purpose or effect of unreasonably interfering with an individual's work performance or creating an intimidating, hostile, or offensive working environment [4].

Management has a duty to create and maintain an atmosphere that does not tolerate sexual harassment on the part of supervisors, employees, customers, and suppliers.

Minorities

Employees in the restaurant industry continue to mirror the population as a whole. African-Americans and those of Hispanic origin accounted for 10 and 6 percent, respectively, of all restaurant industry employees in 1983. By 1997 the figures were 12 and 16 percent, respectively [5]. Each segment accounts for 9 percent of foodservice- and lodging-industry managers.

In 2000, one of every four people living in the United States is a member of a minority group. This is a significant change from past decades [6]. Non-Hispanic whites, who made up 79 percent of the workforce in 1990, will account for a lower 65 percent of entrants into the labor pool between 1990 and 2005. Hispanics will account for 16 percent of entrants, largely attributed to high levels of immigration. Thirteen percent of workforce entrants between 1990 and 2005 will be black, and 6 percent will be Asian [7].

For Hispanics the cultural and language barriers make their success in the workplace more difficult. Among many Hispanics the tradition of a male-dominated, traditional society can place significant pressures on Hispanic women as they seek the security and independence that working out-

Women in the Workplace

The restaurant business has experienced tremendous growth due to women entering the workplace; however, this trend is ending and may even be reversing according to a study by Donaldson, Lufkin & Jenrette, an investment firm in New York. The rate at which women entered the workforce since World War II has had a tremendous effect on the entire economy, but that growth has leveled off. In fact, it is not a temporary stoppage and it may even start trending downward. This change is reported to be secular, lasting for at least a ten-year period.

As more women entered the workforce post-war, at-home meal preparation declined. For single parents and dual-income households, preparing meals became secondary to boosting the household income. The movement of women into the labor force became one of the largest and profound demographic and economic changes this country has seen. The number of women in the work place has grown an average of 1.8% each year from 1980 into the early 1990s.

The sheer number of women in the work force had many consequences. Many brand names enjoy sales growth as consumers lacking time learned to trust certain brands as an efficient way to get the quality and consistency they had come to know. As consumers realized that they need help with meal preparation, more and more began to go out to eat or ordering food to go. The trend not only gave businesses growing pricing power and encouraged better margins and business expansion. The number of restaurant locations increased from 155,000 in 1972 to 815,000 in 1999.

Unfortunately for restaurant operators, starting with the early 1990s, the number of households with two or more earners is growing at only about a third of its previous growth—0.5 percent versus 1.6 percent. The number of one-earner households is growing at a rate of 1.8 percent today compared to a declining rate of –0.2 percent as seen in the 1980s. Women are beginning to choose to stay home and the trend is moving toward households with more time than money.

The implications of the demographic shift are enormous on operators. The number of people seeking meal preparation outside of the home could greatly decrease. As the number of entrants into the industry slows, restaurants will no longer be restrained from price hikes. In many years, industry price increases have not even kept up with inflation rates, which has encouraged operators to contain prices and use value as their primary selling point.

Source: "Back to the Future: New Study Shows More Women Staying Home May Hurt Dining Dollars." *Nation's Restaurant News*, v. 33, n. 8, February 22, 1999, p. 27.

Hispanic Employees

Hispanic workers make up the largest minority or ethnic group of employees in the foodservice industry. These workers are alleviating the severe shortage of employees in the restaurant business, especially in the back-of-the-house for casual dining eateries. Hispanic employees have always been a good source of labor for restaurant companies, but the availability and prominence of these minority employees has grown dramatically in the table-service business for the past five years.

The rise in Hispanic employees is occurring for a number of social and economic factors. Members of Hispanic groups have gravitated to foodservice jobs because of minimum wage increases; welfare reform and the strong national economy have prompted members of other low-income minority and ethnic groups to seek entry-level employment in nonfoodservice industries.

Across the country more and more Hispanics are appearing in the restaurant business as entrepreneurs, corporate executives, general managers, executive chefs, sous chefs, and line cooks. However, Hispanic labor still dominates entry-level positions such as porters, runners, or dishwashers. Most operators can tell numerous tales of Hispanic employees whose loyalty and commitment in their jobs lead to rewarding advances from busboys to executive chefs and even unit managers.

According to Peggy Marshall-Mimms, a spokesperson for Metromedia Restaurant Group, the company is recruiting so many Hispanic employees that they have begun to publish their training manuals in Spanish. At Darden Restaurants, known for its Red Lobster and Olive Garden chains, a large percentage of its kitchens are operated and supervised by Hispanic employees. Red Lobster's president and CEO, Dick Rivera, is Hispanic and a 27-year veteran of foodservice.

Regardless of the achievements of many prominent Hispanics in the field, many industry observers accuse the casual dining segment of abusing its Hispanics employees. The abuse, they claim, stems from Hispanics' language limitations and unfamiliarity with labor laws. "To Henry Tamarin, president of the Hotel Employees and Restaurant Employees International Union, Local 100, in New York City, Hispanics are becoming a new class of indentured servants for operators who can't find workers elsewhere and who resent the salary demand and preconceptions of culinary graduates."

(continued)

quick bite 12.3
Hispanic Employees (*continued*)

Hispanics in Foodservice: One Kitchen as Microcosm

To assess the prominent role Spanish-speaking workers have played in the success of six-unit B.R. Guest Inc., a New York City-based casual-dinner-house operator, the company did a mini-census of its Hispanic employees, their positions and countries of origin. Following is a snapshot of results from one B.R. Guest restaurant, its popular Blue Water Grill in Union Square.

Name	Position	Birthplace
Luis G. Nieto*	Executive sous chef	Colombia
Guillermo Trejo	Sous chef	Mexico
Ricardo Aucapina	Sushi chef	Mexico
Roelio Gil	Line cook	Mexico
Juan Carlos	Line cook	Ecuador
"Ortega"	Line cook	Ecuador
Felipe Rojas	Line cook	Mexico
David Lopez	Line cook	Mexico
Bruno Alontes	Pantry	Mexico
Miquel Oropeza	Pantry	Mexico

*Nieto graduated from the government-sponsored Restaurant Hotel School in Bogota, Columbia. He worked as sous chef at the Italian Community Club in Colombia, leaving in 1993 to work on the ill-fated Achilee Lauro cruise ship. He came to the United States and worked initially at LaReserve in Manhattan.

Source: Prewitt, Milford. "Hispanics Find Job Niche in Restaurant Industry." *Nation's Restaurant News*, v. 33, n. 5, February 1, 1999, pp. 41–46.

side the home can bring. This is particularly evident for female managers supervising employees with such an orientation.

Businesses can require that English only be spoken under very narrowly drawn guidelines. Taking a proactive approach and realizing that it is difficult to manage someone if it is impossible to communicate with that person, some companies are teaching English to their employees while supervisors are encouraged to learn Spanish.

To attract and keep employees it is important to understand what motivates them and to develop an atmosphere that reinforces these things. At the risk of generalizing, it is true that most Hispanics place a high value on the family. Because unemployment rates in Hispanic areas are high, regular work is valued and contributes to the self-esteem and status of adult males.

Urging employees to have families visit the operation can make the employee feel that the family is assimilated into the workplace, thereby heightening the importance of the employee's work.

Immigrants

It is estimated that a minimum of 450,000 immigrants a year enter the United States legally, while an additional 100,000 to 300,000 come in illegally every year [8].

California, Texas, and New York account for more than half of all foreign-born residents, 20 percent of all recent immigrants live in the Los Angeles area [9].

Under the Immigration Reform and Control Act of 1986 it is unlawful for an employer to knowingly hire any alien not authorized to work in the United States. Irrespective of legal issues, hiring illegal aliens begins the employer–employee relationship with a lie.

"Illegals live in a world of lies. They are not liars, but theirs is a world of lies. They have to live—to eat—and to eat they have to say things that others want to hear. If a boss asks if they are here legally, they say they are. But they know that the boss knows they are lying and the boss is lying when he acts like he believes him" [19].

---

 q u i c k   b i t e   1 2 . 4
Immigration Law

Here are some commonly asked questions about immigration law:

1. When do I fill out the employment eligibility verification form?
   - Up to three days after the employee starts work.
2. Am I responsible for determining if the documents are real?
   - No, if the documents "on their face" appear to be genuine.
3. How long do I need to keep the I-9 forms?
   - Three years. If employees stay longer than three years, you must hold on to the I-9 form for one year after he or she leaves.
4. What if INS finds an illegal worker?
   - If you complete and retain all I-9 forms, you cannot be penalized unless INS can show that you knew about the illegal status of the worker.
5. What are the penalties?
   - Fines range from $100 to $1000 per violation. Fines for knowingly hiring an unauthorized worker range from $250 to $10,000 per incident.
6. How can I get more information?
   - Call the Immigration and Naturalization Service at (800) 255-8155.

Source: DiDomenico, Pat. "Immigration Crackdown Targets Restaurateurs," *Restaurants USA*, v. 15, n. 4, April 1995, pp. 8–9.

Restaurateurs have to ask themselves whether or not this is the best way to begin a relationship.

Older Employees

By 2010 about one in every five persons will be 55 or older—and almost one in three by 2030. Older employees represent a marketing tool for companies faced with increasing numbers of older customers. More than half of all working adults indicate a desire to work beyond the standard retirement age.

Advances in medicine have resulted in greater numbers of healthier older people. Older people tend to be "more dependable, have lower absenteeism, are punctual, . . . show good judgment based on their past experience, interact well with others, and show greater motivation due to increased job satisfaction and less job-related stress" [11]. They are not as adaptable and creative as younger employees.

An outreach program is necessary to attract older employees. Although most national studies indicate that they tend to prefer part-time employment and flexible work schedules, this finding is not supported by studies in the food-service industry. Older people identify with people younger than themselves. Advertisements showing people about 10 years younger than the age group sought are more likely to be successful.

Seniors are motivated by the desire for social interaction followed by having a purpose in life. Stressing the importance of interacting with customers and other employees and letting them know that their experience is appreciated are important factors in attracting this employee group. The fast food companies—led by McDonalds and KFC (the former Kentucky Fried Chicken)—have done a particularly good job of reaching out to older employees.

According to the American Association of Retired Persons, to be successful, training should be related directly to the job for which the person is being trained, should be given only for jobs that the employee has a chance of getting, should be active rather than passive, should be self-paced and individualized, and is more effective if short-term rather than a longer-term program.

Part-Timers

A major reason that many companies like to hire part-timers is that they typically do not pay them benefits. Benefits may add as much as one-third to the labor bill. In 1997 the median staffing levels for limited service fast food restaurants was five full-time employees and 12 part-timers. The figures for full-service restaurants with an average check of less than $10.00 and those with an average check of $10.00 or more was 12 full-time employees and 16 part-timers and 18 full-time and 25 part-timers respectively [12].

The importance of benefits was noted in a survey of restaurant operators. The most frequently mentioned changes in benefits mentioned by operators were establishing a 401(K) program, improving health insurance, providing profit sharing, instituting a pension plan, and increasing employees' share of benefit costs. More than half provided meals free of charge, while an additional

quick bite 12.5
Gen X Employees

Many rumors and ill-founded beliefs exist about Gen X-ers, also known as "busters," who were born between 1965 and 1976. Many hospitality managers feel that Gen X-ers are uninterested in their job and seem unable to communicate effectively with customers and other employees. These beliefs are not really true as a rule of thumb. However, Gen X-ers do have unique ideas about work and life and understanding these philosophies can help operators to work effectively with this generation.

The arrival of home computers, ATMs, automated telephone systems and Internet shopping has had an increasing impact on personalized service and customer expectations. Yet, because many young adults today have spent more hours than any other generation in front of the television and in the world of virtual reality, they have had less of the human-to-human contact needed to develop the people skills and team player attitude needed for good customer service.

Service expectations are increasing. However, customers complain that workers seem dissatisfied in their jobs. Servers don't know how to relate or communicate with strangers and seem removed and uneager to help.

Millions of people boast the importance of customer service, yet few really understand what it is about. Today's customer is interested in attitude, communication, knowledge, appearance, standards and initiative. Some effective ways to improve customer service in the hospitality industry is to assist employees in: 1) developing a positive attitude about themselves, 2) seeking opportunities to serve customers, 3) communicating effectively with customers, 4) becoming more positive and powerful representatives of the business, 5) listening more attentively to customer needs, 6) developing a professional service manner and 7) maintaining a neat and professional appearance. One hospitality professor claims that many Gen X-ers just don't have the basic skills required to deliver exceptional service to their customers.

In general, busters say that they prefer to work alone as opposed to in teams. Experts believe that this attitude comes from single-parent family experiences as well as from a focus on computers and technology. Gen X-ers have spent more time alone playing on computers and watching TV. They love to have fun and hate routine. They crave creative stimuli. Many Gen X-ers have not attended college, but have extensive technological knowledge.

Quality of life is a huge issue for Gen X-ers, they are not interested in climbing the corporate ladder; they will not be a slave to an organization. This attitude may result from companies that no longer promote moving through the system and instead make the message that "there is no job security here"

(*continued*)

clear. Yet, these corporations are continually pushing Gen X-ers for more productivity. These employees have also watched their parents sacrifice to rise up the corporate ranks only to be downsized, re-engineered, restructured, or eliminated. Those whose parents did reach the top often were taught that it is not all it's cracked up to be at the top.

Therefore, Gen X-ers have developed a belief that work is for pay and quality of life is what really matters. They are determined to work for good wages and to enjoy their leisure time. Employers need to respect those values and seek new and innovative ways to encourage these employees to focus on service. This generation's desire for a good quality of life does not mean that they don't have solid work ethics or aren't interested in working or success. However, lifestyle is very important; titles, prestige and power are not. Gen X-ers do not idolize workaholics; smart X-ers focus on the main objective and work towards it.

Source: Booth, Fran A. "Back to the Basics: Generation X Needs to Connect to People, Not Just Computers." *Nation's Restaurant News,* v. 33, n. 12, March 22, 1999, pp. 30, 66.

12 percent paid partially for them. Ninety percent of the hourly employees at foodservice companies with sales of $1 million or more a year receive meals and paid vacations, while more than 80 percent of the companies offered medical/surgical coverage. Forty-four percent gave Christmas bonuses, while one in eight offered maternity leave [13].

Part-time employees tend to be less loyal to the company, have higher turnover rates, and must be trained more often and supervised more closely. However, they can be laid off with less risk of lawsuits and/or unemployment compensation claims. They can be more eager to work, as they work fewer hours per day than do full-time employees. They may also be more willing to perform any job given to them. It is important to hire people who really want to work part-time. Employees will often say they are happy with part-time hours in order to get a start with a company. If the manager accepts this and continues to give few hours, the employee may become dissatisfied.

The orientation and training programs for part-time employees should be the same as those for full-timers. Although they only work for a few hours a day, those hours tend to be when the business is busiest. They do not have the luxury of slack business periods to get accustomed to the operation. It is therefore important that the training they receive be given during those slack periods and also be sufficiently rigorous to allow them to perform when business is busiest. Finally, they should be treated like full-time employees. People who are treated as second-class employees will act accordingly.

Disabled Employees

In 1990 the Americans with Disabilities Act (ADA) was signed into law. This law guarantees civil rights protection to persons with disabilities. For example, it is illegal to treat a disabled employee differently than any other employee, refuse to hire or promote qualified individuals because of a disability, put disabled employees into lower-paying jobs, or pay them at a different pay level [14].

The ADA defines a person with a disability to be one who has "a physical or mental impairment that substantially limits one or more major life activities" [15], who has a history of such an impairment, and/or who is perceived as having a disability. Individuals with disabilities, who may be customers or employees, are entitled to "reasonable accommodation" from a restaurant. Reasonable accommodations include removing barriers in the workplace, such as rearranging furniture to provide access aisles; providing auxiliary aids and services, such as an adapted computer or occasional assistance; and modifying policies such as dress codes or flex-time and job restructuring. If the operator can show that the accommodation will create an "undue hardship"—it will be a significant hardship or expense—the change is not required.

Barriers present in the operation must be removed if this can be done without much difficulty or expense. This might include such things as [16]:

- Providing a minimum of one accessible marked parking space per 25 parking spaces in the lot
- Providing the accessible spaces closest to the accessible entrance
- Ensuring an unobstructed path of travel from the on-site parking to the restaurant entry
- Having continuous handrails at both sides of all stairways
- Having flashing lights and audible signals on all alarms
- Ensuring that pathways to foodservice areas are free of stairs
- Ensuring that service is available at accessible tables or counters within the same area
- Ensuring that the same menu is available in an accessible space as is served in a mezzanine or raised or sunken dining area
- Ensuring that all rest rooms, and some telephones and drinking fountains, are fully accessible

Table 12.1 contains reasonable accommodations made by Hardee's in the development of their Creatively Applying People's Abilities (CAP) program in an attempt to employ 2,000 persons with disabilities by 1996.

There may be more than physical barriers to overcome in hiring the handicapped. There may by resentment and apprehension from existing employees. A communications program to orient new and existing employees to each other will help the transition into the workplace.

The number of people with disabilities employed as restaurant employees increased from 14,000 in 1980 to 19,000 in 1990 [17]. In 1991, over 25 percent of operators employed people regarded as retarded or learning disabled, while nearly

Table 12.1   Reasonable Accommodations: Hardee's CAP Program

Disability	Job Duty	Accommodation
Auditory hallucinations	Maintenance	Job coach, flexible schedule, management education on disability
Emotional disability	Cashier	Knowledge of medication effect
Hearing and speech impairment	Maintenance	Sign language, job restructure
	Host/hostess	Job restructure, job reassignment
Mental disability	Fried chicken preparation	Job coach, group training, transportation during inclement weather
	Host/hostess	Restructured job, additional training time, color-coded bar towels
Orthopedic impairment (arms)	Crew	Flexible schedule
Alcohol abuse		Supervisor meetings and counseling, Alcoholics Anonymous
Physical disability Paraplegic (legs)	Front-line cashier	No heavy lifting, curb cut, flexible schedule

Source: William F. Jaffe, "Integrating the Disabled Employee into the Quick-Service Restaurant: The Enclave Model," *Hospitality & Tourism Educator,* v. 6, n. 2, Spring 1994, p. 19.

one-fourth employed persons with a physical disability such as sight or hearing impairment. About 5 percent employed persons with an emotional disability.

McDonalds, KFC, Hardee's, Pizza Hut, and Friendly's are just some of the companies that have taken the lead in organizing programs aimed at employing the disabled. The McJobs program at McDonalds, for example, has graduated more than 1,000 employees since 1989 from their training program.

About 9 in 10 of these restaurateurs rated the dependability of their employees with disabilities as excellent or good compared to employees who were not disabled. About 7 in 10 rate the productivity of disabled employees as excellent or good compared to those without disabilities [18].

The Friendly Restaurant Company has a four-step process to help ensure a successful program. This program involves:

- Identifying company needs
- Identifying community resources
- Establishing a mutual relationship
- Building the relationship and understanding the pitfalls

Many jobs within the company are routine, repetitive, mechanical, and/or tedious. They are also the jobs that account for much, if not most, of the turnover in the business. The mentally handicapped or retarded person may be perfectly satisfied to handle these types of jobs which the company has the hardest time keeping filled. Dishwasher, stock clerk, bus help, kitchen help, sorter, janitor, and truck help may be particularly appropriate.

The employment options used most in integrating employees with disabilities into the workplace are individual worksites, enclaves, and work crews [19]. In an individual work site a person with a disability works at a community site with a support person. A group of no more than eight people working within a regular industry comprises an enclave, while groups of no more than eight people who perform specialized contract services are termed work crews. There is no consensus as to the most effective method of integration. A Marriott study of the three methods concluded that the individual worksite was most beneficial, while the enclave approach was of marginal benefit and sometimes harmful to the employee. Other studies outside the hospitality field have found the enclave to be the most effective method.

To build the relationship, management must first evaluate the employee to determine the type of work that he or she is best suited to handle. The employee may need the manager's help in overcoming uncertainties in interacting with others. Orientation and training techniques may have to be adapted to the disability of the employee. It is important that the manager, rather than another employee, supervise the training directly. Many handicapped employees adjust better to a new job situation if they feel they have the full support of the manager. Direct supervision of training is one way to demonstrate this.

A continuous schedule of positive reinforcement may be required to develop a new behavior. Meals, drinks, and verbal praise will, in many cases, be more effective than money in motivating mentally handicapped persons if they lack a realistic conception of the worth of money.

A variety of community organizations are available to assist in finding and placing handicapped employees. Contact with one or more specialized agencies to find out what they do will help establish the mutual relationship necessary for a successful hire.

THE REGULATORY ENVIRONMENT: EQUAL EMPLOYMENT OPPORTUNITY

In hiring employees, managers have to operate within an environment of laws and regulations that have been developed by government. In recent decades equal employment opportunity has received more attention than any other in the field of human resource management. Equal employment opportunity involves the "employment of individuals in a fair and unbiased manner" [20].

Federal Laws

A variety of federal laws have been enacted that affect equal employment opportunity. The major ones are [21]:

- Equal Pay Act of 1963, which requires employers to pay equal pay for equal work regardless of sex. Jobs are considered equal when they entail essentially "the same skill, effort and responsibility under similar working conditions and in the same establishment" [22].
- Title VII of the Civil Rights Act of 1964 (amended 1972), which prohibits discrimination in employment on the basis of race, color, religion, sex, or national origin.
- Age Discrimination in Employment Act of 1967 (amended 1986), which prohibits discrimination against people 40 years or older in areas of employment because of age.
- Pregnancy Discrimination Act of 1978, which prohibits discrimination against pregnant women in employment if they are capable of performing their job.

These laws cover all private employers engaged in interstate commerce who have a minimum of 15 employees working 20 or more weeks a year.

In addition, companies that are agencies of or contractors with the federal government are subject to various laws and executive orders. Such companies might be foodservice operators who have the contract to provide foodservice at a government facility. The more important regulations are [23]:

- Vocational Rehabilitation Act of 1973 (amended in 1974), which prohibits federal contractors from discriminating against handicapped individuals and requires them to develop affirmative action plans to hire and promote such people.
- Vietnam Era Veterans Readjustment Assistance Act of 1974, which prohibits discrimination against Vietnam era veterans for contractors with government contracts of $10,000 or more and requires affirmative action programs to advance such people.

Various other executive orders have been created to extend the same protection indicated above to employees of contractors to the federal government.

In addition to federal laws, most states and many other local governments have passed laws prohibiting discrimination in employment. Managers are advised to check with local and state agencies to determine the specific laws applicable to them.

Bona Fide Occupational Qualification

If an employer can show that discrimination on the basis of age, religion, sex, or national origin is justified by nature of the job itself, they can claim a bona fide occupational qualification (BFOQ). Claiming that, for example, hiring a woman instead of a man is a business necessity has been defined very narrowly by the courts. It would be appropriate, for example, to have males only as attendants in a men's bathroom.

Sexual Harassment

Sexual harassment is defined by the Equal Employment Opportunity Commission as "unwelcome advances, requests for sexual favors, and other verbal or physical conduct of a sexual nature." It is illegal when it is determined that such conduct interferes with the work performance of an employee or when it creates a hostile work environment. Although there have been some reported cases of sexual harassment of a male by a female, the vast majority of problems occur when a male supervisor, employee, customer, or supplier is accused of harassing a female.

The employer is held responsible for sexual harassment when he or she knows or should have known about it and did not prevent it or take corrective action. An effective sexual harassment policy should include the following [24]:

1. Develop a comprehensive company-wide policy announced to all employees and indicating that sexual harassment will not be tolerated.
2. Provide training sessions for all supervisors to explain the legal requirements and the company policy.
3. Establish a formal complaint system indicating how employees can make charges without fear of retribution and how charges will be investigated and resolved.
4. Take immediate action on receipt of a complaint.
5. Take immediate and consistent disciplinary action once a charge has been substantiated.
6. Follow up on all cases to assure a satisfactory resolution.

Affirmative Action

Affirmative action programs require employers to institute programs and to correct past discriminatory practices. To comply, employers must make an affirmative effort to find, hire, train, and promote employees of protected groups. Employers who have federal contracts greater than $50,000 are required to have affirmative action programs.

The basic steps in developing an effective affirmative action program are [25]:

1. Develop an equal employment policy and affirmative action program in writing.
2. Assign responsibility and the authority to go with it to a senior manager to implement the program.
3. Publicize the program.
4. Identify the number of minority and female employees by department and job classification.

5. Develop goals and timetables to increase, where necessary, the number of minorities and females.
6. Develop and implement specific programs to meet the set goals.
7. Develop an audit program to monitor and evaluate progress.
8. Develop programs to support the effort.

RECRUITING EMPLOYEES

Job Analysis

A job analysis, a periodic analysis of every distinct job in the operation, is crucial to a successful human resources management program. Figure 12.1 illustrates the relationship and importance of a job analysis to other personnel-related tasks. Before managers can hire an employee, they need to know what they should be looking for. A listing of the knowledge, skills, and abilities required to perform a job is known as a job specification.

The job specification for a particular job comes from a document that lays out the purpose, scope, and major duties and responsibilities of a particular job. This document is called a job description. The job description is developed as a result of a job analysis. The analysis of a job is the basis for developing performance standards for that job. In fact, performance standards for the job cannot be developed until and unless a job analysis has been completed.

Performance standards tell the employees "how well they are expected to perform" [26]. They are job descriptions translated into measurable form. The standards of performance expected for the job set the stage for appraising the performance of the employee performing that job. In other words, there is no foundation for firing an employee for not performing the job unless clear performance standards have been developed. These standards can only come from having conducted a job analysis.

An orientation program will include an introduction to the important facets of a job while training seeks to develop the employee's ability to perform that job. Neither can be done unless the manager can identify the important aspects of the job. This knowledge comes after analyzing the job.

One facet of a motivated workforce is one that feels they are being treated in a fair and equitable manner relative to their pay. Many suggest that the more important the job to the company, the more someone who performs in that job should be paid. Job evaluation evaluates the relative worth of every job in the operation. Job evaluation typically uses job descriptions as the basis for determining job worth. As noted above, job descriptions are the outcome of a job analysis program.

Analysis Process

A job analysis can be carried out in several ways. First, the manager can observe the employee performing the job. While necessary as part of the process, it is not a good idea to rely solely on this method. Employees may adjust the speed of

Figure 12.1 Relationship between job analysis and personnel-related functions.

How many smiling faces does a company need? *Source:* Robert Christie Mill.

their work if they are aware that they are being watched. The result may distort the number of employees needed. Direct observation does not reveal the mental processes used to perform a job. Some additional input is necessary.

An interview with the person doing the job is usually used as a supplement to direct observation. Employees may be asked to list, in chronological order, everything they do as part of their job. There may also be distortions with this type of review. The worker may exaggerate the importance of the job, or a poor attitude may diminish the importance of the tasks performed. Employees may forget parts of the job or may be performing tasks that should not be part of the job but were inherited from past jobholders.

An interview with the employee's supervisor might take care of any potential problems faced in the methods mentioned above. There is the possibility that the supervisor might be unclear about what should be done, but generally speaking, supervisory input will round out the picture supplied by personal observation and employee interview.

Tasks. The first step in the job analysis is to develop a job list, an inventory of the tasks associated with the job. These are limited to "how-to" items.

For a garde-manger or cold-meat chef, a job list might indicate that the employee should be able to [27]:

1. Plan future meals
2. Carve cold meats
3. Prepare various dishes
4. Prepare sandwiches

The job list for a food server might read [28] as follows:

1. Greet and seat restaurant guests
2. Serve water; light candles
3. Take beverage orders and serve drinks
4. Present the food menu and beverage list
5. Assist customers in making food and beverage selections
6. Place orders in the kitchen
7. Serve food and beverage items ordered and clear table between courses
8. Present bill
9. Perform other duties as assigned

Job Breakdown. For each item on the job task list, a detailed job breakdown will indicate what is to be done, how it is to be done, and why each step is important. A fast food operation may need 40 to 60 job breakdowns, each one to three pages in length. The time required initially is well worth the effort.

The completed job breakdown serves as a listing of standard operating procedures for the restaurant in addition to being the basis for training new employees in how to perform in the way that management wants.

Job Description. As noted above, the job description lays out the purpose, scope, and major duties and responsibilities of a particular job. Between 68 and 72 percent of tableservice restaurants—depending upon average check—report that they have written job descriptions [29]. As a minimum it should include the following [30]:

1. Job title
2. Title of immediate supervisor
3. Job summary: 20 to 30 words identifying the purposes of the job
4. Essential functions: what should be done; percentage of time spent on each; equipment used; types of materials handled
5. Reporting relationships: to whom jobholder reports; who reports to jobholder
6. Qualification standards: personal and professional qualifications; skills, education, and experience required; physical and mental demands; amount of responsibility; personal characteristics for job success

A job analysis should be updated periodically. Often, a restaurant will initiate a change of theme or menu without updating the job descriptions required to perform the work. As the operation changes, so will the jobs and the type of employees needed to perform them.

A job analysis may pave the way for a restructuring of employees. It may turn out that some employees are performing jobs that can be done by others. Some may be performing tasks that have been made redundant. Although this is not the major reason for conducting a job analysis, it is probably the reason many employees are fearful of such an effort—they think management will use the results to eliminate jobs. It is important that whoever conducts the job analysis realize the potential concerns of the employees and the impact they might have on their willingness to participate honestly in the process.

THE HIRING PROCESS

A television advertisement for oil filters features an auto repairman who examines a car and finds that because the oil filter was not replaced on a regular basis, the car needs a new engine. The tag line is "You can pay me now, or you can pay me later." The message is that investing a little time and effort up front will save money in the future. The same can be said about hiring employees. Managers who invest little time or effort in selecting employees are likely to have more problems in the future: problems such as absenteeism, high turnover, pilfering, and low productivity. Although restaurant operators cite employee referrals, walk-ins, and newspaper ads as the most effective methods for attracting new employees [31], additional steps can be taken in the hiring process. Each step taken costs time and money but reveals more information about potential employees. That, in essence, is the cost-benefit decision that each employer must make when determining a hiring process. Will the cost of taking this action result in a better hire that will bring the operation cost savings or increased sales sufficient to justify the cost of hiring? If the answer is "yes," take the time and effort to collect the additional information; if the answer is "no," forgo that step in the process.

Next we outline a variety of steps in the hiring process. For many operators this list will seem too costly both in terms of time and money. Others willingly spend the time and money up front in the belief that careful hiring will produce better profitability in the future. The steps and the percentage of tableservice restaurant operators who say they do them are [32]:

- Preliminary interview
- Completion of application form: 94–97%
- Employment tests
    Personality test: 23–28%
    Skills test: 15–43%
    Job simulation: 18–21%
    Assessment center: 4–8%
- Interview in human resources department
    Structured interview: 91–96%
- Background investigation
    Background check: 53–67%
    Reference check: 85–94%
- Medical examination
    Drug test: 8–20%
- Preliminary selection in human resources department
- Supervisory interview
- Realistic job preview
- Hiring decision

(Note: The range varies by average check.)

Preliminary Interview

Very often, prospective applicants will call or come into the restaurant wishing to know if there are any openings. The preliminary interview might be no more than a first impression as to what job the person is interested in, whether there are openings, and whether the applicant seems like a good fit for such a job.

While it is true that first impressions mean a lot, it is probably wise to err on the side of including rather than excluding candidates. The fact that someone is willing to inquire about jobs shows a certain amount of initiative.

Completing the Application Form

In reviewing a completed application certain cues will indicate whether or not a candidate should be considered further. Some of the red flags to consider are:

- Has the candidate had too many jobs in the past? A history of job hopping may indicate someone who cannot be happy at any one thing or someone who cannot keep a job.
- Lack of progress in previous jobs. Employees who have not been promoted and/or who have not received pay increases over time may lack the ambition and/or skills to perform at higher levels.
- The reasons for gaps in employment history need to be explored. The reasons may be legitimate—a return to school—or questionable—spent time in prison.
- Questionable reasons for leaving jobs.
- Inconsistency in career path. People who have worked in a variety of food-service sectors (fast food, fine dining, cafeterias) may not really know what they want to do.
- A messy application with misspellings and erasures can indicate an employee whose work habits are equally messy and undisciplined.
- Illegible handwriting that goes above or below the lines may indicate physical problems.
- Does the handwriting on the application match the signature? Some applicants get friends to complete the application for them if they feel they cannot do it themselves.

Employment Tests

Selection tests are used to provide an objective means of measuring abilities or characteristics. In the restaurant business, because of ready access to cash and supplies, there are potential problems with employee theft; other customer-contact positions require employees with empathy and an outgoing personality. Many argue that properly constructed tests can identify employees who have the characteristics necessary for specific positions.

Various laws and regulations governing tests used in the United States have been developed at three levels:

- At the federal level most of the laws are embodied in Title VII of the Civil Rights Act of 1964 and related EEOC regulations, in particular the Uniform Guidelines for Employment Selection Procedures.
- Regulations at the state level tend to follow federal guidelines but may add other, more stringent requirements.
- Professional standards are established by the American Psychological Association, American Guidance of Personnel Association, and the National Measurement Association.

The purpose of these regulations is to ensure that job applicants are not subject to discrimination or unfair, arbitrary rejection.

To be useful a test must be:

- Sensitive, so that it distinguishes between people who possess the characteristics and those who do not.
- Standardized, so that benchmark scores have been identified on a representative and sizable sample of people for whom it is intended and against whom an applicant's scores will be compared.
- Reliable, so that it always measures the same thing.
- Valid, so that it measures what it is intended to measure.

Validity can be either concurrent or predictive. To establish concurrent validity, existing employees are tested and their test scores recorded. Their job performance is also evaluated and noted. The test score of each employee is then compared to how well the person performs on the job to determine whether or not there is a significant relationship between the two. If there is a significant relationship—those who score well on the test perform well on the job, and vice versa—the test is valid and can be used on future applicants as a predictor of future job success.

With predictive validity all applicants are tested and the test scores noted but they are not used to determine whether or not to hire. Applicants are hired on the basis of other methods, such as an interview. After a period of time the performance of each employee is evaluated and the person's job performance is compared to his or her test scores. If there is a significant relationship between test score and job performance, predictive validity exists and the test can be used on future applicants as a predictor of job success.

Although written integrity tests are controversial, the American Psychological Association has given them qualified support, indicating that most of the evidence supports the idea that some of the tests do work. Tests are more likely to work if they meet the four criteria noted above.

Three companies—London House, Reid Psychological Systems, and Stanton—account for 70 percent of the integrity test market and tend to have the strongest research support. Reid Psychological Systems, for example, claims reliability coefficients of 0.90 on internal consistency and 0.78 on test–retest reliability. Concurrent vailidity has been measured in four studies at 0.43 (twice), 0.62, and 0.39. This compares favorably with average validity scores over several thousand studies for personality tests of 0.30. Predictive validity scores have also been impressive.

According to Reid, people who possess integrity [33]:

- Value their self-concepts and personal reputation as honest persons
- Value integrity in their friends and associates
- Avoid thoughts or situations related to theft, deceit, or inappropriate behavior
- Are willing to discipline other people or themselves for violating socially accepted standards of honest conduct

Can You Self-Monitor?

A useful test to identify service-oriented employees is the Self-Monitoring Scale. Developed by Mark Snyder of the University of Minnesota, someone who is defined as a high self-monitor, having picked up cues in the environment, can control and modify his or her behavior and expressions successfully based on the behavior and expressions that are most appropriate. Such a person would be better able to adjust his or her behavior to meet the needs of customers. In addition, high self-monitors have a higher level of persuasive communications skills.

With use of the scale, Snyder reports a 70 percent correlation in identifying self-monitors. Following is the 18-item Self-Monitoring Scale together with the typical replies of high-self-monitoring individuals. (Some observers suggest using a Likert-type scale rather than a simple true–false.)

1. I find it hard to imitate the behavior of other people. (F)
2. At parties and social gatherings, I do not attempt to do or say things that others will like. (F)
3. I can only argue for ideas which I already believe. (F)
4. I can make impromptu speeches even on topics about which I have almost no information. (T)
5. I guess I put on a show to impress or entertain others. (T)
6. I would probably make a good actor. (T)
7. In a group of people I am rarely the center of attention. (F)
8. In different situations and with different people, I often act like very different persons. (T)
9. I am not particularly good at making other people like me. (F)
10. I'm not always the person I appear to be. (T)
11. I would not change my opinions (or the way I do things) in order to please someone or win their favor. (F)
12. I have considered being an entertainer. (T)
13. I have always been good at games like charades or improvisational settings. (T)
14. I have trouble changing my behavior to suit different people and different situations. (F)
15. At a party I let others keep the jokes and the stories going. (F)
16. I feel a bit awkward in public and do not show up quite as well as I should. (F)
17. I can look anyone in the eye and tell a lie (if for a right end). (T)
18. I may deceive people by being friendly when I really dislike them. (T)

Source: Samenfink, William W. "Identifying the Service Potential of an Employee through the Use of the Self-Monitoring Scale." *Hospitality Research Journal*, v. 15, n. 2, 1992, pp. 1–10.

In addition to the integrity attitude test, others are available, including:

- Substance use attitudes
- Substance use history
- Sales productivity
- Service relations
- Numerical skills
- Social conduct history
- Work/education history

These tests vary in price from $16.50 to $25.00 each, the unit cost getting progressively smaller as the number used increases. (This section should not be taken as an endorsement of Reid Psychological Systems. It is published as an example of what one company offers in the area of employee testing.)

A special form of testing is that done through assessment centers. Over the course of several days candidates go through a variety of tests, case studies, and job simulations. Because of the high cost involved, the use of assessment centers is usually reserved for management positions.

Interview in Human Resources Department

Where a foodservice company has a corporate human resources department, the individual manager can expect assistance in interviewing employees. The basic breakdown of responsibility is that whoever is better able to do the job should do the job. Human resource professionals have specialized knowledge in the area of selecting qualified applicants within the existing regulatory environment. Managers would do well to utilize that expertise. A typical breakdown of responsibilities regarding interviewing is that the personnel or human resource manager would:

- Develop legal, effective interviewing techniques
- Train managers in selection interviewing
- Provide interview formats and tests
- Send qualified employees to managers who want to do the final interview

The line manager or supervisor, on the other hand, would typically:

- Decide whether or not to do the final interview (most will, rightly, want to)
- Do the actual final interviewing and hiring where appropriate
- Provide feedback to personnel on hiring decisions and reasons for not hiring

The interview is the most widely used and probably the most subjective method used in selecting employees. It has been demonstrated, for example, that [34]:

- Negative information brought out during the interview is weighed too heavily and positive information not weighed heavily enough.
- A favorable–unfavorable information sequence of information resulted in better applicant ratings than did an unfavorable–favorable sequence.
- Interviewers have an "ideal" stereotypical candidate against which they compare candidates. This ideal is a composite of the interviewer's perception of the characteristics of successful jobholders.
- Visual cues are often regarded as more important than verbal cues in reaching conclusions.
- The interviewer's rating of candidates, in part, depends on the quality of the other candidates being interviewed at the same time.

The interview is the best method for determining whether or not candidates possess certain characteristics, such as self-confidence, effectiveness in expressing oneself, and sociability, factors that are especially important in customer-contact positions. For this reason it is recommended as part of the hiring process. However, there are ways to improve its effectiveness.

There are three steps in preparing for the interview [35]. The interviewer should be selected, the place where the interview will take place must be identified, and time should be planned to preview the application.

In a corporation, human resource managers may be responsible for an initial screening of candidates. However, line management should have the responsibility for making the final hiring decision. Whoever conducts the interview should have a complete understanding of what the job entails, in addition to the skills, knowledge, and abilities required to perform that job. The former comes from a job description, the latter from a job specification. In addition, the interviewer must be objective, an excellent judge of people, a good listener, and an excellent representative of the operation. The interview is not only an opportunity to select employees; it is a way to represent the restaurant to people in the community. Even if an applicant is not hired, the person interviewed will leave with some kind of an impression about the company based on the type of interview that he or she had. That impression can be positive or negative. Some people have left interviews indicating that "Not only would I never work for that restaurant; I would never eat there and will tell all my friends to avoid eating there."

Care should be taken in selecting a time and place conducive to making an objective decision on whether or not a candidate is a proper fit for a job. Interviews should be scheduled when the interviewer can devote her or his time exclusively to the task at hand without interruptions. Sitting at a table in the restaurant can be a good idea as long as the manager makes it clear that they are not to be disturbed. This setting gives the interviewee a chance to see part of the operation.

The application form and additional screening information should be reviewed before the interview begins. A list of appropriate questions should also be developed prior to the interview. Many companies have found that a structured interview is most effective. In a structured interview, questions are developed based on the most important and most time-consuming duties of the job, and all candidates are asked those questions. Questions might be situational ("What would you do if . . . ?"), cover job knowledge ("How is a 'rusty nail' made?"), consist of a simulation ("Show me how you would clear this table"), or deal with employee requirements for the position. The interview may be part oral, part written, and part physical, and sample answers to the questions to be asked should be developed beforehand.

Developed along the lines suggested above, a structured interview is more likely to be objective and nondiscriminatory compared to unplanned interviews.

---

 quick bite 12.7
How to Use a Structured Interview Guide

The interview is the best suited and most widely used selection method in the restaurant industry. Structured interviews are one way to improve the reliability and validity of an interview. A structured interview is a "face-to-face encounter where the interviewer uses an identical set of predetermined questions with each applicant." The following questions were found to be useful in selecting swing managers for fast-food operations:

1. Tell me about two or three people you work with at _____ with whom you have to interact "differently." Perhaps these people were new to the organization, older workers, or disabled.
2. Tell me about two or three situations where you had to deal with a difficult customer. How did you know they were unhappy? How did you handle them?
3. Tell me about some problem situations (other than unhappy customers) that you've encountered on the job. How did you handle them? Would you handle them the same way again?
4. Have you been able to make any parts of your job easier or more rewarding? How?
5. Describe some of the times you tried to persuade or influence other crew members or members of the management team. What did you do? How did it turn out?
6. Describe some situations where you did more than was expected on the job.

Source: MacHatton, Michael T. and Lynne E. Baltzer, "Quality Personnel Selection: Using a Structured Interview Guide to Improve Selection of Managers," *Hospitality Research Journal,* v. 18, n. 1, 1994, pp. 77–99.

Questions focus on what is important in performing the job. Writing the questions down together with sample answers ensures that everyone is asked the same questions and that the interviewer has thought about the answer that is preferred. Inexperienced interviewers will often ask a question and fail to listen to the candidate's answer, as they have to formulate the next question in their mind while the candidate is answering the first.

One problem with a structured interview is that the structure itself can mean that potentially good candidates can be lost because of the lack of flexibility of the interview itself. Responses that do not conform to the sample answers developed should not be discarded if, in fact, they are good and legitimate.

First impressions are very important. It is often a mistake to judge someone based only on appearances and first impressions. However, someone who comes to an interview late, lights a cigarette without asking for permission, and has dirty shoes and/or messy hair certainly does not seem too interested in the job.

Some small talk is useful to get the interviewee relaxed. The application form should have been reviewed immediately prior to the interview but should not be consulted during the interview, to avoid a stilted question-and-answer session.

During the body of the interview the objective is to get the person being interviewed to do most of the talking. The interviewer has an idea (from the job description and job specification) of what is needed. By listening to the responses of the interviewee, the interviewer is better able to evaluate whether or not that person is the right one for the job.

People can perform a job if they have the skills and the motivation. Many positions in a restaurant are not highly skilled jobs or require skills that can be taught readily on the job. The manager must decide whether it is more important to hire attitude and train skills rather than vice versa. Particularly for front-of-the-house jobs, it is better and easier to hire attitude. It is difficult to identify the basic values, ethics, and motivation of someone rather than the extent to which the person possesses specific skills. Here are some examples that will help [36].

1. "Tell me about your first job." When a person started work can be a good indication of their work values and motivation. It does not matter so much whether or not the job was restaurant related. What is important is the reason they went to work and what they got out of the experience.
2. "What was your class schedule in school?" The restaurant business is one that is physically demanding. People who had trouble getting up before an 11 o'clock class may not have the energy level needed for your business.
3. "When was the first time you sold anything?" (for server positions).
4. "Tell me about your experience as a customer in our restaurant or in one of our competitors' restaurants." Their response will indicate what they think of customer service and what is required to satisfy a guest.
5. "Who are your heroes or best friends? Why?" (or best friends) are and why. We tend to look up to people we admire. The answer to this question will indicate what the interviewee's values are.

6. When hiring someone who will take reservations over the phone, interview them over the phone. That way you will find out how they really sound to potential customers. If they pass this test, interview them in person.

7. "What were customers like in the last place you worked?" Again, this will indicate true feelings about the importance of customers.

8. "Who was the best (and worst) manager you ever had, and why?" This will give an indication of how well or how poorly this person works with people in positions of authority.

9. "If you could have improved anything about your last job, what would it have been?" Exceptional employees are those who express their interest in the job by continually seeking ways to improve it and others within the operation.

10. "Why should we hire you?" Some employees feel that the world owes them a living. Others, the kind you want, believe that they can contribute something positive to the operation.

Once the interviewer's questions have been exhausted, it is time to ask the applicant if she or he has any questions. It is doubtful that everything could have been covered to the interviewee's satisfaction, so some kind of response should be expected. In fact, if the applicant has no questions, it probably indicates a lack of interest in the job. The number and type of questions asked can also give a clue as to what is important to this person.

Questions can be either direct or indirect. Direct questions are those that require a one- or two-word answer ("When did you leave your last job?"). They are useful for collecting large amounts of information very quickly. However, for a real evaluation, indirect questions (for example, "Why did you leave your last job?") are better, because they require that the applicant talk more to answer the question completely. Remember, the objective is to get the applicant to talk.

It may be necessary to probe the answer to a question. A probe is an attempt to elicit more information from the interviewee if the initial answer to a question is considered vague. If it is to work, the probe should seek to confirm, clarify, and/or promote further discussion. Probing can come only if the interviewer actively listens to the initial response to learn that it does not give a complete answer to the question.

There are certain questions that employers cannot lawfully ask. Topics should be avoided that could discriminate against employees on the basis of federally protected categories. Businesses cannot discriminate on the basis of race, ethnic background, origin, color, gender, age (over 40), handicap, military experience, and religion. Additional state and local laws have been enacted to protect additional groups of people. Basically, it comes down to this: Ask questions that deal solely with a person's ability to do the job—and nothing else. A person may be asked whether or not they have the legal right to work in the United States; they cannot be asked whether or not they or their parents are naturalized citizens. They can be asked which high school they attended but not when they went there. They can be asked if they have ever been convicted of a crime but not whether they have ever been arrested for a crime.

　　　　Restaurant Management: Customers, Operations, and Employees

quick bite 12.8
Road to the Top: Regynald Washington

General Manager; President and Chief Executive

According to general manager of food and beverage at Epcot Center in Lake Buena Vista, Florida, Regynald Washington, "We lose sleep at night if a guest leaves our facility unhappy." His job includes oversight of 12 full-service and 10 quick-service restaurants, 21 outdoor food outlets and a multi-million dollar event catering organization. These foodservice options at Epcot provide guests with recipes from Canada, China, France, Germany, Italy, Japan, Mexico, Morocco, Norway, the United Kingdom, and the United States.

Washington's main focus since he joined Epcot has been bringing together a diverse group of independent operators, according to George Kalogridis, vice president of Epcot. "Regynald meets with them regularly to ensure we're on the same page, philosophically. The respect that he's developed with that group is truly admirable," say Kalogridis.

Washington earned his bachelor's degree from Florida International University in international hotel and restaurant administration. However, he credits a great deal of his success to his first position at Concessions International. According to Washington, "Concessions International was very small when I started, and I wore a lot of hats." Co-workers describe Washington as quality-minded and people-oriented, with a great sense of humor and a good head for business.

With over 2,500 employees in the foodservice division, Washington stresses the importance of leadership. He espouses a back-to-basics approach, doing everything necessary to run a great restaurant first. Priorities include making guests happy, proper staffing, and things as simple and extremely important as making sure hot food is hot and cold food is cold.

Washington's platform for management includes three approaches in addition to back-to-basics. His second priority is financial results and making sure every manager and chef understands the financial elements of their area. Thirdly, Washington focuses on developing not properties, but people. He helps employees move forward, grow and continually learn new things. And finally, Washington focuses on having fun through building cohesive teams.

Source: Smyth, Whit. "Regynald Washington: Epcot's Chief of Food & Beverage Says Pleasing Customers Is No Mickey Mouse Operation." *Nation's Restaurant News,* v. 33, n. 4, pp. 216–217.

Background Investigation

The value of a reference check is the belief that past experience on the job is the best predictor of future job performance. It is, however, increasingly difficult to get worthwhile feedback about prior job experience. Applicants will only give the names of people who might be expected to give glowing references. The best source of past performance is to check with previous supervisors. There are two potential problems. First, because of the high turnover in this business, it may be difficult to locate references from even several months back. Second, previous employers may be reluctant to give detailed information on previous employees. There have been cases where employees who did not get a job have turned around and sued previous employers for giving a negative reference. People who are familiar with the law may be reluctant to do more than give the former employee's date of hire, date of departure, and job title.

Because of the usefulness of a reference from a previous supervisor, it is recommended that managers continue to give honest evaluations of their past employees. This advice is given in the hope that the manager who gives evaluations will receive them from others when requested.

There are some guidelines that, if followed, will help keep managers out of trouble from disgruntled employees [37].

- Don't volunteer information; respond only to specific requests. Before responding, telephone the inquirer to check on the validity of the request.
- Direct all communications only to persons who have a specific interest in that information.
- State that the information being given is confidential and should be treated as such.
- If possible, obtain written consent from the employee.
- Provide only information that relates to the job and job performance in question.
- Avoid vague statements (such as "She was careless at times").
- Document all released information.
- Clearly label all subjective statements based on personal opinions and feelings.
- When providing information negative to the employee, give the reasons why and specify the incidents.
- Avoid answering questions "off the record."

When requesting a reference, the most important things to check are [38]:

- Employment dates
- Job title
- Primary job duties and responsibilities
- Applicant's performance compared to others
- Attendance and lateness records
- Applicant's ability to get along with fellow employees and managers
- Amount of supervision required

- Quality of applicant's work
- Motivation and enthusiasm toward the job
- Starting and final pay
- Reason for leaving
- Anything else of significance

It would also be useful to find out if the previous employer would rehire the person. It is worth asking this question, although if the person giving the interview knows anything about the law, he or she will probably answer "It is against company policy to rehire previous employees." In addition to reference checking, employers may wish to check criminal records, driving records, Workers' Compensation records, federal court records, and educational records if it is deemed important.

Specialized companies will check these types of records for a fee, but it is possible to obtain a great deal of information yourself simply by using public records. Criminal records at the county or state level can be checked over the telephone. The state motor vehicle office will provide driving records. Workers' Compensation records, available through the state, will indicate past job injuries together with whether or not an employee has been cleared to return to work. Such records cannot be used to discriminate against an applicant who has made compensation claims at other places. Federal court records can also be accessed, while educational records are checked through the appropriate educational institution. Information from such background checks can be used as part of the selection process only if it is job related and is applied to every candidate.

Medical Examination

State agencies require medical clearances for all food handlers. An increasing number of companies will test new employees for drug use. Although controversial, drug testing has generally been upheld by the courts as long as it is applied to every job candidate for every position.

Preliminary Selection in Human Resources Department

At this point it would be appropriate for the personnel department, having screened prospective employees, to make a preliminary cut of employees deemed inappropriate. The remainder would be cleared for interviews with line managers who would make the final decision.

Supervisory Interview

The guidelines given above for interviewing with people from the personnel department are equally appropriate for interviewing with line management.

Realistic Job Preview

Often, the manager will be interviewing an excellent candidate, someone who will really make a difference to the operation. At other times she will be in somewhat of a panic to fill a position. In either or both cases, there is a tendency to sell the job to the applicant as something better than it really is. In such a situation the initial job expectations are set too high. The applicant might be told that no more than a 45-hour week will be required and that two days off a week are standard. The job will be viewed as attractive and there will be a high rate of job acceptance.

quick bite 12.10
Restaurant Workforce in 2010

According to the National Restaurant Association the most likely developments regarding the restaurant workforce in 2010 are:

- More women and minorities will move into upper management.
- There will be greater cultural diversity in the workplace.
- Employees will demand more free time and a better family lifestyle.
- Compensation plans will be developed to keep key employees.
- Pay will be more incentive-based and benefits will seek to encourage employee loyalty.
- Lack of employees will prevent some companies from growing.

Source: Restaurant Industry 2010: The Road Ahead (Washington, D.C.: National Restaurant Association, 1999), p. 12.

Once on the job, however, the newly hired employee realizes that all is not as promised. The employee becomes dissatisfied, less motivated, and may quit. In the short run a body has been found; in the long run, there is increased turnover.

A realistic job preview, on the other hand, presents an accurate picture of the job and its conditions as part of the hiring process. The job may or may not be attractive to applicants and there will probably be a lower rate of job acceptance than that described above. Of the smaller percentage of applicants who do accept the job, however, a greater number will find that the job is, in fact, as represented. They will tend to be more satisfied, more motivated, and will stay longer than the group discussed above.

Hiring Decision

It is important that the hiring decision be made in a timely manner and that applicants be made aware of that date. If an applicant is well qualified for the job, any delay in making the decision may mean that the person will find employment elsewhere.

Informing both those who will receive job offers and those who will not makes for good public relations and keeps those who did not get the job interested in applying for other opportunities within the operation for which they might be better suited.

In making a job offer the following elements should be covered [39]:

- Position title
- Person to whom to report
- Salary or pay

- Shift
- Starting date
- Starting time
- Ending time
- Days off
- Equipment needed
- Clothing required
- Meal arrangements
- Parking
- When to come for processing of personnel forms

The working relationship will be easier if it begins on the right foot. This means making the new employee feel welcome and preparing existing employees for the new arrival. Involving existing employees before a new worker shows up will help ease the difficulties associated with getting to know and work with the new person.

ENDNOTES

1. "The People Behind the Jobs," *Restaurants USA,* February 1999, p. 41.

2. National Restaurant Association, *Foodservice Manager 2000, Current Issues Report* (Washington, DC: National Restaurant Association, 1992), p. 19.

3. "Minorities Make an Impact," *Restaurants USA,* September 1998, p. 43.

4. Karen Eich Drummond, *Human Resource Management for the Hospitality Industry* (New York: Van Nostrand Reinhold, 1990), p. 230.

5. "Minorities Make an Impact," *Restaurants USA,* September 1998, p. 42.

6. Johnston and Packer, *Workers for the 21st Century,* p. 89.

7. National Restaurant Association, *Foodservice Manager 2000,* p. 19.

8. Johnston and Packer, *Workers for the 21st Century,* pp. 92–93.

9. Ibid., p. 92.

10. Paul Ehrlich, Loy Bilderback, and Anne H. Ehrlich, *The Golden Door* (New York: Ballantine Books, 1979), p. 242.

11. Mill, *Managing for Productivity in the Hospitality Industry,* p. 19.

12. "Adding Up Employees," *Restaurants USA,* November 1998, p. 45.

13. National Restaurant Association, *Foodservice Manager 2000,* p. 28.

14. William F. Jaffe, "Integrating the Disabled Employee into the Quick-Service Restaurant: The Enclave Model," *Hospitality & Tourism Educator,* vol. 6, no. 2, Spring 1994, p. 15.

15. National Restaurant Association, *Americans with Disabilities Act: Answers for Foodservice Operators* (Washington, DC: National Restaurant Association, 1992), p. 2.

16. Ibid., pp. 8–18.

17. National Restaurant Association, *Foodservice Manager 2000,* p. 27.

18. Ibid., p. 27.

19. Jaffe, "Integrating the Disabled Employee into the Quick-Service Restaurant," p. 19.

20. Arthur W. Sherman Jr., George W. Bohlander, and Herbert J. Chudren, *Managing Human Resources,* 8th ed. (Cincinnati, OH: South-Western Publishing Co., 1988), p. 63.

21. David Wheelhouse, *Managing Human Resources in the Hospitality Industry* (East Lansing, MI: Educational Institute of the American Hotel and Motel Association, 1989), p. 67.

22. Ibid., p. 66.

23. Ibid., p. 71.

24. Ibid., p. 79.

25. EEOC, *Affirmative Action and Equal Employment: A Guidebook for Employers,* vol. 1 (Washington, DC: Equal Employment Opportunity Commission, 1974), pp. 16–17.

26. Lewis C. Forrest, *Training for the Hospitality Industry* (East Lansing, MI: Educational Institute of the American Hotel and Motel Association, 1983), p. 56.

27. Donald Lundberg, *The Management of People in Hotels and Restaurants,* 5th ed. (Dubuque, IA: Wm. C. Brown Company, 1992), p. 85.

28. Forrest, *Training for the Hospitality Industry,* p. 41.

29. "Addressing the Needs of a Diverse Work Force," *Restaurants USA,* October 1997, p. 42.

30. Ibid., p. 53.

31. National Restaurant Association, *1998 Restaurant Industry Operations Report* (Washington, DC: National Restaurant Association and Deloitte & Touche LLP, 1998), p. 9.

32. Sherman et al., Managing Human Resources, p. 160. Bruce Grindy, "Hooking and Keeping Employees," *Restaurants USA,* October 1998, p. 24.

33. Reid Research Report, unpublished promotional booklet, undated.

34. Sherman et al., *Managing Human Resources,* p. 172.

35. Wheelhouse, *Managing Human Resources in the Hospitality Industry,* pp. 176–183.

36. Bill From and Len Schlesinger, *The Real Heroes of Business* (New York: Doubleday, 1994), pp. 323–333.

37. J. D. Bell, J. Castagnera, and J. P. Young, "Employment References: Do You Know the Law?" *Personnel Journal,* vol. 63, no. 2, February 1984, pp. 32–36.

38. Karen Eich Drummond, *Human Resource Management for the Hospitality Industry* (New York: Van Nostrand Reinhold, 1990), p. 33.

39. Wheelhouse, *Managing Human Resources in the Hospitality Industry,* p. 119.

CHAPTER THIRTEEN

TRAINING AND DEVELOPMENT

learning objectives

By the end of this chapter you should be able to:

1. Design an effective orientation program.

2. Compare and contrast the various training methods.

3. Design, implement, and evaluate an effective training program.

4. Develop the skills necessary to become an effective trainer.

5. List the elements of a strong employee and management development program.

The previous semester, several students had tried an experiment. Back in their restaurants they inserted the words "for you" into every sentence, even when it sounded silly, as in "I'd be happy to get a fresh cup of coffee for you," or "Is this steak done all right for you?" Their tips increased 20 percent.
Jeffrey Steingarten, *The Man Who Ate Everything.*

Source: Steingarten, Jeffrey, *The Man Who Ate Everything* (New York, NY: Vintage Books, 1997).

Hot Concepts: Rodizio Grill

Meat lovers can often feel left out in today's age of consistently adding new vegetarian entrées to the menu. The owners and operators of Denver, Colorado-based Rodizio Restaurants International, Inc, call Rodizio's Grill a meat-eater's haven. The company currently runs five units each with annual sales of $2 million to $5.2 million. Average checks at the Brazilian churrascaria themed restaurants run about $12.50 for lunch and $20 for dinner.

Patrons feel as though they are in a Brazilian-style steak house and experience a completely unique dining atmosphere at Rodizio Grill. An exhibition-style rotisserie and grill fill the center of the restaurant. Guests begin their meal with appetizers including glazed bananas and polenta sticks. A thirty-five-item salad bar provides them with their veggies. And when they are finally ready for the main course they turn over a wooden dowel at the edge of their table from red to green in order to have the meat come.

The wait staff is costumed in a gaucho, a Brazilian rancher's outfit and they appear at customers' tables with a variety of meats. Customers select from the variety of beef, chicken, pork and fish presented by the server. The meats are served in an all-you-can-eat format and another turn of the dowel to green signals to the server that a guest would like another helping. The unusual serving style set to Brazilian music invites guests "to let loose, eat to their hearts' content and become Brazilian for the night."

According to president and chief executive, as well as native Brazilian, Ivan Utrera, customers are transformed by the end of their first visit. "They come in, sit down and are very quiet. Yet, by the end of the meal they turn Brazilian. They're speaking with their hands, talking and having a great time." The history of the churrascaria explains the atmosphere of the grill. Very much like our Thanksgiving, Brazilian settlers who had fled from Germany and Italy gathered a couple of times a year to celebrate settling in the temperate region with rich and fertile soil, fit for raising livestock.

Part of the appeal of Rodizio's is not only the "eatertainment" effect of the skewered meat but also the food quality. Customers are coming to the restaurant because of the variety. They can select what they want from a variety of items placed in front of them, making very little effort involved in the process. According to Rodizio's director of operations, Scott A. Henley, "They truly get to sit back and relax without having to make a lot of decisions and everything kind of comes to them, and they feel like a king or queen."

Source: Strauss, Karyn. "Rodizio Grill: Churrascaria Carves It's Niche in Steak Segment." *Nation's Restaurant News*, May 17, 1999, v. 33, n. 20, pp. 72–74.

EMPLOYEE ORIENTATION

Orientation is "the formal process of familiarizing new employees with the organization, their job, and the work unit" [1]. Conducted properly, orientation will give employees the knowledge necessary for them to be successful in an operation.

It is generally recognized that a well-run orientation program will help [2]:

- Lower turnover
- Increase productivity
- Improve employee morale
- Lower recruiting and training costs
- Facilitate learning
- Reduce the level of anxiety of new employees

As noted above, a comprehensive orientation program should cover three major areas: the organization, the job, and the work unit. The following elements are typical of a comprehensive program [3]:

The organization:
1. Description of the operation's history, size, and objectives
2. Company standards regarding job behavior and performance
3. Conditions of employment regarding such things as hours of work and pay periods
4. Key management and the chain of command

The purpose of this segment is to let employees see the "big picture" of what the company stands for. In so doing, employees will get a feeling for how their job fits into the entire operation and realize the history and tradition behind what the operation does.

The job:
5. Detailing the duties and responsibilities of the job and its importance to the entire organization
6. Explaining the training to be given
7. Explaining how performance will be evaluated
8. Sanitation and safety regulations

The objective of this segment is to let employees know what a "normal" workday looks like.

The work unit:
9. Introduce them to fellow employees
10. Immediate contact in dealing with problems

11. Tour of the entire operation
12. Rules, regulations, and policies

The Old Spaghetti Factory includes the following items in their orientation program [4]:

- Brief history of the company and store
- Customer philosophy
- Names of managers
- Name of trainer
- Schedule and scheduling
- Where to park
- Attendance and tardiness
- No-solicitation rule (prohibits employees from selling any products or services or from distributing literature on the premises without prior approval from the employer; designed to prevent unions from distributing union literature in the restaurant)
- How to sign in
- Meals
- Wage and raise policy
- Payday and paycheck procedure
- House and safety rules
- Grooming and uniform standards
- Other store rules
- Training schedule
- Handwashing and sanitizing

It is as important to prepare existing employees for the new hire as vice versa. Employees may be suspicious of new hires and will wonder if and how a new employee will affect them and their job. This important section aims to make new employees feel like they belong.

There is a danger in exposing the new hire to too much information over a short period of time. For a new employee, the first day is especially stressful: dealing with a work environment, employees, supervisors, and customers who are different. In such a situation the employee may be unable to absorb much additional information. Nevertheless, the first few days of contact between the employee and the company will set the tone for the longer-term relationship.

To combat potential problems of information overload, employees are given much of the information in writing in the form of an employee handbook. They are then asked to sign a declaration indicating that they have received this information. In this way the company protects itself against future employee

quick bite 13.2
Orientation Manual

Many operators are providing workers with an employee manual as part of their orientation. Here is an example of an outline for such a manual:

A. Operational Procedures
   1. Clock-in
   2. Smoking
   3. Horseplay
   4. Phone calls
   5. Answering the phone
   6. Solicitations
   7. Paychecks
   8. Advances
   9. Absences/tardiness
   10. Personal property
   11. Personal business
   12. Age requirements
   13. Accidents
   14. Customer complaints
   15. Employee meals
   16. Breaks
   17. Parking
   18. Scheduling
   19. Dress code
B. Personal Hygiene
   1. Hair
   2. Clothing
   3. Face
   4. Hands
   5. Fingernails
   6. Washing hands
C. Employee Benefits
   1. Insurance
   2. Promotions
   3. Training
   4. Uniforms
   5. Vacations
D. Menu Breakdown
E. Greeting, Seating, and Table Service
F. Abbreviations
G. Employee Agreement

Source: Bailey, A. Dyal. "The Quick Way to Produce an Employee Manual," *Restaurants USA,* v. 12, n. 8, September 1992, pp. 16–18.

claims that they were not told certain information. This is particularly important for those employees who have to enforce company rules.

The final part of an orientation program is the evaluation and follow-up. Too often the assumption is made that because employees have been through the program, they have absorbed the information. The objective is, in fact, to have them absorb certain information deemed important by management. Some companies will test employees several weeks after the orientation to determine whether or not the information has been taken in.

EMPLOYEE TRAINING AND DEVELOPMENT

Importance of Training

There are some in the industry who see training as a cost rather than an investment. When sales drop, any training that is currently being done is stopped altogether. They argue that given the turnover rate in the industry, there is little point in training employees who will invariably leave. They argue that they are, in essence, training employees for others.

This argument fails to recognize that employees may be leaving, in part, because management has not invested the time, money, or energy in them, the employees. A well-trained group of employees should result in a reduction of costs, stress, turnover, and absenteeism and a corresponding increase in efficiency and customer satisfaction.

---

 quick bite 13.3
Cost of Turnover

Here are the costs directly related to turnover:

1. Advertising and recruiting
2. Time spent on recruiting
3. Orientation and training
4. Overtime for existing employees
5. Support items such as uniforms and wine openers

Here are the indirect costs of turnover:

1. Lack of productivity in new employee
2. Loss of reputation and goodwill
3. Waste and breakage
4. More accidents
5. Lack of teamwork
6. Decreased motivation among existing staff

Source: Carbone, Loret. "Less Employee Turnover: The Hidden Key to Profitability," *Nation's Restaurant News*, March 20, 1995, p. 50; Theresa Howard, "New Strategies for Tomorrow's Workforce," *Nation's Restaurant News*, March 20, 1995, p. 63.

In order to remain competitive in the upcoming fast-food wars of the new millennium, Taco Bell introduced a systemwide retraining effort aimed at 7,000 managers. Taco Bell in an unprecedented step gathered managers to improve their employee-manager communication and to reward front-line staff for superior service.

The "Leaders Millennium Expo" was a national convention consisting of Tricon Global Restaurants' 7,300-unit chain of Mexican fast-food restaurants. The convention addressed menu and operational strategies which Taco Bell conceived to make ready its managers for the ongoing market-share battle between the quick-service restaurants that is sure to wage into the next millennium. Taco Bell's far-reaching training program underlines the corporate philosophy that the restaurant manager is the number one organizational leader.

Taco Bell's new training program—known as CHAMPS for Cleanliness, Hospitality, Accuracy, Maintenance, Product quality and Speed of service—stresses the importance of crew motivation and recognition. Taco Bell hopes to have the program instituted in its 5,000 domestic units and 1,800 kiosks and other nontraditional sales outlets by July of 1999.

One reason for the huge retraining effort by the chain is the shift in ownership Taco Bell has seen as well as the changing management structure. Taco Bell has shifted from a predominately franchisor-owned chain to approximately 80% ownership by franchisees. The chain's former owner PepsiCo Inc., had made Taco Bell unit managers responsible for "portfolios" of satellite businesses supported by Taco Bell restaurants. However, PepsiCo.'s strategy was reversed in 1997 when GMs were placed back in the restaurants and regional supervisors loads were reduced to between eight and ten restaurants versus 35 restaurants as previously required.

The CHAMPS training program is a group-training design that guides up to 10 employees per session through an interactive series of "learning maps." According to one franchisee, the program allows the restaurant general manager the opportunity to empower and reward their crew and teaches them more about the business and customers needs and wants.

Source: Spector, Amy. "Taco Bell Launches Sweeping 'CHAMPS' Retraining Effort." *Nation's Restaurant News,* v. 33, n. 12, March 22, 1999, pp. 4, 92.

Responsibility for Training

The person responsible for training will depend on the size of the organization and how it is structured. For a restaurant that is part of a chain or a unit part of a larger organization, line managers will be supported by staff people in a human resource department with specialized expertise in training.

Such staff people can be called upon to [5]:

- Assist line managers in developing training programs
- Conduct general training programs focusing on such general topics as supervisory techniques and time management
- Coordinate various elements of training, such as the use of outside speakers and seminars and directing programs of succession planning and cross-training
- Research, monitor, and evaluate training

Even if there is staff assistance, the unit manager bears the ultimate responsibility for training new employees. At the independent unit level the unit manager does not have the benefit of specialized staff assistance. The general manager of a restaurant will not necessarily carry out the actual training. The training itself is best done by someone who understands the performance standards required for the job and is able to pass those skills on to others. Often, that person is the department manager.

TRAINING PROCESS

Training can be defined as "any procedure initiated by an organization to foster learning among organizational members" [6]. Training is done initially to bring new hires up to the standards required by the company. Beyond this, as the job or the market changes, there will be a need to establish training programs to adjust operations to the new situation.

There are several steps involved in developing a training program [7]:

1. Conduct a needs assessment.
2. Determine learning objectives.
3. Develop the overall training program.
4. Develop individual training lessons.
5. Conduct the training.
6. Evaluate.
7. Follow up.

Needs Assessment

The purpose of a needs assessment is to determine what types of training are needed. Assessment can be done at three levels [8]: organizational analysis, task analysis, and person analysis.

The organizational analysis looks at the company as a whole and in light of company goals, resources, and the external environment in which it operates, suggests where the training emphasis should be. For example, the courts have increased their attention on the topic of sexual harassment. In light of this environmental influence, an organizational analysis might suggest supervisory training in this area.

A task analysis involves designing the content of a training program based on the duties involved in a job. A job description is one document that results from having conducted a job analysis. The job description indicates the most important and time-consuming tasks involved in performing that job. Performance standards will then be developed for every important part of the job. These performance standards represent the level of performance required for that job. A person analysis then determines what knowledge, skills, and attitudes are required to perform the job successfully. People hired for that job must either possess these skills or must be trained in them. The need for training can also come from accident records, personal observation, exit interviews, customer complaints, and employee evaluations.

Learning Objectives

Learning objectives should be SMART: specific, measurable, achievable, realistic, and time-bound. Both manager and employee will then know up front what is to be done, the level of performance that is to be achieved, and when it is to be accomplished.

Training Program

The complete training program can then be laid out. The training necessary for a specific job comes from an analysis of that job. A job analysis identifies the important tasks that make up that job. This is what people performing the job must be able to do. If an employee is hired without the ability to perform one or more of these tasks, the task must be taught to the employee. The program will identify what is to be taught, when, where, how, and to whom it is to be taught, together with an estimate of the cost involved.

Earlier, the process for conducting a job analysis was identified. The process involves developing [9]:

- A job list
- A job breakdown
- A job description
- A job specification

A job list is an inventory of all the tasks that must be performed as part of that job. For example, a job list for a food server might include the following, among others [10]:

- Greeting and seating restaurant guests
- Serving water; lighting candles
- Taking beverage orders and serving drinks
- Presenting the food menu and beverage list
- Assisting guests in making food and beverage selections

A job breakdown is then prepared for each task on the job list. The job
breakdown indicates how the task should be performed. It comprises four parts:
what is to be done, what materials are needed, how it is to be done, and why
that step is important.

The task of "assisting guests in making food and beverage selections"
might involve six steps [11]:

1. Approach the table.
2. Take cocktail order.
3. Serve cocktails.
4. Check back for a second cocktail.
5. Take the food order.
6. Take the wine order.

Each item would then be described in more detail as to the procedures for performing the task, any materials that might be needed, and why the specified procedures are important. The first step might look like this [12]:

WHAT TO DO
Approach the table.

HOW TO DO IT
Stand erect. Look at the guest, smile, and greet them pleasantly. Introduce yourself. If you know their names, use them when you greet them. Be courteous.

WHY IT IS IMPORTANT
You "win" the table by your first contact when you are pleasant and personable.

From the job breakdown a description of the job can be developed and used to write a job specification: a list of the knowledge, skills, and abilities needed by someone to perform the job. When employees are hired, their existing knowledge, skill, and abilities can be compared to those in the job specification to identify shortcomings. These items form the basis for the tasks that employees have to be trained to perform. The specifics are to be found in the job breakdown. These will also serve later as the performance standards to determine the extent to which employees are performing up to the level required by the restaurant.

Training Lessons

The entire training program is then divided into segments and a lesson plan developed for each segment. Typically, classroom training sessions should last from 15 to 30 minutes. The training lesson will identify a learning objective for that session and suggest which techniques should be used to meet that objective.

Conducting the Training

At this point it is necessary to select someone to do the training. Typically, that task is left to the immediate supervisor or a fellow employee. Just because someone knows how to perform a job or has responsibility for seeing that the job is performed well does not mean that the person will be effective in training another person to perform the task effectively.

According to Wheelhouse [13], effective trainers are:

- Good judges of people
- Objective
- Aware of, understand, and accept the differences in people
- Good at listening and communicating

Answer these questions to determine how good a trainer you are:

1. Do you spend as much time in preparation as in instruction?
2. Have you prepared job breakdowns for what you will teach?
3. Do you explain to employees how they will benefit from the training?
4. Before training, do you find out what the employee already knows?
5. Do you lay out a timetable for the training?
6. Do you accept that there will be times when you will notice no progress?
7. Do you expect that employees will learn at different rates?
8. Do you show and tell how to do the task?
9. When mistakes are made, do you point out what the employee did right before correcting their mistakes?
10. Do you give clear instructions?
11. Do you ask the employee to attempt the task while explaining it to you?
12. Do you praise frequently?

Note: The answer should be "yes" to all these questions. What skills and attitudes are necessary to adopt these behaviors? Do you have them?

Source: Forrest, Jr., Lewis C. *Training for the Hospitality Industry* (East Lansing, MI: Educational Institute of the American Hotel and Motel Association, 1983), p. 107.

- Good role models for the department
- Optimistic and enthusiastic about the job, the department, and the company

If a fellow employee is asked to take on the role of trainer, that person should be compensated financially and given positive recognition within the operation. A server acting as trainer will be able to serve fewer customers and will have fewer tips. Extra pay and recognition should be given to make up for this shortfall.

Evaluation

This next step in the process determines the extent to which the training objectives have been met. The success of the training can be measured at various levels [14]. At the first and most basic level the trainee's reaction can be measured: Did they like the program? Next, their knowledge level can be measured: Did they learn the new information? Even better is to evaluate behavior and/or attitude: Do the employees demonstrate new behaviors and/or attitudes on the job that can be traced to the training received? Finally, and most important, was the training cost-effective: Was the cost of the training outweighed by a resulting increase in employee productivity?

Follow-up

Follow-up is necessary to ensure that the skills taught are used constantly. Supervisors can follow up through coaching—checking that the results of a training program are improving employee performance and either giving positive feedback when it is happening or correcting that performance, when necessary, in a way that will improve the performance of the employee.

PRINCIPLES OF LEARNING

There is a difference between training and learning. Often, it is assumed that because training takes place, the trainees have learned. Learning does not take place until and unless the information that was part of the training program was received, understood, and internalized. Thus for training to be effective, it has to be designed such that it helps trainees learn. By identifying how people learn and designing training programs with these principles in mind, trainees will be more likely to learn.

Intention to Learn

People will not learn unless they want to. The trainer's role is to help supply that motivation by letting the trainee know the importance of the information about to be presented. Employees need to know what's in it for them. It may be that learning how to perform a new task will increase tips, help the employee get a promotion, or give them more status within the operation. The task is to find out what is important to the employee and to show how actively participating in the training will help the employee satisfy that need.

Whole Learning

Learning is improved if the entire job or task is shown in relation to other jobs and the task to be taught is then broken down into its constituent parts. Known as whole or Gestalt learning, the idea is that a trainee will better comprehend the task if she or he knows where that task fits into the entire operation. When training a dishwasher, for example, one would first explain how and where the dirty dishes come from, how they are cleaned, and what happens to them once they leave the dishwasher's control. By adding an explanation as to the importance of having clean dishes, the person being taught the job now has a frame of reference for learning the specific steps involved in producing clean dishes.

Reinforcement

People act in ways that are rewarding to them. Rewards can be external—pay increase, promotion, verbal praise—or internal—a feeling of accomplishment. Trainers should find out what rewards are important to the trainee and reinforce positive behavior using these rewards to get more of the same behavior.

Positive reinforcement—a reward for doing something right—is more effective than punishment—an action to punish the person for doing something wrong. Reinforcement is improved when the reward is given as soon as possible after the action. Praising a hostess immediately after she helps a family calm a child fretting at the dinner table is more effective in reinforcing the behavior than waiting until the end of the shift.

Practice

The saying goes: "Practice makes perfect." Some would adapt this to say: "Perfect practice makes perfect." The point, however, is that repeating the newly learned skill will improve the performance of that skill. Further, active practice is more effective than reading or listening.

Spaced versus Massed Practice

Retention is improved when new material is spread out over several sessions rather than being condensed into fewer, longer sessions. If, for example, it is estimated that a new job will require eight hours of training, the trainee will learn better if there are two hours of instruction in the new job each day for four days rather than one eight-hour day of new material.

Learning Curve

People learn at different rates. There appear to be three patterns by which learning takes place. The learning of most routine jobs follows a decreasing returns pattern, wherein a rapid increase in the skill level is followed by a tapering off in the rate of improvement as the trainee's rate of performance stabilizes at a "normal" rate.

When someone is learning a completely unfamiliar job, the increasing returns pattern is common. This learning curve starts out very slowly and increases with more instruction and practice.

The S-shaped curve is one where the trainee's performance starts out slowly, improves rapidly, then tails off. It is common with difficult tasks that also require the trainee to become familiar with the basics of the job.

With all three patterns, trainees will have periods of growth and times when performance seems to have flattened. This leveling off of performance can be discouraging for many trainees unless they are told that this is normal. Positive encouragement at these times is necessary for long-term growth in job performance.

Behavior Modeling

One of the most effective ways in which people learn is through behavior modeling: watching other people perform the task and copying their behavior. It is particularly good for situations where trainees have to learn specific information and then apply it in practice.

TRAINING METHODS

There are three general types of training: learner-controlled, individual, and group instruction [15].

Learner-Controlled Instruction

In learner-controlled or self-instruction programs, employees learn individually, at their own pace. It is training without a trainer. Whether a videotape presentation, a programmed instruction manual, or a computer-interactive program, trainees use them at times convenient to them. Because the training message is consistent, they are considered to be the best method for training standardized routines to employees.

Depending upon the average check in the restaurants, anywhere from 31 to 47 percent of operations use video-supported training while 28 to 34 percent utilize classroom training. Comparable figures for computer-interactive and CD-ROM supported methods are 16 to 19 percent and 1 to 5 percent, respectively [16].

Such programs are particularly appropriate for teaching repetitive tasks, when there are many employees doing the same job, where turnover is high, and/or when there are large numbers of temporary employees who must be trained [17]. There is a downside, however: The initial cost is high in terms of time and dollars to develop the program. When procedures change, the program is out of date and must be redone.

According to Forrest, there are nine characteristics of learner-controlled instruction [18]:

1. Self-direction
2. Performance-based expectations
3. Contract learning
4. Learning environment
5. Printed resource materials
6. Demonstration of mastery
7. Feedback
8. Self-pacing and sequencing
9. Challenge and bypass

Self-Direction

The process of learner-controlled instruction is controlled by the trainee. The objective is to learn the material efficiently and effectively. Some take the view that this type of program can only be effective with trainees who are self-directed. These companies prescreen employees to eliminate any who are not. The advantage to the trainee from this process is that not only are the tasks learned but employees identify how to make solid, responsible decisions while managing their time.

Performance-Based Expectations. In a typical training schedule, trainees spend a period of time on one job before moving on to another. In learner-controlled instruction, trainees move on to other tasks after they have mastered the performance of that task. They need to be told what tasks they will have to perform and what level of competence defines mastery. The performance standards for a particular job could double as the competency level for that job.

Contract Learning. A learning contract serves as an agreement between the employee and the trainer and is a record of employee performance. The trainer, by signing the document, agrees to assist the employee in achieving the competencies defined. Once the trainer is convinced that the competencies have been developed, the contract is signed to that effect. A written contract formalizes the process and helps ensure that both trainer and trainee take it seriously.

A typical contract contains [19]:

- A competency statement: a learning objective, what the trainee will be able to do
- Learning activities for developing the competence: knowledge that must be developed and skills acquired by the trainee
- Evaluation guides: minimum performance standards for each competency
- Resources: printed information available to the trainee
- Agreements and certification: places for trainer signatures

Learning Environment. Learner-controlled instruction takes place on the job during actual working conditions.

Printed Resource Materials. As noted above, the trainee must be supplied with written materials indicating the standard operating procedures and company standards for performing the job for which he or she is being trained. In this way, any observed deviations between the way the job is supposed to be done and how it is actually being performed can be noted and corrections made.

Demonstration of Mastery. Trainees show that they have met the expectations laid out earlier when they show that they have mastered the tasks or competencies in the learning contract. Then, and only then, can they move on to learn other parts of the job. In a program where employees spend a certain amount of time in a department, they may have learned the task but must stay in that department until it is time to move to the next stage.

Feedback. When the trainer signs off on a specific competency the trainee is given specific, timely, and positive feedback on his or her performance. This type of feedback has been shown to aid in learning and performance.

Self-Pacing and Sequencing. Trainees learn at their own speed and construct the training in a way that makes sense to them. Because of this element of control, it is argued, they will learn faster and will remember better what they have learned.

Challenge and Bypass. Because employees learn at different speeds, a time-based training program is designed to accommodate slower learners. For an employee who has had significant experience or who can learn faster than others, such a program can mean they will spend time on a task that they have already mastered. Learner-controlled instruction allows them to move quickly through tasks they already have experience with and move on to competencies that are new to them. They are thus less likely to be bored by "old" material.

Individual Training

The most commonly used individual training method is on-the-job training. It is fast, flexible, and inexpensive. Four steps are involved: preparation, presentation, practice, and feedback.

Preparation. Preparation includes the development of what is to be taught, how it is to be taught, why it is important, and the standards to be achieved. The job is broken down into its parts, which are then listed in terms of importance. For example, the job of a restaurant cashier might be described as [20]:

Ensures that each guest leaves the restaurant satisfied by being friendly, fast, accurate, and helping other employees if needed, while maintaining a pleasant appearance and a clean work area. Accountable for all cash, guest checks, charges, and related reports for the restaurant during the shift.

The elements or parts of the job are:

- Friendliness
- Appearance
- Teamwork
- Opening duties
- Operating duties
- Closing duties
- Reports
- Equipment

Each element can form the basis for a separate training module.

Presentation. A good presentation consists of several steps. The trainee will probably be experiencing some stress as a result of having to learn something new. It would, therefore, be a good idea to say or do something to put the employee at ease. The trainer should introduce himself or herself, giving enough background to justify why he or she is qualified to be doing the training. The trainer would then explain what is to be taught and why it is important. These two items are intended to motivate the employee to learn what is to be taught. Next, the trainer should find out what the trainee already knows about the task at hand in order to communicate at a level appropriate to the trainee.

The entire job would then be explained with a description of how and where it fits into the entire operation. This gives a context for the task to be covered. When people know how their job relates to the overall organization, they are more likely to understand its importance. The job is then demonstrated at normal pace, then more slowly. As this is happening, the trainer explains what is being done and why it is important that the job be done in this way. The trainee can be asked specific questions as this is going on, to determine whether she or he understands.

Practice. When the trainee practices the new task, the objective is to concentrate first on accuracy, then on speed of completion. The trainee performs the job, explaining what he or she is doing and why each step is important. By having the trainee articulate the steps in this way, the trainer tests that the employee does, in fact, understand the importance of what is being done.

Feedback. Feedback is necessary to ensure that the employee continues to perform the job the way it should be done. People perform better and learn more effectively with positive feedback than with negative feedback. A word of praise works better than a rebuke. When an employee does something wrong it is important to focus on *what* went wrong rather than on *who* did something amiss.

Some trainers will work with an employee to perform a task, then once the employee has demonstrated the job correctly will move on to work with other employees. When feedback goes from continuous reinforcement to no reinforcement it is likely that the behavior will stop or that performance will go down. To maintain that performance, periodic reinforcement is required. This will probably be the task of the employee's supervisor. The same principles regarding the importance of positive feedback hold when supervising the employee as when training that person.

Group Training

Group training is particularly effective for teaching human relations skills. It can be used when a number of employees are to be trained in the same task. A common mistake that trainers make when dealing with groups is to rely on a lecture format. Because this is the format they have been exposed to themselves as students, they feel most comfortable with it as trainers. However, especially when working with adults, participation increases motivation and learning.

A variety of participatory techniques are available to increase both trainee motivation and learning. Brainstorming gets trainees involved in coming up with new ideas or in providing solutions to problems. In small groups, participants attempt to come up with as many ideas as possible. Initially, there is no criticism of ideas. Once a list of ideas has been developed, the ideas are explored as to their feasibility.

Case studies are situations taken from real life. The situation is explained in writing and, through discussion, trainees identify the problem and attempt to come up with a solution. The actual solution is less important than the process the group went through in arriving at it.

In a role-play situation, trainees are given background information and asked to act out a situation. It may involve such things as responding to a situation where the customer complains about the food.

A simulation is the practice of skills in the work area itself. Prior to the official opening of a new restaurant, the staff may have a preopening in which an invited list of customers eat at the restaurant as a trial run to the actual opening.

---

quick bite 13.7
Career Path

Industry professionals have espoused the benefits and solid career foundation that a restaurant job can give to America's youth. Employees can gain the work ethics of punctuality and professionalism through work schedules and a workplace setting. Communication skills, fiscal responsibility and respect for authority can be learned from a good manager. According to NRA research, one-third of adults have worked in the dining room or kitchen of a restaurant. However, the connection that a job in the foodservice industry can lead to future success is often missed in the public arena.

However, major players in the industry are working hard to make the message that restaurant jobs can lead to success more mainstream. McDonalds along with their ad agency, DDB Needham in Chicago created a commercial that shows men and women of all ethnic backgrounds happily working at a McDonalds. As the commercial focuses on each of the employees, a description of that individual's future job is written on the screen. Some of the job titles include future professional basketball player, orthodontist, air traffic controller, software tycoon, vice president of human resources, second grade teacher and to identify true diversity, future grandmother.

Not only does McDonald's ad serve as a recruitment piece, but also dispels the stereotype of the industry as home to the dead-end "hamburger-flipping," "pizza-slinging" jobs. The ad shows McDonalds jobs as the starting point for numerous possibilities for talented individuals. Unfortunately, the commercial does not represent a foodservice executive suggesting that the foodservice industry itself lacks opportunities. Many of the industry's leaders began on the front lines rather than in entry-level management positions.

Median salaries for managers in the foodservice and lodging industry have risen at a respectable rate of 8.3 percent between 1997 and 1998, which is double the average growth in median salaries of all employees in executive, administrative, and managerial occupations. The median annual salary for unit managers was $32,495 with a $4,000 bonus in 1998 and the average median salary increased with sales volumes. Executive chefs' median annual salary reached $40,000 with a $4,000 bonus, while that for district managers was $45,000 with an $8,000 bonus. Regional managers receive a median annual salary of $52,962 with a $12,000 bonus.

Source: "From Beginning to End, Foodservice Industry Offers Students a Career Path, Not Just a Job." *Nation's Restaurant News,* v. 33, n. 11, March 15, 1999, p. 35.

CAREER DEVELOPMENT

Employee Development

One answer to the problem of employee turnover is a career development program. Such a program involves assisting employees at all levels to determine their career goals and working with them to achieve such goals. To the extent that employees leave an operation because of the lack of opportunities to advance, such a program should help provide opportunities for growth.

A career development program should apply to all employees, not just managers. Too many managers assume that someone who washes dishes for a living has no desire to anything but that for the rest of his or her life. There are people who are good at what they do and have no desire to be moved or promoted to another job. They should not be looked down on but, as long as they are solid contributors to the operation, should be rewarded and appreciated. For those employees at all levels who do want something better or different for themselves, a career development program will help them get there. At the same time, such a program can serve as a motivational device for existing employees that can help increase productivity while reducing turnover.

A career development program consists of [21]:

- Identifying the objectives and needs of the business
- Identifying the personal goals and needs of employees
- Developing an action plan to match the employees' needs with those of the organization
- Providing feedback and guidance to carry out the plan

Management Development

It is important to offer training for management as well as for employees. A typical management training program revolves around three things [22]:

- Training existing managers
- Promoting people from within
- Developing programs for management trainees

Succession Planning. Many companies use succession planning to identify what type of training is required. Succession planning is "a formal process in which plans are developed to ensure that replacements can be readily identified to fill key positions in your organization" [23].

Such a program involves tracking the key positions with the operation and identifying the feeder jobs for each of these key positions. A feeder job is one from which the jobholder can be promoted into a key position. The short- and long-term staffing needs of the operation are then determined to identify how many managers are needed and when they will be required. Those people in the operation who are potentially capable of being promoted into management are

quick bite 13.8
Road to the Top: Steve Ells

Founder and Chief Executive

Founder and chief executive of 18-unit, Denver-based Chipotle Mexican Grill, Steve Ells learned to love food at a young age. He began to experience a variety of cuisines traveling across Europe and the States with his family. According to Ells, while other kids were watching cartoons, he was watching cooking shows. Although he grew up in the junk food generation, Ells developed a liking for clean, natural and classic cuisine. This attraction to fresh ingredients, classic culinary technique and a sharp-edge, modern environment enticed Ells to open his first restaurant in 1993.

In addition to his bachelor's degree in art history from University of Colorado, Boulder, Ells received classic training from The Culinary Institute of America. He also worked with Jeremiah Tower at Star's San Francisco. Applying his love for food and classical training to Mexican peasant food earned the first Chipotle's Mexican Grill near the University of Denver's campus immediate recognition. The new quick-service concept bloomed in Denver and spread to Kansas City, Missouri, in 1998. Ells has plans to open corporate units in Chicago; Cleveland and Columbus, Ohio; Minneapolis; Phoenix; and Washington, D.C.

Food is not the only concern of Ells though, he is also one of the rare operators who believes that design can actually contribute to the bottom line, according to Brand Gould, director of design and development for the chain. Ells credits his training in fine dining for his focus on atmosphere and the small details including what the right amount of ice for a beverage is. The food at Chipotle's is artful in itself and the packaging is creative. The giant flour tortilla does not serve as Chipotle's burritos wrapper; instead a second wrap of tin foil creates a hand-held portable meal.

Ells enjoys taking simple ingredients like chicken, pork, beef, peppers and onions and combining them with a style of cooking using unique twists including lime juice and roasted chiles. A great deal of Chipotle's appeal comes from the mix of fresh ingredients and a fresh look. The concept even earned the attention of corporate giant, McDonalds, who bought a small stake in the company, providing resources to grow into more markets. And according to Ells, the biggest challenge now is maintain food quality and character during the expansion of the chain.

Source: Ruggless, Ron. "Steve Ells: Taking Quick Service to New Levels of Sophistication at Chipotle Mexican Grill." *Nation's Restaurant News*, v. 33, n. 4, pp. 68, 77.

Hot Skills

Background/Education and Hotel, Restaurant,
and Institutional Management Schools 2000

Managers will need both better interpersonal and communication skills at the turn of the century. The need for these skills increase as human resource challenges increase and cultural diversity grows. As a result, industry experts agree that technical skills are not as important for a manager in 2000.

Managers will be required to handle multiple duties, often at the same time, but they must present calmness to employees and customers at all times. Managers will need to be more democratic than autocratic, which requires a great deal of flexibility. However, managers in 2000 will not be required to have advanced degrees.

HRI schools are an important part of the industry's future as they emphasize more management and leadership skills as well as internship programs, business and computer courses and continuing education. These schools have also begun to place more emphasis on "on-the-job training." HRI schools are also expected to increase in number in the new millennium.

The Top Five Most Likely Developments for Managers
in Background/Education for 2000:

1. Need for interpersonal skills
2. Communication skills is the greatest need
3. Need for multi-tasking ability
4. Must use a democratic management style
5. Need for flexible personality

The Top Five Most Likely Developments for HRI Schools for 2000:

1. Place more emphasis on leadership and management
2. More computer training available
3. Will seek more qualified instructors
4. Will provide internship programs
5. Will emphasize manager's continuing education

Adapted from: National Restaurant Association, *Foodservice Manager 2000* (Washington, D.C.:, National Restaurant Association, 1992).

then identified and, for each, an estimate of promotion potential is made. For each person an evaluation is made as to whether or not they are promotable and, if so, when. For each key position two or three alternative successors are identified in case of turnover.

For each employee identified as promotable, a list of needed skills is drawn up and a timetable established for the development of these skills. This list, updated every six months, forms the basis for the type and amount of management training to be done. The list also lets management know the extent to which additional management will have to be found outside the organization.

At the same time that the company is evaluating its managers, each individual should be developing a personalized career development plan. The questions to ask are these [24]:

- What are my career goals?
- What are my options for career development?
- What skills and abilities do I need to acquire?
- What plans do I need to make to move toward my goals?
- What will be my implementation steps and timetable?

Methods.   The methods used to develop managers can be done on or off the job. It is imperative that whichever methods are chosen, they be planned rather than left to chance. The oldest method of development is that of coaching. This term refers to the ongoing, daily instruction provided by a superior. Some people are better than others at developing subordinates. Managers need training in how to develop their staff effectively. Job rotation is another common tool for developing management talent. This involves moving an employee into different positions in a planned manner to allow the trainee to develop additional

---

 quick bite 1 3 . 1 0
Education and Training in 2010

According to the National Restaurant Association the most likely developments regarding the education and training in 2010 are:

- Trainging and communications will be the key to retaining employees.
- More management will be provided on how to manage a diverse workforce and how to solve problems.
- Employee certification will become more important.
- Restaurant managers will be more highly educated.

Source: Restaurant Industry 2010: The Road Ahead (Washington, D.C.: National Restaurant Association, 1999), p. 12.

skills and knowledge. Larger organizations have the option of giving managers committee assignments or positions as "assistant to," to encourage their development.

ENDNOTES

1. Arthur W. Sherman, George W. Bohlande, and Herbert J. Chudren, *Managing Human Resources,* 8th ed. (Cincinnati, OH: South-Western Publishing Co., 1988), p. 194.

2. Ibid., p. 194.

3. Ibid., p. 197.

4. Vincent H. Eade, *Human Resource Management in the Hospitality Industry* (Scottsdale, AZ: Gorsuch Scarisbrick, Publishers, 1993), p. 180.

5. David Wheelhouse, *Managing for Human Resources in the Hospitality Industry* (East Lansing, MI: Educational Institute of the American Hotel and Motel Association, 1989), pp. 146–147.

6. Sherman et al., *Managing Human Resources,* p. 199.

7. Karen Eich Drummond, *Human Resource Management for the Hospitality Industry* (New York: Van Nostrand Reinhold, 1990), pp. 68–78.

8. Sherman et al., *Managing Human Resources,* p. 201.

9. Lewis C. Forrest, *Training for the Hospitality Industry* (East Lansing, MI: Educational Institute of the American Hotel and Motel Association, 1983), p. 40.

10. Ibid., p. 41.

11. Ibid., pp. 45–46.

12. Ibid., p. 45.

13. Wheelhouse, *Managing for Human Resources in the Hospitality Industry,* pp. 148–149.

14. Mary L. Tanke, *Human Resources Management for the Hospitality Industry* (Albany, NY: Delmar Publishers, 1990), p. 75.

15. Wheelhouse, *Managing for Human Resources in the Hospitality Industry,* p. 154.

16. Bruce Grindy, "Hooking and Keeping Employees," *Restaurants USA,* October 1998, p. 26.

17. Wheelhouse, *Managing for Human Resources in the Hospitality Industry,* p. 154.

18. Forrest, *Training for the Hospitality Industry,* pp. 112–116.

19. Ibid., pp. 113–114.

20. Wheelhouse, *Managing for Human Resources in the Hospitality Industry,* p. 155.

21. Tanke, *Human Resources Management for the Hospitality Industry,* p. 198.

22. Wheelhouse, *Managing for Human Resources in the Hospitality Industry,* p. 176.

23. Tanke, *Human Resources Management for the Hospitality Industry,* p. 80.

24. Ibid., p. 193.

CHAPTER FOURTEEN

MOTIVATING
THE EMPLOYEE

learning objectives

By the end of this chapter you should be able to:

1. Suggest what causes employees to behave the way they do.

2. Suggest how management can channel and maintain employee behavior through implementing various process theories of motivation.

3. Identify the six dimensions of organizational climate outlined below.

4. Describe how to implement successfully the following in a restaurant operation:
   • Management by objectives
   • Job redesign
   • Positive reinforcement
   • A climate of trust

5. Summarize the major theories of leadership, indicating how they can be applied to a restaurant situation.

If anything goes bad, I did it.

If anything goes semi-good, then we did it.

If anything goes real good, then you did it.

That's all it takes to get people to win football games.
Paul "Bear" Bryant, *The Manager's Book of Quotations.*

---

quick bite 14.1
Hot Concepts: Roly Poly

Linda Wolf, creator of the original Roly Poly sandwich wrap, got the idea for her creation while working in a Tex-Mex restaurant and visiting a friend often who worked in a deli across the street. Wolf has served her tortilla-wrapped sandwiches at a number of restaurants she has owned, but she didn't open a location to serve the sandwiches alone until two years ago.

Wolf and her partner Julie Reid have made progress fast, opening 40 units in two years. The stores vary in location from Tempe, Arizona to Concord, Massachusetts and each has average annual sales from $250,000 to $500,000. The stores are available on a franchise basis. The two owners hope to open 150 new stores over the next five years. The two owners designed the units and sandwiches to be as simple as possible since they felt it would be difficult to train and teach other people.

According to Wolf, "We knew the biggest challenge in trying to grow the business would be to keep the concept the same. So we really tried to simplify and remove as many moving parts as we could. We definitely wanted to make build-out user friendly." They succeeded in their plan for simplicity, it seems. Each unit is only 800 to 1,000 square feet. The only equipment required is a sandwich press, a roll-ready counter top and refrigeration units. Any one location depending on size can roll from 200 to 500 sandwiches a day.

The concept focuses on healthy foods although that was not the plan. According to Reid, "It was driven by flavor, but it just happened that the combinations turned out low in fat and calories because there is no frying, no butter and no oil. Sandwiches run from $4.50 to $6.50 and feature quality ingredients like artichoke hearts, chutney, apple butter and avocados. A half sandwich is also offered for $2.99, which turned out to be a good alternative for customers on college campuses, and for those customers on the go.

The chain has a database of over 400 sandwich ideas. Many of these 400 ideas often become specials; however, the menu is actually made up of 50 core items. Favorites of customers include Santa Fe Chicken, Basil Cashew Chicken and Ultimate Veggie. Many of these items, including the Ultimate Veggie, contain up to 13 different ingredients, but roll up into a neat, transportable meal.

Source: Battaglia, Andy. "Roly Poly: Rolling out sandwiches in a style all its own." *Nation's Restaurant News*, May 17, 1999, v. 33, n. 20, pp. 76–80.

Roly Poly

EMPLOYEE MOTIVATION

The Role of Managers

Managers cannot motivate employees—motivation comes from within. However, managers are responsible for providing a climate within which employees are motivated to perform. Many managers do not agree that it is their responsibility to motivate employees. They believe that it is the responsibility of employees to "bend" to the needs of the company. If they do not, they are fired. From a purely economic viewpoint this approach is bad management. Treating employees in an arbitrary, inflexible manner will guarantee that the operation will suffer high turnover as increasing numbers of employees decide that they cannot put up with such treatment. Even if they stay, there is a good chance that productivity will go down and absenteeism and pilfering will rise as employees seek to "get even" with the company for perceived slights.

When an employee joins a company there is an implied, and sometimes an explicit, contract. The employee puts forth time and effort in order to receive pay; the company gives the security of a job in return for that effort.

Although every person is an individual, the operation cannot adapt to each employee. There has to be a middle ground wherein management is flexible to employee needs while realizing that the objective is to run a profitable operation. At the same time, employees must sacrifice some of their independence and the satisfaction of their individual needs to the good of the company. An understanding of what motivates employees is critical to getting employees to perform in a productive manner.

We begin the chapter with a survey of the major theories of motivation and propose an inclusive model of organizational climate that builds on these theories. Utilizing this model, managers can implement a comprehensive approach to developing and maintaining a motivated team of employees.

Theories of Motivation

A complete discussion of motivation must cover the following:

- What causes behavior?
- What channels behavior?
- How is behavior sustained?

Content Theories.   Content theories are concerned with what causes behavior. Four such theories that have gained acceptance to one degree or another are Maslow's need-hierarchy theory, Alderfer's ERG theory, Murray's acquired needs theory, and Herzberg's two-factor theory.

Maslow.   Psychologist Abraham H. Maslow focused on a person's basic needs and the relative order of their importance. He identified a hierarchy of needs as follows:

1. Physical: the need for food and shelter.
2. Safety and belonging: the need for protection from people and/or the environment. This person would be cautious, avoiding risk and planning for the future.
3. Social: the need for love and belonging. This person will have high social needs, like people, wish to be a team player, and want to be accepted.
4. Esteem: the need for self-respect and the respect of others. People seeking the respect of others would seek attention and thrive on publicity and praise. They would be aware of status symbols and desire material things.
5. Self-actualization: the need to meet one's potential. Such people are interested in making creative contributions and want a challenging work environment.

Maslow's hierarchy of needs suggests that lower-level needs must be satisfied for the most part before a person can be concerned with the satisfaction of higher-level needs. A corollary of this is that once a need has primarily been satisfied, it ceases to motivate the person.

It is difficult to identify where money comes into this picture. For some, money is necessary to satisfy basic needs and is regarded as crucial to meeting physiological needs. For others, money is seen as a status symbol. The problem for those using this theory to identify needs is that it may be thought that money no longer motivates a person making a considerable salary, as their basic needs have been taken care of. For the person who sees money as a way of keeping score with the world, money will continue to be important as a motivator long after basic needs are taken care of.

Managers should attempt to determine what needs employees are seeking to satisfy and create an environment that gives employees opportunities to satisfy them. Consider the restaurant that hired Sarah as a bookkeeper. Sarah had been a stay-at-home wife for 25 years, raising the children. Bored at home, she decided to get a part-time job. After only a few weeks at work, management noticed that Sarah was forever venturing out of the office to visit with the servers and cooks. The result was that the work of the other employees was interrupted while Sarah's job duties were left unfinished. Management could have fired Sarah. Instead, a thoughtful discussion with her indicated that the main reason she took the job was the desire to interact with others. Her husband was doing well financially, so money was not a prime factor in her decision to reenter the job market. Management gave Sarah a job as hostess and now has a personable greeter, a satisfied employee, and customers who are delighted with the service they receive.

Alderfer.   Alderfer proposed three need categories: existence, relatedness, and growth. The first—existence—similar to Maslow's physiological and safety needs; the second—relatedness—involves relationships with others and is similar to the safety, social and ego-esteem needs of Maslow; and the third—growth—is similar to self-esteem and self-actualization. According to Alderfer, more than one need can operate at a time. He also proposes that in addition to a hierarchy effect, people who are frustrated in their ability to satisfy a higher-level need may regress to become more concerned with the fulfillment of lower-level needs.

Murray.   Murray suggests that a large part of performance can be explained by a person's need for achievement. People with a high achievement motivation prefer moderate risk, are persistent, take personal responsibility for their performance, need feedback on how well they are performing, and are innovative [1]. Conversely, people with low achievement needs take high risks.

David McClelland, a student of Murray's, sees motivation as a function of three needs: the need for affiliation, the need for power, and the need for achievement. Those with a high need for power want to control, dominate, or otherwise have an impact on others. Power can be individualized power or socialized power. In the former situation, people want power for its own sake. They desire the emotional feelings they get from applying power. Socialized power comes from using one's influence to attain objectives that will benefit everyone. Obviously, the latter behavior makes for a more effective manager.

These motives are developed through learning. In other words, people learn to behave in ways rewarding to them.

Herzberg.   Herzberg identified two aspects affecting the work of an employee: hygiene factors and motivators. The absence of hygiene factors will result in employee dissatisfaction, but their presence will not result in a motivated employee. The most important hygiene factors are [2]:

- Company policy and administration
- Supervision

- Salary
- Interpersonal relations
- Working conditions

---

quick bite 14.2
Motivation & Recognition

Although many government agencies report the unemployment rate at about four percent, the reality is that the unemployment rate for restaurant managers is zero. Not only are unemployment numbers working against operators, but demographics are as well. By the year 2000, there will be 31.7 million less men and women between the ages of 24 and 34 in the U.S. than there were in 1988. The implication for the restaurant industry is severe considering that this is the primary age group for restaurant managers. An additional challenge for operators is the attrition rate of managers. Today, a student with a degree in computer science or business can earn up to $50,000 right out of school and have their weekends free. However, compensation is not the only benefit sought by restaurant managers. Many are also seeking quality of life and acknowledgment.

Operators who properly acknowledge and compensate their managers can avoid what is known in the industry as the "counteroffer syndrome." The counteroffer occurs when a manager feels that he or she is doing a good job and feels that they are worth more than they are paid. The manager feels under-valued, under-appreciated or under-challenged. As a result, the manager seeks other employment in the market and most likely will be offered a better package. And most operators will react with a counteroffer in order to keep the manager at their venue.

This reaction on the part of the operator is a poor way to deal with the situation. The counteroffer sends two dangerous messages. The first is that if a manager threatens to leave an organization, he or she will get a raise. The second is that a manager must resign in order for the operator to acknowledge his or her real value. It is a wise move for restaurateurs to compensate managers fairly, conduct timely salary reviews and compare their compensation and benefits packages to others in and outside the foodservice industry.

Operators must acknowledge the efforts of their best managers including working long hours on weekends and holidays, working extra shifts, and acting as ambassadors for their operations and the industry. Managers supervise businesses in an extremely complex, demanding and competitive environment; they provide leadership and training to employees and service to customers. Unless operators begin to become proactive in terms of compensation and appreciation, it could possibly cripple the entire restaurant industry.

Source: Tolman, Dan. "Be Proactive and Appreciate Your Managers." *Nation's Restaurant News,* v. 33, n. 2, February 11, 1999, p. 22.

Motivators are the factors whose presence will act to motivate the employee. The most important motivators are [3]:

- Achievement
- Recognition
- The work itself
- Responsibility
- Advancement

Herzberg believes that the key to motivating employees is to enrich jobs such that they provide employees with work that is interesting and meaningful. The content theories described above would indicate that [4]:

1. Individuals prioritize needs and act in an attempt to satisfy them.
2. More than one level of need may be operable at any one time. If higher-level needs cannot be satisfied, the satisfaction of lower-level needs takes on greater importance.
3. Much of an employee's performance can be explained by the need for achievement.
4. Certain factors—motivators—motivate people; others—hygiene factors—do not. However, the absence of the latter will result in dissatisfaction.

Process Theories.   Process theories are concerned with what channels behavior and how that behavior can be sustained. Four theories will be discussed: equity theory, expectancy theory, reinforcement theory, and goal-setting theory.

Equity Theory.   Equity theory considers that people look at what they put into the job relative to what they get out of the job and compare both to others. If they perceive that there is an inequitable situation, they will work to reduce the inequity. The greater the inequity, the stronger will be the motivation to reduce it.

There are a number of ways to reduce a perceived inequity. People can [5]:

- Reduce what they put into the job
- Seek more rewards for their effort
- Delude themselves into believing that the situation is equitable
- Leave or be absent from a job
- Get others to lower their efforts
- Change the basis of comparison

People will choose the course of action easiest for them.

The key points in this theory are that people make comparisons; that what they perceive or believe (rather than what may actually exist) is what is important; and that their reaction can be one of several.

Expectancy Theory.   According to expectancy theory, employees are motivated to produce to the extent that they believe they will receive a reward important to them. They will put forward more effort, leading to greater productivity, for which they will receive a reward important to them. The effort is diminished if:

1. The reward is unimportant to them.
2. They do not believe that they will get the reward.

This means that the manager needs to know what is important to the employee and must also convince the employee that he or she can be trusted to provide the reward.

Tying expectancy theory into Herzberg, hygiene factors such as working conditions are seen as less motivating than such things as a promotion. We can speculate, therefore, on the relative impact on performance of employees or promising to improve working conditions compared to the promise of a promotion. The latter, it is suggested, would act as a greater motivating factor.

Expectancy theory can also be examined relative to Maslow. Effort on the part of the employee leads to the employee performing if he or she believes that there will be a reward important to the employee, a reward that will, to some extent, satisfy needs important to the employee.

Reinforcement Theory.   Reinforcement theory is based on the idea that performance improves when it is rewarded or reinforced. This idea of modifying people's behavior says that people behave in ways that are rewarding to them. By rewarding existing behavior, that behavior will be encouraged and repeated.

Something in the environment (antecedent) stimulates behavior for which there is a consequence. Behavior can be "managed" by managing antecedents and providing the appropriate consequences. Managing antecedents can be done by removing barriers that hinder the completion of a good job or by providing aids that help employees do a good job [6]. Barriers might be such things as training deficiencies or confusing policies or rules. Factors that help get the job done might include clear plans and instructions and realistic deadlines.

There are four types of consequences to a particular behavior: positive reinforcement, negative reinforcement, extinction (no consequences), and punishment. Positive reinforcement—catching somebody doing something good and rewarding them—is generally accepted as the most potent consequence in shaping future behavior.

Goal-setting Theory.   Goal-setting theory states that setting or accepting more difficult goals results in higher performance than the setting or acceptance of easier goals. Employees will set goals for themselves if management does not. Therefore, management should get involved in raising employee goals.

The foregoing theories would indicate that [7]:

1. People compare what they put into their work and what they get out of it to the inputs and outputs of others.

2. People will expend effort to the extent that they believe they will receive rewards important to them.
3. Behavior can be shaped by a system of rewarding desired behavior and punishing undesirable behavior. Positive reinforcement of desirable behavior is a stronger motivator than is punishment of undesirable behavior.
4. Having a specific goal increases performance; having a difficult (yet attainable) goal results in higher performance than will having an easy goal.

ORGANIZATIONAL CLIMATE [8]

Bearing in mind the various theories as to what motivates employees, the manager's role is to provide the climate within the organization that will motivate employees to perform. The organizational climate is how it "feels" to work there. The organizational climate:

1. Consists of a set of properties of the work environment.
2. Is based on the perceptions of the people who work there.
3. Influences the motivation and behavior of employees, depending on how they perceive the climate [9].

These points indicate that it is possible to describe and measure the climate within an organization in terms of a number of dimensions. In this chapter we will go on to suggest six dimensions of climate. The point is also made that it is the perception of the employees, not management, that is important in defining climate. The employees' perception of what exists within a company may be the same or different from what is actually occurring in the company. However, it is the employees' perception, right or wrong, that is important. Finally, it is the employees' perception that will influence to what extent employees are motivated as well as how they behave. If, for example, an employee perceives that management does not set high service standards (even if the standards actually are high), she or he may decide: "If management does not care about the service, why should I?"

Dimensions of Climate

Research has resulted in descriptions of climate in anywhere from four to seven dimensions. One well-respected model is that of the Forum Corporation [10]. In this model the climate of an organization is described in terms of six dimensions: three dealing with performance, three with development. The performance dimensions are clarity, commitment, and standards. The development dimensions are responsibility, recognition, and teamwork.

Performance Dimensions. The first performance dimension is that of clarity. Clarity refers to how well employees understand the goals and policies of a company, in addition to how clear they are about their own jobs. It is the feeling that things are organized and run smoothly. For example, when employees are not given a written job description but are told to "watch Joe and learn from him," they are probably unclear about what they should be doing and would give the climate a low score on this dimension.

Many managers do not tell employees enough about the overall goals of the operation. They may feel that employees do not care. However, many employees do care. The result is that these employees do not know what is important to the company. If they do not know what is important, they will not know how to act in certain situations. For example, if a customer complains about the way a steak is cooked, what should the employee do? A restaurant that is concerned primarily with customer satisfaction would want the employee to correct the situation in favor of the customer. A company more concerned with cost control might have the employee try to convince the customer that the steak was prepared the way the customer ordered it.

Commitment, the second performance dimension, is the extent to which employees continually feel committed to achieving the goals of the company, the extent to which they accept goals as being realistic, the extent to which they are involved in the setting of such goals, and the extent to which their performance is continually evaluated against the goals of the organization. Companies have certain goals, such as profitability, return on investment, customer satisfaction, and cleanliness. These goals are achieved (or not achieved) by the efforts of the employees. The goals of the restaurant can be met only if employees are committed to achieving them. The greater the commitment, the more likely it is that the objective will be achieved.

The final performance dimension is standards. Standards measure the degree to which employees feel that management emphasizes the setting of high standards of performance and the extent to which they feel pressure to continually improve their performance. Employees may have higher standards than does the company. For example, in a restaurant that is very bottom-line oriented, concessions may be made in the areas of customer service, equipment maintenance, and employee training. Management may think that their standards—low costs and high profits—are high.

Employees may feel that company standards—cut back on service, maintenance, and training—are low. This influences how they feel toward the company and may well affect their performance. In *In Search of Excellence,* the authors compared the bottom lines of companies that emphasized financial objectives such as profit and return on investment with those that stressed nonfinancial objectives such as customer satisfaction or quality [11]. They found that the latter actually produced better bottom-line results than did the companies that stressed financial objectives. One explanation is that fewer layers of employees can relate to the financial objectives of the operation; they are unlikely to be personally involved in getting a return on investment or participating in a profit-sharing program. Many more layers of employees can relate to something like customer satisfaction: When they go out as customers, they know what it means to be satisfied.

Development Dimensions. Responsibility, the first development dimension, is the feeling employees have that they are personally responsible for the work they do, that supervisors encourage them to take the initiative, and that they have a real sense of autonomy. The employee who has to check with the boss before he or she can do anything does not have this.

The second development dimension is recognition, the feeling that employees are rewarded for doing good work rather than receiving criticism and punishment as the predominant form of feedback. In a climate such as this, rewards and recognition outweigh threats and criticism, there is in place a promotion system that helps the best person get promoted, and the restaurant has a reward structure related to excellence of performance. When we hear "the boss wants to see you," most of us immediately think, "What did I do wrong?" A major reason for this is the idea of management by exception. Under this accounting term, targets are set and, if met, the business is on target and no remedial action need be taken. If sales or cost projections are out of line, however, a red flag goes up to initiate corrective management action. Similarly, in dealing with employees, if employees are performing the way they should, the manager—with many demands on her time—will pass over that employee to concentrate on those who are not performing up to standard. The result is that the only time employees hear from management is when things go wrong. Under this type of climate, employees may actually perform negatively in order to receive some feedback, even if it is criticism. An absence of feedback is even more punishing than is punishment.

Teamwork is the third development dimension. This is the perception of belonging to an organization that is cohesive, one where people trust one another, where employees feel personal loyalty and the sense that they belong to the company. It is the feeling of us working together, rather than us versus them, whether that be management versus employees or kitchen versus dining room.

DEVELOPING A PRODUCTIVE ORGANIZATIONAL CLIMATE

There is a problem within the operation when employees are dissatisfied enough with their jobs that the dissatisfaction affects their job performance. That dissatisfaction comes when there is a gap between what employees want in terms of clarity, commitment, standards, responsibility, recognition, and teamwork and what they perceive they are getting in terms of those dimensions.

Just what do employees want? According to the *Industry of Choice* report [12] employees have 20 employment needs called "Deal Breakers"—job characteristics so important employees would change jobs because of them. They are characterized as human resource practices and elements dealing with the organizational culture.

In order of importance, they are:

Human Resource Practices Deal Breakers

1. A regular paycheck
2. A safe place to work

3. A clean place to work
4. Competitive wage or salary
5. The right equipment to do my job
6. Having enough employees to handle the workload
7. Health insurance
8. Working enough hours
9. Paid vacation
10. Worker's-compensation insurance

Organizational Culture Deal Breakers

1. Having a boss who is fair (Recognition)
2. Having a boss who doesn't embarrass or make fun of me (Recognition)
3. Having a boss who treats others like he/she would like to be treated (Recognition)
4. Feeling like the company treats employees fairly (Recognition)
5. Feeling like I do my job well (Commitment)
6. Having a boss with whom I get along (Teamwork)

---

 q u i c k   b i t e   1 4 . 3
Employee Satisfaction

The wants and needs of today's employees are as diverse as the employees themselves. Restaurateurs are beginning to give employee satisfaction serious consideration in their strategic planning and resource allocation. One way to increase employee satisfaction is to offer a competitive wage. However, the needs of restaurant employees include much more than high pay. Employment attributes that are so important that they could cause an employee to leave a job can be divided into two categories: Human Resource Practices and Organizational Culture.

Human resource practices include formal compensation policies, benefits, schedules, workload and other factors that management can control. The four most important human resource practices include a regular paycheck, a safe workplace, a clean place to work and competitive wage or salary (in that order). Organizational culture deals with shared values and behavioral norms influenced by management that employees experience on the job—especially at the unit level. The top four issues that deal with organizational culture all involve "fairness" of management.

Source: "1999 Highlights." *Restaurants USA,* v. 18, n. 11, December 1998, p. F7.

7. Being treated as an adult, even when I make a mistake (Recognition)
8. Feeling like the company is well managed (Standards)
9. Feeling like everybody does his/her part to keep things running smoothly (Teamwork)

Categorizing these statements in terms of the dimensions of organizational climate, the overwhelming importance of the recognition factor stands out.

It is suggested that a four-pronged approach to dealing with employees will produce an organizational climate that will motivate employees to perform. The four guiding principles of this system are management by objectives, job re-design, positive reinforcement, and the development of trust. In the following sections we look at how these concepts relate to employee motivation.

Management by Objectives

Properly implemented, a philosophy of management by objectives should take care of situations where there is a discrepancy between what employees want relative to clarity, commitment, and/or standards and what they feel they get.

Management by objectives (MBO) can be defined as a managerial process in which managers and employees join in pursuit of specific, mutually agreed-upon goals of limited duration, through a plan of action that is monitored in ap-praisal sessions following mutually determined standards of performance [13]. The definition above indicates that:

1. Manager and subordinate agree on company and personal objectives for the subordinate.
2. The objectives are for a specified period of time, usually a year.
3. Objectives should be specific and measurable.
4. The subordinate prepares a plan of action that is reviewed by the manager.
5. At the end of the time period there is a formal appraisal process to indicate the extent to which the objectives have been met.

The evidence is mixed as to whether or not MBO works. Conceptually, the idea appears sound. Objectives should be set; manager and employee should agree as to what the important objectives are; manager and employee should agree on what is to be measured; the plan of action designed to achieve the objectives should be monitored; and there should be a session at the end of a specified period at which the employee's efforts are evaluated. Despite mixed results regarding the overall effectiveness of the concept, there is general agreement that the mere setting of goals improves performance. MBO also assumes that people will work toward goals to which they are com-mitted. That commitment comes from being involved in the process of setting the objectives.

Implementing the Concept

A program of management by objectives is most appropriate when there are problems with clarity, commitment, or standards. Clarity, it will be recalled, indicates how well employees understand the company's goals and policies and feel that things are organized and running smoothly.

Commitment indicates how strongly employees feel about achieving company goals. To what extent do they accept these goals, see them as realistic, get involved in setting them, and have their performance evaluated against them?

Standards indicate the emphasis that management puts on a high quality of performance. How much pressure exists to improve performance?

Clarity. How will a properly implemented program of MBO improve these three dimensions of climate? When management involves employees in the objective-setting process it becomes clear to employees what objectives are important and the role that they, the employees, play relative to management in achieving these objectives.

In many cases, management has done a poor job of communicating the objectives that are important to a company. The manager or supervisor is the key link between the company and the employee. The objective of the company is to make a profit; the employee is seeking satisfaction from the job. How are these brought together? To maximize profit, the company must determine the key result areas that must be emphasized; what employee behavior is necessary in those key areas; whether employee performance matches the behavioral objectives set; and how to communicate to employees the results of their efforts, following up with praise, coaching, or remedial actions.

At the same time, the employee has several questions: What is really expected of me? How far am I expected to go? How good is good? How am I doing? It seems that the best performance and highest degree of goal attainment exist when there is agreement between manager and employee as to the content of the employee's job.

Objectives can be set in a variety of ways. The manager could come in one morning and say "We've had a number of complaints about the quality of service in the restaurant. From now on, I want you to pick up the pace to improve the job that you do." Will employees know what is expected of them? On the other hand, the manager could hold an employee meeting, announce that there are problems with the level of service, and solicit ideas from the employees about what is causing the complaints and how they can be resolved. The point is that when management and employees discuss in specific terms what they should focus on, employees are clear about what they should do and what they can expect from management.

Standards. But what about the level of standards that would be set when employees are involved? A fair amount of research indicates that participative rather than assigned goals leads to setting higher goals and, in turn, to higher performance. In particular, some studies indicate that participative goal setting has produced higher goals among minorities and the less educated.

If we assume that most employees want to do a good job, it is fair to say that when involved in the setting of objectives, most employees will set objectives they can be proud of. Thus, involving employees may very well produce standards higher than if management alone had set them.

Commitment.   Generally, employees resist making commitments to goals for two reasons: They do not feel that they are capable of reaching a goal because they lack confidence, ability, or knowledge, or because they see no personal benefit or gain in terms of money, promotion, personal pride, recognition, or whatever is important to them. This relates to the concept of expectancy theory.

By allowing employees to participate, it gives employees a feeling of control over the process that they might not ordinarily have had in their lives. Steak & Ale has found that commitment is improved when [14]:

- Decisions are made as far down the company ranks as possible.
- People are told the whys and hows of change.
- People are informed about how well the company is doing.
- Employee input is sought.
- Employees' individuality is respected.
- The focus of leadership styles is on helping people perform.

Although management has to take primary responsibility for determining the key results areas, employees can be involved in helping set objectives for these key areas.

Let us return to the earlier problem with service. A manager might ask: "What would a server do that would have you say 'That is excellent service'? What would a server do that would have you say 'That is terrible service'?" Employees could easily come up with a list of specifics. They might say that excellent service includes such things as:

- Calling regular customers by name
- Seating customers right away
- Smiling at customers

Terrible service might include such things as:

- Forgetting who ordered what
- Not making eye contact
- Being slow to bring the check

Management can go on to ask for input on how long it should be before a customer's presence is recognized, before they should be given a menu, before they receive the drinks and the meals they ordered, which customers should be smiled at (everyone!), who should get eye contact, and so on. The result will be a series of objectives—employees should make eye contact with and smile at every customer, drinks should be delivered within 4 minutes of being ordered, and servers should always remember who ordered what—that employees are committed to achieve because they have been involved in setting them. Ideally, the standards set will be high (who is going to suggest low service standards?), and they will be clear as to exactly what they are expected to do.

Evaluating Employee Performance. Once set, the objectives become the performance standards against which employee performance will be evaluated. Next, management will monitor employee performance.

In deciding which method to use, various criteria should be kept in mind. First, the method should validate the selection techniques used. If an effective selection method is in place, an appraisal method should show a significant percentage of employees meeting the performance objectives of the job. If this does not happen, it indicates that the selection method is faulty and/or the appraisal method is poor.

Another purpose of an appraisal method is to provide a rationale for making personnel decisions. It is important that the method selected be legally defensible. In this regard it should be based on an analysis of job requirements. Ratings should be documented and employees should have a formal appeal procedure.

A variety of methods are commonly used. Performance can be evaluated through direct indices or personal traits against set objectives or behaviorally an-

---

 quick bite 14.4

Improving Performance

Here are some ways to get better performance from employees:

1. Hire the values you are looking for.
2. Find out why employees are not performing and ask what you can do to help them do a better job.
3. Tell employees in writing what you expect.
4. Give employees clear performance standards.
5. Make sure that employees have the tools to do the job.
6. Get employee input on what behaviors they (the employees) should be engaged in.
7. Have employees come up with 10 "house rules."
8. Train, coach, evaluate, and reward the behaviors identified above.
9. Improve your feedback by dealing with the problems that are within an employee's control, think through what you will say and how you will say it, and be specific about behaviors rather than attitudes.

Source: Losyk, Bob. "How to Improve Employee Work Performance," *Restaurants USA,* v. 15, n. 2, February 1995, pp. 12–14.

---

chored rating scales. Direct indices are objective and can be well documented. Servers may be evaluated on the basis of number of appetizers sold, for example. Direct indices, however, cannot take into account how well employees deal with customers and fellow employees.

In the personal trait method, characteristics are identified that are considered to be an important part of the job—such as creativity, dependability, and initiative—and the employee is evaluated on the extent to which he or she possesses them. A major problem here is the subjectivity involved. The extent to which a person is creative is open to a great deal of interpretation and argument.

Behaviorally anchored rating scales (BARS) are very compatible with a program of MBO. Whereas management by objectives focuses on the end result, BARS stresses the means to reach the end. In a BARS program the behavior necessary to reach the set objective is specified and the employee evaluated on the extent to which the behavior is displayed. Take, for example, the objective of selling more appetizers. Employees may be unable to sell a customer on buying an appetizer because they lack the training or because the customer is just not that hungry. Thus, through no fault of their own, the objective is not met. BARS identifies whether or not the employees do what they should, within their power, to get the sale.

The behaviors necessary for successful suggestive selling need to be identified. Success in selling probably comes from displaying a knowledge of items on the menu, suggesting items to every customer while maintaining eye contact and smiling, and describing those items using language that paints a desirable picture. This is another area in which employee involvement can be sought. Given a few minutes and some encouragement, employees can come up with several types of behavior that would encourage or discourage the sale of extra items. These behavioral objectives or anchors become the behavioral standards against which employees will be measured.

The ratings scale is typically displayed on a single page with various scale points, ranging from excellent to unacceptable. For each scale point there are behavioral statements representing the behavior that will probably lead to that level of performance. By observing the behavior, a manager can determine whether the employee behaved in a way that would lead to the objective being met.

BARS are useful for several reasons. They focus on behavior, what employees actually do in their jobs. They stress only those things over which an employee has control. Employees have no control over whether a customer buys dessert; they do have control over whether they ask the person to buy. Specifying behavior tells employees what to do to be given a rating of excellent; employees can then adjust their behavior accordingly. If they do not perform as desired, managers can also be specific about what the employees did wrong.

Although this method is time-consuming and costly to develop, BARS makes it easier for managers to implement the last part of the MBO process, providing employee feedback.

Providing Employee Feedback.   Employees need to know how they are doing. Many managers view the appraisal session with as much trepidation as does the employee. It may be especially difficult and uncomfortable if the subordinate is older or has more experience than the manager.

Restaurant Management: Customers, Operations, and Employees

Most people enjoy giving good feedback (although they may not do enough of this). However, it can be difficult to tell employees they are not doing so well. One reason is that the manager has little or no objective data on which to base an evaluation. With BARS the manager can indicate the specific objective things that the employee did or did not do.

Having employees evaluate themselves prior to the appraisal interview with the manager provides a basis for discussion of any differences in the ratings. In some cases, managers may be surprised that employees are regarding their own shortcomings. It is also a good idea to give the employee the manager's basic evaluation one to three days prior to the appraisal interview. This allows the employee to get over the initial defensiveness that comes from a negative appraisal and to approach the interview more objectively.

It can be argued that a formal annual evaluation is of questionable value. Some research is available to show that in annual interviews, praise has no effect, while criticism brings on defensive reactions that in some cases result in decreased performance in the future. For this reason it is suggested that coaching be a day-to-day activity, not once a year.

The actual interview can take one of several formats. In the tell-and-sell interview, the objective is to communicate the manager's evaluation of the employee and persuade the employee to improve. The manager acts as judge. This approach is most likely to work when the employee respects the manager and feels that the manager is, in fact, qualified to pass judgment on his or her performance.

A second approach is the tell-and-listen interview. The task is to communicate the evaluation while giving the employee an opportunity to react to it. The manager still plays the role of judge but spends time listening to the employee and attempting to summarize the employee's reactions.

In the problem-solving interview, the approach is to stimulate growth and development within the employee rather than focus on past behavior. In the role of helper, the manager uses exploratory questions to identify new ideas from the employee on how performance can be improved. This does not mean that performance is not evaluated. It does mean that the focus is not on how the employee has failed, but rather, on why the employee has failed and what has to change for her or him to succeed.

While the potential for change is great, the interview is unsuccessful if the employee is unable or unwilling to bring forward ideas. Additionally, the interview may not go the way the manager thought it would. The employee may identify changes the employer is unwilling or unable to consider.

Job Redesign

When employees rate their job low on "responsibility," they are saying that they do not feel personally responsible for the work that they do, that supervisors do not encourage them to take the initiative, and that they do not have a real sense of autonomy. When the level of responsibility felt is less than the level desired, there is a problem. The answer lies in redesigning the "problem" jobs.

quick bite 14.5
No More Idle Time

Because of uneven demand, there will be times when employees are not working up to capacity. Here are some thoughts on how to make the most of all your employees' time:

1. Compress the schedule. Note when your first customer arrives and when the last one leaves and compare with your employees' work schedule. Can preopening activities be done by the closing staff?
2. Reexamine the hours of operation. Don't keep your employees hanging around if the business doesn't warrant it.
3. Keep a logbook that includes operational changes, customer comments, and inspirational thoughts. Have employees review it during downtimes.
4. Provide incentives for dull, repetitive tasks. Pay extra for the times when employees perform cleaning jobs.
5. Brainstorm new dishes, marketing ideas, or solutions to operational problems.

Source: Solomon, Jay. "Making the Most of Idle Time," *Restaurants USA*, v. 13, n. 7, August 1993, pp. 18–19.

Definition. The classical approach to designing jobs held that productivity would be increased by task specialization. Additionally, by simplifying jobs, costs would be reduced because management could avoid paying for a difficult skill that was used only sparingly in the performance of a piece of work.

More recently, with a workforce that is increasingly educated and demanding, there has developed the thought that low-skill, monotonous jobs will lead to boredom and job dissatisfaction, which, it is argued, will lead to lateness, absenteeism, and reduced performance on the job. Thus the move to job redesign is to accomplish two things: task efficiency and human satisfaction.

The objectives of a program of job redesign are to design jobs to help the company get work done in the most productive way possible while helping satisfy employee needs for a good-quality work life by fashioning jobs that are interesting, challenging, and provide opportunities for employee accomplishment.

Job redesign, then, assumes that employees want jobs that are interesting, challenging, and provide opportunities for employee accomplishment. Employees who cannot or will not handle such a job are likely to become confused and frustrated at being asked to think rather than just perform. When employees feel that they are being given insufficient responsibility, when they are in a job that they feel is monotonous, segmented, and routine, the job is a good candidate to be redesigned.

There are two common redesign strategies: job enlargement and job enrichment. Job enlargement—horizontal job loading—involves adding more tasks to the individual job to provide a greater variety of tasks for the person doing the job. Adding one meaningless task to another meaningless task is like adding zero to zero. The answer is still zero.

Job enrichment—vertical job loading—enriches the job by taking some of the tasks performed by management and adding them to the job of the employee. Traditionally, management has planned the work, the employee performs it, and management decides whether or not it has been performed correctly. Vertical job loading seeks to build into people's jobs some of the planning and/or control functions usually performed by managers.

A program of job enrichment fits in well with a number of the motivational theories noted above. Herzberg's work indicates that 80 percent of job satisfaction comes from achievement, recognition, and responsibility. Job enrichment can be seen as an outgrowth of this model.

Behavioralists believe that reinforcement is the key to achieve performance. They view job design as a way of making the job more intrinsically rewarding, thus leading to higher levels of performance. Others feel that cues received from the environment are diffused over areas of the brain to arouse and activate the person. The greater the variety and stimulation in a job, the higher the state of arousal and the greater the motivation.

As noted above, expectancy theory holds that a person will behave in a certain way if he or she believes that such behavior will result in an important outcome. This theory indicates that the worker perceives that an enriched job will lead to an intrinsic reward, so the employee is committed to the job and performs better if such rewards (challenge, responsibility, etc.) are regarded as important by the employee.

Implementation. The manager's task is to organize the tasks involved in performing the job and the relationships between the person doing the job and the supervisor, any subordinates, and all fellow employees, to produce jobs that will be performed in an efficient manner while contributing to employee satisfaction.

Employee Satisfaction. Behavioral scientists have found that three factors are critical to satisfaction and motivation on the job. Employees must feel that what they are doing is meaningful in terms of their own set of values, they must feel personally responsible for the outcome, and they must learn how well they are performing.

If, for example, a server feels that serving food is demeaning, the person is unlikely to feel good about the job, the company, or himself. It is difficult for a person to give good service when feeling this way. In a kitchen organized such that several cooks are involved in preparing a particular dish, the fact that no one has total responsibility for the outcome diminishes the rewards of the job. Finally, consider the typical relationship between kitchen and dining room. Cooks prepare the meal and hand it over to servers to give to the customer. If they get no feedback from either the customer or management, their job satisfaction goes down. Brian Watts, managing director of the catering facilities at the Bank of

England, found that the quality of food improved noticeably when he redesigned the cooks' job to serve customers the food they had cooked in the kitchen.

Throughout this segment there has been talk of employee job satisfaction and motivation. No links have been established between job satisfaction and productivity. However, there are links between job satisfaction and such things as absenteeism, lateness, and turnover. These things cost the operation money. It can be safely assumed that anything that will improve job satisfaction will reduce costs in terms of the items mentioned above. Additionally, it is not hard to accept that employees who feel a level of dissatisfaction with their jobs will be unable to give truly hospitable service to customers.

Basic Job Dimensions. Every job has five basic dimensions that affect whether or not the job produces any of the three factors noted above. How meaningful the job appears to the person doing it depends on three of these dimensions: the variety of skills used, task identity, and task significance. The more skills that are used in performing a job, the more meaningful the job appears to the employee performing it. The job seems more important because it requires more skills. It is also less boring because of the variety of skills required. Skill variety can be improved by such things as combining tasks and/or adding customer contact to a job that did not require such contact previously. For example, instead of one person washing dishes for an eight-hour shift, perhaps they could wash dishes for four hours and bus dishes for four hours. Enlarging the job adds variety while allowing the dishwasher to get to the front of the house and interact with the customers.

Such a technique also relates to task identity, the extent to which the job entails doing something from beginning to end. The more that employees are involved in a job from beginning to end, the more motivated they are about what they are doing. The busser who takes dirty dishes into the kitchen does not see what happens to them after they are left with the dishwasher. By doing both jobs, the flow of dishes from use to reuse is seen in its totality. This technique may also improve relations between two employees who bicker over who should do what in the interaction of their jobs. Bussers can make the dishwasher's job easier or more difficult, depending on how they arrange the dirty dishes as they are cleared from the tables. Dishwashers, on the other hand, do not see the hectic pace in the dining room. Seeing the job "from the other side" can produce more-understanding employees.

Task significance refers to the way a job affects others in a substantial way. The more employees feel that what they are doing affects the overall goal of the restaurant in a substantial way, the more satisfaction they get from what they are doing. Before Disney employees are allowed to sell popcorn or clean Main Street, they must undergo a training program that emphasizes what they do in relation to customer satisfaction. The street cleaners are very visible to visitors and therefore, they are asked numerous questions. They are told that an important part of their job is acting as a Disney "Ambassador" in addition to their crucial role of keeping the place clean. On the other hand, what message does a manager send to back-of-the-house employees when she or he spends little or no time behind the scenes, preferring to be out front with customers?

What is said, or communicated, nonverbally is also important. Saying such things as: "I don't know how you can stand this job for eight hours a day" lets the employee know exactly what is thought about the job. If the job is so bad, what does that say to the employee about the person doing the job? If employees are told: "You start as a hostess and if you work out and when we get an opening, we'll move you into a server's position," they learn that much is thought of the hostess position. It is better if they are told: "We have found that you will benefit from starting out in this position. You will have a chance to work with all of our servers and see how this operation works. You set the tone for the customer's experience because you make that first impression. When you get your own station, you'll have a better understanding of the way the restaurant operates." Taking those who burnish the silverware up to see the banquet room when it is set up for a party allows them to see how the silverware adds to the look of the room.

The fourth basic characteristic of a job is the amount of autonomy involved in it. The more autonomy that workers experience, the more personal responsibility they will feel for the outcome of the work. Employees in highly autonomous jobs know that they are responsible for success or failure. The management trainee who has to consult the manual for the answer to problems is taught to use the book as a crutch for judgment and initiative. The employee is not responsible for customer satisfaction; the manual is. When employees are given the responsibility and the autonomy to solve customer problems, they feel more responsible. This concept of employee empowerment pushes decision making down to the lowest possible level. Suppose, for example, that a customer complains about the length of time that he or she waits for the order to come. Many restaurants have a policy by which employees refer all complaints to a manager who seeks to appease the customer. When employees are empowered, they have, within certain boundaries, the latitude to take care of the problem. Whoever receives a complaint has ownership of it until it is solved. The server may offer to discount the meal or give a complimentary dessert to appease the customer. The feeling of control over the satisfaction of the customer will, for most employees, translate into more positive feelings about the job.

The last job dimension is feedback. The more feedback employees receive, the better they know how they are performing. For employees in tipped positions feedback comes regularly in terms of the amount of tips they receive. Management must pay more attention to nontipped employees who get little or no customer feedback.

Employee Growth Needs.   Research results on the relationship between job satisfaction and the growth needs of employees have been mixed. Although some results show that the strength of growth needs moderates the amount of job satisfaction experienced, other studies show no effect. It appears that job satisfaction can be increased for all employees, but the increase is greater for those who have strong needs for growth.

Leadership Style.   Managers can affect employee job satisfaction and performance through the style of leadership they adopt. The appropriate leadership style depends on the scope of the job and the growth needs of the employee performing that job [15]. When an employee has high growth needs and is performing a job high in variety (a high-scope job), participative management with a great deal of autonomy for the employee would be appropriate.

When a job is varied but the employee has a low need for growth, the manager should provide direction in planning, organizing, and controlling the work of the employee.

When an employee with high growth needs is performing a task that is not fulfilling, frustration and dissatisfaction probably result. Supportive leadership will be necessary to produce a satisfied and productive employee.

When an employee with low growth needs is performing a dull and repetitive task, performance should be monitored but the manager need not supervise the employee closely. As long as the job is being performed to the level required, little or no interference from the manager is needed. This maintenance leadership style is appropriate until performance or satisfaction problems arise, in which case more direction or support can be given.

Positive Reinforcement

When employees rate a company climate low on "recognition," they are saying that they feel criticized and punished when they do something wrong rather than praised and rewarded when they do something right. The "solution"—positive reinforcement—assumes that people behave in a way that is most rewarding to them. Management can improve employees' performance by providing appropriate consequences to employee behavior. Research does seem to show that positive reinforcement works better than negative reinforcement in producing and maintaining behavior.

Punishment. Many managers overrely on punishment as a means of shaping employee behavior. Punishment seeks to eliminate negative behavior by applying negative consequences to that behavior. An employee comes in late. The employee is told: "If you come in late again this month, you will be fired." The negative behavior is the lateness; the punishment is being fired; the objective is to reduce or eliminate the negative behavior—to stop the lateness.

There are several problems with an overreliance on punishment. It may eliminate the behavior. However, it may, instead, result in avoidance behavior. Our tardy employee wakes up late. Instead of coming in late and being fired, the employee may call in sick and not come in at all. Or consider the chef who is told: "Don't let me catch you with your food costs this high again." Under his breath the chef may mutter: "Don't worry, you won't catch me." The result may be actions that suppress rather than eliminate the negative behavior. There is also the problem that if employees hear from management only when things go wrong, a negative climate results.

Positive Reinforcement. Positive reinforcement seeks to increase the occurrence of positive behavior by providing desirable consequences for that behavior. Let us return to our tardy employee. Positive reinforcement occurs when the employee is told that at the end of each week, all employees who have a perfect attendance record will be eligible for a prize drawing. The idea is to reward the desired behavior.

quick bite 14.6
Building Employee Morale

It's not the big problems that cause problems with employees—it's the little things. Here are some ideas on how to improve employee morale by concentrating on the little things:

1. Listen attentively to your employees.
2. Don't use "cute" names such as "Hon" and "Dear."
3. Build an atmosphere of trust by acknowledging their ideas even if you don't take action on them.
4. Be honest with employees.
5. Show flexibility in scheduling.
6. Remember the basics—provide comfortable uniforms and keep the bathrooms stocked.
7. Train employees to give them the confidence to handle problems.
8. Make sure that everyone knows the goal and the rules.
9. Treat your employees like family. Bill Fromm says, "If you want the customer to be treated like a king, treat your people like royalty."
10. Find and utilize all of your employees' talents for things outside their specific jobs.
11. Put a simple, sincere note in with the paycheck.
12. Publicize letters of appreciation.

Source: Liparulo, Robert. "Building Employee Morale," *Restaurants USA,* v. 12, n. 8, September 1992, pp. 12–14.

Implementation. The starting point is an audit of existing performance in behavioral terms. We may note, for example, that servers do not suggest dessert after customers are finished with the entree.

Next, management identifies what objectives it wishes to see accomplished. Carrying the dessert example through, a goal may be set of having servers sell 10 desserts a shift.

The next step is to identify the behaviors necessary to achieve the objectives. To sell desserts it is necessary to:

- Know what desserts are being offered.
- Suggest to every customer that they have a dessert.
- Describe the desserts accurately and in a way that is likely to induce purchase.

If employees do these three things, it is more likely that they will sell desserts than if they do not do these things.

The fifth step is the key to the success of positive reinforcement—reinforcing the behavior. Several types of reinforcement are possible. Continuous reinforcement involves reacting to the behavior every time it occurs. This is the type of reinforcement received when we put coins in a soda machine. Every time the correct amount of money goes into the slot, a soda appears. Continuous reinforcement is necessary to establish a new behavior.

Related to this is the idea of fixed and variable or intermittent reinforcement. Fixed reinforcement involves getting feedback on a set schedule in terms of time or number of actions. The most obvious example of fixed reinforcement is the weekly or biweekly paycheck. Because that check comes once a week, it becomes expected and, as a consequence, can lose its effect as a motivator. Intermittent reinforcement is given on an irregular basis.

In terms of motivation, variable or intermittent reinforcement is more effective in sustaining already established behavior. Consider the soda machine compared to the slot machine. If you put coins in the soda machine and nothing happens, you may give up and leave, muttering under your breath; or you may kick the machine; or if you are thirsty enough, you may put more coins in the slot. But if nothing still happens, will you put more change in? Probably not. We are used to a continuous schedule of reinforcement. When we go from continuous reinforcement to no reinforcement, the behavior stops.

Management will often work with employees to improve their behavior. After lots of work, lots of coaching, and lots of reinforcement, an employee's behavior begins to improve. But then the manager goes to work with another employee whose behavior needs to improve. Getting no more reinforcement, the first employee's new behavior may disappear.

Consider the slot machine. We put in some coins but get no response. Do we put in more? Of course! The behavior is continued far longer than we would feed the soda machine because we know that at some time there will be a worthwhile payoff. The intermittent variable response of the slot machine keeps the behavior going.

As the fifth step in the process, employees are encouraged to keep a record of their own work. This self-assessment means that employees themselves continuously reinforce their own behavior. Every time the server sells a dessert, she or he makes a note of it. The reinforcement is immediate. In this way the server sees the relationship between the behavior and the consequence. The success interval, or the distance between the behavior and the measurement, is shortened.

Finally, the supervisor looks at the performance of the employee and praises the positive aspects. For reinforcement to work, the employee has to see the relationship between the behavior and the consequence. With continuous reinforcement, it has to be as immediate as possible. It also has to be meaningful to the employee. The priorities of a waitress struggling as a single parent to raise two children are different from those of a college student working for "fun money."

Development of Trust

The last of the six dimensions of organizational climate to be considered is teamwork. This is the feeling of belonging to an organization characterized by cohesion, mutual warmth, and support, trust, and pride. Such employees trust and respect each other while feeling personal loyalty and a sense of belonging to the company. When employees perceive teamwork to be low, it is management's responsibility to instill a feeling of trust and loyalty.

Organizational Commitment. What factors determine whether or not an employee will be loyal to a company? There are various models of organizational commitment which determine the factors that influence how and why employees are tuned in to the needs of the company. In these models there are several common ideas. The main factors that influence a person's commitment are investments, reciprocity, lack of alternatives, and identification.

As people invest more deeply in a company in time, energy, and commitment, the less they are likely to leave as they accept future rewards—promotions, for example—for their contributions. If they leave the company, their investment will not be recovered.

The idea of reciprocity is based on the assumption that if employees feel they are getting more than they deserve—that the rewards of the job are more than expected—they will remain with the operation to repay this debt through future performance.

Lack of alternatives means that the more specific skills become to a company, the less opportunity is available to use those skills outside the operation. This is not very important, however, in the restaurant industry, where the job in one restaurant differs little from that in another.

Identification is defined as the linking of one's social identity to one's work. As identification increases, change becomes harder and commitment is strengthened.

Implementation: Management Style. Management's task is to integrate the employee with the company in such a way that there is evidence of mutual warmth and support. In a climate where truth and respect are present, employee feelings of belonging and loyalty will result.

Managers can implement such a climate by the style and behaviors they adopt. Many contemporary managers have idealized models in their imagination akin to the heroic manager: the conquering leader who rescues helpless, disorganized employees from all problems and leaves only when all has been accomplished by his or her own courage, intelligence, and skill. The helpless subordinates continue with their mundane tasks until another problem arises and the hero returns.

It is the feeling of control over themselves, but primarily over others, that creates this vision. When crises arise at work and tough decisions are called for, many managers feel responsible for knowing what the problem is, developing the solution, and exerting control over the situation.

When managers perceive their employees to be helpless and incapable and take full control, they elicit reciprocal behavior from their employees. Subordi-

Trends—Developing a Caring Culture

The first step to creating a caring culture is to formalize a mission statement or a declaration of long-term goals. It is essential that each employee in the organization understands and "buys into" the mission statement. It is also imperative that employees are shown how important they are to the overall success of the organization. Management must support and guide employees to reach their workplace goals.

A caring culture requires a "hands-on," or interactive, style of management, a style that facilitates open communication between managers and employees. A reward system also contributes to a caring culture. To improve overall business, management should encourage employees by offering financial incentives and/or public recognition for superior performance.

Creating a caring culture enhances a business's ability to retain employees, ultimately leading to greater profitability. Another positive result of a caring culture is the development of goodwill ambassadors for the restaurant industry as a whole.

A Caring Culture Checklist

	Limited-Service	Tableservice <$25	Tableservice >$25
√ Written Mission Statement			
Percent that have a written mission statement	72%	40%	46%
√ Remind Employees of Mission Statement			
How often employees are reminded of mission statement (1 = never, 10 = daily) Hourly	4.5	5.5	6.1
Salaried	6.2	6.4	6.3
√ Have "Hands-On" Management Style			
Rating of management style (1 = completely hands-off, 10 = completely hands on)	7.7	8.3	8.5
√ Foster Open Relationships			
Manager/employee relationship (1 = hierarchical and structured, 10 = unstructured and collaborative)	5.2	6.0	6.2
√ Empower Hourly Employees			
Level of input hourly employees have on policy setting (1 = no authority, 10 = complete authority)	3.5	4.9	4.6

(continued)

Trends—Developing a Caring Culture (*continued*)

	Limited-Service	Tableservice <$25	Tableservice >$25
√ Give Incentives for Superior Performance			
Percent of respondents offering:			
• Rewards for salaried employees			
Bonuses	94%	66%	66%
Profit-Sharing	44%	21%	26%
• Rewards for hourly employees			
Bonuses	42%	52%	52%
Profit-Sharing	21%	12%	20%
√ Recognize Superior Performance			
Percent of respondents offering:			
• Recognition of salaried employees			
Individual Recognition	65%	26%	33%
Group Recognition	51%	13%	14%
• Recognition of hourly employees			
Individual Recognition	67%	33%	37%
Group Recognition	50%	16%	19%
√ Give Employees an Ownership Stake in the Business			
Percent of respondents that have employees with an ownership stake	21%	12%	12%

The Results

Employees work for a longer tenure.			
Median Tenure for:			
Hourly Employees	6–11 mos.	2 –3.9 yrs.	2 –3.9 yrs.
Salaried Employees	4 + yrs.	4 + yrs.	2 –3.9 yrs.
Former employees have a positive view of the industry.			
Operators' views of former employees' satisfaction (1 = completely unsatisfied, 10 = completely satisfied)	6.2	7.0	7.5

Source: "1999 Highlights." *Restaurants USA,* v. 18, n. 11, December 1998, pp. F5–F6.

nates retreat to a defense of their narrow interests as managers exert complete control.

The key is for managers to act as developers, people with a strong employee-centered image. Managers learn to have impact without exerting total control, to be helpful without having all the answers, and to be powerful without needing to dominate.

The developer–manager model consists of three components that must be nurtured to achieve productive excellence: interdependence, interpersonal skills, and commitment to an overriding departmental goal. Within the operation there is a high degree of interdependence among departments and a constant stream of changes, both internal and external. This is especially true in the restaurant industry, where the satisfaction of the customer depends on the performance of many people in many departments. Managers must develop a method to handle this interdependence.

The solution is to build a team that shares the responsibility for managing departments. It is a joint responsibility group that shares in making the basic decisions and influences each member to a high level of performance. Building such a team leads to greater subordinate commitment and motivation. Joint responsibility increases individual challenge and potential learning and growth. Development occurs in technical and managerial skills. Research has indicated that groups make better decisions than individuals do when the problem is complex.

The second component in being a developer–manager is the importance of interpersonal skills. Daily interaction can be used to encourage and enhance growth in subordinates. Coaching from the developer–manager helps build competence. In this way, behavioral problems can be turned into an opportunity for growth.

The third component is getting employees committed to the overriding goal of the department. The goal unites employees because it is a vision they can share and work toward. Employees do not work for money alone; the goal generates reasons that make the work worthwhile. It is the achievement made toward the goal and the appreciation of the extra effort that become rewarding to the employee.

Implementation: Management Behavior.   The day-to-day behavior of managers nurtures or destroys a climate of trust and loyalty. Employees are constantly looking to determine the extent to which they should be on their guard in dealing with management. The more they perceive management as being threatening, the more time they will spend on their own emotional defenses. The more they perceive an atmosphere in which they can grow, the more emotion they can devote to the job.

Certain behaviors that management can develop encourage trust on the part of the employee.

1. Encourage employees to express doubts, feelings, and concerns. In some companies, expressing doubt about a management course of action is liable to have that person labeled a traitor to the operation. In such an atmosphere, creative ideas are stifled.

2. Tell employees the reasons behind requests. When people understand why they are being asked to perform rather than just being told what to do, they feel that management has a greater respect for them. Consequently, they respect management more and perform better.

3. When something goes wrong, be more concerned about what happened and how to prevent it than in finding and punishing the guilty party. This does not mean permitting or encouraging slackness. It does mean that the focus is on problem solving, including the participation of the affected parties, rather than on assigning blame.

4. Encourage employees to come to you for assistance while helping them to develop independent judgment.

5. Be candid about the person to whom you are talking, but never gossip about anyone. Managers are never off the record.

LEADERS AND MANAGERS

Throughout this chapter we have referred to supervisors as "managers" while suggesting at times that they exhibit a "leadership" style. There is a difference between a manager and a leader. According to Bennis and Nanus [16], most organizations are managed, not led. They, among others, promote the idea that what is increasingly needed are leaders, not managers. It is useful, therefore, to look at some ideas of what constitutes a leader and to relate these ideas to the task of motivating employees.

Leadership Theories

Leadership theories have evolved over the years. Trait theories, popular from the 1920s to the 1950s, focused on the role of personal characteristics such as intelligence and dominance. Beginning in the 1950s, we saw the development of behavioral theories which suggested that the effectiveness of leaders comes from what they do rather than the personal characteristics they possess. Another development is that of situational theories—the idea that the characteristics of employees and the situation the business is in must be considered when developing an effective leadership strategy.

Trait Theories. While early studies attempting to identify personal characteristics that made for successful leaders were inconsistent, later reviews have identified more consistent results. It appears that the following are important [17]:

- Vigor and persistence in the pursuit of goals
- Self-confidence
- Ability to influence others
- Ability to tolerate frustration

Taken together, they give a fuzzy picture of the personality of a leader. Although it is now felt that personality is part of being a leader, it is no longer accepted that the existence of various traits will make a person a leader, and vice versa.

Behavioral Theories.   Because trait theories were unable to identify what made a leader effective, the focus turned to an examination of the behaviors that seemed to work.

Early studies at the University of Michigan found that production-centered supervision, where the focus was on getting the job done, actually produced less than did employee-centered supervision, where the accent was on developing high goals and focusing highly enthusiastic attention on the employees who did the work.

A research team at Ohio State University identified two similar dimensions of supervisory behavior—consideration and structure—which were popularized by Blake and Mouton as the managerial grid. Two dimensions—consideration for production and consideration for people—were placed on a grid to form five possible supervisory styles [18]:

1. Country club management: where there is a high concern for people and a low concern for production. There is a friendly atmosphere at work and little pressure to perform.
2. Impoverished management: where there is a low concern for both people and production. Those in the organization put forth just enough effort to keep their jobs.
3. Organization management: where there is average concern for both people and production. There is a balance between getting out the work and keeping morale at a satisfactory level.
4. Authority-obedience: a workplace characterized by a very efficient workforce in which employees are expected to conform to the needs of the company.
5. Team management: where there is a high concern for both people and production. Employees see themselves as having a common purpose with the company and, as such, are committed to perform well.

In an attempt to synthesize earlier work, Gary P. Yukl identified the following measurable behaviors which, when used under specific conditions, will produce effective leadership [19]:

Performance emphasis	Consideration
Inspiration	Praise–recognition
Structuring reward contingencies	Decision participation
Autonomy delegation	Role clarification
Goal setting	Training–coaching
Problem solving	Information dissemination

Planning

Work facilitation

Interaction facilitation

Criticism–discipline

Coordinating

Representation

Conflict management

Situational (Contingency) Theories. Aware that neither trait nor behavioral theories adequately explained what makes a leader, attention turned to the importance of situational variables. Basically, such theories say that there is

---

q u i c k   b i t e   1 4 . 8
Road to the Top: Thomas C. Kish

Vice President, Information and Support Services

Technology is increasingly important in the restaurant industry and Thomas Kish understands this idea very well. The Management Information Systems chief of Papa John's International, Kish realizes all too well the fast-paced change in information technology. Kish learned many of his adaptation skills from his numerous family moves as his father advanced through jobs in an insurance company. Kish moved from his birthplace in Winter Park, Florida, to homes in California, Oklahoma, Illinois, Pennsylvania, and Houston, Texas, where he currently resides.

Thomas Kish at the age of 33 years is responsible for the successful and rapid technological implementations for Papa John's International (PJI). Papa John's Louisville, Kentucky-based pizza chain operates and franchised over 1,900 restaurants and they are growing at a staggering pace.

Kish oversaw the chain's implementation of PeopleSoft software for human resources and payroll. The new technology standardized the way in which the chain's 14,000 employees are compensated. The implementation only took about 4 months. Kish credits the major success to his dynamic team. Kish reports directly to Blaine Hurst, president, and oversees 140 employees in three divisions including Field Systems, Technical Operations and an Enterprise Group.

Kish earned the position after consulting for the firm in 1995. After joining the company full-time Kish and his team developed and deployed a customized front-and back-of-the-house solution in only 22 months. The system was later trademarked by PJI as the "Papa John's PROFIT System." Kish earned a BS in mechanical engineering from the University of Texas at Austin and claims that his three years working for Andersen Consulting was better experience than getting an MBA.

Source: Rubinstein, Ed. "Papa John's Tom Kish: Ensuring that Better Systems Make for Better Operations." *Nation's Restaurant News,* v. 33, n. 6, February 8, 1999, p. 43.

no single style of leadership that will be effective in every situation. To be effective, leaders must adapt their behavior to changing situations.

Fiedler's contingency leadership model states that group performance is a function of both the leader and the leadership situation. The extent to which the leader is task or relationship oriented is a measure of the motivational system of the leader. The leadership situation consists of three things [20]:

---

quick bite 14.9
Hot Skills

Working Conditions 2000

Managers themselves will change in 2000 as they find career development to be more important. Managers will also focus more on their lifestyles and improving their quality of life. Managers in the future will receive salaries and benefits that are more competitive and most will enjoy better working conditions than previously encountered.

Managers in 2000 are likely to have more education and as a result receive higher compensation levels and more respect from the public and their peers. However, industry experts do not expect the hours worked by managers to decrease significantly. One reason for this is the increased hours units will operate in order to stay competitive.

Managers in 2000 will also face higher levels of stress than ever before due to the increasingly competitive nature of the industry. These managers, however, will also earn increased rewards. Stress training will become an important part of the manager's education.

The Top 10 Most Likely Developments for Managers in Working Conditions for 2000

1. More education required
2. Career development increasingly important
3. Healthy lifestyle plays a bigger role
4. Quality of life issues are met better
5. More competitive salaries and benefits
6. Increasing partnership with owners
7. Salary and benefits equal with other retail industries
8. Work is more satisfying
9. Longer hours remain required
10. Receive better working conditions

Adapted from: National Restaurant Association, *Foodservice Manager 2000* (Washington, D.C.: National Restaurant Association, 1992).

1. Leader–member relations (the extent to which the group trusts and likes the leader and is willing to follow her or his instructions)
2. The extent to which the task is structured
3. Position power

The first factor is the most important. Fiedler's research has shown that task-oriented leaders are most effective where they have power by virtue of their position, good relations with the group, and a job to be done that is well structured. Relationship-oriented leaders are most effective where the situation is moderately favorable or unfavorable to the leader. These might be situations where the leader is accepted but the job objectives are vague or where the task is structured but the leader is not accepted. The major lesson to be learned from this theory is that a style of leadership that is effective under one set of circumstances may not work under a different set of conditions.

The path–goal theory identifies two variables to be taken into account when deciding on an appropriate leadership style: employee characteristics and characteristics of the work environment. Preliminary findings indicate that [21]:

- A directive style of leadership is effective when the work situation is vague.
- Supportive leadership works best on employees who have jobs that are stressful, frustrating, or dissatisfying.
- Employees prefer a participative style of leadership in jobs that are not repetitive and which involve the ego of the employee.

Four points can be made regarding leadership theories [22]:

1. There is no universally accepted approach to studying leadership.
2. There are some personal characteristics that differentiate effective leaders from ineffective leaders.
3. There are two accepted dimensions of leadership:
   a. Employee—or relationship—oriented; (consideration)
   b. Production—or task—oriented; (structure)
4. Leadership effectiveness is some function of a leader's personal characteristics and behaviors, the feelings of the employees toward the leader, the type of job, relationships within the work group, and the organizational climate.

ENDNOTES

1. Craig C. Pinder, *Work Motivation: Theories, Issues and Applications* (Glenview, IL: Scott, Foresman and Company, 1984), p. 63; David C. McClelland, *Human Motivation* (Glenview, IL: Scott, Foresman and Company, 1985), pp. 595–596.

2. Auren Uris, *101 of the Greatest Ideas in Management* (New York: John Wiley & Sons, 1986), p. 26.

3. Ibid., p. 26.

4. Arthur W. Sherman, George W. Bohlander, and Herbert J. Chudren, *Managing Human Resources,* 8th ed. (Cincinnati, OH: South-Western Publishing Co., 1988), p. 304.

5. Ibid., p. 299.

6. Ibid., p. 302.

7. Ibid., p. 304.

8. This material has been taken from Robert Christie Mill, *Managing for Productivity in the Hospitality Industry* (New York: Van Nostrand Reinhold, 1989), Chapters 6–10.

9. George H. Litwin, and Robert A. Stringer, Jr., *Motivation and Organizational Climate* (Cambridge, MA: Harvard University Press, 1968).

10. Forum Corporation, *The Language of Organizational Climate,* unpublished monograph, 1979.

11. Thomas T. Peters and Robert H. Waterman, *In Search of Excellence* (New York: Harper & Row, 1982).

12. Bruce Grindy, "Hooking and Keeping Employees," *Restaurants USA,* October 1998, p. 25.

13. M. C. McConkie, "A Classification of the Goal-Setting and Appraisal Process in MBO," *Academy of Management Review,* vol. 4, no. 1, 1979, p. 29.

14. Mill, *Managing for Productivity in the Hospitality Industry,* pp. 143–144.

15. Ricky W. Griffen, "Relationships among Individual, Task Design and Leader Behavior," *Academy of Management Journal,* vol. 23, no. 4, 1980, p. 667.

16. Warren Bennis and Burt Nanus, *Leaders: The Strategies for Taking Charge* (New York: Harper & Row Publishers, 1985), p. 218.

17. Marc G. Singer, *Human Resource Management* (Boston: PWS-Kent Publishing Company, 1990), pp. 353–354.

18. Ibid., p. 356.

19. Gary P. Yukl, *Leadership in Organizations* (Upper Saddle River, NJ: Prentice Hall, 1981), pp. 121–125.

20. Singer, *Human Resource Management,* pp. 356–357.

21. Ibid., p. 358.

22. Ibid., p. 359.

CHAPTER FIFTEEN

RESTAURANT MANAGER 2000

learning objective

By the end of this chapter you should be able to:

1. Identify the major skills and knowledge that will be required of restaurant managers in the new millennium.

> *Studies ... document that today's young work force is motivated not just by dollar compensation but by the opportunity to make decisions on the job and to grow. But in many cases, the young support staffer's sense of direction is clouded by unrealistic expectations of rapid career advancement coupled with the frustrating perceptions that the present job holds no opportunities for improvement.*
> Paul Blesing, quoted in *Training and Development Journal*

THE STUDY

In 1991 the National Restaurant Association began a study to determine the skills needed for a foodservice manager in the year 2000. The methodology used was a Delphi study. A panel of experts was put together comprising the board of directors of the National Restaurant Association, the board of trustees of the Educational Foundation of the National Restaurant Association, human resources professionals and training directors belonging to the Council of Hotel and Restaurant Trainers, educators belonging to the Council on Hotel, Restaurant

Hot Concepts: Tin Star

Veterans from Brinker International and Canyon Café have come together to introduce a new "fast casual" concept named Tin Star, which is expected to bring many new ideas to the service and menu playing fields. The first Tin Star prototype opened in January 1999 near downtown Dallas. The restaurant is comprised of 2,600 square feet and 125 seats.

The new concept's operations encompass several quirky ideas including the following:

- Menu items are priced to include tax and only render change in quarters.
- Orders are taken by wait staff in line, not at a counter.
- Condiments are provided at an open, center-of-the-room station to complement the menu's exciting Southwestern tastes.

The restaurant's menu is comprised of primarily tacos, pizzas, rellenos, salads and soups. A small assortment of wines and beers is also available at Tin Star. The store opens at 7 A.M. for breakfast, serving a variety of tacos. Other items include the Cheeseburger Taco for $6, which includes all the traditional fixings inside a flour tortilla, and the $7 spicy Texas Batter Chicken Salad that includes lettuce, blue cheese crumbles, diced pickled beets, cashews, apple chunks and a Texas Cabernet vinaigrette.

Tin Star effectively combines fast food with casual dining by limiting all menu items to $9 or less, taking orders from people in line, offering complimentary quesadillas to waiting customers and using hard plastic dinnerware and stainless flatware. According to Rich Hicks, operations director and veteran of Macaroni Grill, a customer does not need wait staff to feel like they have had great service and a good experience. In order to keep the energy level high Tin Star's operators brought the kitchen to the front of the restaurant.

Tin Star hopes to appeal to consumers who are finding it more and more necessary to save time. And as more people find themselves eating on the run, they do not want to lose quality or service expectations. Tin Star will undertake the challenge of satisfying demanding and time conscious customers in an upscale setting with downscale pricing.

Source: Ruggless, Ron. "Brinker, Canyon Café Vets Debut 'Fast-Casual' Tin Star." *Nation's Restaurant News*, v. 33, n. 1, January 4, 1999, p. 8.

and Institutional Education, state restaurant association executives, independent and chain operators, consultants, and other foodservice industry experts.

Panelists were asked to list any issues they believed would be important to foodservice managers at the turn of the century. Broad categories of topics were identified and a questionnaire sent to all panelists asking them to identify the importance of the various items discovered in the first phase of the project. The results are qualitative and subjective rather than quantitative and were published in 1992 [1].

THE FINDINGS

The Manager's Job

In 1988 the National Restaurant Association identified the basic functional areas of a restaurant manager's job [2]. That report identified nine functional areas rank ordered in terms of importance as follows:

1. *Cost control and financial management:* monitoring, controlling, and reporting on store profitability indicators.
2. *Supervising shift operations:* running each shift efficiently and effectively.
3. *Organizing and planning each shift:* preparing for the shift so that it will run smoothly.
4. *Unit coordination and control:* communication among and between managers, supervisors, and other resources within the organization.
5. *Customer relations:* improving the dining experience for customers.
6. *Motivating employee performance:* improving the performance of employees.
7. *Employing and developing crew members:* obtaining, selecting, training, and keeping employees.
8. *Communicating with outside sources:* keeping in touch with corporate and community sources outside the unit.
9. *Monitoring and maintaining facility and equipment:* keeping physical assets operational and in compliance with internal and external regulations and laws.

Three of these nine were found in the Delphi study as being of most importance: supervising shift operations, employing and developing crew members, and motivating employee performance.

In the following sections we examine major findings in each of the following areas:

- Administration
- Finance
- Human resources
- Facility maintenance

- Sanitation and food safety
- Service
- Marketing
- Food and beverage
- Working conditions
- Background and education
- Industry trends

---

quick bite 15.2
Time Management

Operators must learn to manage restaurant, family, social and community obligations. According to NRA research, almost 75% of restaurant operators work at least 50 hours per week. Almost 10% of restaurateurs work 80 hours or more—twice the standard workweek. Not only do operators work hard, 9 out of 10 operators also participate in community activities. Although it takes long hours and hard work to be a successful restaurateur, it is important that operators find a balance between working hard and working so hard that their family and health is effected. The following steps can help restaurateurs save money, energy and time:

- Do it right the first time

   It is easy to tell when restaurants make good use of their time or if they need help with time management. Time management is a quality issue in restaurants because if something is cooked wrong and is sent back it throws off the entire kitchen. The first step to using time more efficiently is to get organized. A set of policies and procedures will help operators to organize time most efficiently. One time-saving policy is one that deals with supplier shortages; the policy should include which ingredients can be substituted in case of a emergency and which cannot.

- Clean up the clutter

   According to one time management specialist, 60% of papers on a desk and 80% of the paper in files can be discarded. He also urges operators to make use of computer technology. One extremely useful software tool for managers is contact-management software that acts as a to-do list and an electronic Rolodex. Installing electronic point-of-service and accounting systems can also greatly increase the efficiency and accuracy of operations.

(continued)

quick bite 15.2
Time Management (*continued*)

- Prioritize important efforts

  Learning to prioritize tasks can help operators streamline their workload. It is essential to set a schedule for tasks that must be accomplished and adhere to it. One of the best ways for restaurateurs to save time is to delegate tasks that others can do. Two great time-saving resources are an administrative assistant to help with paperwork and an advertising agency or consultant to deal with advertising offers and requests.

- Divide and conquer

  One advisor suggests that there are three types of restaurateurs: front-of-house focused (spend 90% of their time on the floor), back-of-house focused (hide in the office looking at numbers) and crisis management focused (need a series of crises in order to survive). In order to be efficient and successful, operators must learn to greet customers during peak hours, do paperwork during off-hours and manage as proactively as possible to avoid crisis situations. One way to evaluate where a manager is spending too much time is to log daily activities.

Source: Apfel, Ira. "How to Avoid a Time-management Meltdown." *Restaurants USA*, v. 19, n. 1, January 1999, pp. 23–26.

Administration

In the area of administration, the most likely development, according to panelists, is that managers will have to become computer proficient. As more operations move to comprehensive computer-based information, managers will have to be able to find, oversee, and use information from a variety of databases on a regular basis. Managers will use computers to perform a variety of tasks, from scheduling employees and forecasting customer demand to collecting sales data and keeping inventories.

Second, managers will increasingly have to supervise a more culturally diverse workforce. Managers will have to become more sensitive to the characteristics of different cultures and customs. Many felt that managers who are bilingual will be at an advantage in communicating with, and therefore motivating, their employees.

Third, managers will be more involved in teaching and training their employees. This will require them to develop better communication skills to enable them to do a better job in interacting with employees. Specific skills would include "public speaking, presentation, interpersonal skills and leadership abilities" [3]. More time will be spent training employees and less time dealing with paper.

quick bite 15.3
Single-Unit to Multi-Unit Management

First-level multi-unit managers employed by 10 fast-service organizations identified the importance of various dimensions of their jobs as (1) restaurant operations, (2) human resource management, (3) financial management, (4) marketing, and (5) facilities and safety management. The last two were perceived as being significantly less important than the other dimensions.

Managers had most trouble in human resource management in making the transition from single-unit to multiunit management. This was also the area in which they found themselves spending an increased amount of time. Specifically, managers suggested the following as problems:

- How to manage managers
- How to use different motivational techniques
- How to work with different personalities
- How to read behaviors
- How to communicate effectively
- How to solve problems through people
- How to coach and develop subordinates
- How to evaluate performance and take disciplinary action
- How to get unit managers to achieve high performance standards

They felt they needed more training in the areas of human resource management and marketing. The following marketing training needs were felt to be most important.

- Implementing local-store promotional programs
- Determining the effectiveness of promotional programs
- Identifying the appropriate products to promote
- Developing economic profiles of market areas and assessing competition
- Developing radio ads and buying media
- Developing in-house marketing and promotion programs

Source: Mone, Mark A. and W. Terry Umbreit. "Making the Transition from Single-Unit to Multi-Unit Fast-Service Management: What Are the Requisite Skills and Educational Needs?" *Hospitality Education and Research Journal,* v. 13, n. 3, 1989, pp. 319–331.

quick bite 15.4
General Manger Personalities

A study of 19 general managers working for a restaurant company indicated that as a whole, they exhibited the following personality traits:

- "Can-do" attitude
- Acceptance of challenges
- Tendency to overestimate their abilities
- May come across as arrogant
- Unlikely to say: "I don't know," "I need help," "I was wrong"

They have a high energy level and tend to overload their agendas, thereby making it difficult to attend to details. A highly competitive group, they take the initiative, keep score, and are rarely satisfied with a given level of accomplishment. They have a tendency to do everything themselves at the expense of delegating to others. They are outgoing and exhibit a need to control others. Rather disciplined and predictable, they tend to play by the rules. Their analytical ability dominates their skill in following through on their ideas. They are able to handle the countless pressures of the job by their ability to pay attention to what is going on under the most difficult of circumstances.

This group scored as high on confidence, extroversion, and ability to control their attention as any group of top executives in other industries and are as competitive as Olympic athletes and the Navy's SEALS.

Source: Pratt, Robin W. and David L. Whitney. "Attentional and Interpersonal Characteristics of Restaurant General Managers in Comparison with Other Groups of Interest," *Hospitality Research Journal,* v. 15, n. 1, 1991, pp. 9–24.

Finance

The reason that managers will need more computer skills is that operations, primarily the chains, will increasingly have on-line computer-based financial systems. Point-of-sale systems and other electronic tools will "make the manager's more traditional accounting responsibilities more obsolete at the turn of the century" [4]. Managers who are able to perform spreadsheet analysis will be more effective in understanding and reporting on a unit's financial condition.

A second major thought is that managers are more likely to have their pay linked to performance through bonuses and incentives. Managers will continue to assume responsibility for achieving bottom-line results. In addition, however, they will be given more responsibility for managing costs as well as sales. As an example, they will be expected to take more responsibility in reducing workers' compensation claims.

The American Restaurateur: Part One

The results of a survey of 18,000 owners and foodservice companies nation-wide revealed a picture of the American restaurateur. Here are some of the findings:

1. How many hours a week do you work?

Work Hours/Week	Table Service[a]	Quick Service[a]
30 or less	3%	5%
31 to 40	5%	10%
41 to 49	9%	14%
50 to 59	16%	22%
60 to 69	27%	29%
70 to 79	21%	13%
80 or more	16%	3%
No answer	3%	5%

[a]Numbers may not equal 100% because of rounding.

Taking one day off a week (or none) is the norm and vacations are infrequent.

2. What was your first job in foodservice?

Position	Male	Female
Management	26%	23%
Back of the house (table service)	33%	16%
Front of the house (table service)	22%	43%
Crew person or supervisor	9%	9%
No response	10%	9%

According to 40 percent of the respondents, their first job was in foodservice; they are twice as likely as the general population to have begun in foodservice. They started as a dishwasher (16 percent), busperson (10 percent), cook (10 percent), or server (9 percent). Most owners worked their way to the top.

Source: "The American Restaurateur," *Restaurants USA,* v. 11, n. 3, 1994, pp. 8–11, 17–24.

Human Resources

Human resources will become increasingly important to tomorrow's managers. They will have to move from being authoritarian to becoming coaches and develop better people skills for dealing with employees as well as customers. It is expected that finding qualified employees will be more difficult.

More attention will be paid to reducing turnover and keeping qualified employees. The manager's task will be to create a climate within the operation that will foster team spirit and motivate workers. This will involve such things as

---

quick bite 15.6
What Do Managers Do?

Additional Job Responsibilities Performed By Some Foodservice Professionals

Position	Additional Responsibilities Can Include
Executive chef	Kitchen manager
	Chef
	Catering manager
	Pastry chef
	Head of distribution/catering
Food and beverage director	Banquet manager
	Catering manager
	Dining room manager
	Head of distribution/purchasing
	Head of operations
Unit manager	Head of training
	Dining room manager
	Kitchen manager
	Food and beverage director
	Head of personnel/human resources
Owner	President/chief executive officer
	Chief financial manager
	Chief operating officer
	Treasurer
	Head of marketing

Source: National Restaurant Association, *Compensation of Salaried Personnel in Foodservice, 1994,* reported by Hudson Riehle, "Chef's Compensation Varies by Responsibilities," *Restaurants USA,* v. 14, n. 4, April 1994, pp. 40–42.

---

quick bite 15.7
The American Restaurateur: Part Two

Here are some additional results from the survey of 18,000 owners, and food-service companies nationwide about the American restaurateur:

1. What activities do you especially like doing?

Leisure Activity	Restaurant Operators	General Public	Difference
Eating out in restaurants	61%	40%	+21%
Cooking	34%	22%	+12%
Traveling on weekends	41%	31%	+10%
Getting prepared for work	15%	6%	+9%
Spending time with family	80%	72%	+8%
Home repairs and improvement	22%	15%	+7%
Spending time by yourself	37%	32%	+5%
Spending time with friends	56%	53%	+3%
Going out for entertainment	42%	41%	+1%
Reading magazines	34%	33%	+1%
Reading books	36%	38%	+1%
Grocery shopping	8%	11%	−3%
Hobbies	35%	39%	−4%
Entertaining guests	29%	34%	−5%
Napping	14%	20%	−6%
Browsing in stores	14%	21%	−7%
Watching television	26%	36%	−10%

2. What is your favorite thing to eat?

- Sandwich: hamburger
- Entree: beef or veal
- Ethnic: Italian
- Appetizer: shellfish
- Dessert: ice cream

(continued)

quick bite 15.7
The American Restaurateur: Part Two (*continued*)

3. Do you love your job?

Statement	Percentage Who Agree Or Strongly Agree
I am proud of my accomplishments	93%
I am satisfied with my career	79%
I am proud of the foodservice industry	73%
If I had to do it over again, I would choose a career in foodservice	54%
I would recommend a career in foodservice to my children	38%

Older restaurateurs are more likely than younger ones to recommend a food-service career to their children. Quick-service operators are more satisfied than are table service operators with the tangible rewards of their jobs (income, hours worked, benefits, and job security). Table service operators, on the other hand, are more satisfied than quick-service operators with the intangible rewards of the job, such as interaction with staff and the satisfaction of making a contribution to society.

Source: "The American Restaurateur", *Restaurants USA*, v. 11, n. 3, 1994, pp. 8–11, 17–24.

paying on the basis of performance, and providing better fringe benefits, improved work schedules, ongoing training, extensive evaluations, and better retirement benefits.

Facility Management

Mangers will get more involved in waste management and recycling. This will cover such things as ensuring that recyclable materials are properly sorted and helping encourage recycling by consumers. In this regard operators will have to become more familiar with government regulations regarding waste management.

Safety and security will also be a concern. Because of increasingly high liability costs, managers, with safety committees made up of employees, will be more aware of security issues both within and immediately outside their units.

Third, there will be a greater emphasis on the implementation of preventive maintenance programs as a way of reducing maintenance and repair costs.

Sanitation and Food Safety

Increasingly, restaurant managers will have to have a sanitation certificate. Most states will require sanitation testing. In addition, managers will have to communicate the importance of this topic to employees, who will receive more training in this area. It is expected that more natural cleaning agents will be developed as a consequence of restrictions on the use of pesticides and cleaners.

Service

As service increasingly becomes a method of differentiating one restaurant from another, managers will have to become adept to getting feedback from customers and providing service to an increasingly diverse customer base. To allow employees to deliver the level of service needed, managers will have to empower them, giving them the training to be flexible in dealing with customers as well as the authority to handle requests and complaints. This means that managers will spend more time on customer relations and on setting the standards required to ensure that employees perform to the level needed to produce satisfied customers. They will spend more time talking to customers to get feedback on the service provided and giving that feedback to employees.

Marketing

Success in marketing will come from the manager's ability to understand and satisfy local tastes. To accomplish this, managers will have to understand the desires of neighborhood and local customers. They will be given greater latitude in implementing plans to accomplish this.

Within chain operations corporate staff will retain control over "creative development, market research, and media purchasing" [5]. However, managers will be given the lead in conducting local and in-store marketing efforts. This will include teaching employees to sell suggestively. Managers will require more expertise in advertising and public relations in order to reach their local target markets effectively.

Food and Beverage

As consumers become more knowledgeable about nutrition, managers will have to develop more expertise about the nutritional content of ingredients and menu items. Quality control and product consistency will grow in importance. As a way of cutting down on costs, inventory control will become an even greater concern. In line with greater flexibility at the local level, mangers will be given more authority to promote specific food and beverage items.

Working Conditions

Although the number of hours worked per week is not expected to decline, managers will have a better quality of life. Salaries and benefits will become more competitive, and mangers will have more formal education. The job will continue to be stressful, although training in how to deal with stress on the job may help managers deal with this issue.

Background and Education

To deal with a more diverse customer and employee base, managers will need better interpersonal and communication skills. A manager will be more of a generalist and less of a specialist, creating the climate necessary to accomplish

---

quick bite 15.8
Road to the Top: Tom Ryan

Vice President of Menu Management

Tom Ryan has accepted the challenge of making the McDonald's menu more appealing to consumers' increasingly sophisticated palates. As the vice president of menu management at McDonald's Corp., Ryan has instituted a customer-focused approach to product development and is attempting to add new flavorful menu items into the chain's menu mix.

Ryan has instituted several tests of new products across the country. Most of these products are expected to roll out either regionally or nationally. Ryan's department includes 35 researchers and gives McDonald's marketing department real items that they can use to compete in today's intense competition.

According to Ryan, he has the best job in the company: "I get involved with everything from the long-range planning right down to the specific tactics—how much mayonnaise should be on this thing." The fact that Ryan loves his job so much influences everyone who works with him. According to Claire Babrowski, senior vice president of restaurant systems, "To watch those people work with him, you almost wonder how they can be enjoying their jobs so much."

Ryan prepared for his career by earning a bachelor's degree in food science, a master's degree in lipid toxicology, a doctoral degree in flavor science with a minor in marketing, all from Michigan State University. He began his career at Procter & Gamble and Pillsbury before moving to a restaurant career at Pizza Hut. After spending time at Pizza Hut, KFC and Long John Silver's, Ryan developed a reputation for being persistent in his focus on consumer feedback.

Ryan feels that the most important opinions about McDonald's menu items come from the consumers. Ryan's focus on consumer attitudes is a welcome change at McDonald's after the operations-driven Arch Deluxe failure.

Source: Hamstra, Mark. "Tom Ryan: Using a Customer-Focused Approach to Redefine McDonald's Menu Management." *Nation's Restaurant News*, v. 33, no. 4, Jaunuary 24, 1999, pp. 184–186.

---

the profit objectives of the unit. Managers will have to become more democratic and flexible in dealing with employees and be able to "present an image of grace under pressure to both staff and customers" [6].

Industry Needs

More managers will be needed in casual dining table services, nursing care, and fast food, whereas fewer positions will be available in military foodservice and fine dining.

---

 quick bite 15.9
Hot Skills

Educational Priorities 2000

In order to successfully run an operation in 2000, managers need more administrative capabilities. Industry experts ranked communication and leadership as two of the most important skills. Managers need these skills to deal with the challenges they will continue to face.

Managers need to be more skilled in human resources tools as well. Managers must be able to effectively train, motivate, build teams and supervise their employees. These four items are essential to the duties of a manager.

When industry experts were asked to rank the top ten educational priorities for managers with the coming of the new millennium, seven of the ten priorities mentioned included administrative or human resources topics. Other important educational priorities they mentioned include customer relations, food handling and cost controls.

The Top 10 Educational Priorities for Managers

1. Communication
2. Leadership
3. Customer relations
4. Training
5. Motivation
6. Team building
7. Supervision
8. Food handling
9. Cost controlling
10. Recruitment/selection

Adapted from: Foodservice Manager 2000 (Washington, D.C.: National Restaurant Association, 1992).

Restaurant Management: Customers, Operations, and Employees

The Bottom Line

Managers who implement the principles and practices outlined in this book, paying special attention to the areas noted in this chapter, will lead the industry in the next decade. Good luck in your efforts!

ENDNOTES

1. The entire report can be ordered from the National Restaurant Association, 1200 Seventeenth Street NW, Washington, DC 20036-3097; telephone (800) 424-5156 or (202) 331-5960.

2. "Job Analysis Report for Unit Manager and Assistant Manager," Educational Foundation of the National Restaurant Association, November 1988.

3. National Restaurant Association, *Foodservice Manager 2000*, Current Issues Report, (Washington, DC: National Restaurant Association, 1992), p. 5.

4. Ibid., p. 8.

5. Ibid., p. 14.

6. Ibid., p. 16.

INDEX